GENDER IN THE EARLY
MEDIEVAL WORLD

D1452056

Gender analysis is one of the most probing ways to understand both power and cultural strategies in pre-industrial societies. In this book, sixteen scholars on the cutting edge of their disciplines explore the ideas and expressions of gender that characterised the centuries from *c.* 300 to 900 in milieux ranging from York to Baghdad, via Rome and Constantinople. Deploying a variety of disciplines and perspectives, they draw on the evidence of material culture as well as texts to demonstrate the wide range of gender identities that informed the social, political and imaginary worlds of these centuries. The essays make clear that although the fixed point in the gender systems of the period was constituted by the hegemonic masculinity of the ruling elite, marginalised groups, often invisible as historical subjects in their own right, were omnipresent in, and critical to, the gendered discourses which buttressed assertions of power.

LESLIE BRUBAKER is Reader in Byzantine Art History and Director of the Centre for Byzantine Studies at the Institute of Archaeology and Antiquity, University of Birmingham. Her many publications on Byzantine culture include *Vision and Meaning in Ninth-Century Byzantium* (Cambridge, 1999) and *Byzantium in the Iconoclast Era: The Sources* (2001).

JULIA M. H. SMITH is Reader in Medieval History at the University of St Andrews. She has published extensively on early medieval history and her books include *Province and Empire: Brittany and the Carolingians* (Cambridge, 1992) and *Early Medieval Rome and the Christian West* (ed., Leiden 2000).

GENDER IN THE EARLY MEDIEVAL WORLD

East and west, 300–900

EDITED BY

LESLIE BRUBAKER AND JULIA M. H. SMITH

CAMBRIDGE
UNIVERSITY PRESS

PUBLISHED BY THE PRESS SYNDICATE OF THE UNIVERSITY OF CAMBRIDGE
The Pitt Building, Trumpington Street, Cambridge, United Kingdom

CAMBRIDGE UNIVERSITY PRESS
The Edinburgh Building, Cambridge, CB2 2RU, UK
40 West 20th Street, New York, NY 10011–4211, USA
477 Williamstown Road, Port Melbourne, VIC 3207, Australia
Ruiz de Alarcón 13, 28014 Madrid, Spain
Dock House, The Waterfront, Cape Town 8001, South Africa

http://www.cambridge.org

First published 2004

Printed in the United Kingdom at the University Press, Cambridge

Typeface Adobe Garamond 11/12.5 pt.   *System* LaTeX 2ε   [TB]

A catalogue record for this book is available from the British Library

Library of Congress Cataloguing in Publication data
Gender in the early medieval world: east and west, 300–900 / edited by Leslie Brubaker
and Julia M. H. Smith.
p.   cm.
Includes bibliographical references and index.
ISBN 0 521 81347 6 – ISBN 0 521 01327 5 (pbk)
1. Sex role – Europe – History – To 1500.   2. Women – Europe – History – To 1500.   3. Men –
Europe – History – To 1500.   4. Europe – Social conditions – To 1492.   5. Feminist theory.
I. Brubaker, Leslie.   II. Smith, Julia M. H.
HQ1075.5.E85G46   2004
305.3′094 – dc22   2003069751

ISBN 0 521 81347 6 hardback
ISBN 0 521 01327 5 paperback

Contents

Illustrations

Contributors

JULIA BRAY, Professor of Arabic, University of Paris 8, Saint-Denis

LESLIE BRUBAKER, Reader in Byzantine Art History and Director of the Centre for Byzantine Studies, University of Birmingham

NADIA MARIA EL CHEIKH, Associate Professor in History, American University of Beirut

LYNDA COON, Associate Professor of History, University of Arkansas

BONNIE EFFROS, Associate Professor of History, State University of New York at Binghamton

DAWN HADLEY, Senior Lecturer in Historical Archaeology, University of Sheffield

MARY HARLOW, Lecturer in Roman History, University of Birmingham

YITZHAK HEN, Professor of Medieval History, Ben-Gurion University of the Negev

MAYKE DE JONG, Professor of Medieval History, University of Utrecht

GISELA MUSCHIOL, Professor of Medieval and Modern Ecclesiastical History, University of Bonn

JANET L. NELSON, Professor of Medieval History, King's College London

WALTER POHL, Director of the Institute for Medieval Research, Vienna

JULIA M. H. SMITH, Reader in Mediaeval History, University of St Andrews

SHAUN TOUGHER, Lecturer in Ancient History, Cardiff University

MARTHA VINSON, Associate Professor of Classical Studies, Indiana University

IAN WOOD, Professor of Medieval History, University of Leeds

Acknowledgements

In the first instance, the editors wish to thank Tom Noble for providing the original inspiration behind this collection of essays when he asked why five years' work by a team of international experts studying 'The Transformation of the Roman World' had paid virtually no attention to either social relations or men's and women's experiences during and after late antiquity. Our initial response to that lacuna was to run a strand of sessions on 'Gender and the Transformation of the Roman World' at the Leeds International Medieval Congress in 2000. Several articles in this volume had a preliminary airing on that occasion; alongside them we have added other specially commissioned contributions. Bringing these papers together into a coherent whole has been a collective undertaking: we thank our contributors for their care in commenting on each other's chapters and their understanding of the time that such a collaborative project invariably takes. In addition, we gratefully acknowledge the stimulating contribution of everyone who participated in the Leeds panels and of those who aided the transition from conference to book: Melissa Aubin, Tom Brown, Averil Cameron, Wendy Davies, Hans-Werner Goetz, Guy Halsall, Heinrich Härke, Anne-Marie Helvétius, Judith Herrin, Michel Kaplan, Rosamond McKitterick, Daniel Praet, Barbara Rosenwein, Pauline Stafford and Nicholas Stoodley. We are also deeply indebted to William Davies at Cambridge University Press for his support throughout all stages of this project. In steering this volume through production, Alison Powell has coped smoothly with unforeseen circumstances and has helped us greatly. Last but not least, we appreciate the incisive editorial advice and domestic support of Chris Wickham and Hamish Scott.

Abbreviations

AASS	*Acta Sanctorum quotquot toto orbe coluntur*, ed. J. Bollandus *et al.* (Antwerp, Brussels and Paris, 1643–1940; 3rd edn Paris, 1863–70)
CCCM	Corpus Christianorum, Continuatio Medievalis
CCSL	Corpus Christianorum, Series Latina
CSEL	Corpus Scriptorum Ecclesiasticorum Latinorum
CT	*Codex Theodosianus*
DOP	*Dumbarton Oaks Papers*
EME	*Early Medieval Europe*
JESHO	*Journal of the Economic and Social History of the Orient*
JÖB	*Jahrbuch der Österreichische Byzantinistik*
JRS	*Journal of Roman Studies*
MGH	*Monumenta Germaniae Historica*
AA	*Auctores Antiquissimi*
Cap.	*Capitularia. Legum sectio II*
Conc.	*Concilia. Legum sectio III*
Epp.	*Epistolae*
Poet.	*Poetae Latini Aevi Carolini*
SRG	*Scriptores Rerum Germanicarum in usum scholarum separatim editi*
SRL	*Scriptores Rerum Langobardicarum et Italicarum*
SRM	*Scriptores Rerum Merovingicarum*
SS	*Scriptores*
PG	*Patrologia Cursus Completus, Series Graeca*, ed. J.-P. Migne, 161 vols. (Paris, 1857–66)
PL	*Patrologia Cursus Completus, Series Latina*, ed. J.-P. Migne, 221 vols. (Paris, 1844–65)
SC	Sources Chrétiennes
SHA	*Scriptores Historiae Augustae*

CHAPTER I

Introduction: gendering the early medieval world

Julia M. H. Smith

In recent years few subjects have attracted as much attention – or as much hostility – as 'gender'. Fewer still are the concepts whose meaning and significance are more hotly debated. Uncomfortable, subversive, threatening, contentious, it is also provocative, creative, multivalent and of immense analytic vigour. How can it help students of past societies achieve a fuller grasp of their subject? This volume of essays by leading specialists in a range of complementary disciplines answers this question with respect to the society of the late Roman empire and its successor civilisations, Byzantine, Islamic and western European. Through the prism of gender, these papers offer new perspectives on the institutions and ideologies of government, the allocation of economic resources, individual and collective identities, religious beliefs and practices, family life, death and burial, and the writing of history during the centuries from AD 300 to 900. Together, they argue for the ubiquity of gender in the ordering of social existence throughout this period.

The essays which follow are diverse in subject and pluralist in approach. It is fitting that they should be so, for they are located at the intersection of two fields of research which are different in focus but alike in liveliness and diversity. Simultaneously but separately, both fields took centre stage in academic debates from the early 1970s onwards. In 1971, Peter Brown's *The World of Late Antiquity: From Marcus Aurelius to Muhammad* not only gave common currency to the expression 'late antiquity' for the centuries from *c.* AD 250 to 800, but inaugurated a thorough re-evaluation of this period and set the research agenda for a whole generation of scholars.[1] The following year, Ann Oakley's *Sex, Gender and Society* launched a different

---

[1] For assessments of its impact, see Peter Brown, G. W. Bowersock, Averil Cameron, Elizabeth A. Clark, Albrecht Dihle, Garth Fowden, Peter Heather, Philip Rousseau, Aline Rouselle, Hjalmar Torp and Ian Wood, '*SO* Debate: the world of late antiquity revisited', *Symbolae Osloenses* 72 (1997), pp. 5–90; Richard Lim and Carole Straw (eds.), *The Past Before Us: The Challenge of New Historiographies of Late Antiquity* (Berkeley, forthcoming).

intellectual revolution by turning the attention of political activists and scholars alike to the implications of the socially constructed asymmetries and differences between men and women. *Gender in the Early Medieval World: East and West, 300–900* brings the two together by addressing the period of late antiquity with the methodology of gender studies.

For this double hinterland let us first turn our attention to the period in question. *The World of Late Antiquity* deliberately subverted conventional disciplinary boundaries between classical studies and Islamic studies and between ancient and medieval history. It marked out the Roman empire which emerged from the mid-third-century crisis as an empire with a political and cultural order fundamentally revised since the Principate (the first two centuries of the common era). It made religion – paganisms, Judaism, Christianity, Islam – the province as much of the social historian as of the theologian. And it ended forever the negative evaluation of the later imperial centuries which Edward Gibbon's *Decline and Fall of the Roman Empire* had made central to the grand narratives of Enlightenment and post-Enlightenment historiography. 'Late antiquity' thus signifies a world substantively different from prior times but not thereby in decline or decadence, as traditional paradigms of Roman history had mandated. It indicates too a cultural tradition and heritage which continued in many guises long after all the Roman empire except its north-eastern quadrant (the Byzantine empire) had ceased to be under Roman rule, a heritage as central to early Islamic society as to the emerging 'barbarian' successor kingdoms in the former western provinces of the Roman empire. In altering historical periodisation, *The World of Late Antiquity* revealed a coherence in the post-Roman early Middle Ages which had hitherto been lacking. That coherence renders it otiose to try to delimit the 'late antique' from the 'early medieval'; for most of the period covered by our essays, these terms are effectively interchangeable.

Scholars of the late and post-Roman worlds benefit greatly from the exceptionally rich and varied corpus of texts and material culture surviving from these centuries. Admittedly, distribution across place and time is uneven, but, in western Europe at least, any graph of surviving words per century would certainly show sharp peaks for the periods *c.* 350–450 and again *c.* 750–850. In Byzantium, the peaks are somewhat differently constituted – *c.* 350–550 and *c.* 800 on – while the Islamic world begins to generate massive textual evidence from the end of the eighth century. In part, these inconsistencies even out when we turn to material remains. The revisionist perspectives ushered in by *The World of Late Antiquity* coincided with new methodological approaches to visual communication, and a huge upsurge in the quantity and quality of material evidence available as archaeologists began to pay serious attention to periods and cultures other than the prehistoric or the classical. Increasing interest in urbanism and settlement patterns coincided with archaeological opportunities presented by the 1960s post-war reconstruction of European cities, the rapid modernisation of Middle Eastern cities and the growth of historical preservation and heritage movements. Together with rapidly developing scientific techniques of field research and laboratory analysis, these have effected multiple, overlapping transformations in late antique studies during four decades. As a result, the natural and built environments within which the women and men of the early medieval centuries lived, their technologies and trade routes, diseases and life expectancies, funerary practices and religious places are known to us as never before.

The textual and material evidence from the late and post-Roman worlds informs diverse and wide-ranging debates. Some of these concern the impact of first Christianity then Islam on the ancient societies of the Mediterranean. Others address the causes and consequences of political change, whether the crumbling of imperial rule in the western provinces which were subjected to Germanic migration and settlement, its transformation into the caliphate around the southern and eastern shores of the Mediterranean by Muslim conquerors, or its reshaping in Byzantine regions where Roman rule persisted for many centuries to come. Differently put, the formation of new identities, whether social, religious or ethnic, stands close to the heart of much recent work in this field. So too does the expression of those shifting identities in such institutions as family, city, kingdom or caliphate. The reception and renegotiation of Rome's legacy in the Islamic, Byzantine and western culture provinces is another long-standing subject of enquiry, as much concerned with the textual as with the material inheritance. Attention to the knowledge these texts transmit is now supplemented by exposing the discourses they sustain, just as artisanal, archaeological and architectural remains are interrogated for the identities and ideologies they betray as much as for their styles, motifs and technologies. All approaches stress that the late Roman and early medieval world was characterised by societies, cultures and polities in flux, however disputed the causes and consequences of those changes remain. Common to all debates, however, is an emphasis on symbiosis not caesura in both present-day scholarly circles and the political and cultural life of the period from 300 to 900.

'At the crossroads of many histories': thus the *Guide to the Post-classical World* characterised these centuries in 1999, a generation after the publication of *The World of Late Antiquity*.[2] This *Guide* stands as a survey of a subject which hardly existed prior to 1971. Prefacing its alphabetically arranged entries, eleven introductory essays offer an overview of several key directions in late antique studies. Worth attention – as much for what is omitted as included – they are: 'Remaking the past'; 'Sacred landscapes'; 'Philosophical tradition and the self'; 'Religious communities'; 'Barbarians and ethnicity'; 'War and violence'; 'Empire building'; 'Christian triumph and controversy'; 'Islam'; 'The good life'; 'Habitat'.[3] Each reader can draw up an alternative contents list; for our purposes there are two significant silences. The first concerns markers of individual or group identity other than those of religion or ethnicity, such as status, class or sexual identity. The second is the human body in both its lifecycle from reproduction to death and its public presentation through moulding, dress, deportment and language. The central lacuna of this compendium is, in effect, the social and discursive construction of sexual difference.

That is the subject of this book of essays. We approach it by means of 'gender'. This is not a thing or object waiting to be discovered, whether in the ground or a dusty archive. Rather, like 'class' or 'race', it is a concept capable of being put to various uses. As such it is inevitably shorthand, a single word that hints at possibilities and complications. And, like many other concepts used by historians, it has its own history – of shifting meanings and contested significances.[4] At its simplest it refers to the disparities in all societies between the social roles permitted to men and women together with the wider cultural meanings associated with masculinity and femininity.

This has not always been its meaning, however. The English word 'gender' is from the common Latin word *genus* (Greek: *genos*). Meaning a

---

[2] Introduction, in G. W. Bowersock, Peter Brown and Oleg Grabar (eds.), *Late Antiquity: A Guide to the Postclassical World* (Cambridge, MA, 1999), p. xiii.

[3] In addition to the extensive bibliographical guidance supplied in the *Guide to the Postclassical World*, consult the following for up-to-date interpretations: *Cambridge Ancient History*, vol. XIII: *The Late Empire, AD 337–425*, ed. Averil Cameron and Peter Garnsey, and vol. XIV: *Late Antiquity: Empire and Successors, 425–600*, ed. Averil Cameron, Bryan Ward-Perkins and Michael Whitby (Cambridge, 1998–2000); *New Cambridge Medieval History*, vol. II: *c.700–900*, ed. Rosamond McKitterick (Cambridge, 1995); *The Byzantine and Early Islamic Near East*, vol. I: *Problems in the Literary Source Material*, ed. Averil Cameron and Lawrence Conrad, vol. II: *Land Use and Settlement Patterns*, ed. G. R. D. King and Averil Cameron, and vol. III: *States, Resources and Armies*, ed. Lawrence Conrad and Averil Cameron (Princeton, 1992–95). The numerous volumes of essays under the general editorship of Ian Wood in the ongoing series Transformation of the Roman World (Leiden, 1997–) are also relevant.

[4] The full history of the concept remains to be written; for a clear outline of its development within the historical profession see K. Canning, 'Gender history', in *International Encyclopaedia of the Social and Behavioral Sciences*, vol. IX (Amsterdam, 2001), pp. 6006–11; 'Gender history: the evolution of a concept', in Robert Shoemaker and Mary Vincent (eds.), *Gender and History in Western Europe* (London, 1998), pp. 1–20. On its contested significance, see the preface to Joan Scott, *Gender and the Politics of History*, revised edn (New York, 1999), and Penelope Corfield, 'History and the challenge of gender history', *Rethinking History* 1 (1997), pp. 241–58.

'category, class or kind', *genus* is etymologically closely related to *gens*, 'a biological descent group, a race or people', and *gignere*, 'to beget', and thus has connotations of procreation as much as of categorisation. Amongst its many uses in antiquity, *genus* was the grammarian's term for the classification of all nouns and adjectives into groups including 'male', 'female', 'neuter' and 'common'. The grammarian Servius (*c.* 370–*c.* 430) explained it thus:

> Genders are so called from that which they generate, and thus there are only two principal genders, masculine and feminine, for biological reproduction generates these two alone. Genders [of words], however, are either natural or assigned by authoritative social usage. Natural genders are words such as 'man' or 'woman'; those assigned by authoritative social usage are words such as 'wall' [*hic paries*: masculine] or 'window' [*haec fenestra*: feminine]. We recognise that these things do not have any natural sex, but we follow the sex which authority has established. The remaining genders, however, derive from the aforementioned, namely neuter, which is neither masculine nor feminine; common, which is both masculine and feminine; inclusive, which includes all the aforementioned genders, and finally epicene, which refers to creatures of either sex.[5]

With this complex semantic field referring to modes of categorising, both arbitrary (grammatical) and natural (biological), *genus* had passed into Middle English as 'gender' by the fourteenth century.[6] Primarily (although not exclusively) a grammarian's term, 'gender' must have puzzled generations of grammar school children curious as to why a window should be feminine but a wall masculine. Thus the term remained until the mid-twentieth century, when anglophone psychoanalysts turned their attention towards individuals whose social personality and sense of individual identity were discordant with their physiological sex. Disregarding the word's etymological roots, they found 'gender' a convenient word for categorising these individuals' social role, as distinct from their genital anatomy.[7]

---

[5] *Commentarius in artem Donati*, ed. H. Keil, *Grammatici Latini*, vol. IV (Leipzig, 1864), pp. 407–8: 'Genera dicta sunt ab eo, quod generant, atque ideo duo sunt tantum genera principalia, masculinum et feminum. Haec enim sexus tantum generat. Genera autem aut naturalia sunt, aut ex auctoritate descendunt: naturalia sunt, ut vir mulier; auctoritate descendunt, ut hic paries, haec fenestra. In his enim naturalem nullum intellegimus sexum, sed eum sequimur, quem firmavit auctoritas. Cetera vero genera a superioribus veniunt, ut est neutrum, quod nec masculinum est nec feminum, commune, quod et masculinum et feminem, omne, quod omnia supra dicta continet genera, epicoenon vero, quod confusum continet sexum.' I am grateful to Karla Pollmann for discussion of this passage.

[6] *Oxford English Dictionary*, online edition, sv 'gender'.

[7] The Englishness of this word is important: no other language is capable of a similar sharp semantic distinction between 'sex' and 'gender'. Cf. Gisela Bock, 'Challenging dichotomies: perspectives on women's history', in Karen Offen, Ruth Roach Pierson and Jane Rendall (eds.), *Writing Women's*

Thanks to Ann Oakley's *Sex, Gender and Society*, this meaning was taken up in the early phases of the 'second-wave' feminist movement, and from there spread rapidly throughout the social sciences, always referring to the socially organised relationship of women to men.[8]

Its adoption by historians owes much to Joan Scott's immensely influential paper of 1986, 'Gender: a useful category of historical analysis'.[9] Since then, its conceptual and historical elaboration has been rapid, notably so in the USA. On the one hand, a renewed emphasis on the use of language to organise knowledge about sexual difference has entered historical scholarship under the influence of post-modern literary theories.[10] On the other hand, historians have followed sociologists in exploring the relational aspects of gender from men's perspectives, thus opening up to analysis the cultural production of masculinities and the organisation of power hierarchies between different groups of men.[11] Notable here has been R. W. Connell's elaboration of the notion of 'hegemonic masculinity'. This refers to a dynamic masculinity which lacks fixed content but is rather the culturally specific legitimation of the dominant form of masculinity within any particular gender order, by which femininities and other masculinities are marginalised or subordinated.[12]

Loosed from its earlier grammatical moorings, the word 'gender' has developed additional related but variant meanings. Sometimes regarded as synonymous with 'sex', it is more widely used to designate humans as

---

History: International Perspectives (Basingstoke, 1991), pp. 1–23 esp. p. 9, and Ruth Roded, *Women in Islam and the Middle East* (London, 1999), p. 14.

[8] Ann Oakley has commented on the context in which she developed this usage in 'A brief history of gender', in Ann Oakley and Juliet Mitchell (eds.), *Who's Afraid of Feminism? Seeing through the Backlash* (New York, 1997), pp. 29–55 esp. pp. 31–3.

[9] First published in *American Historical Review* 91 (1986), pp. 1053–75; reprinted in Scott, *Gender and the Politics of History*, pp. 28–50 and Joan Scott (ed.), *Feminism and History* (Oxford, 1996), pp. 152–80.

[10] Pertinent to the period covered in these essays are Kate Cooper, 'Insinuations of womanly influence: an aspect of the Christianization of the Roman Aristocracy', *JRS* 82 (1992), pp. 113–27; Elizabeth Clark, 'The lady vanishes: dilemmas of a feminist historian after the "linguistic turn"', *Church History* 67 (1998), pp. 1–31; Gabrielle Spiegel, 'History, historicism and the social logic of the text in the Middle Ages', *Speculum* 65 (1990), pp. 59–86.

[11] The article which opened up this subect was T. Carrigan, R. W. Connell and J. Lee, 'Toward a new sociology of masculinity', *Theory and Society* 14 (1985), pp. 551–604 (reprinted in H. Brod (ed.), *The Making of Masculinities* (Cambridge, MA, 1987), pp. 63–100 and, abbreviated, in Rachel Adams and David Savran (eds.), *The Masculinity Studies Reader* (Malden, MA, 2002), pp. 99–118). For an up-to-date overview of recent work on masculinity within a contemporary British perspective, see Stephen M. Whitehead, *Men and Masculinities: Key Themes and New Directions* (Cambridge, 2002). Its emergence as a subject of historical enquiry was prompted by Michael Roper and John Tosh (eds.), *Manful Assertions: Masculinities in Britain since 1800* (London, 1991). See also John Tosh, 'What should historians do with masculinity?', *History Workshop Journal* 38 (1994), pp. 179–202; reprinted in Shoemaker and Vincent (eds.), *Gender and History*, pp. 64–85. For further bibliography, see note 26 below.

[12] See further R. W. Connell, *Masculinities* (Cambridge, 1995), pp. 76–81.

belonging to one of two groups, either male or female. Common usage thus often blurs the distinction between biological and cultural categories, and is at variance with the meaning of the term established as normative in the social sciences from the 1970s onwards but unwittingly analogous to the word's etymological root.[13] In this context, 'gender history' has often been women's history passing under a new name. 'Today', Ann Oakley comments, looking back on the political career of the word she had launched a generation previously, 'gender slips uneasily between being merely another word for sex and a contested political term'.[14]

Its contested nature stems directly from the fact that it is inherently political. Many of the conceptual advances stemmed explicitly from the political engagement of their originators, whether within the women's movement of the 1960s–80s or within more recent gay rights movements, pro-feminist men's groups and a wide range of minority rights political interest groups. Even more importantly, gender is in essence about power relationships and the language which legitimates or denies their existence. A gendered approach insists upon attention to hierarchies of power, and in so doing takes equal notice of institutional, cultural and discursive mechanisms of exclusion and inclusion. Additionally, it exposes understandings of the sexed human body as culturally conditioned. In dismantling any lingering idea of the 'naturalness' of gender, it contributes a sharpened sense of the ways in which even at a physiological level the sexed body is a malleable object of a politics of power and interpretation.[15] In sum, whether we focus on socio-political modalities or on language as the medium which represents and interprets the world, the self and the human body, the concept of 'gender' indicates the rejection of any notion that 'male' and 'female' are essential, natural and objective distinctions. It divorces the gendered individual from genital anatomy, and in place of biological determinism it substitutes language, social situation and power.

Gender politics and gender studies originated in a specific political context – the final three decades of the twentieth century in the secularised western world. In that environment, they have become intimately associated with some of the fundamental issues of modern and post-modern philosophy: the nature and production of language, knowledge, power and selfhood. But because of that very context, 'gender' has also encountered

---

[13] For a discussion of this slippage and its methodological implications, see Joan Scott, 'Some more reflections on gender and politics', in the revised edition of her *Gender and the Politics of History*, pp. 199–222.

[14] Oakley, 'Brief history', p. 30.

[15] Anne Fausto-Sterling, *Myths of Gender: Biological Theories about Men and Women* (New York, 1985); Fausto-Sterling, *Sexing the Body: Gender Politics and the Construction of Sexuality* (New York, 2000).

powerful challenges which have delayed its impact, renegotiated its terms or even denied it any validity at all.[16] Whether propounded by opponents of secularisation or of westernising paradigms of political and social development, these refutations have constrained the development of concepts of gender, rendering their acceptance patchy. Even within the western world, gender studies are construed as far more radical in some countries and institutions than in others. The essays in this volume indirectly reflect this: our authors write in a wide range of specific political situations ranging from the American to the Middle Eastern, and in various religious milieux as well as self-consciously secular contexts. Although some write from a position of greater personal involvement in the politics of social equality than others, all of us know that the scholar as much as the object of study is gendered, and that none of us can deny our own bodily subjectivity or personal experience of gender.

Nevertheless, we all engage with a common understanding of 'gender', agreeing that it is both a method of analysing past societies and also a subject of study within them. Although some of the chapters which follow incline to one rather than the other, most deploy both together. As a group of essays, they take as their domain the human body, social institutions (family, marriage, church, state) and the rhetorics of sexuality; as their method, they search out both implicit and explicit ways in which sexual differences informed politics, culture, society and religion in the late Roman empire and its successor civilisations.

The driving impulse behind the spread of the concept of gender has been contemporary political action, and historians' efforts to explain the formation of modern, western gender systems have tended to concentrate their energies in the period from the French Revolution onwards.[17] Nevertheless, historians, political theorists and sociologists alike are now far more sensitive than they were in the 1970s and early 1980s to the absence of any universals underlying the modern, western gender order. Indeed, anthropologists have made it abundantly clear how very different gendered roles, discursive practices and understandings of the sexed human body are in other cultures.[18] There is now a general recognition that gender is historically contingent, expressed through and interacting with the cultural

---

[16] Cf. Scott, *Gender and the Politics of History* (revised edn), pp. ix–xiii, 211–18; Roded, *Women in Islam*, pp. 9–18; Barbara L. Marshall, *Configuring Gender: Explorations in Theory and Politics* (Peterborough, Ont., 2000), pp. 144–9.

[17] See, for example, the essays collected together by Shoemaker and Vincent (eds.), *Gender and History*.

[18] Of the vast literature, key works include Michele Rosaldo and Louise Lamphere (eds.), *Women, Culture and Society* (Stanford, 1974); Rayna Reiter (ed.), *Toward an Anthropology of Women* (Stanford, 1975); Carol MacCormack and Marilyn Strathern (eds.), *Nature, Culture and Gender* (Cambridge,

resources and social matrix particular to any given time and place. All that is remarkably constant is the presence of gender differences in all known human societies. Beyond that, gender is fluid, subject to constant challenge and reformulation, multivalent not monolithic and not easily susceptible to generalisation.

Approaching the centuries between AD 300 and 900 with this in mind, we also build on recent scholarship on women, men and sexuality in classical, western medieval, early Islamic and Byzantine societies. Over the past generation, this has followed a trajectory similar to that of women's and gender history in general, although with some notable modulations. Broadly speaking, there have been three historiographical phases since the 1970s. The initial one drew attention to women within existing modes of historical analysis and identified the realities of women's lives with their concomitant modes of subordination. The second phase was marked by conceptualisations of the distinctiveness of women's lives and cultural expressions which either established new interpretive agendas or claimed a different historical space for women. Most recently, attention to the social and cultural formations of gender relations has followed, somewhat belatedly, the agenda outlined above.[19]

In the early phase of women's history, in which the keynote was 'becoming visible', the women of some historical periods were nevertheless far more visible than of others. The comparative invisibility of women in traditional Eurasian societies contributed to retarding their emergence as historical subjects in their own right: the women of the centuries and cultures featured in this book were notably absent from the general histories of women composed in the 1970s–80s.[20] By the time the women of late antiquity, Byzantium and the early medieval west were gaining scholarly attention

1980); Sherry Ortner and Harriet Whitehead (eds.), *Sexual Meanings: The Cultural Construction of Gender and Sexuality* (Cambridge, 1981); M. Strathern, *The Gender of the Gift* (Berkeley, 1988); Andrea Cornwall and Nancy Lindisfarne (eds.), *Dislocating Masculinity: Comparative Ethnographies* (London, 1994); Sherry Ortner, *Making Gender: The Politics and Erotics of Culture* (Boston, 1996).

[19] For overviews see Olwen Hufton, 'Women, gender and the *fin de siècle*', in Michael Bentley (ed.), *Companion to Historiography* (London, 1997), pp. 929–40, and Johanna Alberti, *Gender and the Historian* (Harlow, 2002). Note Hufton's comments on the differing American and European trajectories of women's and gender studies. Historiographical trends in classical and medieval studies are sketched by Allen J. Frantzen, 'When women aren't enough', in Nancy F. Partner (ed.), *Studying Medieval Women* (Cambridge, MA, 1993), pp. 143–69 esp. pp. 145–50; Liz James, 'Introduction: women's studies, gender studies, Byzantine studies', in L. James (ed.), *Women, Men and Eunuchs* (London, 1977), pp. xi–xxiv, and Maria Wyke, 'Introduction', in M. Wyke (ed.), *Gender and the Body in the Ancient Mediterranean* (Oxford, 1998), pp. 1–7. For a different framing of the literature, consult Janet L. Nelson, 'Family, gender and sexuality in the Middle Ages', in Bentley (ed.), *Companion to Historiography*, pp. 153–76.

[20] Neither Renate Bridenthal and Claudia Coonz, *Becoming Visible: Women in European History*, 1st edn (Boston, 1977), nor Bonnie S. Anderson and Judith P. Zinsser, *A History of Their Own: Women*

in the late 1980s and early 1990s, it had become problematic to study the women of more recent historical periods as a single, relatively homogeneous group at all.[21] Indeed, medieval Islamic women could be described as 'becoming visible' only as recently as 1999.[22] For the period and cultures under discussion here it is possible to fracture the category of 'women' along lines of ethnicity, status and class, but the extreme scarcity of any direct evidence for women's activities and experiences makes attempts to dissolve it into multiple subjectivities exceptionally difficult.

Instead, scholarly impulse has come from rather different directions, on the one hand the institutional and theological history of Christianity and on the other the history of sexuality. From the 1960s onwards, attention to the role of women within contemporary churches, Catholic and Protestant alike, prompted both re-evaluation of the roles of women within the early Christian church and reappraisal – often searing – of the development of patristic teaching about women and gender order.[23] One consequence of this has been lay and academic fascination with the high-profile women saints of late antique and medieval Christianity; another, a sophisticated body of scholarship on the gendered aspects of Christian ethical and moral teachings.[24] To the extent that injunctions to sexual abstinence – and indeed

in Europe from Prehistory to the Present, 2 vols. (New York, 1988), nor Whitney Chadwick, Women, Art and Society, 2nd edn (London, 1996) devotes more than a handful of pages to them.

[21] Cf. Denise Riley, 'Am I that Name?' Feminism and the Category of 'Women' in History (Basingstoke, 1988).

Groundbreaking titles on women c. 300 to 900 include Averil Cameron and Amélie Kuhrt (eds.), Images of Women in Antiquity (London, 1983); Pauline Stafford, Queens, Concubines and Dowagers: The King's Wife in the Early Middle Ages (London, 1983); Christine Fell, Women in Anglo-Saxon England (London, 1984); Suzanne F. Wemple, Women in Frankish Society: Marriage and the Cloister, 500–900 (Philadelphia, 1985); Storia delle donne in occidente, vol. I: L'Antichità, ed. Pauline Schmitt Pantel (Rome, 1990) [English translation: A History of Women in the West, vol. I: From Ancient Goddesses to Christian Saints (Cambridge, MA, 1992)]; Storia delle donne in occidente, vol. II: Il Medioevo, ed. Christiane Klapisch-Zuber (Rome, 1990); [English translation: A History of Women in the West, vol. II: Silences of the Middle Ages (Cambridge, MA, 1992)]; Joëlle Beaucamp, Le Statut de la femme à Byzance, IVe–VIIe siècle, 2 vols. (Paris, 1990–2); Werner Affeldt (ed.), Frauen in Spätantike und Frühmittelalter: Lebensbedingungen – Lebensnormen – Lebensformen (Sigmaringen, 1990); Gillian Clark, Women in Late Antiquity (Oxford, 1993); Léonie Archer, Susan Fischler and Maria Wyke (eds.), Women in Ancient Societies: An Illusion of the Night (London, 1994). For an overall assessment, see Julia M. H. Smith, 'Did women have a transformation of the Roman world?', in P. Stafford and A. B. Mulder-Bakker (eds.), Gendering the Middle Ages (Oxford, 2001) [also published as a special issue of Gender and History 12, 3 (2000)], pp. 22–41.

[22] Cf. Gavin R. G. Hambly, 'Introduction. Becoming visible: medieval Islamic women in history and historiography', in Hambly (ed.), Women in the Medieval Islamic World (Basingstoke, 1999), pp. 3–27. See also Nikki R. Keddie and Beth Baron (eds.), Women in Middle Eastern History: Shifting Boundaries in Sex and Gender (New Haven, 1991).

[23] For example, Rosemary R. Ruether, Religion and Sexism: Images of Women in the Jewish and Christian Traditions (New York, 1974); Elisabeth Schüssler Fiorenza, In Memory of Her: A Feminist Theological Reconstruction of Christian Origins (New York, 1983).

[24] A short selection: Caroline Walker Bynum, 'Women's stories, women's symbols: a critique of Victor Turner's theory of liminality', in R. L. Moore and F. E. Reynolds (eds.), Anthropology and the

permanent chastity – are central to the latter, the stimulus of patristic studies intersected with the markedly different impulse offered by the work of Michel Foucault on the ethics of sexual self-fashioning in the ancient world. In 1984, the second volume of his *Histoire de la sexualité, L'Usage des plaisirs*, took fifth- and fourth-century BC Greece as the locus of an argument about the ideological nature of the apparent 'naturalness' of modern western heterosexuality; the third volume, *Le Souci de soi*, extended his interest in the contribution of sexuality to the shaping of male modes of being into the first and second centuries AD.[25] The second volume in particular administered an electric shock to classical studies, a jolt which rapidly affected late antiquity too.[26] If Foucault made the social construction of the male body central to understandings of citizenship and selfhood throughout the entire ancient world, the reaction provoked by his notorious gender-blindness has prompted the rapid development of fully gendered analyses of classical and patristic masculinities.[27]

Hitherto, understanding of men, women and gender in the post-classical period has tended to focus on the textually rich decades of the fourth to fifth centuries, when Christian discourses of self, power and morality were debated with articulate passion and enduring norms were established. The essays in this book extend a gendered perspective far more widely, into periods and places which are not all as well documented. Notably, our geographical and religious contexts are not limited to the rapidly Christianising world of the late Roman empire. Effros takes as her subject the pre-literate peoples who found new homes for themselves within the boundaries of

---

Study of Religion (Chicago, 1984), pp. 105–25; James A. Brundage, *Law, Sex and Christian Society in Medieval Europe* (Chicago, 1987); Benedicta Ward, *Harlots of the Desert: A Study of Repentance in Early Monastic Sources* (London, 1987); Susanna Elm, *Virgins of God: The Making of Asceticism in Late Antiquity* (Oxford, 1994); Kate Cooper, *The Virgin and the Bride: Idealized Womanhood in Late Antiquity* (Cambridge, MA, 1996); Lynda Coon, *Sacred Fictions: Holy Women and Hagiography in Late Antiquity* (Philadelphia, 1997); Elizabeth Clark, *Reading Renunciation: Asceticism and Scripture in Early Christianity* (Princeton, 1999); Anke Bernau, Ruth Evans and Sarah Salih (eds.), *Medieval Virginities* (Cardiff, 2003).

[25] English translations by Robert Hurley, *The Use of Pleasure* (Harmondsworth, 1986) and *The Care of the Self* (Harmondsworth, 1986).

[26] For critiques by ancient and late antique historians, see Averil Cameron, 'Redrawing the map: early Christian territory after Foucault', *JRS* 76 (1986), pp. 266–71, and Lin Foxhall, 'Pandora unbound: a feminist critique of Foucault's *History of Sexuality*', in Cornwall and Lindisfarne (eds.), *Dislocating Masculinity*, pp. 133–47.

[27] Clare Lees (ed.), *Medieval Masculinities* (Minneapolis, 1994); J. J. Cohen and B. Wheeler (eds.), *Becoming Male in the Middle Ages* (New York, 1997); Lin Foxhall and John Salmon (eds.), *Thinking Men: Masculinity and Self-Representation in the Classical Tradition* (London, 1998); Foxhall and Salmon (eds.), *When Men Were Men: Masculinity, Power and Identity in Classical Antiquity* (London, 1998); D. M. Hadley (ed.), *Masculinity in Medieval Europe* (London, 1999); Virginia Burrus, *Begotten Not Made: Conceiving Manhood in Late Antiquity* (Stanford, 2000); Mathew Kuefler, *The Manly Eunuch: Masculinity, Gender Ambiguity and Christian Ideology in Late Antiquity* (Chicago, 2001).

empire but persisted, for a while, with their traditional ways of dispos-
ing of the dead by burying them richly dressed and in furnished graves.
Bray and El Cheikh both extend gendered methodology into early Islamic
society, and Coon explores Jewish notions of priestly identity as the background to her work on ninth-century Christian images of the gender of the
clergy.

Moreover, many of our contributors present source material previously
excluded from discussions of gender history in these centuries. Three
authors draw on material and art historical evidence: Harlow finds visual
images an important source for understanding the dress codes associated
with elite masculinity in the third to sixth centuries, whilst Effros and
Hadley both work with funerary archaeology, the former in the context
of 'migration age' settlements in western Europe, the latter in Anglo-
Saxon England. Effros exposes the inappropriate gendered assumptions
of much modern scholarship by doubting whether women's dress can provide a secure guide to ethnic identity and thereby challenging assumed
links between material culture and ethnicity in fifth-century Gaul. Hadley
argues that, notwithstanding the gradual impact of Christianity on burial
rites, the expression of gender identity through Anglo-Saxon burial practices fluctuated between the fifth and tenth centuries, and that funerary
expression of martial masculinity was a recurrent feature at times of great
social stress and political crisis.

Others find richness in neglected written sources. Two authors turn a
gendered gaze on Christian texts not generally interrogated from this perspective because of the highly technical and deeply conservative nature of
their genres: Muschiol on liturgy and Coon on biblical exegesis. By contrast,
Wood finds in bare genealogies a fertile source for the gendered manipulation of lineages of power and dynasty, whilst Tougher exploits administrative lists for their insights into a form of masculinity entirely absent
from the history and sociology of masculinities in more recent times – the
eunuch.

We balance contributions on new sources with ones which pose new
questions to topics which have always been the object of historical enquiry –
royal and imperial courts, the Christian church, family and marriage.
Several chapters address courts from varying perspectives: power and rulership, cultural production, dynastic reproduction. As an ensemble, these
chapters make clear that gender is the connective tissue between these
seemingly different themes. Whilst Hen examines the evidence for women's
modes of patronising cultural production and finds a considerable degree
of gender complementarity in Merovingian courts, Pohl highlights the role

of Lombard queens in conferring dynastic legitimation, ordering social memory and commissioning historical commemoration of the Lombard people and their kings. Nelson extends this discussion by investigating royal women's agency in the reproduction of cultural value systems in the early medieval west and arguing that women as well as men were key agents in the 'civilising process'.

Marriage emerges as a crucial vector for cultural reproduction and political legitimation in many of our chapters. Nevertheless, it is equally evident from them that the ways in which early medieval authors deployed gendered stereotypes or wrote in ways which systematically occluded female subjectivity have to be unravelled before a full understanding of the gender differences and complementarities of dynastic marriages and court politics can be appreciated. Notably, Wood complements Pohl's analysis of Lombard queens by demonstrating how the female ancestors of the Carolingian kings not only conveyed dynastic legitimacy but also transmitted crucial claims to land and power to their male relatives, in ways which eighth-century writers and modern historians alike have consistently overlooked. In contrast, Brubaker dissects a literary account of the Byzantine empress Theodora, who was the contemporary of some of the civilising western queens discussed by Nelson, and demonstrates how a famous text whose denunciation of female conduct is conventionally read as essentially factual is in essence a rhetorically constructed fiction. By demonstrating the text's use of standard stereotyping of female sexual transgression to vilify the reigning emperor, Brubaker argues that the gendered stereotyping of the empress cannot be separated from that of the emperor, for the two are mutually reinforcing, to devastating political ends.

Brubaker's conclusions are complemented by El Cheikh's demonstration of the disjuncture between the textual representation and the political realities of a woman's influence in the court of an early tenth-century caliph of Baghdad. Not until the gendered rhetoric of both medieval and modern Arab historians has been picked apart can the career of an able woman, a slave in origin and mother of the reigning caliph, be understood and the scope of female agency assessed. Stripped of rhetorical denigration, the ability of Shaghab to govern effectively from the private, residential quarters of the palace (the harem) becomes evident. In this case, not husband and wife but mother and son form the gendered pair equally central to political action and gendered text. Coupled chapters by Vinson and de Jong about 'bride shows' – literary narratives of emperors selecting their bride from among the participants in a female beauty parade – extend the arguments about courts, gender and political influence still further. Together, they demonstrate how textual discourses about gendered morality and the ideal wife simultaneously construct and reflect court life and dynastic legitimacy in the ninth century, both Byzantine (Vinson) and western (de Jong). As a group, these chapters all put a gendered understanding of dynastic politics at the centre of late antique, early medieval, western, Islamic and Byzantine court life by indicating the ways in which female agency and men's political imperatives are refracted in the same texts through complex literary strategies. Together, they warn us of the gender games which authors play. They alert us to the discursive power of gendered commonplaces. In so doing, they reinforce a notable theme of the volume, the complex relationships between textual representations and political 'realities'.

A secondary theme in Vinson's and de Jong's discussion of purported bride shows is the reformulation of early medieval gender roles under the impact of Christianity. This becomes the main focus of two chapters which each offer a distinctive approach to the history of the Christian church. Muschiol examines the extent to which the formal liturgical rituals of worship encoded changing understandings of gender relationships, and also points to the ways in which changing ritual contributed to reorganising gender roles. Coon, on the other hand, provides an exposition of the rhetorics of the fecundity of priestly chastity in a ninth-century monastery. She demonstrates the malleability of strongly gendered language by analysing how feminine imagery contributed to organising an understanding of masculine, priestly prowess. By contrast, images and realities of gender roles in early Islam are Bray's subject. Although the cultural specifics of the early Islamic Arab world were different from those of the early medieval Christian west, the reorganisation of gender roles is likewise an aspect of religious conversion and associated societal changes.

Bray's analysis is concerned as much with the imaginative reorderings of social and gender hierarchies in poetry as with the actual reorganisation of Arab society in the eighth and ninth centuries. She finds poetic images of socially marginal women – slaves – a particularly sensitive index of changing forms of Arab masculinity, thus further emphasising the integral, subtle links between constructions of masculinity and femininity and also between gender and other forms of social distinction, in this case legal status. Pohl, on the other hand, searches out the intersection of discourses of gender with those of ethnicity in late antiquity and the early medieval west. He brings to our attention images of Amazons and other women warriors. Through literary representations of these embodiments of otherness, Pohl argues, cultural boundaries could be affirmed and gender hierarchy maintained in situations where both were in flux. Like Bray, Pohl emphasises the deep levels of meaning contained within literary texts' imaginative reorderings of gender hierarchies at times of major socio-political change.

Taken together, the chapters in this book require us to revise our understanding of the early medieval world in several ways. In the first place, they expose serious fallacies within the common knowledge frequently recycled in textbooks. Effros demonstrates that many of the maps of 'barbarian' migration routes and settlement patterns are without secure interpretive foundation. Similarly, Wood points out that the genealogical tables which accompany accounts of the Carolingian dynasty's rise to power are fundamentally misleading and must be reconceived. Rid of these outmoded props, the history of the early medieval west will have to be visualised and conceptualised very differently.[28] El Cheikh and Brubaker both make clear the way in which Islamicists and Byzantinists have continued to recycle as truthful narratives which are so tendentious as to be wrong or, at best, misconceived. They emphasise that it remains all too easy for modern scholars to reiterate the gender prejudices of their medieval sources. It takes their skilful approach to identify discursive practices, medieval and modern, which occlude or disempower women, and to make apparent the gendered nature of the narratives which they sustain.

Instead of master narratives, the embodied self is central to the arguments offered here. This emerges in two ways. First, understanding of sexual physiology in the ancient world was quite different from post-Enlightenment interpretations, for it rooted gendered morality directly in physiology.[29] The Christian Middle Ages reinforced this inheritance with an externalised ethical code projected straight on to the human body.[30] Hence, as Vinson and de Jong both show, the morally pure wife was also the most beautiful, for external appearance was the outer manifestation of inner moral character. Yet, as de Jong also stresses, bodily appearance required careful interpretation, for beauty might also betoken lack of modesty and a wanton disposition.

---

[28] Similar arguments concerning the high and late medieval west are offered in Mary C. Erler and Maryanne Kowaleski (eds.), *Gendering the Master Narrative: Women and Power in the Middle Ages* (Ithaca, NY, 2003).

[29] Thomas Laqueur, *Making Sex: Body and Gender from the Greeks to Freud* (Cambridge, MA, 1990); Mary Harlow, 'In the name of the father: procreation, paternity and patriarchy', in Foxhall and Salmon (eds.), *Thinking Men*, pp. 155–69.

[30] Peter Brown, *The Body and Society: Men, Women and Sexual Renunciation in Early Christianity* (New York, 1988); Joan Cadden, *Meanings of Sex Difference in the Middle Ages: Medicine, Science and Culture* (Cambridge, 1993); Julia M. H. Smith, 'Gender and ideology in the early Middle Ages', in R. N. Swanson (ed.), *Gender and Christian Religion*, Studies in Church History 34 (Woodbridge, 1998), pp. 51–73.

Nor was the distinction of 'male' and 'female' analogous to that of the modern world. Tougher's discussion of eunuchs reminds us that the male body of late antiquity, Byzantium and medieval Islam was adjustable, liable to surgical reshaping for political ends. The inherent social and moral implications of that medical intervention inform the ambivalence with which others wrote about eunuchs in the Byzantine world. These feminised men also remind us that instead of a gender polarity of male and female, Roman and post-Roman ideas of sexual distinction formed a broad spectrum of possibilities.[31] As Tougher also indicates, the notion of a 'third gender' is no recent anthropological construct, but a late antique way of classifying eunuchs. That this spectrum also took discursive form is the conclusion to be drawn from the contributions of Pohl and Coon. These both focus on the early medieval west, where indigenous eunuchism was lacking, but where both virile woman warriors and fecund, virginal men able to generate sons existed in textual form. As Pohl and Coon show respectively, the language of masculinity applied to Amazons as convincingly as the language of birthing and pregnancy fitted chaste priests.

Not only surgery, but language and discourse inscribed gender on the early medieval body. Costume – dress, jewellery and portable objects betokening status – was equally potent, as Harlow, Effros and Hadley agree. Male costume, Harlow stresses, was a way of negotiating power and identity in late antiquity that had to cope not only with the gender ambiguity of brightly coloured silks but also with the cultural ambiguity of barbarian-inspired trousers. Choice of female costume in the post-Roman west, Effros argues, involved issues of ethnic identity, agency and cultural assimilation which the archaeological record and extant textual sources cannot fully reveal. For Hadley, committing a person to the grave in Anglo-Saxon England implied decisions about whether to mark status through gendered clothing and grave goods, during ceremonies in which the audience can be presumed to have been at least as important as the deceased. Inscribed on stone memorials, decisions about gendered displays of costume could endure for many centuries. The point that emerges is that costume could mark far more than merely the gender identity of the body which it clothed. The dress codes for court eunuchs (Tougher), Christian priests

---

[31] As argued with respect to early Icelandic society by Carol J. Clover, 'Regardless of their sex: men, women and power in early Northern Europe', in Partner (ed.), *Studying Medieval Women*, pp. 61–85, and with respect to early Islam by Everett K. Rowson, 'Gender irregularity as entertainment: institutionalised transvestism at the caliphal court in medieval Baghdad', in Sharon Farmer and Carol Braun Pasternack (eds.), *Gender and Difference in the Middle Ages* (Minneapolis, 2003), pp. 45–72.

(Coon) and Amazons (Pohl) variously signalled one or more of their wearers' occupation, status and ethnicity. Clothing could also be interpreted as marking depravity or virtue, the transgression or adherence to cultural and moral norms and expectations. We encounter here what Judith Butler has labelled the 'performative' nature of gender identity.[32]

Social fashioning and discursive interpretation of the human body thus constitute one of the ways in which gender was produced and interpreted in the early medieval world. But human encounters are of course socially organised, and thus our contributors give equal attention to those institutions where gender informed social relationships. Particularly evident here is the gendered regulation of space, whether in the caliphal palace with its attached harem (El Cheikh), the imperial Byzantine palace with its *gynaikonitis* (women's quarters), the male monastery (Coon) or the chancel of a community church (Muschiol). These were the places of holiness or courtliness, where the efficacy of ritual purity on the one hand, or of the politics of power on the other, called for particular attention to the maintenance of gender boundaries. Those boundaries rested on the presumption that neither political nor sacred power was to be wielded by women or eunuchs but only by fertile men, whether as kings and emperors or as priests and caliphs.

However much gender difference blocked women and subordinate men from the exercise of power, these boundaries were nevertheless negotiable to a degree. A holy woman's convent could function as an outpost of a western court or as a centre of familial politics in its own right (Nelson, Wood), whilst Byzantine and Islamic eunuchs were regularly entrusted with high administrative office and might also have privileged access to *gynaikonitis* and harem (Tougher, El Cheikh). Indeed, at the elite level, we can detect a degree of gender complementarity, whether in lavishly furnished burials of the fifth and sixth centuries (Effros, Hadley), in participation in the liturgy and in the patronage of cultural production in Merovingian Gaul (Muschiol, Hen), in the generation and transmission of cultural values (Nelson) or even in subjection to vitriolic invective (Brubaker). Early medieval gender order was often as fluid in practice as it was rigid in theory.

It was also as much discursive as performative or institutional, as many of our contributors rightly insist. As such, it infused explicit ideologies and organised perceptions of individuals' behaviour (Pohl, Brubaker, Vinson, Bray, El Cheikh, de Jong, Coon). With their firm physiological groundings, discourses of gender remained less liable to change than performative or

---

[32] Judith Butler, *Gender Trouble: Feminism and the Subversion of Identity*, 2nd edition (London, 1999).

institutional manifestations of gender. But as we unravel them, we must always remember that mastery of literacy was one of the ways in which hegemonic masculinity reproduced itself in the ancient and medieval worlds, and that the texts in which gender ideology was embedded were, for the most part, generated by those centres which had most at stake in the maintenance of hierarchies of power, whether sacred or secular.

The political, religious and social transformations which characterised the centuries from *c.* 300 to *c.* 900 were accompanied by upheaval and renegotiation of gender systems. Not surprisingly, therefore, fluidities and pluralisms mark the ideas and expressions of gender which we meet in this book. It is nevertheless possible to point to continuities and uniformities in the organisation and expression of gender in the late Roman and early Byzantine, Islamic and medieval worlds.

One of those is the restricted range of social roles in which we can observe women. At elite level, they feature in this book only as wives and mothers or, in Christian times, as nuns. At a lower social level, we occasionally encounter them as courtesans, slaves and prostitutes. We may note too the intellectual efforts which several contributors have to make to uncover traces of female agency even at elite level (El Cheikh, Effros, Nelson, Muschiol, Hen). Alongside these women, however, we meet elite men as senators, warriors and bureaucrats as well as kings, emperors and caliphs. All were generally husbands and fathers, often highly visible within textual and/or material evidence. Chaste Christian priests and eunuchs, Byzantine and Islamic, both occupied distinctive roles within this elite, the former claiming a unique spiritual potency, the latter of essential utility but ambiguous social evaluation. The restricted range of women's social roles contrasts sharply, however, with the wide range of imaginative forms which women's lives could take in poetic, political, religious and historical texts. As for men, we encounter the inverse: a much narrower range of imaginative masculinities accompanied the varied constructions of masculinity actualised in social practice.

Simply to invoke the gender asymmetry typical of traditional societies would not be an adequate explanation of this. Though we may agree that male authors within the centuries from 300 to 900 often found women 'good to think with', this observation also lacks full explanatory utility.[33] We should turn instead to the fixed point in late antique and early medieval

---

[33] Cf. Janet L. Nelson, 'Women and the Word in the earlier Middle Ages', in W. J. Shiels and D. Wood (eds.), *Women in the Church*, Studies in Church History 27 (Oxford, 1990), pp. 53–78 at p. 58 (reprinted in Janet L. Nelson, *The Frankish World, 750–900* (London, 1996), pp. 199–221); Catherine

gender systems: the hegemonic masculinity of the ruling elite of the day. This was the reference point for all other expressions of gender identity in both discourse and practice, whatever the particular cultural content and social form of that elite masculinity might be. In many of our chapters, elite masculinity emerges as the most unstable element in the post-classical gender order, the most in need of frequent reaffirmation. The particular mode of hegemonic masculinity of any given moment faced challenges from those it marginalised, whether barbarians, elite women, eunuchs, slaves or political opponents. Men responded to these challenges by investing in material and discursive reinforcements to their hegemony. Whether this investment was in personal adornment (Harlow), political invective against transgressing women (Brubaker, de Jong, El Cheikh) and effeminate eunuchs (Tougher), commemorative funerary stones (Hadley), narratives about terrifying women warriors (Pohl) or poetic romances about courtesans turned soul-mates (Bray), our contributors agree that it was greatest, and the results most historically conspicuous, at moments of greatest social stress or political dislocation. The gendered arguments which all these texts and monuments contain emphasise that even hegemonic masculinity was relative, performed in relation to those it marginalised as 'other', reduced to subordination or disparaged as weak.

To conclude that the manifold textual and material constructions of gender in the early medieval world were always context specific but nevertheless betray fundamental structural and discursive similarities is therefore not at all a contradiction in terms. Furthermore, despite the virtual invisibility of most women as historical subjects in their own right, they were nevertheless omnipresent in the gendered discourses which buttressed men's precarious assertions of power. Inasmuch as the study of gender has the capacity to 'revise our concepts of humanity and nature, and enlarge our sense of the human predicament',[34] we publish these essays as a contribution to that end.

Cubitt, 'Virginity and misogyny in tenth- and eleventh-century England', *Gender and History* 12 (2000), pp. 1–32 at p. 15.

[34] Jill K. Conway, Susan C. Bourque and Joan W. Scott, 'Introduction: the concept of gender', *Daedalus* 116 pt 4 (1987), pp. xxi–xxix at p. xxix.

PART I

Gender in late antique, Byzantine and Islamic societies

CHAPTER 2

Gender and ethnicity in the early Middle Ages

Walter Pohl

Surprisingly little research has been done so far to connect gender and ethnicity in the early Middle Ages, even though research in both fields has moved in parallel directions.[1] Until fairly recently, both categories have been regarded as firmly grounded in biological terms. One was born man or woman, Goth or Roman, English or French. Only in recent decades has this biological determinism been largely abandoned in scholarship, although it has hardly been shattered in popular opinions and sometimes still lingers over scholarly debates. Both gender and ethnicity were (and still are) cultural constructs, but they were rarely perceived as such. Because they seem to be 'natural' boundaries, the cultural codification, or identification, necessary to maintain them is never transparent. In antiquity and the Middle Ages, just as in modern research well into the twentieth century, ethnicity was regarded as a matter of descent, so that our contemporary sources tend to picture it that way even where that is clearly fictive. That has made it difficult to study how the ethnic cohesion of early medieval peoples was achieved.

Paradoxically, in studies of late antique and early medieval ethnicity (including my own) the change of paradigm – culturally constructed instead of biologically determined – has not led to a systematic interest in the relationship between gender and ethnicity, or to analysis of the parallels in their construction. In part, this may be explained as a reaction to the old paradigm. If birth confers ethnic identity, mothers play a key role, which has been exploited by all sorts of racist ideologies. At some stage, historians need to step past all those ethnically distinct mothers to see what else could confer ethnicity. When we look in the sources for traces of the historical process of the creation of ethnicity, mostly we find information about warrior groups and about the stories old men tell. Both taken together

---

[1] Recent overviews: P. J. Geary, *The Myth of Nations* (Princeton, 2002); W. Pohl, 'Aux origines d'une Europe ethnique', *Annales: Histoire, Sciences Sociales*, forthcoming.

constitute the Wenskus model of a kernel of tradition, with all its merit
and its limitations: a small core group that preserved the ethnic memories
of a people, which could expand quickly under favourable circumstances,
especially under the leadership of a successful warrior king.[2] The Wenskus
model of ethnogenesis has been modified and refined, and some of its
initial shortcomings have been removed.[3] But the role of women, and of
gender, in ethnic processes needs further study. Did the 'recollections of
the elders' and the exploits of war bands give shape to ethnic identities
without female participation? The purpose of this paper is to look at both
elements from a gender perspective to show that the construction of ethnic
and of gender identities is in fact related and intertwined, and should
be looked at in conjunction. The role of women in origin myths will
be discussed in the second part of this chapter: in what ways were women
'good to remember with', and how did women contribute to the shaping of
such social memories? The first part of the chapter will deal with fighting
women, both as gendered fantasies expressed through the ancient myth
of the Amazons, and as possible barbarian realities that stimulated such
perceptions.

AMAZONS — GENDER TRANSGRESSION AND ETHNIC IDENTITY

The *Historia Augusta*, written around AD 400, offers a detailed and fictive
description of Aurelian's triumph thought to have taken place in the 270s
after the emperor's victory over Zenobia of Palmyra and other enemies.
In this account, Aurelian rode up to the Capitol in a chariot which had
belonged to a king of the Goths and was drawn by four stags, followed by
exotic animals, gladiators and captives from the barbarian tribes, among
them Arabs, Indians, Persians, Goths, Franks and Vandals. 'There were
also led along ten women, who, fighting in male attire, had been captured
among the Goths after many others had been killed; a placard declared
these women to be of the people of the Amazons (*de Amazonum genere*) —
for placards are borne before all, displaying the names of their people
(*praelati sunt tituli gentium nomina continentes*).'[4]

---

[2] R. Wenskus, *Stammesbildung und Verfassung*, 2nd edn (Cologne, 1977); developed further by
H. Wolfram, *Die Goten*, 4th edn (Munich, 2000); English edn, *History of the Goths* (Berkeley, 1988).
[3] W. Pohl, 'Tradition, Ethnogenese und literarische Gestaltung: eine Zwischenbilanz', in K. Brunner
and B. Merta (eds.), *Ethnogenese und Überlieferung* (Vienna, 1994), pp. 9–26; see the criticism of
Wenskus in A. Gillett (ed.), *On Barbarian Identity: Critical Approaches to Ethnicity in the Early Middle
Ages* (Turnhout, 2002) with the response by W. Pohl, 'Ethnicity, theory and tradition: a response', in
ibid., pp. 221–40.
[4] *SHA*, *Aurelianus* 33–4, ed. A. Chastagnol (Paris, 1994), p. 1004.

The name Amazons told an old story. Fighting women were classed as a people of their own, though at the same time we are told that they 'had been captured among the Goths'. This paradox can tell us much about the way in which barbarian identities were perceived in the late Roman empire, and in which this otherness served to reinforce Roman self-perception. For ancient society, the Amazons were, as Josine Blok has put it, an emblem of otherness.[5] But at the same time, the images they evoked were complex and contradictory; to regard the Amazons as a people opened up a field of ambiguities and paradox. The 'breastless' women, as the Greeks understood the name, were mythological figures already attested, under their queen Penthesileia, in the *Iliad*;[6] several cities in Asia Minor, for instance Ephesos, claimed to have been founded by Amazons.[7] In the age of Herodotos, the mythological women warriors from a distant heroic age reappeared in ethnographic perceptions. Tales about Sarmatian *oiorpata*, as those fighting women were called, seem to correspond somehow with the archaeological evidence, for about one-fifth of weapons found are from female graves.[8] Herodotos took some pains to bridge the gap between legends from Asia Minor and ethnographic observations in Scythia.[9] As we shall see, this fundamental tension between myth, ethnography and barbarian realities was never really resolved.[10] The Amazon myth provided a narrative matrix to accommodate fighting barbarian women, and influenced perceptions of powerful women even when they were not called Amazons. At the same time, it served to express moral judgements that had little to do with those distant barbarians.

In the sixth century AD, Prokopios still dealt with Herodotos' problem of localizing an Amazon people.[11] He decided (against Strabo's opinion) that they had come from the steppes near the Caucasus and then migrated to Asia Minor, and not vice versa. 'Today', he explains, 'nowhere in the vicinity

---

[5] J. H. Blok, *The Early Amazons* (Leiden, 1995), p. vii.

[6] Homer, *Iliad* III.181; IV.185. For a recent discussion, K. Dowden, 'The Amazons: development and function', *Führer des Rheinischen Landesmuseums in Bonn* 140 (1997), pp. 97–128; see also W. B. Tyrell, *Amazons: A Study in Athenian Mythmaking* (London, 1984).

[7] These civic origin legends were still known in late antiquity: e.g. Jordanes, *Getica* xx.107, ed. T. Mommsen, *MGH AA* v, 1 (Berlin, repr. 1982), pp. 53–138, here p. 85; *Exordia Scythica*, ed. T. Mommsen, *MGH AA* xi (Berlin, 1894), pp. 314–21, here n. 13, p. 315.

[8] R. Rolle, 'Oiorpata', *Materialhefte zur Ur- und Frühgeschichte Niedersachsens* 16 (1980), pp. 275–94.

[9] The fundamental account is Herodotos, IV.110–17, ed. A. D. Godley (Cambridge, MA, repr. 1982), vol. II, pp. 308–17. Blok, *The Early Amazons*; R. Bichler, 'Herodots Frauenbild und seine Vorstellung über die Sexualsitten der Völker', in R. Rollinger and C. Ulf (eds.), *Geschlechterrollen und Frauenbild in der Perspektive antiker Autoren* (Innsbruck, 1999), pp. 13–56.

[10] Cf. U. Wenskus, 'Amazonen zwischen Mythos und Ethnographie', in S. Klettenhammer and E. Pöder (eds.), *Das Geschlecht, das sich (un)eins ist?* (Innsbruck, 1999), pp. 63–72.

[11] Prokopios, *Wars* VIII.3, 5–11, ed. H. B. Dewing, 7 vols. (Cambridge, MA, 1953–54), vol. V, pp. 74–9.

of the Caucasus range is any memory of the Amazons preserved.'[12] In Asia Minor, on the contrary, several cities claimed to have been founded by the Amazons. The written evidence was contradictory, and therefore Prokopios relied, most interestingly, on myths and memories as clues to early history. That means that he was more convinced by the 'internal' Amazon as a source for civic identities than by the 'external', barbarian one. But then a further problem arose: had Amazons really disappeared long ago, or could they have survived somewhere? This question was repeatedly discussed by early medieval authors, with different results. Prokopios explicitly based 'my judgement on what has actually taken place in my time'. After battles with the Huns, dead women had been found on the battlefield. But, as he claims, 'no other army of women . . . has made its appearance in any locality of Asia or Europe'.[13] In the seventh century, Isidore of Seville in his *Etymologies* was positive that Amazons did not exist any more, because they had been destroyed by Achilles, Herakles and Alexander the Great.[14] Paul the Deacon, in his *Historia Langobardorum* written before 796,[15] after relating an Amazon legend supposed to have occurred during the migration of the Lombards, voiced his doubts in similar fashion:

From all that is known from the ancient histories it is evident that the people of the Amazons was destroyed long before this could have happened; except perhaps because the places where these deeds were reported to have taken place were not sufficiently known to the historiographers and were hardly published by any of them, it could have come about that up to those times a race of women of that kind might have maintained itself there. For I also heard some say that a people of those women exist in the innermost regions of Germania to this day.[16]

The complicated syntax seems to indicate how uncomfortable Paul, the monk, was with the possibility that Amazons might really have played a part in the prehistory of his people, one of the several instances when there is a polyphony of contemporary debates in his text.[17] It was not impossible that in the timeless world of barbarians, far from civilisation and history, mythological peoples had survived. If the troublesome Amazons could not

---

[12] Prokopios, *Wars* VIII.3, 11, p. 78.   [13] Prokopios, *Wars* VIII.3, 11, pp. 76–8.

[14] Isidore, *Etymologiae* IX.2, 64, ed. W. M. Lindsay, 2 vols. (Oxford, 1911), vol. I, p. 352.

[15] W. Pohl, 'Paulus Diaconus und die "Historia Langobardorum": Text und Tradition', in A. Scharer and G. Scheibelreiter (eds.), *Historiographie im frühen Mittelalter* (Vienna, 1994), pp. 375–405; Pohl, 'Paolo Diacono e la costruzione dell'identità longobarda', in P. Chiesa (ed.), *Paolo Diacono – uno scrittore fra tradizione Longobarda e rinnovamento Carolingio* (Udine, 2000), pp. 413–26.

[16] Paul the Deacon, *Historia Langobardorum* I.15, ed. L. Bethmann and G. Waitz, *MGH SRL* (Hanover, 1878), pp. 12–187, here pp. 54–5.

[17] Pohl, 'Paulus Diaconus'.

be confined to a distant past, then at least they had to be at a safe distance. Only the place had changed: instead of the steppes beyond the Black Sea it was the innermost Germania.

For civilised observers, it was clear that Amazons could only exist far away in place or time, or both. For Adam of Bremen at the end of the eleventh century, there was a place on the Baltic Sea 'that is now called the land of women'.[18] In early Christian Ireland, the mythical 'Land of Women' who beguiled the hero Bran by charms and trickery but were otherwise quite peaceful and hospitable was far away across the sea, and the bands of fighting women who had challenged even the great heroes of Irish legend such as Cú Chulainn were located in a remote heroic age.[19] In ancient and medieval cosmology, the Amazons were located on the margins of the world, beyond the barbarians, where fantastic animals also lingered. On medieval world maps, Amazons are pictured beyond the Tanais river among the griffins, the dog-headed *cynocephali* and the peoples of the Apocalypse, Gog and Magog.[20] During the later middle ages, they were gradually moved even farther into Asia, until in the sixteenth century they were transferred to the unknown regions of South America, and that is why the Amazon river has its name.

Although the Amazons were thus pictured as 'the Other', the moral judgements expressed by late antique and early medieval authors are often not purely negative. Many authors, among them Justin, Orosius, Jordanes and Prokopios, explained that, initially, they had been left behind when all their men were killed in a battle and thus they had been forced to fight for their survival on their own. But after their initial victory, they began to despise men and marriage altogether, so that 'they embarked instead on an enterprise unparalleled in the whole of history, the building of a state without men and then actually defending it themselves'.[21] The Christian apologist Orosius used the Amazons as an argument that the sack of Rome by the Goths in AD 410, a few years before he wrote, had not been any worse than barbarian raids in the pagan period. 'Oh what grief, it is the shame

[18] Adam of Bremen, *Gesta Hammaburgensis Ecclesiae Pontificum* IV.20, ed. R. Buchner, *Quellen des 9. und 11. Jahrhunderts zur Geschichte der Hamburgischen Kirche und des Reiches* (Darmstadt, 1961), p. 456.

[19] L. Bitel, *Land of Women: Tales of Sex and Gender from Early Ireland* (Ithaca, NY, 1996), pp. 161–4.

[20] For instance twice on the Ebstorf map: cf. I. Baumgärtner, 'Biblical, mythical and foreign women: texts and images on medieval world maps', in P. M. Barber and P. D. A. Harvey (eds.), *The Hereford and Other Mappaemundi* (London, forthcoming).

[21] Justin, *Epitome of the Philippic History of Pompeius Trogus* II.4, 6, trans. J. C. Yardley (Atlanta, GA, 1994), p. 29.

of human error', begins his conclusion to the Amazon chapter: women
warriors are a thoroughly pagan phenomenon.[22] The ideological potential
of the Amazon myth becomes clear in such diatribes. What begins as an
understandable reaction to the loss of their husbands quickly gets out of
control, owing to the lack of the consolation that the church could now
offer to widows (as Orosius implies), and both Europe and Asia are left at
the mercy of warrior women. This Christianisation of the Amazon myth
opened up new space for its contemporary use: the shameful error of the
Amazons was still possible wherever paganism reigned and men failed, for
whatever reason, to control women.

Orosius' account became a model for many early medieval authors.[23]
Jordanes, in his *Gothic History*, gives the Amazon myth an ideological turn
rather different from Orosius: he pictures them as Gothic women, so that
their victories become part of the glorious achievements of the Goths.[24]
Like ancient cities, many medieval peoples claimed to have originated from
Amazons, or at least asserted that Amazons had played some part in their
early history. Distant in time, these female origins still provided a focus
for later identities, as will be discussed in the second part of this chapter.
Amazons were, and had to be, barbarians, but they could easily be the
barbarians in one's own past and often came to represent the stage before
these barbarians had been civilised, and the conflicts involved in reaching a
civilised and gendered order from which certain types of female agency and
behaviour had to be expelled. These contradictions are obvious in Jordanes,
for he also mentions a battle between the Goths and the Amazons.[25] The
exclusion of improper femininity takes yet another form in his narrative:
the *haliurunnae*, Gothic witches, are chased out into the wilderness where
they mate with unclean spirits of the steppe; from this union, the Huns
originate – almost a parody of the Sarmatian origin story in Herodotos.[26]
At the end of his Amazon chapter, Jordanes deems it necessary to offer a

---

[22] Justin, *Epitome* II.4, p. 29; Orosius, *Historiae* I.15–16, ed. A. Lippold, *Le storie contro i pagani* (Milan, 1976), pp. 76–9.

[23] E.g. Jordanes, *Getica* v.44, p. 65; the *Exordia Scythica*, pp. 314–21, a text added to some manuscripts of Isidore of Seville; and the enigmatic eighth-century *Cosmography of Aethicus Ister*, c. 6, ed. O. Prinz, MGH Quellen zur Geistesgeschichte 14 (Munich, 1993), pp. 178–81.

[24] Jordanes, *Getica* VII.49–52, pp. 67–8; VIII.56–8, p. 69. A connection between Getae-Goths and Amazons had also been established by Claudian, ed. M. Platnauer, 2 vols. (Cambridge, MA, 1922): *In Eutropium* I, vv. 240–2, vol. I, p. 156; *De Raptu Proserpinae* II, v. 62, p. 322. Sidonius Apollinaris, *Carmina*, ed. C. Luetjohann, *MGH AA* VIII (Berlin, 1887), IX, vv. 94–100, p. 220; XIII, vv. 11–13, p. 231; XV, vv. 141–3, p. 237, on the other hand, places them in lists of animals and fantastic creatures inspired by the Herakles myth.

[25] Jordanes, *Getica* v.44, p. 65.

[26] H. Wolfram, 'Origo gentis', in *Reallexikon der Germanischen Altertumskunde* 22 (2003), pp. 174–8.

rhetorical excuse for dealing with the Amazons at such length: 'But do not say: "He has begun to tell about the men of the Goths; why does he dwell on their women for so long?"'[27]

Paul the Deacon and the Lombard origin myth will be discussed at greater length below; fighting Lombard women initially play a positive part, but then inimical Amazons block the way of the wandering Lombards at a river crossing, and not until the Lombard king Lamissio has killed their queen in an underwater fight in the river do they let the Lombards pass. As a hero who has defeated an Amazon queen, Lamissio joins the ranks of Achilles, Herakles, Theseus and Alexander the Great, and no doubt Paul the Deacon's readers were supposed to make the comparison.[28] The seventh-century *Chronicle* of Fredegar brought the Amazons into some relationship with the Frankish origin legend from Troy, at least implicitly: *Amazones Priamo tolere subsidium. Exinde origo Francorum fuit* – when the Amazons withdrew their support from the Trojans, these were defeated, and thus had to flee to become the Franks.[29] Aethicus Ister claimed that the Amazons' weapons were of such high quality that later on, among other peoples, Scythians, Franks and Trojans learnt from them. In the beginning of the twelfth century, Cosmas of Prague assumed that the Amazons had once lived in Bohemia, where they dressed, fought and hunted like men, and even founded their own city, Devin, the 'city of girls'; but Libuše, their queen, had to be removed from power to pave the way for the rule of the Přemyslids.[30]

These examples demonstrate the power of ethnic narrative: if fighting women existed, they were likely to be designated as Amazons. The mere name evoked an elaborate narrative with two alternative endings, one allowing for the Amazons' contemporary appearance, the other one not. Nobody in late antiquity succeeded in making the Amazon myth a basis for political power, therefore we know of the Amazons as an imaginary people. The ambiguous Amazon myth could be used for very different aims. The various stories that had circulated in Greek antiquity, indeed a cluster of

---

[27] Jordanes, *Getica* IX.58, p. 70. See P. J. Geary, 'Cur in feminas tamdiu perseverat?', in W. Pohl (ed.), *Die Suche nach den Ursprüngen* (forthcoming).

[28] W. Goffart, *The Narrators of Barbarian History* (Princeton, 1988), p. 383, makes Lamissio 'Paul's own creation'. See, however, W. Pohl, 'Origo gentis (Langobarden)', in *Reallexikon der Germanischen Altertumskunde* 22 (2003), pp. 183–8.

[29] Fredegar, *Chronicon* II.4, ed. B. Krusch, *MGH SRM* II (Hanover, 1888), p. 45. This is inserted into the *Chronicle* of Jerome. Fredegar's compilation places Amazonia in the vicinity of Armenia and Media: Fredegar, *Chronicon* I.5, p. 21.

[30] Cosmas of Prague, *Chronica Boemorum* I.4, ed. B. Bretholz, *MGH SRG* n.s. II (Hanover, repr. 1980), pp. 10–12. See Wolfram, 'Origo gentis'.

heroic legends making use of the popular stereotype, had in the course of antiquity been brought into a precarious and rather contradictory synthesis. Civic origin legends and accounts of barbarian otherness had been balanced in complicated migration legends to which some of the greatest heroes of ancient myth and history served as anchors in place and time. In late antiquity, Christendom sharpened the concepts of 'pagan' otherness and thus redrew the map of inclusion and exclusion in which the Amazon myth could acquire new meanings. This did not mean that a new story had to be told. Many late antique and early medieval authors rehearsed at least key elements of the old story, still placing it in a remote past. But its ambiguity and its inner contradictions kept the story alive, so that many texts are in fact polyphonic and contain traces of controversy on the subject. These controversies then facilitated the integration of contemporary material into a story that obviously had happened long ago, by way of comparison or allowing for a survival in regions so distant that ancient authors had passed them over in silence; for instance, in 'innermost Germany'.

Can we grasp any barbarian realities in these legends? Perhaps it is exactly the contradictory nature of the 'puzzling evidence' that late antique and early medieval authors had to deal with that makes their reports more credible. It seems that among barbarians in antiquity and the early middle ages, fighting women 'in male attire' were not imaginary at all. Barbarian women on the battlefield are prominent in most Roman authors who deal with the wars fought against the Cimbri and Teutons, the armies of Ariovistus in Gaul or the Germanic peoples east of the Rhine. Indeed, a majority of all available sources about Germanic women before AD 238 deal with women at war.[31] These are variously described as taking part in the fighting, spurring on their men on the battlefield, abusing or killing them after defeat, defending their camp against victorious enemies or killing their children and themselves lest they should be taken captive.[32] Perhaps it is not astonishing that women spinning receive less attention, although we may safely assume that barbarian women spent more time with the spindle than with the sword. Ammianus Marcellinus, in the late fourth century, wrote about the Gauls:

---

[31] This can easily be checked using the excellent index of the sourcebook edited by H. W. Goetz and K. W. Welwei, *Altes Germanien*, 2 vols. (Darmstadt, 1995).

[32] E.g. Plutarch, *Marius* 19, 9; 27, 2, vol. I, p. 248; Caesar, *De Bello Gallico* I, 51, 3, vol. I, p. 300; Tacitus, *Germania*, 8, vol. I, p. 132; Tacitus, *Historiae* 4, 18, vol. II, p. 190 (all ed. Goetz and Welwei, *Altes Germanien*); Orosius, *Historiae* 6, 21, 17, ed. Lippold, p. 228; W. Pohl, *Die Germanen* (Munich, 2000), p. 76.

When in the course of a dispute, any of them calls in his wife, a creature with gleaming eyes much stronger than her husband, they are more than a match for a whole group of foreigners; especially when the woman, with swollen neck and gnashing teeth, swings her great white arms and begins to deliver a rain of punches mixed with kicks, like missiles launched by the twisted strings of a catapult.[33]

Here we are in a genre rather different from heroic epic in which the Amazons first made their appearance. Explicit rhetoric was not the only textual strategy used to remind men where women's place was: often, irony, against both women and barbarian men, would suffice.

To contemporaries, the existence of female warriors was attested by their dead bodies found after a battle, which is, for instance, reported from the Gothic raids in the Balkans in the third century.[34] A less-known example is the thwarted attack of Slavs in dug-out canoes along the Golden Horn during the Avar siege of Constantinople in 626: according to Nikephoros, writing about 150 years later, 'among the dead bodies, one could even observe those of Slavic women'.[35] Ironically, the Byzantines believed that a woman, the Virgin Mary, had defended their city: the *Chronicon Paschale* has the Avar khagan say prior to his departure: 'I see a woman in a stately dress rushing about the wall all alone.'[36] The Christian image of women allowed for some martial elements.

Archaeological evidence for women buried with weapons in the early Middle Ages is not as substantial as in the case of the Sarmatians, but it can be found.[37] Extraordinary features are sixteen graves of seventh- and eighth-century Avar women buried with horses which were found in southern Slovakia and which lacked typically female grave goods such as distaff and needle-case; female horse burials from the period also occur in other parts of eastern Europe and central Asia, though usually without weapons.[38] Bonnie Effros (in this volume) warns us not to overlook the possibility that even more women were buried with weapons (or men with 'female' objects), which may go unrecognised because of object-based sexing of the skeletons.[39] Warrior women are a question not only of male perceptions,

[33] Ammianus Marcellinus xv.12, 1, ed. J. C. Rolfe, 3 vols. (Cambridge, MA, 1950–52), vol. 1, p. 194.
[34] Wolfram, *Goten*, pp. 394–5.
[35] Nikephoros, *Breviarium Historicum* 13, ed. C. Mango (Washington, DC, 1990), p. 60.
[36] *Chronicon Paschale* a. 626, trans. M. and M. Whitby (Liverpool, 1989), p. 180.
[37] R. Gilchrist, *Gender and Archaeology* (London, 1999), pp. 67–71; Sarmatians: Rolle, 'Oiorpata'.
[38] Z. Čilinská, 'Die awarenzeitlichen Frauengräber mit Pferdebestattung in der Slowakei', in *A Wosinsky Mór Múzeum Evkönyve* 15 (Szekszárd, 1990), pp. 135–46; W. Pohl, *Die Awaren* (Munich, 1988), p. 306.
[39] See also G. Halsall, 'Material culture, sex, gender and transgression in sixth-century Gaul', in L. Bevan (ed.), *Indecent Exposure: Sexuality, Society and the Archaeological Record* (Glasgow, 2001), n. 10.

but also of female agency, although it is hard to judge whether the written sources and the evidence of objects from the warrior sphere in female graves represent symbolic transgressions, exceptional cases or the regular occurrence of female warriors in certain cultures.

For male authors, women who 'converted their appearance into male habitus', 'put toughness before allure, aimed at conflicts instead of kisses, tasted blood, not lips, sought the clash of arms rather than the arm's embrace, fitted to weapons hands which should have been weaving', as Saxo Grammaticus says about fighting women who once lived in Denmark, adding that they 'were forgetful of their true selves'.[40] Rarely do we find the idea that fighting women represented a world turned upside down so clearly expressed.[41] Women who put toughness before allure may have been common in a barbarian world where toughness was the better option for survival. A warrior society more or less required, or at least allowed, transgression of conventional gender roles, and we may assume that not only Christian authors felt the need for a good dose of rhetoric to reiterate social boundaries: let women kiss while men kill.

In the post-Roman kingdoms, female violence was also restricted by legislation. The edict of the Lombard king Rothari in 643 stated that a woman could not be tried for armed irruption into someone's house, 'for it seems absurd that a woman, free or slave, could commit a forceful act with arms as if she was a man'.[42] Another of Rothari's clauses treats a similar issue quite differently: 'If a free woman participates in a brawl (*scandalum*) while men are struggling, and if she inflicts some blow or injury and perhaps in turn is struck and killed', the higher compensation normally required for women does not apply, 'since she had participated in a struggle in a manner dishonourable for women'.[43] There is little doubt that this addition to Rothari's code was based on a case that had actually happened. In the Burgundian Code, 'if a woman has gone forth from her own courtyard to fight' and suffers some injury, she forfeits all compensation altogether.[44]

---

[40] Saxo Grammaticus, *Gesta Danorum*, ed. J. Olrik and H. Raeder, vol. I, 2nd edn (Copenhagen, 1931), p. 192; J. Jesch, *Women in the Viking Age* (Woodbridge, 1991), p. 176.

[41] Usually, this passage has been read as just another proof that fighting women were common among the Vikings: see, for instance, Gilchrist, *Gender and Archaeology*, p. 69.

[42] *Leges Langobardorum*, Edictus Rothari 278, ed. F. Bluhme, *MGH Leges* IV (Stuttgart, repr. 1964), p. 67.

[43] *Leges Langobardorum*, Edictus Rothari 378, ed. Bluhme, p. 88. Cf. R. Balzaretti, '"These are things that men do, not women": the social regulation of female violence in Lombard Italy', in G. Halsall (ed.), *Violence and Society in the Early Medieval West* (Woodbridge, 1998), pp. 175–92.

[44] *Liber Constitutionum* 92, 2, trans. F. Drew (Philadelphia, 1976), p. 82. For female violence and the Salic law, N. Gradowicz-Pancer, 'De-gendering female violence: Merovingian female honour as an exchange of violence', *EME* 11, 1 (2002), pp. 1–18, here pp. 17–18.

These were transgressions of the gender dichotomy which pervaded that most male of all social domains, violence. A male society reacted by suspending the legal protection otherwise valid for women. The law-code does not imply any further consequences of the ensuing paradox. Those had been projected in the language of myth, creating a space of alterity that invited, and still invites, reflection and debate. Fighting women are an excellent test case to study the social dynamic of violence in ancient societies, and the way in which it established or challenged social distinctions.[45] Furthermore, they can shed light on the mechanisms of inclusion and exclusion that ancient and medieval societies maintained, and on the constructions of social categories in general. Amazons were located on the margin not because they represented a very remote concern. They impersonated a lingering presence that threatened the assignment of social roles in the heart of the classical and the early medieval world. The frequent representations in ancient art of the *Amazonomachia*, the battle against the Amazons, demonstrate that this was not a minor concern. They continued into the Byzantine period, where Amazon warriors are a common textile pattern.

In many other contexts, the Amazon myth preserved its capacity to express the paradox of gender boundaries and at the same time redraw them where they threatened to become blurred. Male dress is one of the recurrent elements in descriptions of fighting women. As Homer observed, the Amazons are men's equals, at least as long as they fight.[46] But when they lie dead, they are women, and in an instant, the mechanisms of exclusion collapse, as in the epic Aithiopis after Achilles has slain Penthesileia, and Thersites mocks him that he was in fact in love with her.[47]

The ambiguity of the female body when it lacked the social signs normally attached to it (clothes, ornaments, make-up, etc.) was a threat that only subsided when the 'wrong' signs had been removed, and the 'wrong' behaviour stopped. The death of the Amazon was one way to reaffirm the proper order of gender.[48] But that apparently seemed an unpleasant solution to many. The representations of *Amazonomachia* often depict very feminine women with full breasts and flowing hair. The feminine Amazon was not a pure projection either; the graves of armed Sarmatian women also contain a number of typically female objects, among them make-up and

---

[45] In general, see Halsall (ed.), *Violence and Society*; C. Dauphin and A. Farge (eds.), *De la violence et des femmes* (Paris, 1997).
[46] Homer, *Iliad* iii.181; vi.185.   [47] Blok, *The Early Amazons*, pp. 195–6.
[48] For the attraction of dead women for male writers, see E. Bronfman, *Over Her Dead Body: Death, Femininity and the Aesthetic* (Manchester, 1992).

little mirrors.[49] The erotic element in the Amazon myth can also be directly linked with gender transgression, as in the story of Commodus wanting to dress up as an Amazon for the arena just as his favourite mistress had done.[50] In late antiquity, court poets exploited the romantic underside of the Amazon myth, for instance Claudian in his verses on the marriage of Honorius:

Hadst thou over the heights of the snowy Caucasus gone against the cruel Amazons in all thy beauty, that warrior band had fled the fight and called to mind again their proper sex; Hippolyta, amid the trumpets' din, forgetful of her sire, had weakly laid aside her drawn battle-axe, and with half-bared breast loosed the girdle all Hercules' strength availed not to loose. Thy beauty alone would have ended the war.[51]

Unlikely flattery for an emperor with a crooked neck, indeed; but it shows how the sexual imagery of the Amazon legend could be used to draw strong images of masculinity. The half-bared breast as an erotic image, however, competed with the masculine elements in the Amazons. To be an Amazon proper required mutilation – one breast had to be cut off, or burnt away, a procedure from which the name 'without breasts' derived, as Isidore knew.[52]

Throughout classical antiquity and the Middle Ages, fighting women tended to be subsumed under a general mythological model that allotted them an identity apart; ethnic boundaries served to exclude what gender boundaries could not contain.[53] This is significant for the construction both of femininity and of ethnicity. The late antique concept of ethnicity allowed for a female ethnic identity. It is, however, an extreme case that allows us to test the flexibility of the concept, then and now. Late antique Amazons often fight *virili habitu*, in male attire, and do not appear to be women; their femininity can only be detected after the battle, when they lie dead or have been captured. Thus, their ethnic identity only becomes obvious when their sex is revealed; before that, they are perceived as Goths, Slavs or whatever barbarian people they belong to. Amazon ethnicity cuts across other ethnic identities. That being an Amazon is an ethnic definition and not simply a mythological designation for fighting women of all nations, however, is clear from the placard indicating the *gentis nomen* carried in front of them in Aurelian's triumph. It is no coincidence that the anonymous

---

[49] Rolle, 'Oiorpata'; Wenskus, 'Amazonen', p. 66.

[50] *SHA, Commodus Antoninus* 11, 9, ed. Chastagnol, p. 234.

[51] Claudian, *Fescennia de nuptiis Honorii Augusti*, vv. 30–7, ed. Platnauer, vol. II, p. 231.

[52] Isidore, *Etymologiae* 9, 2, 64, ed. Lindsay, vol. I, p. 352: 'id est sine mamma'.

[53] See also W. Müller-Funk, 'Von den Differenzen von Differenzen', in Müller-Funk (ed.), *Macht, Geschlechter, Differenz* (Vienna, 1994), pp. 152–73.

author of the *Historia Augusta* specifically mentions the carrying of the *tituli* in this case, to identify the most elusive of all peoples. In this case, the true self and the outward appearance are in contradiction. Here, ethnic identity is in fact defined by this contradiction: women acting like men. One might even say that, to contemporary eyes, Amazons have female sex and male gender. They thus belong to a trans-gender group, along with eunuchs, hermaphrodites, or cross-dressing transsexuals.[54] The connection with eunuchs was made by contemporaries. Claudian (d. *c.* 404) wrote in his invective against Eutropius: 'If eunuchs shall give judgement and determine laws, then let men card wool and live like the Amazons, confusion and licence dispossessing the order of nature.'[55] Fredegar's *Chronicle* reports, in the mid-seventh century, the fantasy that the general Belisarios was married to an Amazon from a brothel in Constantinople (while the general Narses was a eunuch).[56]

As always, looking for paradox is a good way to test our categories. Fighting women are such a case: they affirm and transgress models of gender and ethnicity at the same time. Seen through Roman eyes, they represented a non-hegemonic, marginal form of femininity, which however tended to grab the limelight. Rather than claiming, in the wake of women's history of the seventies (the 'women-in' approach, as Liz James has aptly called it),[57] that late antique barbarians were a haven for strong and aggressive women, I would argue that Roman perceptions of the barbarians allowed for, or even promoted, a certain blurring of gender – and ethnic – roles. Consequently, strong and aggressive women of the Roman world could be qualified as barbarian: gendered and cultural prejudices overlap. Christianity adapted this model and charged it with further meanings. Now, paganism was held responsible for the 'shame' of female warriors, which further reinforced the ties between the stereotypes of the barbarian and the Amazon. In turn, these perceptions could be used to denounce powerful women in the Christian

---

[54] Cf. M. E. Wiesner-Hanks, *Gender in History* (Oxford, 2001), p. 159. Eunuchs: M. Kuefler, *The Manly Eunuch* (Chiacago, 2001), esp. pp. 245–82; S. F. Tougher, 'Byzantine eunuchs: an overview', in James (ed.), *Women, Men and Eunuchs*, pp. 168–84; and Tougher, chapter 4 below. For a theoretical approach to non-binary gender, see J. Butler, *Gender Trouble: Feminism and the Subversion of Identity* (London, 1990), esp. pp. 16–25; Butler, *Bodies that Matter* (London, 1993). It is no coincidence that Greek ethnography and medical literature also made much of Scythian eunuchs (e.g. Herodotus 1.105; IV.67): owing to the climate, men were less male and women less female, see U. Wenskus, 'Geschlechterrollen und Verwandtes in der pseudo-hippokratischen Schrift *Über die Umwelt*', in Rollinger and Ulf (eds.), *Geschlechterrollen*, pp. 173–86, here pp. 180–1.

[55] Claudian, *In Eutropium* 1, vv. 497–9, ed. Platnauer, vol. 1, p. 175.

[56] Fredegar, *Chronicon* 11.62, ed. Krusch, pp. 85–7; the emperor Justinian is supposed to have married the second sister. Belisarios' Amazon wife then helped him to subdue the Vandal kingdom.

[57] James (ed.), *Women, Men and Eunuchs*, p. xii.

world, especially queens (such as Brunhild or Rosamund) or empresses (such as Theodora), as barbarian and shameless.[58]

Still, fighting barbarian women were not only a figment of the Roman imagination. Difficult as it is to judge from barbarian myths recorded in post-Roman kingdoms, it seems that barbarian self-perceptions also gave much space to the question of women and masculinity. Sometimes, aggressive women were demonised, such as Grendel's mother in Beowulf or the Gothic *haliurunnae*, the witches who, according to Jordanes, became the mothers of the Huns. None the less, there are also positive images of women transgressing their gender roles. Both played a surprisingly important part in early medieval origin myths. A good example is the origin legend of the Lombards, or Longobards, which I discuss in the second part of this chapter.

FEMALE MEMORY AND MASCULINE IDENTITY

The seventh-century *Origo gentis Langobardorum* contains a version of the Lombard origin myth, which Paul the Deacon included almost verbatim in his *Historia Langobardorum*.[59] Its core explains how the Lombards were named. The Winnili, led by Gambara and her two sons, are attacked by the Vandals, who have sought the support of Wodan, god of war; he promises victory to whomever he sees first on the battlefield. Gambara asks Frea, Wodan's wife, for help. On her advice, the women line up on the battlefield with their long hair tied in front of their faces to resemble beards. At sunrise, Frea turns Wodan's bed around so that he sees the Winnili. 'Who are these Longbeards (*Longobardi*)?', he asks; Frea answers: 'As you have given them a name, now give them victory as well'.

This story is remarkable for a number of reasons. It is the only genealogy of a post-Roman *gens* that begins with a woman, and Gambara relies on Frea, who outwits Wodan. The long-bearded warriors the god sees are in fact women. Contemporary etymologies ignore that paradox; instead, Isidore explains the name *Langobardi* by their long beards.[60] The relationship between outward sign and ethnic identity could not be more apparent.[61]

---

[58] J. Nelson, 'Queens as Jezebels: Brunhild and Balthild in Merovingian history', in D. Baker (ed.), *Medieval Women* (Oxford, 1978), pp. 31–77 (reprinted in Nelson, *Politics and Ritual in Early Medieval Europe* (London, 1986), pp. 1–48); P. Stafford, *Queens, Concubines and Dowagers*, 2nd edn (London, 1998). For Theodora, see Leslie Brubaker, chapter 5 below.

[59] *Origo gentis Langobardorum* 1, ed. G. Waitz, *MGH SRL*, p. 2; Paul the Deacon, *Historia Langobardorum* 1, 7–10, ed. Waitz, pp. 52–3; W. Pohl, *Werkstätte der Erinnerung* (Vienna and Munich, 2001), pp. 117–22; Pohl, 'Origo gentis (Langobarden)'.

[60] Isidore, *Etymologiae* IX.2, 95, ed. Lindsay, vol. I, p. 356.

[61] The relationship between outward signs and ethnicity in the early Middle Ages is less well attested than ethnographic theory assumes: W. Pohl, 'Telling the difference – signs of ethnic identity', in

But why does the myth replace this interpretation with a reversal of gender roles? Successful myth does not restate the obvious, it sets out to resolve tensions: here, a question of female identity and ethnicity. If the name of the *gens* is taken from a male secondary sexual characteristic, female *Langobardi*, longbeards, constitute a paradox that needs to be resolved. The story explains why women can call themselves Lombards, too.

The female origins of the Lombards, however, are only the point of departure for a male lineage. After the death of Agilmund, Gambara's grandson and first king of the Lombards, Paul the Deacon reintroduces women on the battlefield in a different role, as enemies: Lamissio, the second king, must overcome the Amazons to lead his people across a river.[62] A tradition of scholarship has regarded the Lombard origin myth as a symbolic expression of the transition from an archaic matriarchy to patriarchy, or from the cult of a mother goddess to a god of war.[63] However, these stories were written many centuries after the ethnic origins they relate. In the case of the Lombards, their name is already well attested in the first century AD, so that the powerful women of the Winnili would have to have been remembered for at least 700 years before the myth was written down.

Here, the issue is not the reconstruction of archaic societies, but the significance of the past and of gender in post-Roman kingdoms, and the way in which contemporary problems shaped social memories. Wherever the narratives came from, they mattered to those who chose to recount, rearrange and transmit them. What did these memories mean to those who chose to picture the foundations of their identity in this way? The Lombard origin story had something to do with Lombard identity in Italy; if women played an important role in it, a study of ethnicity needs to take the female element into account.

Female interest and participation in the process of social memory is exceptionally well attested in the case of the Lombards; and women probably played a part in the transmission of the *Origo gentis Langobardorum*.[64] The first known Lombard history, the lost *Historiola* by Secundus of Trento, was probably commissioned by Queen Theodelinda around 610.[65] She also

---

W. Pohl and H. Reimitz (eds.), *Strategies of Distinction* (Leiden, 1998), pp. 17–69. For an introduction to problems of ethnicity see Geary, *The Myth of Nations*.

[62] Paul the Deacon, *Historia Langobardorum* I.15, ed. Waitz, pp. 54–5.

[63] K. Hauck, 'Lebensnormen und Kultmythen in Germanischen Stammes- und Herrschergenealogien', *Saeculum* 6 (1955), pp. 186–223; but see Pohl, 'Origo gentis (Langobarden)'.

[64] P. J. Geary, *Phantoms of Remembrance: Memory and Oblivion in the First Millennium* (Princeton, 1994); J. Fentress and C. Wickham, *Social Memory* (Oxford, 1992); Pohl, 'Paolo Diacono'; Pohl, 'History in fragments. Montecassino's politics of memory', *EME* 10, 3 (2001), pp. 343–74.

[65] Paul the Deacon, *Historia Langobardorum* IV.40, ed. Waitz, p. 133. There is no direct evidence of this commission; but Secundus baptised Theodelinda's son Adaloald and wrote to Pope Gregory on her initiative.

had scenes from the Lombard past painted in her palace at Monza.[66] Leslie
Brubaker has underlined the role of Byzantine empresses in the shaping
of dynastic memory, and Jinty Nelson has stressed similar activities of
Carolingian empresses and queens.[67] Theodelinda, to a certain extent,
shaped the self-perception of the Lombards. She was a Bavarian princess,
but also the granddaughter of King Wacho who had led the Lombards into
Pannonia after 510. She thus conferred the prestige of an ancient dynasty
on two successive husbands, Authari and Agilulf, and later ruled for her son
Adaloald during his minority. When Adaloald was dethroned, her daughter Gundeperga married his two successors, both from families new to the
throne. The female line mattered for legitimacy: in its king-list, the *Origo*
mostly enumerates a king's wives, and their children. In early medieval
genealogies, this is unusual, as Ian Wood emphasises in his contribution to
this volume.

Theodelinda and Gundeperga did not simply serve as passive guarantees
of legitimacy to contested rulers, they played a more active part in the
politics of Lombard identity. Paul the Deacon has Queen Theodelinda,
after the death of her first husband, freely choose a second one, an unusual
way of selecting a ruler in the west.[68] Theodelinda brought about peace
with the Romans and promoted the cultural integration of the Lombards
in their Italian environment. Secundus and Paul the Deacon have created
a positive image of Theodelinda for posterity; Gundeperga met with more
resistance. Fredegar pictures her as often in conflict with her husbands,
who repeatedly accused her of adultery and had her confined; she was also
denounced as *francigena*, of Frankish origin, and thus found defective in
both ethnicity and gender.[69]

As I have argued elsewhere, Gundeperga probably played an important
part in shaping the *Origo*.[70] If so, the early history of the Lombards was
transmitted to us as shaped by two women, both regarded as foreigners

---

[66] Paul the Deacon, *Historia Langobardorum* IV.22, ed. Waitz, p. 124.

[67] L. Brubaker, 'Memories of Helena: patterns in imperial female matronage in the fourth and fifth
centuries', in James (ed.), *Women, Men and Eunuchs*, pp. 52–75; J. L. Nelson, 'Perceptions du pouvoir
chez les historiennes du haut moyen âge', in M. Rouche (ed.), *Les Femmes au moyen âge* (Paris, 1990),
pp. 77–85 and Nelson, chapter 10 below.

[68] Paul the Deacon, *Historia Langobardorum* III.35, ed. Waitz, p. 113. For Theodelinda, see R. Balzaretti,
'Theodelinda, most glorious queen: gender and power in Lombard Italy', *Medieval History Journal* 2,
2 (1999), pp. 183–207; P. Skinner, *Women in Medieval Italian Society 500–1200* (Harlow, 2001),
p. 56.

[69] Fredegar, *Chronicon* IV.51, ed. Krusch, pp. 145–6: 'Gundepergam reginam, parentem Francorum'.
Cf. Paul the Deacon, *Historia Langobardorum* IV.47, ed. Waitz, p. 136.

[70] This explains how the origin legend came to be included in the *Chronicle* of Fredegar: *Chronicon*
III.65, p. 110. See Pohl, 'Paolo Diacono'.

but nevertheless representing the unrivalled prestige of ancient Lombard lineage. This prestige came through the female line, and the *Origo gentis Langobardorum* explained how. Directing the writing of history was a way in which the two women could assert their roles, but these did not go uncontested. Gundeperga's second husband, Rothari, created a different image of the past, listing his sixteen predecessors as kings and his nine forefathers, without mentioning women.[71] But in the long run, through the work of Paul the Deacon who used both Secundus and the *Origo*, the queens' vision of the Lombard past prevailed.

The *Origo gentis Langobardorum* provides some idea of the way in which history was perceived through influential women's eyes. However, this does not mean that it was a female creation, or, even less, that its vision transcended gender stereotypes. What is extraordinary about the Lombard origin myth is the amount of female agency that the narrative implies. But the women fall into well-known categories. Gambara rules as a mother of princes, together with them.[72] This implies a mother's guardianship over her sons, much in the same way as Theodelinda ruled in the name of her son Adaloald during his minority.[73] Yet Paul the Deacon, in one of his few substantial changes to the story of the *Origo*, omits this indication of female rule.[74] He underlines another aspect of her position, wisdom, which is also implicit in the etymology of her name.[75] Wise women among the barbarians are one of the recurrent features in ancient literature, especially in the historiography of the wars fought against Germanic peoples during the early empire. They were compared to the Sibyls; the most prominent of them was Veleda, who resided among the Bructeri in a high tower and supported the rebellion of Civilis in AD 69.[76] Gambara also acted in a sphere in which oracles and prophecy played a role. She was not a virgin like Veleda, but combined the roles of the wise woman/priestess, the mother and the princess/queen.

---

[71] *Edictus Rothari*, Prologue, pp. 1–3.
[72] *Origo gentis Langobardorum* 1, p. 2: 'Ipsi cum matre sua nomine Gambara principatum tenebant super Winniles.'
[73] Paul the Deacon, *Historia Langobardorum* IV.41, p. 133.
[74] Paul the Deacon, *Historia Langobardorum* I.3, p. 49: 'Horum erat ducum mater nomine Gambara.'
[75] W. Haubrichs, 'Amalgamierung und Identität – Langobardische Personennamen in Mythos und Herrschaft', in W. Pohl and P. Erhart (eds.), *Die Langobarden – Herrschaft und Identität* (forthcoming); N. Francovich Onesti, *Vestigia longobarde in Italia*, 2nd edn (Rome, 2000), p. 170.
[76] Tacitus, *Historiae* IV.61; IV.65, ed. Goetz and Welwei, vol. II, pp. 220 and 224. See R. Bruder, *Die Germanische Frau im Lichte der Runeninschriften und der antiken Historiographie* (Berlin, 1974); Pohl, *Germanen*, p. 76.

A display of female power is more likely to occur at the beginning than at the end of an origin story. The outcome is a happy ending for the Lombards, but under male leadership. Wodan 'adopts' the Lombards by his act of name-giving, and they march on under the sole leadership of the two ducal brothers. Paul the Deacon adds a long story about the second king Lamissio. His mother is a whore, *meretrix*, who abandons the baby in a pool, where King Agilmund finds and adopts him, impressed that the boy has immediately grabbed his lance. This motif is more reminiscent of Moses and Romulus than of Nordic saga; and Lamissio's victory over the Amazons also suggests classical models rather than archaic Germanic lore.[77] This need not mean that Paul the Deacon invented it, but it most likely originated among the Lombards in Italy. The Lamissio story directly counters the implications of the name-giving legend. Gambara is a strong mother figure, whereas Lamissio is a motherless child; Gambara's Lombards receive support from the goddess Frea by the turning of a bed, whereas Lamissio is adopted by Agilmund by means of a lance; in the origin story, Lombard warrior women bring victory to their *gens*, whereas the Amazons figure in the Lamissio story as the defeated enemies of the Lombards. The story symbolises the ejection of women from the sphere of war and government. As shown above, this is an element that many *origines gentium* contain. Ethnic identity is rooted in female origins, but then the gender hierarchy has to be symbolically re-established by the expulsion, or the removal from power, of wise and/or warlike women.

A FEW CONCLUSIONS

Whenever women entered male domains and took part in their power games, this was likely to create a stir in discourse: debates about fundamental issues, heated value judgements, strong and paradoxical images, dramatic narratives. Often, women were the objects of textual strategies directed against the blurring of gender roles. In the case of the Amazons, defining fighting women as belonging to a distinct ethnic group was also a way of containing them, confining them to a country distant in space and time. Similarly, many powerful queens were depicted as Jezebels.[78] But as the example of Theodelinda shows, women could also play an active role in

---

[77] Paul the Deacon, *Historia Langobardorum* I.15, p. 55; K. Malone, 'Agelmund and Lamicho', *American Journal of Philology* 47 (1926), pp. 319–46; and Hauck, 'Lebensnormen und Kultmythen', with far-fetched Nordic interpretations; for a critique, see Goffart, *The Narrators of Barbarian History*, pp. 363–6; and Pohl, 'Origo gentis (Langobarden)'.

[78] Nelson, 'Queens as Jezebels'.

the shaping of meanings and memories, and muster intellectual support. The outcome of such debates was not always predictable. Women's role in ethnic processes should not be underestimated. Historians usually equate polyethnicity, for instance, with male mobility, although *alienigenae uxores* (foreign wives), such as Theodelinda or Brunhild, are equally important. Royal brides often arrived with a huge retinue; around AD 500, Theoderic's sister Amalafrida travelled to Carthage with 1000 Gothic warriors to marry the Vandal king Thrasamund.[79] Archaeologists have been more attentive for markers of ethnicity on women, and interpreted female graves with objects from another archaeological culture as those of foreign wives, which probably underrates the complexity of the symbolical language of burial.[80] The example of Theodelinda choosing Agilulf as her husband (however much that may be Paul the Deacon's stylisation of events) shows that women were conceivable not only as objects, but also as subjects of marriage alliances. Her case, and that of Gundeperga, also demonstrates that women could have more than one ethnic identity.

Women played a double role in the construction of ethnic identity. On the one hand, in a society that regarded ethnicity as a matter of descent, mothers had a strong symbolical role in that respect. On the other hand, in a patrilineal and virilocal society, mothers had usually come from somewhere else, and especially in the leading families of a people, that might also mean from another people: the *genetrix* was *alienigena* herself.

Besides, the ethnic identities of early medieval peoples grew in response to a fundamental change of perspective.[81] In the Roman world, the barbarians represented the other, and their perception was charged with images of difference. Amazons were one element of this diversity. From the fifth century onwards, when more or less Romanised barbarians came to rule parts of the Roman empire, they gradually appropriated for themselves the ethnographic discourse once used to describe and explain their otherness. In the end, for instance, Goths or Hungarians came to be proud of their identification with the apocalyptic peoples of Gog and Magog and of the awe these had once inspired, just as a long time ago wealthy cities of Asia Minor had been proud of their foundation by Amazons. Other peoples, on the contrary, sought their origins in the classical world, in Troy

[79] Wolfram, *Goten*, pp. 307–8; however, after Thrasamund's death, Amalafrida and her Goths were killed.
[80] See Bonnie Effros, chapter 9 below, and Pohl, 'Telling the difference'; G. Halsall, 'Social identities and social relationships in early Merovingian Gaul', in I. N. Wood (ed.), *Franks and Alamanni in the Merovingian Period* (Woodbridge, 1999), pp. 141–75.
[81] For an overview, see W. Pohl, *Die Völkerwanderung: Eroberung und Integration* (Stuttgart, 2002).

(the Franks) or with the Macedonians (the Saxons). The often very contradictory origin stories are only a symptom of a complex process of inclusion
and exclusion, of self-identification and new prejudice in which the social
boundaries of the post-Roman world were redrawn. Gothic, Lombard or
Frankish identities were not self-assured and securely rooted in a long and
continuous ethnic history, but had to be maintained through a series of
dramatic demographic and political changes, and in a culturally dominant
late Roman environment.

   This crisis of identity also had its consequences for femininity. Perhaps
it is no coincidence that, in the course of the troubled fifth century,
barbarian women in the west abandoned their age-old style of dress and
adopted another one.[82] At the same time, these transformations also provided unusual opportunities for a number of (mostly royal) women to wield
considerable power and to influence contemporary perceptions.

   Women contributed to the transformations of the early medieval world.
But I certainly do not want to argue, in line with seventies-style women's
history, that the situation of women in the early Middle Ages was not as
bad as we tend to think, and that the strong role of women has simply
been obscured by male-dominated history. Female identities, and female
participation in the politics of identity, were probably more negotiable and
more contradictory than simple models suggest. The reshuffling of social
boundaries and of the corresponding discourse of exclusion and inclusion,
of identity and otherness, also implied a renegotiation of gender roles (and
vice versa). If Goths or Lombards were barbarians, did that mean that they
were likely to have Amazons among their ranks? Or if not, who were the
new barbarians where Amazons might still be found? Could queens be
trusted to hand down the ancient memories of the *gens*? With the support
of Christian intellectuals, women such as Theodelinda were pioneers in
the shaping of new Christian identities for their peoples. But they did not
succeed in establishing a model of powerful and active queens that future
generations could safely continue. Many of the queens who had a strong
position in the sixth century were soon remembered as bad queens. Female
agency remained to some extent an exception, and the consolidation of the
Frankish and the Lombard kingdoms in the seventh century seems to have
reduced the spaces for it.[83]

---

[82] Pohl, 'Telling the difference', pp. 49 ff. and see further Mary Harlow, chapter 3 below.
[83] Although queens continued to have an influential position; see J. L. Nelson, *Rulers and Ruling
  Families in Medieval Europe* (Aldershot, 1999), studies XI–XV; R. Le Jan, *Femmes, pouvoir et société
  dans le haut moyen âge* (Paris, 2001), pp. 21–107; N. Pancer, *Sans peur et sans vergogne: de l'honneur et des
  femmes aux premiers temps mérovingiens* (Paris, 2001), pp. 145–66. Gradowicz-Pancer, 'De-gendering

In a society in which the warrior-aristocrat became the dominant form of masculinity, femininity had to be redefined in relation to the new ideals of controlled violence. Women warriors and Amazons were just one extreme image involved in this debate about the social limits of violence. Legislation to ensure better protection of women through higher *wergeld* (compensation) and other measures were another part of it. But beyond that, a male-dominated society needed to reaffirm female virtues in symbols and token narratives. Early medieval ethnic identities therefore tended to accommodate both barbarian otherness and female otherness, and project them into the past. The narratives that dealt with these tensions are controversial, and their complexity should not be interpreted away. We should not forget that perhaps the most complex and most controversial text known in the period was also by far the most successful one: the Bible.[84] The efforts to construct a Christian society polarised the field in which both gender and ethnic identities developed. Much has yet to be done to understand how these discourses influenced people's lives and identities. Discourse formations, power structures, self-perpetuating systems, the social construction of reality, all these concepts may be used as models and methodological tools. Dramatic narratives and strong images are traces that are still accessible to us, and they seem to indicate a lost world of strong emotions and contradictions that accompanied individual efforts to adapt to a world in which identities were not always easily maintained in the face of overwhelming diversity.[85]

female violence', maintains that Merovingian queens could act violently on the bases of codes of honour shared between men and women. I. N. Wood, 'Fredegar's fables', in Scheibelreiter and Scharer (eds.), *Historiographie im frühen Mittelalter*, pp. 359–66, reads Fredegar's *Chronicle* as a statement against the political influence of Merovingian queens.

[84] On the question of biblical models, see Geary, 'Cur tamdiu in feminas perseverat', and Mayke de Jong, chapter 14 below.

[85] This chapter owes much to discussions with Herwig Wolfram and Patrick Geary who are currently working on similar topics. I am also very grateful to Barbara Rosenwein for help and suggestions.

CHAPTER 3

Clothes maketh the man: power dressing and elite masculinity in the later Roman world

Mary Harlow

This chapter looks at changing expressions of gender during the late Roman world as reflected in the dress of the elite Roman male. Arguably one of the key elements of this period was a blurring of the physical and social frontiers and boundaries that had been thought, by earlier Romans, to be central in the construction of their identity as Roman. In late antiquity previously distinct divisions between Roman and 'barbarian', pagan and Christian, soldier and civilian, elided to create the late Roman man. In terms of dress we might add other important distinctions of east and west, plain and patterned.

The Roman society revealed through its source material, both visual and literary, was male centred and privileged masculine characteristics. Manliness was expressed particularly in military and political virtues. In such a value system the ideal and complete individual was a freeborn, male citizen who behaved in the prescribed manner and looked the part. The image of the toga-clad Roman was not static for the entire period of the Roman empire but its persistence was remarkable in both public sculpture and historical writing. To give a brief example, further elucidated below, a shorthand way to illustrate 'bad' emperors was simply to express their inability to dress correctly. This inability in one aspect of behaviour cast doubts on their capability of carrying out other important aspects of their office, and thus on their manliness in general.[1] Within a system where those virtues specifically deemed masculine are considered normative anything that falls outside that definition is considered inferior and feminised. Masculinity at Rome was tightly defined so as to exclude non-Romans. Slaves,

---

[1] For a brief overview of attitudes to gender in Rome see D. Montserrat, 'Reading gender in the Roman world', in J. Huskinson (ed.), *Experiencing Rome: Culture, Identity and Power in the Roman World* (London, 2000), pp. 153–82; M. Kuefler, *The Manly Eunuch: Masculinity, Gender Ambiguity and Christian Ideology in Late Antiquity* (Chicago, 2001), pp. 19–69. On masculinity and emperors see: Montserrat, 'Reading gender', pp. 156–7; Kuefler, *Manly Eunuch*, pp. 20–1, 57–61. Both use the example of Elagabalus, emperor 218–223.

foreigners, especially 'barbarians', fell short of this definition and were thus often associated with the most obvious inferior group, women. Stereotypical male and female characteristics were defined by opposition: men were rational, self-controlled and hard bodied; women were irrational, lacked control and needed ruling, and soft bodied. Clearly Romans recognised that life was not so simply differentiated, but such divisions served a useful rhetorical and visual tool to create a shared view understood by author and audience. The later Roman empire was a period where the assimilation of things previously defined as distinctly non-Roman was becoming increasingly evident. New influences expressed by incoming individuals and their dress meant that standards that had previously been thought to have fallen short of manliness were becoming the epitome of 'Roman-ness'.

In this chapter pictorial and literary representations are used to assess the type of dress that was considered appropriate for the public representation of the elite male – that is, how the clothing individuals chose to be depicted in expressed messages about their status and gender. A major problem is that the clarity of that message may now be lost to us. Talking about dress is complicated: we face the problem of putting together textile remains, visual representations and literary descriptions. The evidence is therefore highly contextualised. Textile remains come mostly from funerary contexts, so what survives tells us what people chose to be buried in, which may or may not reflect their status, ethnicity or gender.[2] It is also often unclear whether burial clothing is specific to the occasion or simply everyday wear. Visual representations are restrictive in terms of medium but also in terms of audience. While we may trace general changes in dress across a variety of media – mosaics, silver plate, wall paintings, sculpture, book illumination – the nuances of status and rank that were understood by contemporary audiences are harder, if not impossible, for us to read. Literary texts are similarly obscure: while they may describe clothing and discuss appropriate dress they often have a moralising agenda that limits our ability to extract information. Latin writers also tended to adopt the stereotypes of earlier authors, particularly in the characterisation of non-Romans, which may no longer suit the personnel of the empire in their own period.

Apart from the specific limitations of studying a particular historical period, dress as a term can cover a wide definition of attributes. As succinctly put by Barnes and Eicher, dress can identify an individual both geographically and historically. Dress can express membership of a community but also differentiate the individual within that community and

---

[2] See chapters 9 and 16 by Bonnie Effros and Dawn Hadley below.

thus it has properties of both inclusion and exclusion. Dress can be used as a marker of the general social position of a person in society but such a reading is also affected by the gender identification of the dressed person.[3] The fluidity of such a definition means that dress can cover two important, overlapping yet distinct areas of clothing – traditional dress, which we might term costume, and fashion. Traditional dress can be defined as a garment or set of garments worn in a particular way that has existed over a long period of time and undergone relatively little change. The traditional nature of such costume means it can be easily read by contemporaries who understand the signs that signal status, rank, gender and perhaps ethnic origin of the wearer. Observers who share similar cultural backgrounds to the wearer might also further read nuances of political and social affiliations. While such dress can be defined as traditional this does not imply a static array of garments or the resistance to change over time but that certain elements of style are 'fixed', or to use a very seventies but apt term, 'anti-fashion'.[4] The obvious example from the Roman world is the toga – a garment expressive of Roman status and identity which, while retaining the essence of 'toga-ness', still changed over time (see below).

If anti-fashion defines traditional elements in dress, then fashion defines the non-traditional, and elements that have a short-term existence. It is much harder to track changes and nuances in fashion in the past because of this short-term ephemerality but also because of the nature and context of the surviving evidence. Fashion items can, however, be transformed into items of mainstream dress, especially if they serve a purpose, pragmatic or symbolic (or both), for particular social groups. Similarly, traditional elements from the dress codes of external cultures can infiltrate those of their neighbours, usually at first as fashion items, but over time evolving into normal dress. This transformation of non-traditional to traditional (fashion to anti-fashion) occurred in the late Roman world, assisted by the climate of strong external cultural influences and social mobility. These elements came together in the form of 'barbarians', primarily from eastern and northern areas of the empire, whose impact was widespread owing to their presence in the army. It is from this direction that major innovations infiltrated 'traditional' male dress.

This chapter looks at how the traditional Roman dress of tunic and toga was transformed by the intrusion of non-traditional elements, particularly tight, long-sleeved tunics and 'trousers', which went on to become essential

---

[3] R. Barnes and J. B. Eicher (eds.), *Dress and Gender: Making and Meaning* (Oxford, 1992), p. 2.
[4] See T. Polhemus and L. Proctor, *Fashion and Anti-fashion: Towards an Anthropology of Clothing and Adornment* (London, 1978).

elements of medieval dress. I will concentrate on the relationship between dress, gender identity, status and ethnicity, and focus on what became of the quintessential Roman male garment, the toga.

The Romans were quite clear that dress was a significant component of self-identity. In effect, to the Roman eye, you were what you wore – and Romans were the *gens togati*, the race who wore the toga and at the same time was destined to rule the world.[5] They were distinct from non-Roman groups; the *palliati*, those who wore the pallium (a large rectangular mantle, much easier to wear than the elaborately folded toga), which was associated with the Greeks.[6] The term *a toga ad pallium* (from toga to pallium) implied a sinking from a higher position to a lower one. Another non-Roman group identified by their clothing and of significant interest here were the *bracati*: those who wore 'trousers'. These were both non-Romans and non-Greeks, essentially those who lived outside the 'civilised' empire, barbarians of both east and west. Gallia Narbonensis was also known as Gallia Bracata, the name coming to define the people, what they wore, and the geographical area.[7] In the ancient Latin world even the names of items of clothing came to have value-laden, ethnocentric and gendered meanings. In Roman eyes the barbarian lacked the essential qualities of *romanitas* and thus was personified as the inversion of Roman. Barbarians were believed to lack physical and emotional control, and to be irrational – characteristics that were also closely associated with being female.

The Roman need to be clear about such distinctions meant that social rules existed about dress, as is illustrated by certain law codes:

All clothing is men's or children's or women's or that which may be worn by either sex, or that worn by slaves. Men's clothing is that provided for the benefit of the head of the household, such as togas, tunics, cloaks, bedspreads, coverlets and blankets and the like. Children's garments are clothes used only for this purpose, such as *togae praetextae*, coats, Greek-style cloaks and mantles that we provide for our sons. Women's clothes are those acquired for the benefit of the matron of the household, which a man cannot easily use without causing censure, such as robes, wraps, undergarments, head coverings, belts, turbans, which have been acquired with a view to covering the head rather than for their decorative effect, coverlets, and mantles. Clothes adapted to the use of either sex are those which a woman

---

[5] Virgil, *Aeneid* 1.282. All references in this chapter are to Loeb editions unless otherwise stated.

[6] The pallium (Greek: *himation*) was worn by the ordinary (non-office-holding) Roman, as well as being the usual garb of most Greeks. The association with Greeks meant that it was also the garment associated with philosophers. Tertullian argued that it was the most suitable garment for Christians: *De pallio* 6, in Tertullian, *Opera*, CCSL 2 (Turnhout, 1954), pp. 733–50; English trans. S. Thelwall, *The Writings of Tertullian*, vol. III, Ante-Nicene Fathers 18 (Edinburgh, 1870).

[7] Cf. Pliny III.4.5; Cicero, *Fam.* IX.15.2; Juvenal VIII.234.

shares in common with her husband, for instance, where a mantle or cloak is of the type that a man or his wife may use it without criticism, and other garments of this nature. Slaves' clothing is that acquired for dressing the household, such as blankets, tunics, mantles, bed linen, and the like.[8]

This extract comes from a section in Justinian's *Digest* (published in 533) that is concerned with defining the contents of legacies but it gives an idea of how proscriptive the Roman lawmaker could be should he so choose. Certain dress was appropriate for men, and other sorts for women, and to dress inappropriately would cause censure. To insult a person's character through his dress was common rhetorical practice and played a regular part in law court speeches.[9] Likewise dress and the outward appearance of a people, as well as their social systems and behavioural habits, served to create ethnic stereotypes in works of Greek and Latin authors. For instance, according to Suetonius, a rhyme was sung in Rome as Julius Caesar paraded conquered Gauls in his triumphal march through the city that went (loosely translated):

> They've pulled those Gallic trousers down
> They've put on a purple-bordered citizen gown.[10]

By the late third, and certainly early fourth century, the rhyme would have been applicable in reverse – the very items of clothing that the Romans considered symptomatic of barbarian lifestyle had become common currency at the centre of empire. Ancient writers, however, offer relatively little material to show how one can distinguish one barbarian from another

---

[8] 'Vestimenta omnia aut virilia sunt aut puerilia aut muliebria aut communia aut familiarica. Virilia sunt, quae ipsius patris familiae causa parata sunt, veluti togae, tunicae, palliola, vestimenta stragula, amphitaphae et saga reliquaque similia. Puerilia sunt, quae ad nullum alium usum pertinent nisi puerilem, veluti togae praetextae aliculae chlamydes pallia quae filii nostris comparamus. Muliebria sunt, quae matris familiae causa sunt comparata, quibus vir non facile uti potest sine vituperatione, veluti stolae pallia tunicae, capitia zonae mitrae, quae magis capitis tegendi quam ornandi causa sunt comparata, plagulae paenulae. Communia sunt, quibus promiscue utitur mulier cum viro, veluti si eiusmodi paenula palliumve est et reliqua huiusmodi, quibus sine reprehensione vel vir vel uxor utatur. Familiarica sunt, quae ad familiam vestiendam parata sunt, sicut saga tunicae paenulae lintea vestimenta stragula et consimilia.' *Digest* XXXIV.2.23.2. *The Digest of Justinian* (Latin text and English trans.), ed. T. Mommsen, P. Krueger and A. Watson (Philadelphia, 1985).

[9] See for instance J. Heskel, 'Cicero as evidence for attitudes to dress in the late Republic', in J. Sebesta and L. Bonfante (eds.), *The World of Roman Costume* (Madison, WI, 2001), pp. 133–45; A. R. Dyck, 'Dressing to kill: attire as a proof and means of characterization in Cicero's speeches', *Arethusa* 34 (2001), pp. 119–30. Kuefler, *Manly Eunuchs*, pp. 55–7.

[10] 'Galli bracas deposuerunt, latum clavum sumpserunt.' For other examples see e.g. Tacitus, *Germania* 17; Ammianus, XXXI.2 on the Huns. Isidore of Seville, *Etymologiae* XIX.23: *De proprio quarundum gentium habitu*, includes among others Gauls in their cloaks (*linnae*), the Germans in their skins (*renones*) and the Parthians in their baggy trousers (*sarabarae*); ed. W. M. Lindsay, 2 vols. (Oxford, 1911), vol. II, pp. 328–30.

according to dress: they tend to merge into the more, or less, savage/civilised. Some wear almost nothing, others wear skins (and smell), while yet others wear soft fabrics, bright colours, patterned textiles and voluminous styles – the main point is they are all patently not Roman. What we have to keep in mind is that we are looking from the inside out – that is, we have Roman views of what others (non-Romans) might look like, and these views are often themselves derived from other literary texts rather than any real experience.[11]

As noted above, the garment which provided a huge part of Roman self-definition was the toga. It certainly had a very long life as an item of clothing, and existed in various forms from the fourth century BC to the late fifth century AD. However, its popularity throughout this entire period is questionable – and may be misrepresented by the nature of the surviving material. As Stone has shown, it appears that the toga was considered the appropriate costume in which to be represented on public sculpture and as such is overemphasised as the 'typical' dress of the Roman male.[12] However, it was a great marker of status perhaps precisely because it was heavy and difficult to wear correctly, though it was essential to do so. There exists a long tract by the first-century author Quintilian on the subject of rhetoric and behaviour for orators in the public eye, in which dressing correctly is a key part:

I should like the toga itself be round, and well cut to fit; otherwise there are many ways in which it may be unshapely. It is best if the front edge reaches to the middle of the shin, while the back should be higher to correspond with the girdle of the tunic. The fold is most becoming if it falls a little above the bottom of the tunic, and should certainly never fall below it. The fold, which passes obliquely across the body like a belt, under the right shoulder and over the left, should be neither too tight nor too loose. That part of the toga which is arranged last should fall lower; it sits better like that, and is held in place better.[13]

---

[11] See W. Pohl, 'Telling the difference: signs of ethnic identity', in W. Pohl and H. Reimitz (eds.), *Strategies of Ethnic Distinction: The Construction of the Ethnic Communities, 300–800* (Leiden, 1998), pp. 40–51.

[12] S. Stone, 'The toga: from national to ceremonial costume', in Sebesta and Bonfante (eds.), *World of Roman Costume*, pp. 13–45. C. Vout, 'The myth of the toga: understanding Roman dress', *Greece and Rome* 43 (1996), pp. 204–20. The most comprehensive study of the toga in English is still L. Wilson, *The Roman Toga* (Baltimore, 1924); in German, H. R. Goette, *Studien zu römischen Togadarstellungen* (Mainz am Rhein, 1989).

[13] Quintilian, *Institutio Oratoria* XI.3. 'Ipsam togam rotundam esse et apte caesam velim, aliter enim multis modis fiet enormis. Pars eius prior mediis cruribus optime terminatur, posterior eadem portione altius qua cinctura. Sinus decentissimus, si aliquanto supra imam tunicam fuerit; numquam certe sit inferior. Ille, qui sub humero dextro ad sinistrum oblique ducitur velut balteus, nec strangulet nec fluat. Pars togae, quae postea imponitur, sit inferior; nam ita et sedet melius et continetur.'

1 The Brothers Sarcophagus, Museo Nazionale, Naples.

In the first and early second centuries AD the toga clearly marked the citizen from the non-citizen (the Roman male from the non-Roman). It expressed man as civic being, showing the correct *gravitas* in performing his duty to gods, state and family – in short, *pietas*, the essence of male virtue in the classical Roman world, as can be seen on the Brothers Sarcophagus (AD 260) (Fig. 1).[14] Here the same man appears four times, illustrating three different toga styles. At one end he is shown getting married in what is known as the early imperial toga, in the centre he is shown twice, once in the toga with the shoulder 'umbo', popular from the time of Augustus to the third century, and once in the philosopher's pallium. At the other end he is shown as consul in the banded version known as the *toga contabulata*, seen in representations from the mid-second century. This is almost the final stage of the toga as a ceremonial garment; its life as everyday wear seems to have ended long before.[15] The *toga contabulata* is the style seen on the Arch of Constantine in Rome and the obelisk base of Theodosius in Constantinople.[16] While it is clear that the toga was still closely associated with public civic occasions, however, on the obelisk base the emperor and his entourage wear a different style of dress, also considered suitable for public representations by the fourth century. Both styles are exemplified on the ivory diptych of Probianus where on one side he wears the *toga contabulata* and on the other the dress that was to become commonplace in the following century, the long tunic and heavy cloak, the chlamys (Fig. 2).[17]

In late antiquity, beginning in the third century, fundamental changes took place both in the way people dressed and in the ways in which they chose to be represented. The basic garb of loose-sleeved tunic and toga was replaced by a long-sleeved, tighter-fitting tunic, covered by a cloak, and leggings. Probianus' and Stilicho's images, both of AD 400,[18] present the viewer with a multiplicity of meanings, but to an earlier Roman these images would

---

[14] Goette, *Togadarstellungen*, pp. 86–7, 161 for bibliography; pl. 74.2.

[15] For development of toga styles see Stone, 'The toga', pp. 13–45; Goette, *Togadarstellungen*; Wilson, *Roman Toga*.

[16] The classic text for the Arch of Constantine is H. P. L'Orange and A. von Gerken, *Der Spätantike Bildschmuck des Konstantinsbogens* (Berlin, 1939). This was not available to me but the relevant plates can be seen in K. Weitzmann (ed.), *Age of Spirituality* (New York, 1979), p. 68. See also R. Bianchi Bandinelli, *Rome: The Late Empire* (New York, 1971), pls. 69 and 70. For the obelisk base of Theodosius see Bianchi Bandinelli, *Rome*, pls. 335 and 336.

[17] R. Delbrueck, *Die Consulardiptychen und verwandte Denkmäler* (Berlin, 1929), no. 65, pp. 250–6; Weitzmann, *Age of Spirituality*, pp. 55–6.

[18] Diptych of Stilicho: Delbrueck, *Die Consulardiptychen*, no. 63, pp. 242–8; A. Cameron, 'Consular diptychs in their social context: new eastern evidence', *Journal of Roman Archaeology* 11 (1998), pp. 385–403.

2   The Diptych of Probianus.

2 (cont.)

have transmitted two significant messages: the ascendancy of the barbarian and the military. The long sleeves and long trousers, traditional signs of the non-Roman, have replaced the carefully and painstakingly draped garments of the classical period; in the diptych of Stilicho the intrusion of the military and military style dress into the central civic arena is clearly demonstrated (Fig. 5).

To clarify the origins and significance of these changes let us look briefly at the pedigree of each item of clothing in turn.

TUNIC

From earliest times the tunic was the basic male garment for both public and private wear. During the earlier Roman period it had been worn under the toga and even then came under scrutiny: it is clear that except on solemn occasions such as funerals it was worn belted and its length examined. According to Quintilian it should be girt so that the front edge came a little below the knee; in the back to mid-knee. Any lower down the leg and it risked looking too like a female garment, and if above the knee like that of a centurion.[19] Rhetoric such as this does not necessarily reflect daily life but it does indicate that dress was remarked upon and there were dress codes to be observed. During the imperial period the tunic was a rectangular garment, often made in one piece with a slash for the neck; any sleeve, created by the fall of the material down the arm, was incidental. If too long, a tunic denoted a tendency to dress like a woman, and, according to Aulus Gellius, long sleeves were thought to show a marked propensity for weakness and effeminacy.[20] All classes and ages wore a version of the tunic; status, rank and occupation were marked in the type of textile used and any decoration added.

Tunics came in various shapes and sizes. A popular type was known as the dalmatic. It is difficult to fit a strict definition to the dalmatic in this period, but in general it seems to describe a loose wide garment, usually held by a belt, which could, but did not necessarily, have long sleeves. Commodus (emperor 178–193) wore a white silk dalmatic shot with gold threads to the games, an action that provoked much disapproval. According to the *Augustan History* and Cassius Dio, this was inappropriate dress for an emperor on such an occasion when a toga would have been considered correct.[21] A silk dalmatic was also inappropriate because both the fabric and

---

[19] Quintilian, *Institutio Oratoria* XI.3.138–9.   [20] Aulus Gellius, *Attic Nights* 6(7).12.
[21] *Commodus* VIII.8; Cassius Dio LXXII.17.2.

the garment were considered a sign of indulgent luxury and softness, and, by extension, of effeminacy. The message is clear: bad emperors cannot even dress properly.

The early fourth-century mosaics of Piazza Armerina are a good source for information about clothing of the Tetrarchic period (*c.* 300) and illustrate a number of tunics, of different lengths and worn by different classes (Figs. 3 and 4).[22] The tunics appear to be woven of single plain colours, with those in authority wearing white, decorated with the archetypal late antique ornamentation – *segmenta* and *clavi*. These brightly coloured patches were interwoven into areas of fabric and often survive detached from the background fabric.[23] The intricacy and colour of the surviving pieces of textile are as remarkable as the subject matter of their designs which ranges from figurative scenes, including portraits, to Christian and pagan symbols and geometric, floral and animal designs. Use of *segmenta* seems to have cut across class lines: small designs are seen on servants' clothing, more intricate patterns on garments of the upper classes and members of the imperial bureaucracy. Actual tunics found in Egypt and Syria give first-hand evidence of the riot of colour that was now the norm in clothing for all classes. The background colours vary from white, through brown, grey, blue and red[24] and the *segmenta* seem to exhibit a facility for display that was far less restricted than it had been earlier. Quintilian would not have approved of these decorative aspects; he thought a purple stripe was quite enough: 'Again a stripe or some purple in the right place adds a touch of splendour, but a dress with a number of different marks in the weave would suit no one.'[25] These *segmenta* and *clavi* could be defined as fashion decoration that quickly became universal and was subsumed into the mainstream. It is clear that there was a wide variety of choices available. Weavers' pattern books have been discovered that offer a variety of different designs, thus allowing an element of personal taste in the choice of patterning on a garment.[26] It is

[22] See M. L. Rinaldi, 'Il costume romano e i mosaici di Piazza Armerina', *Rivista dell'Istituto Nazionale d'Archeologia e Storia dell'Arte* 13–14 (1964–5), pp. 200–68; G. V. Gentili, 'Piazza Armerina e Faenza. Due mosaici con esaltazioni imperiali', *Bollettino d'Arte* 98 (1996), pp. 1–16.

[23] Such items are often key in museum displays and catalogues, for example: Weitzmann, *Age of Spirituality*, pp. 138–9, 141, 142; T. K. Thomas, 'Costume, fashion and taste in late antique Egypt: "decorative devices" from the textile collection in the Kelsey Museum', *Bulletin, The University of Michigan Museums of Art and Archaeology* 12 (1997–2000), pp. 89–101; A. Lorquin, *Etoffes égyptiennes de l'antiquité tardive du musée George-Labit* (Toulouse and Paris, 1999).

[24] See W. F. Volbach, *Early Decorative Textiles* (London, 1969).

[25] Quintilian VIII.5.28, cited in M. Roberts, *The Jeweled Style: Poetry and Poetics in Late Antiquity* (Ithaca, NY, 1989), p. 115. I thank Thelma Thomas for this reference. See also Thomas, 'Costume, fashion and taste in late antique Egypt', p. 94.

[26] A. Stauffer, 'Cartoons for weavers in Greco-Roman Egypt', in D. M. Bailey (ed.), *Archaeological Research in Roman Egypt*, Journal of Roman Archaeology Supplement 19 (1996), pp. 223–30.

3   The late Roman *dominus* of Piazza Armerina, mosaic detail from
the Hall of the Great Hunt.

these decorated panels and patches that have been the focus of attention for
scholars interested in the history of textiles. They were valued in antiquity
for their intricacy and we find them listed in dowry lists and wills as part of
the stored wealth of the household. The designs themselves may have been
purely ornamental or may have had magical or apotropaic powers. They

4 Men loading a boat, mosaic detail from Piazza Armerina.

may also have been badges of rank, but if so the nuances of meaning are now lost.[27]

Fabrics deemed to be overly decorated had always held implied connotations of corruption for the Romans. Men did wear coloured garments but tended towards the plain rather than the intricately patterned. Wilson, writing in the 1930s, in what is still one of the most influential books on Roman clothing, considered the tunic of this period to have become 'thoroughly orientalised'. Like the Romans, Wilson believed the influences of the east to have a corrupting effect on the morals of the Romans which was reflected in their style of dress: 'This change in the costume of the Roman citizen was alas! a visible expression of the ominous changes taking place in the body politic.'[28] By this she meant the bright colours, use of gold and intricately woven patterns and designs that are evident on the tunic and cloak of Stilicho (Fig. 5). Perhaps she shared the views of Ammianus who regarded the 'tunics embroidered with parti-coloured threads in multiform figure of animals' of the fourth-century Roman aristocracy with distaste:

and in ostentatious finery of apparel, they sweat under heavy cloaks, which they fasten about their necks and bind around their very throats, while the air blows through them because of the excessive lightness of the material; and they lift them up with both hands and wave them with many gestures, especially with their left hands, in order that the over long fringes and the tunics embroidered with parti-coloured threads in multiform figures of animals may be conspicuous.[29]

Stilicho's tunic displays this love of design: it seems to have an all-over pattern, with borders along the lower hem and the wrists; *segmenta* are just visible on the shoulders. The tunic is of knee length, in recognition of Stilicho's military status. It has the long tight sleeves formerly considered barbarian or effeminate but which are now part of mainstream dress. The overall patterning is novel in the representation of a Roman official, civilian or military.

---

[27] H. Maguire, 'Garments pleasing to God: the significance of domestic textile designs in the early Byzantine period', *DOP* 44 (1990), pp. 1–33; Thomas, 'Costume, fashion and taste in late antique Egypt', pp. 95–6 and her references.

[28] L. Wilson, *Clothing of the Ancient Romans* (Baltimore, 1938), p. 68.

[29] Ammianus, XIV.6.9: 'ambitioso vestium cultu ponentes, sudant sub ponderibus lacernarum, quas in collis insertas iugulis ipsis annectunt, nimia subtegminum tenuitate perlabilis, exceptantes eas manu utraque et vexantes crebis agitationibus, maximeque sinistra, ut longiores fimbriae tunicaeque perspicue luceant, varietate liciorum effigiatae in species animalium multiformes'. The extract continues with a comparison with earlier soberly dressed Romans: they are clearly unaware of their forefathers, through whom the greatness of Rome was so far flung. They gained renown not by riches but by fierce wars, and not differing from the common soldier in wealth, mode of life or simplicity of attire, they overcame all obstacles by valour. Ammianus is using a standard rhetorical device of associating excess with moral decline. See also R. MacMullen, 'Some pictures in Ammianus Marcellinus', *Art Bulletin* 46 (1964), pp. 435–55.

5 The Diptych of Stilicho.

By *c.* 400, when the Stilicho ivory was carved, the tunic had evidently come into its own, and was worn by all classes; length, colour and type of fabric marked status difference. All the examples at Piazza Armerina, apart from those in the mythological scenes, have long relatively tight fitting sleeves, which fit snugly at the wrist. It is worn on its own, with or without a cloak. As with the length and colour of tunics, cloaks also seem to work as markers of status and occupation (see below).

CHLAMYS

The elision of civilian and military modes of presentation is evidenced in the wearing of the chlamys by both Probianus and Stilicho (Figs. 2 and 5). This Greek term came also to stand for the Latin *paludamentum*, and describes the ankle-length cloak worn by high-ranking officers in the army.[30] The chlamys was woven with a curved rather than a straight edge. It could be coloured and/or decorated with *tablia* (rectangular blocks of patterning, falling towards the middle of the front and back edges as on the cloaks of Justinian and his entourage, Fig. 7) or, more rarely, with an all-over pattern such as Stilicho's carries.[31] In the third century the ensemble of tunic and chlamys was not yet accepted as appropriate dress for civic occasions at Rome. It was associated with warfare and convention required that it be discarded once the military role was ended. 'Good' emperors recognised this and laid aside the chlamys as a sign of peace once they entered Italy.[32] Gallienus (AD 253–268 – contemporary with the Brothers Sarcophagus) is said to have been the first emperor to appear in the chlamys in Rome, and the implication of this dress for the assessment of his character is evident given the framing of the comment:

so that women ruled better than he . . . at Rome – where emperors always appeared in a toga – he appeared in a purple cloak with jewelled and golden clasps. He wore a man's tunic of purple and gold and provided with sleeves. He used a jewelled sword-belt and he fastened jewels to his bootlaces and then called his boots 'reticulate' [i.e. like caps worn by women and effeminate men].[33]

It should be said in Gallienus' defence that he had an almost uniformly bad press from senatorial historians because one of his first rulings as emperor had been to exclude senators from high army command.

Despite the overelaboration of Gallienus' chlamys, the writer's military preoccupation is worth noting. The dress of the army was influencing civilian dress codes at this point. By the latter part of the third century the chlamys had become acceptable dress for representation. At Piazza Armerina it seems to be worn over a tunic by those in charge – particularly the so-called *dominus*, the most important male figure. This figure is central to the mosaic of the big-game hunt and shares similarities with portraits of

---

[30] In the classical Roman period, the *paludamentum* was a military cloak, usually worn by generals and later emperors. Its associations were martial and it was considered to be part of the garb to be laid aside when returning to civic duties: 'Ut illi, quibus erat moris paludamento mutare praetextam' (Pliny, *Panegyric* LVI.4). As time progressed, the cloak became part of the dress of imperial officials, while the term *paludamentum* came to describe the emperor's cloak.

[31] On cloaks other than the chlamys see J. P. Wild, 'Clothing in the north-western provinces of the Roman Empire', *Bonner Jahrbücher* 168 (1968), pp. 223–6; Wild, 'The clothing of Britannia, Gallia Belgica and Germania inferior', *Aufstieg und Niedergang der römischen Welt*, vol. II, 12.3 (1985), pp. 362–422; A. Croom, *Roman Clothing and Fashion* (Stroud, 2000), pp. 51–4.

[32] E.g. *SHA Hadrian* XXII.

[33] *SHA Gallienus* XVI.4: 'ut etiam mulieres illo melius imperarent . . . cum chlamyde purpurea gemma-tisque fibulis et aureis Romae visus est, ubi semper togati principes videbantur. Purpuream tunicam auratamque virilem eandemque manicatam habuit. Gemmato balteo usus est. Corrigas gemmeas adnexuit, cum campagnos reticulos appellaret.'

the Tetrarchs. The *dominus* wears a three-quarter length chlamys with semi-circular *tablia* (*segmenta*) over a tunic with long, tight sleeves and leggings (see Fig. 3). Originally associated with the military, the chlamys and tunic became the mark of civil officials in the later empire as bureaucrats became subsumed into the military. They are worn by Stilicho, projecting himself as *magister militum* and by Probianus as *Vicarius urbis Romae*. Imperial civil servants held office as part of the militia and over time developed a sort of mufti version of military dress.

The official overtones associated with the wearing of the chlamys are shown by the diptych of Probianus. On the left side, where he is represented as *Vicarius urbis Romae*, he wears the chlamys and long tunic. His official status is emphasised not only by his dress but also by the open codicil, the imperial diploma of office, on his lap. In the lower register two assistants wear similar dress. Decorated *segmenta* are just visible on his tunic at the right shoulder, as are the *tablia* on the cloaks of Probianus' assistants. On the right Probianus sits under an inscription that displays his name and rank *vc* (*vir clarissimus*). Here he wears the *toga contabulata* and is hailed in the lower register by two similarly dressed senators (on whom one can see the back draping of this configuration). Two tunics are now worn under the toga, a longer one with long tight fitting sleeves topped by a slightly shorter one with loose sleeves. The layered tunics look very similar to those shown on the Arch of Constantine and other late antique togate figures.[34]

As the diptych of Probianus and the obelisk base of Theodosius show, the chlamys and tunic did not supersede the toga; neither type was exclusive. None the less, on evidence from the east, Smith has argued that, as a garment of the imperial court and imperial government, the chlamys was used on monuments to differentiate between military offices and those of civilian officials.[35] Both Rome and Constantinople continued to promote dress codes: just prior to Probianus' tenure in office a ruling tried to ensure that men wore the appropriate clothing for the proper occasion:

No senator shall claim for himself a military garb, even without the exception of the early morning hours, provided that he resides within the walls, but he shall lay aside the awe-inspiring military cloak and clothe himself with the sober robes of everyday costume and a civilian cloak. When, moreover, a meeting of the white-robed Order is being held or a case of a senator is being tried at a public hearing of a judge, we command the aforesaid senator to be present clad in his toga.[36]

---

[34] Illustrations in Stone, 'The toga', p. 34; Weitzmann, *Age of Spirituality*, p. 56.

[35] R. R. R. Smith, 'Late antique portraits in a public context: honorific statuary at Aphrodisas in Caria', *JRS* 88 (1999), pp. 155–89.

[36] *CT* xiv.10.1: 'Sine exceptione temporis matutini, dumtaxat intra moenia constitutus, nullus senatorum habitum sibi vindicet militarem, sed chlamydis terrore deposito quieta colobrum ac paenularum

No doubt the lawyers were fighting a rearguard action, as this ruling can only have had meaning if the toga was already being frequently displaced on civic occasions. By the early fifth century the chlamys was the garment that represented imperial authority, and those who wore it, particularly with the cross-bow fastening, were probably displaying their status as office holders, either military or civilian.[37] In images of Christ before Pilate, like that in the Rossano gospels,[38] Pilate almost invariably wears the chlamys/tunic as representation of Roman power, whereas Christ invariably wears a tunic and pallium, but that is another story.

PALLIUM

Proponents of Christianity seem to have used dress as a marker from an early date by rejecting the toga. In catacomb paintings we see much simpler garments, each figure usually wearing a minimally decorated tunic with a pallium or an over-cloak, the *paenula*.[39] In the late second century Tertullian had written *De pallio* in which he waxed lyrical about the advantages of the 'spiritual pallium' over the 'toga of politics'. Tertullian played on a metaphor that was easily recognised by Romans, that to wear the toga suggested close involvement with the civic and political world, while to remove it was a sign of laying down those interests. The pallium (a rectangular cloak of the ordinary person – Greek *himation*) was the garment of the non-political. Tertullian claimed that the toga was a cumbersome and complicated garment not suited to the simple life of the Christian man. He ridiculed Quintilian's instructions and the time spent dressing the toga correctly. The pallium, on the other hand, was simply thrown over the body.[40] The pallium was also the garment associated with the representation of philosophers, those who had chosen to avoid the political world. Tertullian used the image of the pallium and its associations to assert the simple and humble life of the Christian. He reversed the symbol of the

induat vestimenta. Cum autem vel conventus ordinis candidati coeperit agitari vel negotium eius sub publica iudicis sessione cognosci, togatum eundem interesse mandamus.' Issued in Constantinople, AD 382. T. Mommsen (ed.), *Theodosiani Libri XVI* (Berlin, 1904), trans. C. Pharr, *The Theodosian Code and Novels, and the Sirmondian Constitutions* (Princeton, 1952).

[37] Smith, 'Late antique portraits', p. 177; for cross-bow fastenings see E. Swift, *Regionality in Dress Accessories in the Late Roman West* (Montagnac, 2000).

[38] G. Cavallo, J. Gribomat and W. C. Loerke, *I vangeli di Rossano: le minature/The Rossano Gospels: The Miniatures* (Rome, 1987).

[39] The *paenula* was a short hooded cloak. It is the garment worn by the secretaries in the upper register on the right-hand side of the Probianus diptych (Fig. 2).

[40] *De Pallio* 5; L. Coon, *Sacred Fictions: Holy Women and Hagiography in Late Antiquity* (Philadelphia, 1997), p. 58; C. Vout, 'Myth of the toga', *Greece & Rome* 43 (1996), pp. 216–18.

toga, the ultimate sign of 'Roman-ness', so that it came to symbolise moral decline. He described it as burdensome to wear so that it no longer articulated the ideas of simplicity, freedom and citizenship that it once had. Jerome, writing in the fourth century, also used the toga as a tool, advising his senatorial friend, Pammachius, to wear the dark toga of mourning (the toga *pulla*) to the Senate House.[41] Such an act would have been considered inauspicious by traditionalists. The symbolic rejection of the toga, or in Pammachius' case the right style of toga, had an ideological rhetorical purpose that questioned accepted representations of power and status. The power struggle between Christians and Romans used dress as a signifier.

The literary motifs were matched by portrayals of Christ, the apostles and holy men in art. Early representations of Christ developed an iconography which clothed him in the tunic and pallium (*chiton* and *himation*) and this seems to have been almost universally applied in both east and west. He is portrayed with the pallium drawn close around his body with his right arm appearing in the sling of the garment like a philosopher, or with it slung over the left shoulder and wrapped around the body, crossed at waist length at the front and carried over the left arm. Variations on this theme cover almost all the late antique representations of Christ in all kinds of media – manuscripts, wall paintings, mosaics and sculpture – with one exceptional example. A fifth-century sarcophagus, now in the archaeological museum in Istanbul, shows Christ seated in the centre surrounded by four figures. Across his chest he wears what looks like a version of the *toga contabulata*, as seen on the column base of Theodosius, but it transforms itself into a pallium as it falls across his lap. Is this a reworked sarcophagus, modified by an artist who was confused about the iconography of power? Heaven may have looked like a version of the Roman imperial court but Christ did not normally look like a Roman. Dress, and representation of dress, was used as a means of negotiating power between Christians and Romans, just as it was between Romans and the new groups who were assuming power in the political arena.

TROUSERS

In the legislation there was also an attempt to stamp out other styles of dress that were considered less than Roman – trousers (*bracae*) and boots (*tzangae*) were banned from the city of Rome in AD 399 – with the penalty of perpetual exile for disobedience.

[41] Jerome, Letter 66, 6, *PL* 22 col. 642.

Within the venerable city no person shall be allowed to appropriate to himself the use of trousers or boots. But if any man should attempt to contravene this sanction, We command that in accordance with the sentence of the illustrious prefect, the offender shall be stripped of all his resources and delivered into perpetual exile.[42]

This is a very severe penalty and we must question just exactly which groups it was aimed at, particularly as it is clear from the diptych of Stilicho, dated only a year after the publication of this law, that he wears some form of leg covering. Even more interesting is Diocletian's Price Edict, issued a century earlier, in 301, in which a section addressed the pay given to makers of trousers: trousers cannot have been an unfamiliar sight.[43]

Leg coverings were used to help create 'barbarian' identity in Roman art and also to differentiate ethnic groupings. Persians and those from the east were often shown wearing highly coloured and decorated leggings, as in the depictions of the Magi at Ravenna and Santa Maria Maggiore in Rome. Northern barbarians, such as those depicted on Trajan's column or the base of the Arch of Septimius Severus in the Forum Romanum, were often shown in loose but shaped leggings that were tied with thongs at the ankle. The figures are often depicted naked from the waist up, emphasising their conquered status.[44]

Using leggings to depict 'the other' in Roman iconography thus had a long pedigree, and despite the fact that trousers seem to bring out the snobbish in Romans, it is clear that leggings of some sort had been worn by them since the time of Augustus – who obviously felt the cold.[45] Quintilian continued to stress that leggings were only suitable for invalids,[46] and his seems to be the general rhetorical opinion: coverings in the form of leggings, like long sleeves, were considered a mark both of the barbarian and of physical, and by implication of mental, weakness. Soldiers or hunters, as evidenced in the Piazza Armerina mosaics, could wear bindings on thighs and calves as protection. Soldiers wore a form of leg covering when on

---

[42] *CT* XIV.10.2: 'Usum tzangarum adque bracarum intra urbem venerabilem nemini liceat usurpare. Si quis autem contra hanc sanctionem venire temptaverit, sententia viri inlustris praefecti spoliatum eum omnibus facultatibus tradi in perpetuum exilium praecipimus.' Latin text: Mommsen (ed.), *Theodosiani Libri XVI*, trans. Pharr, *Theodosian Code*.

[43] Edict VII.46; 47. The Edict of Diocletian in T. Frank, *An Economic Survey of Ancient Rome*, vol. v (Baltimore, 1940), pp. 310–421.

[44] I. M. Ferris, *Enemies of Rome* (Stroud, 2000); B. Goldman, 'Graeco-Roman dress in Syro-Mesopotamia', in Sebesta and Bonfante (eds.), *World of Roman Costume*, pp. 163–81; R. A. Gergel, 'Costume as geographic indicator: barbarians and prisoners on cuirassed statue breastplates' in *ibid.*, pp. 191–212.

[45] Suetonius, *Augustus* 82.   [46] Quintilian, *Inst. Orat.* XI.3.144.

campaign in northern provinces (visible on Trajan's column) and Severus Alexander gave away gifts of trousers (*bracae*) and boots to soldiers.[47] By the mid-third century, soldiers' normal dress, when on duty but not going into battle, was clearly the forerunner of that worn by Stilicho. The essential elements were a knee-length tunic with long, fitted sleeves, dark trousers, an elaborate belt and a cloak. At this period such dress marked a soldier out from other members of the community.[48] By signifying martial activity, it also meant that certain items of dress, particularly leggings, were not acceptable public wear on civic occasions, unless one was a soldier. Elagobalus, for example, caused great scandal when he appeared in public wearing long decorated trousers.[49] Romans were even more offended by the light loose and patterned trouser of the east (known as *anaxyrides*) than the more modest functional *bracae*.

In the Piazza Armerina mosaics there are many examples of leggings but it is not clear whether they have integral feet or finish at the ankle as those of the 'northern barbarians' do. The leggings in the Piazza Armerina look quite tight fitting, but this may be a convention of the medium of mosaic (Fig. 4); those of Stilicho look similar, while the *bracata* look looser and the *anaxyrides* looser still. The most useful, and perhaps only, example of 'trousers' with integral feet comes from Silistra in Bulgaria (Fig. 6). This is an invaluable cycle of tomb paintings that shows, on separate wall panels, servants bringing items of dress to the master. These include trousers with feet, a tunic, a belt and a chlamys.[50] This would suggest that not only Stilicho but also Probianus, under his longer tunic and hence not visible, wore leggings.

So leggings or trousers of some kind made it through the military into the mainstream of Roman dress. By AD 400 they were worn, despite imperial edicts to the contrary, by officials of the empire, primarily by the military – we cannot deny the military context of Stilicho's diptych – but also by civilian officials who held their offices as militia, and by the sixth century by the emperor. The earliest depiction of an imperial figure in leggings I

[47] *SHA Severus Alexander* XI.6.
[48] S. Janes, 'The community of soldiers', in P. Baker, C. Forcey, S. Jundi and R. Witcher (eds.), *TRAC 98: Proceedings of the Eighth Annual Theoretical Roman Archaeology Conference, Leicester 1998* (Oxford, 1999), pp. 14–25.
[49] Herodian v.3.6 (trans. E. Echols, Berkeley, 1961).
[50] D. P. Dimitrov, 'Le pitture murali del sepolcro romano di Silistra', *Arte Antica e Moderna* 12 (1960), pp. 351–65. Prof. Lise Bender Jørgensen has also shown me illustrations of a find of such a pair of leggings excavated in the nineteenth century in Denmark and I thank her for this reference: C. Engelhardt, *Thorsbjerg Mosefund* (Copenhagen, 1863), pls. 1 and 2.

6   Servant carrying leggings, detail from tomb painting in Silistra, Bulgaria.

have found is a silver plate portrait of Constantius II, dated to the mid-fourth century. Here he is depicted in triumphal military guise, wearing a short tunic decorated with patterned segmenta and edging, with leggings and jewelled shoes.[51]

To return to the image of *Romanitas* presented in the images of Stilicho and Probianus: by contemporary standards there is no doubt that both these men are projecting their membership of the Roman empire and its ruling classes. The way a high-ranking individual could present himself had transformed over the third and fourth centuries. During this period there was an ongoing elision of civil and military and of Roman and non-Roman. The dress of the military had absorbed much from the barbarian repertoire by virtue of the simple fact that most soldiers were barbarians, or descended from them. This had a domino effect as high-ranking soldiers were, or became, members of the elite. Dress items crossed over the military/civilian

[51] J. M. C. Toynbee and K. S. Painter, 'Silver picture plates of late antiquity: AD 300–700', *Archaeologia* 108 (1986), pp. 15–65. The plate shows Constantius making a triumphal entry. It is now in Leningrad State Hermitage Museum (inv. no. 1820/79).

7 Justinian and his entourage, San Vitale, Ravenna.

boundary, a boundary that was in any case becoming blurred as high civilian officials served in a militia, claimed honorific military titles and wore a uniform. So military status was social status and the uniform of the high-ranking soldier (chlamys, tunic, belt and leggings) could be interchangeable with that of the civilian official.

A complete reversal of the oppositions recognisable to earlier Romans had come about: the marks of the barbarian, the long sleeves, fitted tunic, long chlamys and leggings, had by the sixth century become the court dress of the Roman emperor. At Ravenna (Fig. 7) Justinian is portrayed in a knee-length, long-sleeved white tunic with gold decoration, long purple chlamys with decorated *tablion* front and back, black leggings and red shoes. His secular entourage wears plainer but similar garb, the soldiers more brightly coloured uniforms. The churchmen, noticeably, wear neither toga nor chlamys but the tunic and *paenula* that had become standard clerical vestments. On the facing wall the male members of Theodora's court are similarly attired.

The reality of the Italian-born, toga-clad ruler of the world was past its heyday by the mid-second century, but it took until the third and fourth centuries for the new personnel of empire to represent themselves in new ways. By the early fifth century, in the diptychs of Stilicho and Probianus we see the effect of empire on the modes of presentation: both east and west influenced the centre. Those of the outer reaches of empire displaced Italian garments just as personnel from these areas had earlier displaced Italians from positions of power. The integration of new groups and the displacement of the old Roman aristocracy challenged traditional ideas of male identity. These changes were reflected in dress, and as garments and styles previously considered non-Roman became commonplace, over time they became the 'traditional' dress of the Roman emperor.

We have seen in examples above that the character of individuals could be expressed by the interpretation of what they wore. This is, of course, to over-simplify a set of ideas that are very complex in their application but, given the nature of the evidence, we have to work with and exploit the stereo-types that have been left for us. The way we interpret dress is influenced by what we know of a society's preoccupations and prejudices, particularly its attitudes towards certain types of dress and the meanings it ascribes to them. Dress, as stated at the outset of this chapter, is intertwined with concepts of identity and gender. Looking at Stilicho and Justinian's retinue through the earlier prism of the high Roman empire we see the ascendancy of the 'barbarian', or at least the non-Roman. The very elements that were previously considered part of the non-Roman repertoire have been sub-sumed into the mainstream, just as groups that were previously peripheral have become central and have brought with them the memory of their origins. Despite this, it is unclear how far traditional ideas of masculinity are challenged in these images. Roman society was male centred in that it privileged manhood and masculinity; the social transformations of late antiquity did not question this fundamental tenet. The key signifiers of the successful upper-class male remained the virility expressed in military service and the devotion to the state expressed in office-holding.[52] It is not so much that ideals of manhood are challenged here, in that men like Stilicho and Probianus are still portraying themselves in similar positions of military and civil power, but that the way they clothe themselves in these images suggests a transformation of identity. It is not masculinity *per se* that is transformed here but *romanitas*. Concepts of masculinity and of Roman-ness were flexible enough to redress themselves to suit new person-nel of diverse ethnic origins. New men had absorbed and transformed the

---

[52] See Keufler, *Manly Eunuchs*, pp. 37–55, on the relationship between manliness, militarism and political authority.

dominant modes of representation of masculinity into their own image. Where the earlier Roman fought to obscure outside influences, later Roman man embraced them and, in so doing, accepted a transformation both in the individuals who held power and in the way they expressed that power in dress codes.[53]

[53] I would like to thank the following, who have all helped me with this chapter: the Leverhulme foundation for granting me a special Research Fellowship (2000–1) which allowed me to undertake this research, of which this is just the beginning; the Open University (Flexible Fund) who funded my attendance at the Leeds Medieval Conference 2000 where this paper was first given; Chris Wickham, Simon Esmonde-Cleary and Simon Janes who have been willing to read and discuss sections of this chapter.

CHAPTER 4

Social transformation, gender transformation? The court eunuch, 300–900

Shaun Tougher

INTRODUCTION

One of the distinctive features of the later Roman empire was the use of eunuchs at the imperial court.[1] The role of the eunuch in the late Roman court system (*c.* fourth to sixth centuries) has been the subject of significant – and classic – sociological analysis by Keith Hopkins, seeking an answer to why eunuchs became so valued a tool of the late Roman emperors, and also why they became such powerful political players.[2] Hopkins associates the eunuch's emergence as an integral and institutional element of the late Roman court with the reforming emperor Diocletian (284–305), and argues that the development was connected to the general transferral of the position of chamberlain to eunuchs exclusively.[3] He demonstrates

---

[1] See for example J. Long, *Claudian's In Eutropium. Or, How, When, and Why to Slander a Eunuch* (Chapel Hill, 1996); D. Schlinkert, Ordo senatoribus *und* nobilitas: *die Konstitution des Senatsadels in der Spätantike; mit einem Appendix über den* praepositus sacri cubiculi, *den 'allmächtigen' Eunuchen am kaiserlichen Hof,* Hermes Einzelschriften 72 (Stuttgart, 1996), pp. 237–84, and 'Der Hofeunuch in der Spätantike: ein gefährlicher Außenseiter?', *Hermes* 122 (1994), pp. 342–59; H. Scholten, *Der Eunuch in Kaisernähe: zur politischen und sozialen Bedeutung des* praepositus sacri cubiculi *im. 4. und 5. Jahrhundert n. Chr.*, Prismata 5 (Frankfurt, 1995); W. Stevenson, 'The rise of eunuchs in Greco-Roman antiquity', *Journal of the History of Sexuality* 5 (1995), pp. 495–511; S. Tougher, 'Ammianus and the eunuchs', in J. W. Drijvers and D. Hunt (eds.), *The Late Roman World and Its Historian: Interpreting Ammianus Marcellinus* (London, 1999), pp. 64–73. On other aspects of eunuchs in antiquity see for instance M. Beard, 'The Roman and the foreign: the cult of the "Great Mother" in imperial Rome', in N. Thomas and C. Humphrey (eds.), *Shamanism, History, and the State* (Ann Arbor, MI, 1994), pp. 164–90; A. K. Grayson, 'Eunuchs in power: their role in the Assyrian bureaucracy', in M. Dietrich and O. Loretz (eds.), *Vom Alten Orient zum Alten Testament: Festschrift für Wolfram Freiherrn von Soden zum 85. Geburtstag am 19. Juni 1993*, Alter Orient und Altes Testament 240 (Neukirchen, 1995), pp. 85–98; S. Tougher (ed.), *Eunuchs in Antiquity and Beyond* (London, 2002).
[2] K. Hopkins, *Conquerors and Slaves*, Sociological Studies in Roman History 1 (Cambridge, 1978), pp. 172–96 (a version of his earlier 'Eunuchs in politics in the later Roman empire', *Proceedings of the Cambridge Philological Society* 189 (1963), pp. 62–80). See also, however, P. Guyot, *Eunuchen als Sklaven und Freigelassene in der Griechisch-Römischen Antike*, Stuttgarter Beiträge zur Geschichte und Politik 14 (Stuttgart, 1980), pp. 130–76; O. Patterson, *Slavery and Social Death: A Comparative Study* (Cambridge, MA, 1982), esp. pp. 317–24.
[3] Hopkins, *Conquerors and Slaves*, pp. 191–3.

that eunuchs were valued for their loyalty, dependency, mediation and role in imperial pomp, but also for their dispensability.

Despite the value of court eunuchs to later Roman emperors, there is great hostility towards eunuchs demonstrated by the late antique literary sources (particularly in the fourth century), as Hopkins highlights. A famous example is the letter of the Cappadocian Father Basil of Caesarea to Simplicia.[4] The bishop characterises eunuchs as woman-mad, envious, corrupt, quick-tempered, slaves of the belly, avaricious, cruel, lamenting the loss of a dinner, fickle, niggardly, all-receiving, insatiable, mad and jealous. The history of Ammianus Marcellinus and the compilation of the *Historia Augusta* are also noted for their hatred of eunuchs. Ammianus targets his anger mainly at the court of Constantius II (337–361) and the grand chamberlain Eusebius,[5] whilst the *Historia Augusta* denounces the influence of eunuchs at court generally.[6] Notably, hostility to eunuchs could be expressed in gender terms. Basil also describes eunuchs as unwomanly, unmanly and effeminate. Further, eunuchs could be portrayed as an aberration, a third sex. In a speech praising the emperor Julian (361–363) Claudius Mamertinus describes eunuchs as 'exiles from the society of the human race, belonging neither to one sex nor the other'.[7] This is akin to what the emperor Severus Alexander is made to say of eunuchs in the *Historia Augusta*; he asserts that they are 'a third sex of the human race'.[8] Claudian testifies to the same perception in his first invective against Eutropius, the grand chamberlain of Arcadius (395–408); he describes eunuchs as an 'unhappy band . . . whom the male sex has discarded and the female will not adopt'.[9]

Since the Byzantine empire was the continuation of the Roman empire in the east it is unsurprising to find that eunuchs were still a vital element of the imperial court in Constantinople.[10] However, there were changes in the social status and origin of eunuchs between the late Roman and Byzantine periods. In this chapter I explore two particular aspects of the transformation of court eunuchs within the period 300–900, thus considering the

---

[4] For the text see for instance R. J. Deferrari, *Saint Basil: The Letters*, vol. 11 (London, 1928), pp. 228–32.

[5] On Ammianus' views of eunuchs see Tougher, 'Ammianus and the eunuchs', but also G. Sidéris, 'La comédie des castrats. Ammien Marcellin et les eunuques, entre eunocophobie et admiration', *Revue Belge de Philologie et d'Histoire* 78 (2000), pp. 681–717.

[6] See Alan Cameron, 'Eunuchs in the "Historia Augusta"', *Latomus* 24 (1965), pp. 155–8.

[7] *Latin Panegyric* III.19.4: see S. N. C. Lieu (ed.), *The Emperor Julian: Panegyric and Polemic*, 2nd edn (Liverpool, 1989), p. 29.

[8] *SHA* XXIII.4–8.   [9] *In Eutr.* 1.466–7.

[10] See for example R. Guilland's series of studies on the titles and offices of eunuchs at the Byzantine court (inaugurated by his 'Les eunuques dans l'empire byzantin. Etude de titulaire et de prosopographie byzantines', *Revue des Etudes Byzantines* 1 (1943), pp. 197–238) compiled in *Recherches sur les institutions byzantines*, vol. 1, Berliner byzantinische Arbeiten 35 (Berlin, 1967), pp. 165–380.

major group of eunuchs in society.[11] I then relate these transformations back to the issue of the gender identity of eunuchs, considering the view that the social transformations coincided with a gender transformation, as Byzantine eunuchs experienced a shift from a negative to a positive gender identity.

The two social aspects to be addressed first are how the court eunuch transformed in terms of offices and titles held, and how the court eunuch transformed in terms of ethnic origin. The discussion is rooted in, and polarised between, two texts relating to imperial court and administration, texts that date to the opposite ends of my chronological framework. For the later Roman period the text is the notoriously difficult *Notitia Dignitatum*; for the Byzantine period it is the *Kletorologion* of Philotheos.[12] These texts are supplemented by a range of other evidence to secure a fuller picture.

LATE ROMAN COURT EUNUCHS: OFFICE

For the study of late Roman administration a valuable, but complex, tool is the *Notitia Dignitatum*.[13] This Latin 'List of Offices' details the civil and military officials of both the eastern half of the empire and the western half, treated in separate sections. It is taken to reflect the division of the empire between Arcadius and Honorius (the sons of Theodosius I) in 395, and was probably written not long after that, though its exact date is unclear; the western section appears to have fifth-century additions. The text is thought to have been for use in the western empire; the section for the eastern empire certainly lacks detail in places. The exact purpose of the list is not clear; it reveals some interest in the hierarchy of offices, though that is not its only concern.

For the study of eunuchs the list has some relevance, for it includes the office of the *praepositus sacri cubiculi* (grand chamberlain), the most prominent eunuch official of the later Roman empire. Several examples of holders of this post surface in the historiographical evidence, such as Eusebios, Eutherios and Eutropios. Though the *Notitia Dignitatum* is not

---

[11] Most eunuchs were created for court use.   [12] For details of these texts see below.
[13] For this text see for instance R. S. O. Tomlin, '*Notitia Dignitatum*', in S. Hornblower and A. Spawforth (eds.), *The Oxford Classical Dictionary*, 3rd edn (Oxford, 1996), p. 1049; R. Goodburn and P. Bartholomew (eds.), *Aspects of the 'Notitia Dignitatum': Papers Presented to the Conference in Oxford, December 13 to 15, 1974* (Oxford, 1976); A. H. M. Jones, *The Later Roman Empire 284–602: A Social, Economic, and Administrative Survey*, 2 vols. (Oxford, 1964), vol. II, Appendix II, pp. 1417–50; and now M. Kulikowski, 'The *Notitia Dignitatum* as a historical source', *Historia* 49 (2000), pp. 358–77. For an edition see O. Seeck (ed.), *Notitia Dignitatum accedunt notitia urbis Constantinopolitanae et latercula Provinciarum* (Frankfurt, 1962, orig. publ. 1876).

explicit about the physical condition of the holder of the office, it does provide other information. It indicates that the post was to be found in both the eastern and western empire. Also, the placing in the lists reflects the significance of the office. In the eastern list the grand chamberlain is ranked after the praetorian prefects, the prefect of the city of Constantinople and the masters of soldiers,[14] whilst in the western list he is ranked after the praetorian prefects, the prefect of the city of Rome, the master of infantry and the masters of cavalry.[15] However, other valuable information is lost. In the *Notitia Dignitatum* those listed in the initial indices for east and west are usually then treated in separate chapters, giving a brief description of functions and details of subordinate officers and staff. Unfortunately the chapters of the *Notitia Dignitatum* which dealt with the grand chamberlain and the organisation of his staff are missing.[16] We are thus dependent on other sources of information for these details. Of other eunuch offices, Hopkins identifies the *primicerius sacri cubiculi* (superintendent of the sacred bedchamber), and the *castrensis sacri palatii* (chief steward of the palace).[17] These do appear in both ranking lists, though again their status as eunuchs is not explicit. In the separate chapters the details for the *primicerius* are missing for both, whilst those for the *castrensis* are preserved.[18]

TITLE

The *Notitia Dignitatum*'s concern is offices, but it also records details of the senatorial titles held by officials. By AD 400 there were three main titles of distinction; they are, in order of descent, *illustris*, *spectabilis* and *clarissimus*.[19] The *Notitia Dignitatum* records that the grand chamberlain of the east held the rank of *illustris*, again reinforcing the pre-eminence of the position in late Roman society.[20] The text also records that the superintendent of the sacred bedchamber and the chief steward of the palace were *spectabiles*, 'and

---

[14] Seeck (ed.), *Notitia Dignitatum*, p. 1.

[15] Seeck (ed.), *Notitia Dignitatum*, p. 103. On rank see Hopkins, *Conquerors and Slaves*, pp. 174–5; he notes that a similar ranking is found in a western law of 412 (*CT* XI.18.1).

[16] J. E. Dunlap, 'The office of the grand chamberlain in the later Roman and Byzantine empires', in A. E. R. Boak and J. E. Dunlap, *Two Studies in Later Roman and Byzantine Administration* (New York, 1924), p. 202.

[17] Hopkins, *Conquerors and Slaves*, p. 175; Seeck (ed.), *Notitia Dignitatum*: east, nos. 17 and 19, pp. 1, 40–41; west, nos. 15 and 17, p. 103, 158–9.

[18] See Jones, *Later Roman Empire*, vol. 1, p. 567. On the *castrensis* see also E. A. Costa, 'The office of the "castrensis sacri palatii" in the fourth century', *Byzantion* 42 (1972), pp. 358–87. Costa argues that the first eunuch to be *castrensis* was Amantius in the fifth century.

[19] See for instance Jones, *Later Roman Empire*, vol. 1, pp. 528–9.

[20] Seeck (ed.), *Notitia Dignitatum*, p. 30. He has under him the imperial domus of Cappadocia. The folio for the western grand chamberlain is lost: p. 143. The ranking of the grand chamberlain is

thus', says Hopkins, 'were equal in rank, in spite of their origins, to high nobles'.[21]

Dunlap notes that other marks of honour could be won by eunuchs, such as count and patrician.[22] There was also the consulship, but the grand chamberlain Eutropios, under Arkadios, was the only eunuch to earn this distinction.[23]

BYZANTINE COURT EUNUCHS: OFFICE

For the study of Byzantine court eunuchs a vital tool is a late ninth-century Greek text, the so-called *Kletorologion* of Philotheos, written in 899 in the reign of Leo VI (886–912).[24] Philotheos was an *atriklines*, an imperial official whose task it was to organise imperial feasts and ensure that the correct order of precedence was observed with respect to the guests who were invited to such occasions. In his text Philotheos sets out to describe for his fellow *atriklinai* those individuals who could be invited to the imperial feasts, their exact order of precedence at that moment in time, and the prominent feasts of the year to which various combinations of these people would be invited. In the course of the document Philotheos reveals much about the offices, titles and hierarchy of his day. Whilst establishing this system he pays particular attention to the position of eunuchs within it. He lists ten specialised palace offices, reserved for eunuchs, from the top down.[25] These are:

> *parakoimomenos* (head chamberlain) of the emperor
> *protovestiarios* (in charge of imperial wardrobe) of the emperor
> master of the emperor's table
> master of the empress's table
> *papias* (caretaker) of the great palace
> *deuteros* (caretaker) of the great palace
> *pingernes* (waiter) of the emperor

---

attested also by a law dating to 384: *CT* VII.8.3. Dunlap, 'Grand chamberlain', pp. 183–5, argues that the grand chamberlain was ranked as an *illustris* between 382 and 384. For titles held by eunuch officials see also Jones, *Later Roman Empire*, vol. I, pp. 569–70.

[21] Hopkins, *Conquerors and Slaves*, p. 176; Seeck (ed.), *Notitia Dignitatum*, pp. 40–1, 158–9.

[22] Dunlap, 'Grand chamberlain', pp. 195–7.

[23] This occasioned Claudian's infamous invectives on Eutropius: see for instance Long, *Claudian's In Eutropium*.

[24] For the text see N. Oikonomidès, *Les Listes de préséance byzantines des IXe et Xe siècles: introduction, texte, traduction et commentaire*, Le monde byzantin (Paris, 1972), pp. 65–235. See also J. B. Bury, *The Imperial Administrative System in the Ninth Century: With a Revised Text of the Kletorologion of Philotheos* (London, 1911).

[25] Oikonomidès, *Les Listes*, pp. 132–5.

pingernes of the empress
papias of the Magnaura
papias of Daphne

These offices were to be the exclusive preserve of eunuchs; they were not to be filled by non-eunuchs (whom Philotheos defines as 'the bearded'). But Philotheos is quick to point out that eunuchs were not limited to these ten posts. In sharp contrast to the bearded who might in fact occasionally fill a eunuch post,[26] eunuchs were able to be appointed to virtually all other administrative posts, including the *strategoi* (military governors) of the *themes* (provinces). The only exceptions were the posts of eparch (city prefect),[27] *quaestor* (judge and legislator) and *domestikos* (military officer, of which there were several variants).[28]

TITLE

Philotheos also makes clear that eunuchs have their own honours system.
He lists eight titles, from the bottom up:[29]

nipsistarios (ablutions attendant)
koubikoularios (chamberlain)
spatharokoubikoularios (guard-chamberlain)
ostiarios (ceremonial functionary)
primikerios (leading eunuch)
protospatharios (chief guard)
praipositos (chief eunuch)
patrikios (patrician)

It seems that some of these titles were not purely honorific but could carry functions as well.[30] All but two of them are distinct from the titles held by non-eunuchs. In the case of these shared titles (*protospatharios* and *patrikios*) it is interesting to note that the insignia attached to the title could be more elaborate for the eunuch variety; the insignia of the *protospatharios* was a golden collar decorated with precious stones, but with pearls added

---

[26] For example, Basil the Macedonian (later emperor) was the *parakoimomenos* of Michael III (842–867).
[27] Perhaps then Niketas Choniates' detail that a eunuch at the court of Alexios III Angelos (1195–1203) played the role of a mounted eparch during court entertainments has extra significance: see J.-L. van Dieten (ed.), *Nicetae Choniatae Historia*, Corpus Fontium Historiae Byzantinae 11/1 (Berlin, 1975), pp. 508.89–509.4, trans. H. J. Magoulias, *O City of Byzantium, Annals of Niketas Choniatēs*, Byzantine Texts in Translation (Detroit, 1984), pp. 280–1.
[28] For an attempt to explain why eunuchs were barred from these posts see Bury, *Imperial Administrative System*, p. 74.
[29] Oikonomidès, *Les Listes*, pp. 124–9.   [30] Oikonomidès, *Les Listes*, pp. 300–1.

when the holder was a eunuch. It is notable that Philotheos describes the dress appropriate to these two eunuch titles; he does not do the same for the bearded titles, unless it is the insignia itself.[31] It is also worth remarking how these shared title names relate to one another in the complete hierarchy: the eunuch *patrikios* ranks above the bearded *patrikios*.[32]

A COMPARISON OF THE TWO TEXTS

What does a comparison of the two texts reveal about the social transformation of the court eunuch? Although the two texts are different in character, an impression of how the nature of the court eunuch was transformed in certain respects can be gained. By 899 eunuch officials appear to have been more numerous, having their own offices as well as access to most of those of the bearded.[33] They had acquired a separate honours system, in which they could have precedence over their bearded counterparts. Their status had indeed become distinct and enhanced. The early Byzantine administrative system changed greatly between the fifth and ninth centuries, but at what point between the dates of the two texts the position of eunuchs changed is open to debate. Hopkins asserted that other eunuch offices emerged: the Count of the Imperial Estates in Cappadocia (*comes domorum per Cappadociam*), the Count of the Imperial Wardrobe (*comes sacrae vestis*), the Captain of the Bodyguard (*spatharios*) and the Keeper of the

---

[31] The eunuch *protospatharios* wears a white tunic threaded with gold, and a scarlet cloak with stripes on the border woven with gold. The costume of the eunuch *patrikios* only differs from that of the eunuch *protospatharios* by the addition of a loros. For a Byzantine image of a eunuch *patrikios* see the donor frontispiece of the tenth-century Leo Bible, commissioned by Leo the *patrikios*, *praipositos* and *sakellarios*: H. C. Evans and W. D. Wixom (eds.), *The Glory of Byzantium: Art and Culture of the Middle Byzantine Era A.D. 843–1261* (New York, 1997), p. 89. Philotheos also describes the dress of the *nipsistarios*, *koubikoularios* and *primikerios*.

[32] See S. Tougher, 'Byzantine eunuchs: an overview, with special reference to their creation and origin', in L. James (ed.), *Women, Men and Eunuchs* (London, 1997), pp. 181–2 n. 28; Dunlap, 'Grand chamberlain', p. 239. It is not made clear, however, if the eunuch *protospatharioi* precede the bearded *protospatharioi*; they are not identified as a separate group in the relevant section detailing the hierarchy. Note also the evidence of the *Taktikon* produced under Michael III and Theodora: Oikonomidès, *Les Listes*, pp. 41–63. The *patrikios* and *praipositos* is ranked ninth, just after the *synkellos*, and the patrician eunuchs precede all other patricians with office (pp. 46–7). However the eunuch *protospatharioi* do not automatically precede all other *protospatharioi* (pp. 50–1).

[33] Note that in Philotheos the office of *sakellarios* is not identified as a eunuch-only office, though it seems that eunuchs generally held it (e.g. Stephen, Baanes, Leo, Bringas). The role of eunuchs as treasurers seems to have been a traditional one. Plutarch, *Life of Demetrios* 25, records that Lysimachos was furious that Demetrios labelled him a treasurer rather than a king, as he was effectively being called a eunuch given that 'it was the general custom to appoint eunuchs to the post of treasurer'. In the time of Justinian I, the eunuch Narses was a treasurer. Hopkins views the post of *sacellarius* as a eunuch office in the late Roman period: see n. 34 below.

Purse (*sakellarios*).³⁴ He remarked also that 'The number of high positions open to [eunuchs] was still further increased when it became customary for the empress to have a separate Bedchamber with its own complement of high officers.'³⁵ There were also developments in the late Roman ranking system. For instance first- and second-class *illustres* came into being, with the *praepositus sacri cubiculi* belonging to the first class.³⁶ More generally, it is clear that relative ranking could alter over time.³⁷ Dunlap remarked on the changes the administrative system underwent in the sixth century,³⁸ the period often associated with beginning the transformation of Rome to Byzantium, antiquity to the Middle Ages.³⁹ Then one is faced with a comparative lack of knowledge of the history of the seventh and eighth centuries, the so-called Dark Age. The ninth-century texts present a world that had already changed. That the *Notitia Dignitatum* had application for the courts of both east and west (and it is worth pointing out that the fifth-century western court did make use of eunuchs too),⁴⁰ whilst Philotheos' text is solely for the surviving court in Constantinople, underscores this point.

ETHNIC ORIGIN

The comparison of the *Notitia Dignitatum* and Philotheos' *Kletorologion* has additional limitations. Neither addresses my second concern, the changing ethnic origins of court eunuchs. A crucial aspect of late Roman court eunuchs, commented upon by Hopkins, was their status as complete outsiders;⁴¹ they were imported into the society of the Roman empire from foreign territory, with the result that they were forced into a dependent but symbiotic relationship with the emperor, their master.⁴² Having no other social contacts, these eunuchs depended utterly upon the emperor for their well-being, and thus would provide him with the utmost loyalty; the emperor knew this, and in turn would trust and reward his eunuchs. The status of eunuchs as ethnic outsiders was enshrined as an ideal in

³⁴ Hopkins, *Conquerors and Slaves*, p. 176 n. 14.   ³⁵ Hopkins, *Conquerors and Slaves*, p. 176.
³⁶ Hopkins, *Conquerors and Slaves*, p. 175; Dunlap, 'Grand chamberlain', p. 195.
³⁷ Dunlap, 'Grand chamberlain', pp. 185–9.   ³⁸ Dunlap, 'Grand chamberlain', p. 224.
³⁹ E.g. P. Allen and E. Jeffreys (eds.), *The Sixth Century: End or Beginning?*, Byzantina Australiensia 10 (Brisbane, 1996).
⁴⁰ And Dunlap, 'Grand chamberlain', p. 223, also notes evidence for a grand chamberlain at the court of Theoderic, and for a eunuch chamberlain.
⁴¹ Hopkins, *Conquerors and Slaves*, p. 189 and n. 45. This factor can also apply to court eunuchs in other cultures: see S. Tougher, 'In or out? Origins of court eunuchs', in Tougher (ed.), *Eunuchs in Antiquity and Beyond*, pp. 143–59.
⁴² A judgement recently emphasised again by Schlinkert, 'Der Hofeunuch in der Spätantike'.

late Roman imperial legislation.[43] Constantine I (306–337) decreed that no eunuchs were to be created within the Roman empire,[44] whilst Leo I (457–474) revealed the acceptable source of eunuchs, those of foreign nations created outside the Roman empire.[45] Other types of evidence indicate that this ideal had some basis in reality. Aelius Donatus, a *grammaticus* of the fourth century, stated in his commentary on Terence's *The Eunuch* that the majority of eunuchs in the eastern empire came from Armenia,[46] whilst Prokopios reported that under Justinian I (527–565) most eunuchs employed at the imperial court originated in Abasgia, on the eastern shore of the Black Sea.[47] What little we know of the origins of specific eunuchs employed at the late Roman courts provides broad confirmation that they tended to be of foreign extraction. Scholten estimated that there are only six examples of eunuch grand chamberlains for whom information on origin or social status exists.[48] These are Eutherios, an Armenian; Eutropios, an Armenian; Mamas, an Armenian;[49] Antiochos, a Persian;[50] an anonymous Gaul; and Eusebios, a slave. From the extant information, Scholten estimated that for the fourth and fifth centuries the great majority of chamberlains were drawn from Armenia or Persia. If we extend Scholten's chronological boundary beyond the fourth and fifth centuries into the sixth century, the well-known example Narses the Armenian can be added to this list.[51]

At the Byzantine court we also find eunuchs who are ethnic outsiders. For instance there is the infamous Stephen the Persian, active in the late seventh century as treasurer (*sakellarios*) for the emperor Justinian II during his first reign (685–695).[52] In the ninth century we encounter Damianos the

---

[43] On Roman legislation concerning castration from Domitian to Constantine see Guyot, *Eunuchen als Sklaven und Freigelassene*, pp. 45–51.

[44] In a decree to Ursinus the *dux* of Mesopotamia, preserved by Justinian, *Corpus iuris civilis* IV.XLII.

[45] In a decree to Vivianus the praetorian prefect of the east, preserved by Justinian, *Corpus iuris civilis* IV.XLII.

[46] See Guyot, *Eunuchen als Sklaven und Freigelassene*, p. 31; Scholten, *Der Eunuch in Kaisernähe*, p. 28 and n. 124.

[47] Prokopios, *Wars* VIII.3.12–21.

[48] Scholten, *Der Eunuch in Kaisernähe*, esp. pp. 28–33.

[49] Mamas seems not to be a typical slave eunuch, for it is reported that he was castrated for medical reasons. Also, relatives of his were abbots of the monastery of St Theodosius near Jerusalem.

[50] See also G. Greatrex and J. Bardill, 'Antiochus the *praepositus*: a Persian eunuch at the court of Theodosius II', *DOP* 50 (1996), pp. 171–97.

[51] See Prokopios, *Wars* I.15.31.

[52] See C. Mango, *Nikephoros Patriarch of Constantinople Short History. Text, Translation and Commentary*, Dumbarton Oaks Texts 10, Corpus Fontium Historiae Byzantinae 13 (Washington, DC, 1990), ch. 39, pp. 94–5; Theoph. 367, trans. C. Mango and R. Scott, *The Chronicle of Theophanes Confessor: Byzantine and Near Eastern History, AD 284–813* (Oxford, 1997), p. 513. On the fall of Justinian Stephen's fate was to be dragged bound by the feet to the market of the Bull and burned to death: Mango, *Short History*, ch. 40.37–42, pp. 96–8; Theoph. 369, trans. Mango and Scott, *The Chronicle of Theophanes*, p. 515.

Slav, who was chief eunuch (*parakoimomenos*) of the emperor Michael III (842–867).[53] At the very beginning of the tenth century we meet the well-studied case of Samonas the Arab.[54] Samonas worked as a domestic servant in an elite household in Constantinople, before entering imperial service after he informed the emperor Leo VI (886–912) of a plot against his life. He eventually rose to the position of *parakoimomenos*.

But in the case of Byzantium we find the production of native eunuchs also.[55] Evidence for this phenomenon is particularly pronounced not just for the eleventh century, as observed by Ringrose,[56] but also for the late ninth and tenth centuries. This is reflected in general comments and specific cases. The tenth-century Arab writer al-Masudi recorded that the Byzantines, like the Chinese, practised the castration of their own children.[57] This is supported by the story about the background of Constantine the Paphlagonian, *parakoimomenos* in the early tenth century of the emperor Leo VI and then of the empress Zoe Karbonopsina. Constantine was castrated by his father with a view to employment in Constantinople, and our source comments that this was a custom amongst farmers in Paphlagonia.[58] There are other good examples of Byzantine eunuchs. It is notable that several whose origins are known are indeed Paphlagonians, as Paul Magdalino has recently highlighted.[59]

What evidence is there that this transformation in the ethnic origin of court eunuchs had occurred before 900? Again, information is limited, but it suggests that it had begun before the tenth century. From the late eighth/early ninth centuries we have the case of Aetios who served under the empress Eirene (797–802), and who is said to have planned to make

---

[53] See for instance Theophanes Continuatus v.16, in I. Bekker (ed.), *Theophanes Continuatus*, Corpus Scriptorum Historiae Byzantinae (Bonn, 1838), pp. 234.7–9.

[54] See for example S. Tougher, *The Reign of Leo VI (886–912): Politics and People*, The Medieval Mediterranean: Peoples, Economies and Cultures 400–1453, 15 (Leiden, 1997), esp. pp. 197–8.

[55] See Guilland, 'Les eunuques', p. 200. Note also that eunuchs could exist for other reasons. Some are accounted for by castration as punishment, others by birth, some for medical reasons, though perhaps the latter two explanations could cover for deliberate castration. There is also evidence that castration was performed for religious purposes. I hope to explore this in detail elsewhere.

[56] K. M. Ringrose, 'Living in the shadows: eunuchs and gender in Byzantium', in G. Herdt (ed.), *Third Sex, Third Gender: Beyond Sexual Dimorphism in Culture and History* (New York, 1994), p. 511 n. 16; Ringrose, 'Passing the test of sanctity: denial of sexuality and involuntary castration', in L. James (ed.), *Desire and Denial in Byzantium: Papers from the Thirty-First Spring Symposium of Byzantine Studies, University of Sussex, Brighton, March 1997* (Aldershot, 1999), p. 134.

[57] See for example D. Ayalon, 'On the eunuchs in Islam', *Jerusalem Studies in Arabic and Islam* 1 (1979), p. 75, repr. *Outsiders in the Land of Islam: Mamluks, Mongols and Eunuchs* (London, 1988), vol. III.

[58] *Synaxarion of Constantinople*, AASS, Propylaeum Novembris, pp. 721–4.

[59] P. Magdalino, 'Paphlagonians in Byzantine high society', in S. Lampakis (ed.), *Byzantine Asia Minor (6th–12th Cent.)*, Hellenism: Ancient, Medieval, Modern 27 (Athens, 1998), pp. 141–50. See also Tougher, 'Overview', pp. 178–80.

his brother Leo emperor.[60] A little later we encounter Theodore Krateros, who served Theophilos (829–842).[61] How exactly these eunuchs came to be created is not revealed, but that they were employed at court in spite of their Byzantine family ties within the empire suggests that there had been a development in practice. It is useful to return to the case of Constantine the Paphlagonian again, for he was probably made a eunuch in the ninth century; although he was given to Leo by Samonas in 907, he had previously belonged to Basil the *magistros*. The custom which led to his creation thus most likely pre-dated 900.

Indeed Magdalino pushed the custom back in time as far as the sixth century, in an attempt to contextualise the social transformation of the court eunuch from ethnic outsider to home-grown product.[62] He noted that, according to Prokopios, the creation of eunuchs in Abasgia – and thus their importation into the Roman empire – was ended at the command of Justinian,[63] and that the emperor later attempted to outlaw the castration of Romans by Romans.[64] Thus this could be the moment when domestic supply of eunuchs (specifically, for Magdalino, from Paphlagonia) supplanted foreign supply. At first glance this is a seductive argument, but it needs to be recognised that Justinian's concern about the creation of Roman eunuchs was not new. Even in the fourth and fifth centuries Constantine's and Leo's legislation indicates that the ideal of no castration within the empire, and no creation of Roman eunuchs, was not always observed. The repetition of such concerns in the legislation also suggests this.[65] The legislation reveals that the emperors were hoping to stop the practice of creating and selling Roman eunuchs, rather than that they did stop it; the late Roman ideal of foreign eunuchs clearly did not entirely match the reality. The legislation suggests that the court use of eunuchs who were native to the empire became, if not common, at least familiar enough to prompt legal responses well before 900. Whether this situation was aggravated by the factor of the

---

[60] See for instance P. E. Niavis, *The Reign of the Byzantine Emperor Nicephorus I (AD 802–811)*, Historical Monographs 3 (Athens, 1987), pp. 27–8. It is the fact that Aetios has a non-eunuch brother with a career in imperial administration that suggests that he is a native Byzantine.

[61] See for instance Theophanes Continuatus III.23, in Bekker (ed.), *Theophanes Continuatus*, pp. 114–16. Note the use of a family name.

[62] Magdalino, 'Paphlagonians', pp. 149–50.

[63] Prokopios, *Wars* VIII.3.19. The palace eunuch Euphratas, himself an Abasgian, was sent out to relay Justinian's command.

[64] Justinian, *Novel* 142. The law dates to 558, and is addressed to Marthanes, *comites rei privatae*. Gregory of Tours, *The History of the Franks* 10.15, trans. O. M. Dalton, *The History of the Franks by Gregory of Tours*, 2 vols. (Oxford, 1927), vol. II, pp. 446–9, includes a story set in the late sixth century which reveals that castrations were performed in Constantinople, though this is in the context of medical practice.

[65] As Ayalon, 'Eunuchs in Islam', p. 70, appreciates.

lack of supply of eunuchs from Abasgia is a moot point. What is clear is that this transformation can be seen as another feature of the evolution of ancient Rome to medieval Byzantium.

GENDER TRANSFORMATION?

Thus we have witnessed two social transformations in the court eunuch from Rome to Byzantium in the period 300–900. Office and status became more distinct and enhanced, whilst there was also a growth of domestic supply of eunuchs for court use. These transformations have indeed been associated with a further transformation, one of gender. Asserting that 'by the ninth to the twelfth centuries, attitudes and assumptions about eunuchs had changed significantly',[66] Ringrose argues that eunuchs in Byzantium constituted a third gender, but now in a positive sense in strong contrast to the late Roman identity given to eunuchs, which was hostile and constructed eunuchs as men who had been changed into women or as 'unnatural degendered beings'.[67] She declares that 'distinctive roles and sexual status were linked with dress, mannerisms, speech and body language in a way that identified eunuchs as a separate gender'.[68]

Such a generalised position can, however, be questioned. There is hostile Byzantine evidence which matches the negative views of eunuchs found in late antiquity. For instance Photios describes the eunuch John Angourios as a 'human hybrid',[69] whilst the diplomat Leo Choirosphaktes estimates the condition of a eunuch as being as though he had been born of two women.[70] Ringrose considers such hostile comments as merely traditional *topoi*, tending to be found in the historiographical evidence but not in ecclesiastical literature.[71] However we should not ignore the fact that secular literature does not always trot out the hostile classical *topoi*. Further it is clear that ecclesiastical literature can be negative about eunuchs, such as monastic literature.[72]

---

[66] Ringrose, 'Passing the test of sanctity', pp. 123–4.

[67] Ringrose, 'Passing the test of sanctity', p. 137.   [68] Ringrose, 'Living in the shadows', p. 95.

[69] See M. P. Vinson, 'Gender and politics in the post-iconoclastic period: the *lives* of Antony the Younger, the empress Theodora, and the patriarch Ignatios', *Byzantion* 68 (1998), pp. 469–515, at p. 489.

[70] See S. Tougher, 'Images of effeminate men: the case of Byzantine eunuchs', in D. M. Hadley (ed.) *Masculinity in Medieval Europe* (London, 1999), p. 92.

[71] Theophylact of Ochrid's *In Defence of Eunuchs* has a great part to play in the formulation of Ringrose's views.

[72] The ban on admitting eunuchs (as well as boys and youths) to monasteries is recurrent throughout Byzantine history: see for instance J. Patrich, *Sabas, Leader of Palestinian Monasticism: A Comparative Study in Eastern Monasticism, Fourth to Seventh Centuries* (Washington, DC, 1995), p. 274; C.

We can also observe that in the late antique period positive views of eunuchs can be found. A general lessening of hostility towards eunuchs can be detected from the fifth century; for instance the figure of Narses is uncontroversial.[73] Examples of late antique secular views of eunuchs that are in fact positive exist, such as an epigram on Kallinikos, Justinian's chamberlain.[74] In addition it is clear that in late antiquity there were ecclesiastical views which paint a rather different picture of the gender identity of eunuchs, that they are simply men.[75] A recent thesis even postulates that it was the idea of the eunuch that shaped the concept of masculinity in late antiquity.[76]

Thus I am not convinced that a case for gender transformation can be established. I would argue rather that in Byzantium there existed a multiplicity of concurrent gender identities for eunuchs: masculine, feminine, other (both positive and negative). These could be drawn upon according to need and circumstance, and could co-exist in the writings of a single individual.[77] Whilst eunuchs in Byzantium had transformed in some dramatic ways, their gender was still open to a range of interpretations. I favour recognising that a multiplicity of readings of the gender identity of eunuchs exists rather than imposing a single model.

Galatariotou, 'Byzantine *ktetorika typika*: a comparative study', *Revue des Etudes Byzantines* 45 (1987), pp. 77–138 at p. 121.

[73] See for example Jones, *Later Roman Empire*, vol. 1, p. 570.

[74] See G. Sidéris, '"Eunuchs of light". Power, imperial ceremonial and positive representations of eunuchs in Byzantium (4th–12th centuries)', in Tougher (ed.), *Eunuchs in Antiquity and Beyond*, pp. 161–75. It is interesting to note that although Ammianus Marcellinus is generally hostile to court eunuchs he does not seem to express this in terms of gender, as did Claudian and the *Historia Augusta*.

[75] E.g. P. Boulhol and I. Cochelin, 'La réhabilitation de l'eunuque dans l'hagiographie antique (ive–vie siècles)', *Studi di Antichità Cristiana* 48 (1992), pp. 49–76.

[76] M. Kuefler, *The Manly Eunuch: Masculinity, Gender Ambiguity, and Christian Ideology in Late Antiquity* (Chicago, 2001).

[77] The most obvious case is Theophylact of Ochrid, who can both defend and berate eunuchs: see M. Mullett, 'Theophylact of Ochrid's *In defence of eunuchs*', in Tougher (ed.), *Eunuchs in Antiquity and Beyond*, pp. 181–2.

CHAPTER 5

Sex, lies and textuality: the Secret History of Prokopios and the rhetoric of gender in sixth-century Byzantium

Leslie Brubaker

Prokopios of Caesarea, a sixth-century historian closely associated with Justinian and his general Belisarios, is known for three works.[1] The longest is the *History of the Wars*, eight books 'cast in the familiar mould of classical Greek historiography' that celebrate the military campaigns of Justinian.[2] Next comes *Buildings*, a panegyric written in praise of Justinian's building policy.[3] In contrast, Prokopios' *Secret History* is an invective, bent on condemning all that is lauded in the earlier books: Justinian, Belisarios, their wars and their public works.[4] The range of these three texts demonstrates Prokopios' mastery of a wide variety of rhetorical techniques, and his ability to manipulate these techniques to particular ends has been noted by others.[5] As we shall see, in the *Secret History*, Prokopios moulded together two rhetorical strategies of inversion – invective (panegyric inverted) and character assassination based on gender-role reversal – with extraordinary success: the story continues to fascinate the modern reader, and to underpin all modern histories of the period.

The *Secret History* is the modern name given to Prokopios' *Anekdota* ('unpublished notes'), a work written around 550, and certainly during the reign of the Byzantine emperor it eviscerates, Justinian I (527–565). The text is so nasty that, as its name implies, Prokopios can never have

[1] The best assessment remains A. Cameron, *Procopius and the Sixth Century*, Transformation of the Classical Heritage 10 (Berkeley, 1985).

[2] *Procopius 1–5: History of the Wars*, ed. H. Dewing, Loeb Classical Library 48, 81, 107, 173, 217 (Cambridge, MA, 1914–28); discussion in Cameron, *Procopius*, pp. 134–206; quotation *ibid.*, p. x.

[3] *Procopius 7: Buildings*, ed. H. Dewing, Loeb Classical Library 343 (Cambridge, MA, 1940); discussion in Cameron, *Procopius*, pp. 84–112.

[4] *Procopius 6: Secret History*, ed. H. Dewing, Loeb Classical Library 290 (Cambridge, MA, 1935); discussion in Cameron, *Procopius*, pp. 49–83. The contrast has also been noted recently by R. Webb, 'Praise and persuasion: argumentation and audience response in epideictic oratory', in E. Jeffreys (ed.), *Rhetoric in Byzantium* (Aldershot, 2003), p. 134.

[5] See, e.g., G. Downey, 'Procopius on Antioch: a study of method in the *De Aedificiis*', *Byzantion* 14 (1939), pp. 361–78.

intended it to circulate publicly during Justinian's lifetime: if it had, he would certainly have been destroyed socially and probably physically by the emperor's supporters. The work's tone apparently ensured that the *Secret History* remained under wraps for several centuries after its composition. There are no contemporary references to the text, and no indication that others were aware of its existence until the ninth or tenth century.[6]

Modern debates around the text continue to concentrate on whether or not it is 'true', despite Averil Cameron's careful qualifications, published in 1985.[7] This is not an especially useful way to deal with the *Anekdota*. It has been recognised for a century that Prokopios constructed an invective of a type familiar in the Roman and Byzantine world, with a clear and overt agenda in which sexual slander and lies play a starring role.[8] Even so, many scholars have continued to attempt to assess the truth value of the text; or, after noting the formulae involved, have none the less repeated Prokopios' constructs, particularly those that feature the empress Theodora, as 'facts'. The way Prokopios built the characterisations of the main characters, however, makes it clear that 'facts' were not his main concern.

From a methodological point of view, the most curious feature of *Anekdota* scholarship is that, while Prokopios' characterisation of Justinian has never been taken particularly seriously, his picture of Theodora has seemed to require careful analysis. In part, this is because we learn more about Theodora from the *Secret History* than from any other source – though Prokopios devotes far less space to her than to Justinian.[9] But it is also because the prurient sexual slander that Prokopios layers on Theodora and her friends (so at odds with our general notions of Byzantine life)

---

[6] Either no one knew of the work, or any who did failed to mention or copy from it. On its use in the ninth and tenth centuries, see M. Vinson, 'The Christianization of sexual slander: some preliminary observations', in C. Sode and S. Takács (eds.), *Novum Millennium: Studies on Byzantine History and Culture Dedicated to Paul Speck* (Aldershot, 2001), pp. 415–24 at p. 422, and K. Adshead, 'The Secret History of Procopius and its genesis', *Byzantion* 63 (1993), pp. 5–28, esp. pp. 19–27.

[7] Cameron, *Procopius*, pp. 49–83. The most recent consideration of the 'truth value' of the *Secret History* is C. Foss, 'The empress Theodora', *Byzantion* 72 (2002), pp. 141–76. For a summary of the early literature – some of which dismissed the text out of hand – see Adshead, 'Secret History'.

[8] Already in 1888, L. von Ranke, *Weltgeschichte*, vol. IV (Leipzig), pp. 300–12 dismissed most of the *Secret History* as a fanatical rant; it was termed a *Kaiserkritik* by B. Rubin, *Das Zeitalter Iustinians*, vol. I (Berlin, 1960), pp. 197–226, and F. Tinnefeld, *Kategorien der Kaiserkritik in der byzantinischen Historiographie von Prokop bis Niketas Choniates* (Munich, 1971), pp. 29–36; but see the sensible remarks in A. Cameron, 'Early Byzantine Kaiserkritik: two case histories', *Byzantine and Modern Greek Studies* 3 (1977), pp. 1–17. The term has been questioned – e.g. by Adshead, 'Secret History', p. 22 and, most recently, G. Greatrex, 'Procopius the outsider?', in D. Smythe (ed.), *Strangers to Themselves: the Byzantine Outsider* (Aldershot, 2000), pp. 215–28 – but by any name the *Secret History* is an inverted panegyric.

[9] Of the thirty chapters, four (ix, xv–xvii) focus more or less exclusively on Theodora; the imperial couple as a unit star in another (x), and the empress makes brief appearances in chapters xxii, xxv and xxx.

is memorable and has stuck. It has underpinned scholarly understanding of the empress since Gibbon, by modern standards a straightforward misogynist, who urged his readers to ignore 'the malevolent whisper of the *Anekdota*' when it cast aspersions on Justinian and his general Belisarios,[10] but not when it vilified their wives.[11] This construct has been internalised and enshrined in the history books: even the normally laconic Loeb edition of the *Secret History*, where footnotes are usually restricted to concise cross-references, notes on the Greek or brief identifications of persons or places mentioned in the text, contains an extensive footnote that quotes with approval the passage from Gibbon noted above.[12] But to dismiss Prokopios' account of Justinian without comment while treating seriously his portrait of Theodora is intellectually suspect, and ignores the rhetorical tropes of the text.[13]

To Gibbon, the fame and virtue of Justinian and his general Belisarios were 'polluted by the lust and cruelty' of their wives, Theodora and Antonina.[14] This is precisely what Prokopios was attempting to ensure, but his critique of Justinian has been masked by scholars more interested in recovering information about the imperial couple than in analysing the text. As has been recognised for some time, however, sexual slander directed against women is a familiar component of Roman and western medieval invective. Rather than being directed at the woman it slanders – who was, after all, considerably less important in Roman and medieval society than her mate – it is normally channelled through her against a powerful male.[15] More generally, invective is concerned as much (and often more)

---

[10] E. Gibbon, *The History of the Decline and Fall of the Roman Empire*, vol. IV, ed. J. Bury (London, 1896), p. 369.

[11] Gibbon repeats Prokopios' tales about Theodora without a breath of caution: *Decline*, vol. IV, pp. 226–33.

[12] *Procopius* 6, ed. Dewing, pp. 26–7 n. 3.

[13] For a balanced assessment of the *Anekdota* that takes gender into account but has been surprisingly little cited, see E. Fisher, 'Theodora and Antonia', *Arethusa* 11 (1978), pp. 253–80; on Byzantine sexual slander, see Vinson, 'The Christianization of sexual slander'.

[14] Gibbon, *Decline*, vol. IV, pp. 334–5 (also quoted in *Procopius* 6, ed. Dewing, pp. 6–7 n. 2).

[15] L. James, *Empresses and Power in Early Byzantium* (London, 2001), pp. 16–20, on invective directed against empresses. See further J. Nelson, 'Queens as Jezebels: Brunhild and Balthild in Merovingian history', in D. Baker (ed.), *Medieval Women: Essays Dedicated and Presented to Professor Rosalind M. T. Hill*, Studies in Church History, Subsidia 1 (Oxford, 1978), pp. 31–77; repr. in Nelson, *Politics and Ritual in Early Medieval Europe* (London, 1986), pp. 1–48; also Vinson, 'The Christianization of sexual slander'; K. Cooper, 'Insinuations of womanly influence: an aspect of the Christianisation of the Roman aristocracy', *JRS* 82 (1992), pp. 150–64; S. Fischler, 'Social stereotypes and historical analysis: the case of the imperial women at Rome', in L. Archer, S. Fischler and M. Wyke (eds.), *Women in Ancient Societies: An Illusion of the Night* (Houndmills, 1994), pp. 115–33; and, more generally, E. Clark, 'The lady vanishes: dilemmas of a feminist historian after the "linguistic turn"', *Church History* 67 (1998), pp. 1–31. Parallels with Suetonius and Dio Cassius are mooted, but dismissed, by M. Angold, 'Procopius' portrait of Theodora', in *Philhellen: Studies in Honour of Robert Browning* (Venice, 1996), pp. 21–34, esp. pp. 24–5.

with the anxieties of the speaker and/or the speaker's audience as with the actions of the person condemned. How Prokopios characterised Justinian and Theodora is, then, of some importance to our understanding of the text and its author, of assumptions about gender in mid-sixth-century Byzantium and, ultimately, of the historical importance of the imperial couple.

THE NARRATIVE

Prokopios' skill at inverting the rules of panegyric and subverting conventional gender roles determined the impact of the *Secret History*. The first of his tools, panegyric (known to the Byzantines as *enkomion*), followed a formula ascribed to the third-century rhetorician Menander. Its most exalted form, the imperial oration (*basilikos logos*), unfolded in a number of prescribed steps. First came recognitions of the prestige of the emperor's family, his birth – with emphasis on any 'miraculous happenings' associated with this, which the speaker may invent 'because the audience has no choice but to accept the enkomion without examination' – and nurture.[16] Then come accomplishments ('qualities of character not involved with real competitive actions'), followed by actions, subdivided into times of war and times of peace and divided into the four imperial virtues (courage, justice, temperance and wisdom).[17] Fortune – the emperor's success – is next, then comparison with earlier reigns.[18] Finally, in the epilogue, 'you will speak of the prosperity and good fortune of the cities: the markets are full of goods . . . the earth is tilled in peace . . . piety toward God is increased'.[19] Though Prokopios does not always adhere precisely to Menander's order, we shall see that the *Secret History* neatly inverts all of the imperial virtues meant to be incorporated into a *basilikos logos* to create a compelling portrait of Justinian as the antithesis of a good emperor.

Prokopios' understanding of gender roles follows equally well-defined paths. Masculine virtues adhere to Menander's quartet of courage, justice, temperance and wisdom, augmented by the standard Roman male qualities of self-control and pursuit of the common good, and by minor modifications imposed by Christianity (notably chastity outside marriage, Christian piety and philanthropy).[20] Feminine virtues also continue Roman precepts,

---

[16] *Menander Rhetor*, ed. and trans. D. Russell and N. Wilson (Oxford, 1981), pp. 74–83, quotations at pp. 80–82 (371, lines 8–9, 12–14).
[17] *Ibid.*, pp. 82–93, quotation p. 82 (372, lines 3–4).   [18] *Ibid.*, pp. 92–3.
[19] *Ibid.*, pp. 92–5, quotations p. 92 (377, lines 9–14).
[20] Christian imperial virtues were defined around 400 by John Chrysostom, patriarch of Constantinople: see F. Dvornik, *Early Christian and Byzantine Political Philosophy, Origins and Back-*

particularly the ideal of the Roman *matrona*: gentle, modest, and dedicated to family and home.[21] To this are added specific imperial female virtues: the good empress was pious, philanthropic, humble, chaste.[22] The Justinian and Theodora of the *Secret History* stand these gender roles on their heads: just as Justinian is made to play the anti-emperor, the imperial couple invert the ideals of Roman social order.

Prokopios' characterisations are carefully, if broadly, orchestrated and brought into play. The first two (of thirty) chapters of the *Secret History* focus almost exclusively on Belisarios and his wife Antonina.[23] Their relationship anticipates, palely, that of Justinian and Theodora – and damns the imperial couple by association – but is not our concern here. Theodora is briefly introduced in chapter three, Justinian in chapter four, where Justinian-and-Theodora as a unit also makes its first appearance (iv.33) since its obligatory mention at the very beginning of the work. Chapter five concerns Theodora's plan to gain control of Belisarios' and Antonina's fortune by marrying their only daughter to her grandson. The focus of the first five chapters remains the general and his wife (about whom we hear little thereafter), but introduces, interweaves and implicates Justinian and, especially, Theodora in the perverse lifestyle that Prokopios accords them.

Chapter six turns to Justinian and Theodora and, like the panegyric it parodies, begins with the main character's family. The family is represented by Justin and Lupicina/Euphemia, Justinian's uncle and aunt, a ploy that makes it clear that the emperor, and not his wife, was the main target of the *Secret History*. Lupicina/Euphemia is portrayed as 'a slave and a barbarian' (vi.17), an identification that appears in no other source.[24] Whether or not it

ground, vol. II, Dumbarton Oaks Studies 9 (Washington, DC, 1966), p. 695. For further discussion of male virtue in the wake of Christianity, see Cooper, 'Insinuations'; James, *Empresses and Power*, pp. 12–13; and, on the essential continuity of Roman social male roles into the Christian period, M. Harlow, 'In the name of the father: procreation, paternity and patriarchy', and G. Clark, 'The old Adam: the Fathers and the unmaking of masculinity', both in L. Foxhall and J. Salmon (eds.), *Thinking Men: Masculinity and Its Self-Representation in the Classical Tradition* (London, 1998), pp. 155–69 and 170–82. All contain additional bibliography.

[21] The literature on this topic is extensive. See, e.g., Fischler, 'Social stereotypes and historical analysis', esp. pp. 117–21; S. Treggiari, *Roman Marriage: Iusti Coniuges from the Time of Cicero to the Time of Ulpian* (Oxford, 1991); S. Dixon, *The Roman Mother* (London, 1988), all with extensive bibliography.

[22] S. Wood, *Imperial Women: A Study in Public Images, 40 BC–AD 68* (Leiden, 1999); James, *Empresses and Power*, pp. 12–16.

[23] All text references are to the standard edition: *Procopius* 6, ed. Dewing, with parallel Greek text and English translation; as this edition is readily available, I omit citation of the Greek. Many earlier scholars have noted that the first part of the work is distinct from the rest – see e.g. Adshead, 'Secret History', pp. 7–10 (with whose conclusions I do not, however, agree) – but the thematic connection has been rightly stressed by Fisher, 'Theodora and Antonia', esp. pp. 268–70.

[24] J. Martindale (ed.), *The Prosopography of the Later Roman Empire*, vol. II, *AD 395–527* (Cambridge, 1980), p. 423.

is accurate, the classification heralds Prokopios' association of Justinian with slaves and barbarians to emphasise the emperor's lack of *romanitas*.[25] Justin is painted as an illiterate, simple-minded boor with remarkable flaws (vi.11–16, 18–28).[26] Beyond demonstrating that Justinian came from polluted and defective stock, Justin's main function in the larger narrative is to reveal that the family came to power through superhuman intervention. Justin was spared from execution only because the general who was to kill him dreamt three times of 'a creature of enormous size and in other respects too mighty to resemble a man. And this vision enjoined upon him to release the man whom he chanced to imprison' (vi.6–9). Prokopios here gives a twist to Menander's exhortation to invent miraculous origin myths, for it soon becomes clear that the superman responsible for Justin's life, and hence Justinian's elevation to the Byzantine throne, was allied to the powers of evil, not those of good.[27]

Chapter seven concerns the Factions – associations connected with the games in the hippodrome – in Constantinople.[28] As portrayed here, members of the Factions were powerful hooligans who made a mockery of the law and destabilised and corrupted the moral code of Roman citizens. Thus constructed, the *Secret History* makes the advent of Justinian coincide with the rise of social degenerates and the disintegration of the Roman state. Prokopios makes the implication explicit in the chapter's conclusion: the new emperor honours and protects the factionists (vii.40–2), and is in fact worse than they are (vii.39).

Chapter eight provides the basic and entirely negative character sketch of Justinian; chapter nine does the same for Theodora, with particular attention to her sexual depravity, but with a significant admixture of information about her husband's faults. Indeed, since according to the *Secret History* it was bribery in the Factions that lost Theodora's stepfather his job and forced her mother to put her on stage (ix.5), Prokopios' linkage between the corrupt Factions and Justinian in chapter seven indirectly implicates Justinian in his future wife's career as a prostitute. Lupicina/Euphemia returns, still

[25] See p. 96 below.
[26] Prokopios' story of Justin the illiterate who had to use a stencil to sign his name is a trope found earlier in the *Excerpta Valesiana*'s description of Theodoric (in *Ammianus Marcellinus* III, ed. J. Rolfe, Loeb Classical Library 331 (Cambridge, MA, 1939), pp. 556–9), a parallel that serves to remind us that the *Secret History* is not reportage; rather, Prokopios is telling a story using familiar props. I thank Chris Wickham for the reference.
[27] See pp. 89, 93, 97 below. This too may be an inversion of the prophetic – but positive – dream or vision that heralds the birth of saints or the elevation of (later) emperors.
[28] The classic study remains A. Cameron, *Circus Factions: Blues and Greens at Rome and Byzantium* (Oxford, 1976).

a barbarian but now unveiled as a simple, good woman 'far removed from wickedness' (ix.47–8), who did not meddle in government (ix.49): in this, she is the antithesis of Theodora,[29] and Prokopios duly assures us that Lupicina/Euphemia was firmly opposed to Justinian and Theodora's marriage (ix.47). This occurs in chapter ten, which concerns the full liaison of the couple, after which Prokopios explains how Justinian and Theodora worked together for evil.

The four chapters that follow, in which Theodora is barely mentioned, detail Justinian's failings. In chapter eleven, we hear about his senseless wars and persecutions. Chapter twelve tells us how Justinian destroyed members of the Senate – Prokopios' class – and establishes his identification as Lord of the Demons. Chapter thirteen presents a classic set of contrasts, where qualities that should be good are, in Justinian, perverted towards evil.[30] Chapter fourteen purports to show that, under the lawless and self-absorbed Justinian, the administration of affairs in the empire has been thrown into chaos, with all ruled by avarice and greed.

Prokopios then returns to Theodora for three chapters. In chapter fifteen, he reprises some of the themes of chapter nine: Theodora is cruel, wilful, anti-patrician, and self-indulgent; she distorts justice and is the ruin of the state. Chapters sixteen and seventeen interject these same motifs but stress how Theodora perverted her femininity and used gender as a weapon. In the first, Prokopios inserts his understanding of a woman's response to adversity: Theodora is resentful of Amalasuntha, queen of the Goths, and thus has her killed; and, in order to destroy a series of men, she falsely accuses them of sexual crimes (sodomy and homosexuality). Female power here works through jealousy and sexual manipulation; and, in all cases, Prokopios stresses Theodora's secrecy – female power can only work in a 'domesticised' setting. Such secret power is by definition bad power, since power must be public if it is to be legitimate. (This conceit allows Prokopios to present Justinian as pretending ignorance while he none the less pulls in the victims' money, a leitmotif of the *Secret History* that lets him damn the imperial couple for duplicity along with whatever other flaw he is exposing.) Chapter seventeen is structured like a sandwich. At the beginning and at the end, Theodora ruins a man for Justinian's benefit (her husband again feigns ignorance) while in the middle Prokopios runs us

---

[29] So too A. McClanan, 'The empress Theodora and the tradition of women's patronage in the early Byzantine empire', in J. McCash (ed.), *The Cultural Patronage of Medieval Women* (Athens, GA, 1996), pp. 50–72, at p. 60.

[30] This pattern is not used for Theodora; the closest Prokopios comes is parody, on which see p. 92 below.

through the gamut of Theodora's 'female' sins: she forces prostitutes into the Convent of Repentance, destroys the sanctity and honour of marriage for all of her subjects (the specific examples are, of course, drawn from the senatorial class), has her son John murdered (having failed to abort him earlier), and corrupts all women, who now insult their husbands and commit adultery without censure.

Having ended chapter seventeen with Justinian's collusion with his wife, Prokopios devotes the next to demonstrating how the emperor's demonic nature is revealed through the destruction that wars, urban insurrections and natural disasters caused during his reign. The final twelve chapters then focus on Justinian. He absorbs all state and private money (xix); mismanages the administration of Constantinople (xx); sells offices (xxi); allows barbarians to enslave Romans (xxii); ruins land-owners (xxiii); treats the army shamefully and deprives bureaucrats of their revenues (xxiv); destroys trade and devalues the gold coinage (xxv); destroys Byzantine culture and brings suffering to the poor (xxvi); is interested only in money, not orthodoxy (xxvii); alters laws, both those concerning the church (xxviii) and those concerning inheritance (xxix); throws public services into disarray, and, by changing palace rituals, tarnishes respect for the imperial office (xxx).

In this litany of the disasters, Theodora appears occasionally. When Justinian destroys trade, Theodora confiscates imported silks (xxv.19); and as part of the new imperial ritual, all must bow down to her as well as to Justinian (xxx.22–6). Only once, however, is she cast in a major role. In chapter twenty-two, Prokopios explains that all officials appointed by Justinian were disasters, especially Peter Barsymes.[31] According to Prokopios, Peter had cast a spell on Theodora, who 'showed him favour against her will' (xxii.24–5); Prokopios also claims, however, that Theodora approved of Peter's interest in magic, 'for she too from childhood had consorted with magicians and sorcerers' (xxii.26–7). This leads Prokopios to suggest, for the only time in the *Secret History*, that Theodora used magic to make Justinian do her bidding;[32] significantly, he claims that this was possible because the emperor was 'not so right-minded or . . . steadfast in virtue as to be at any time superior to attempts upon him of the kind' (xxii.29): Justinian's weak moral character made him susceptible to Theodora's spells.

---

[31] Prokopios generally avoids biblical references, but it is none the less surprising how little play he makes on the name Barsymes ('son of Simon'); certainly he fails to equate him with Simon Magus.

[32] 'And it is also said that the way she made Justinian tractable was not so much by cajoling him as by applying to him the compulsion of evil spirits' (xxii.28).

The *Secret History* presents a carefully constructed narrative, composed of a series of character sketches, throughout which a number of themes are repeated monotonously. As the Barsymes episode intimates, Theodora's appearances in the *Secret History* usually highlight one of Justinian's flaws. The characterisations of both roles are significant for the ways in which they interlock, and Prokopios manipulates his descriptions to force comparisons that are meant to discredit Justinian. Treating the one without the other distorts Prokopios' method and purpose.

THEODORA

Prokopios' characterisation of Theodora is straightforward. He defines the perfect consort, and makes Theodora its opposite. Justinian 'might have taken his choice of the whole Roman empire and have married that woman who, of all the women in the world, was in the highest degree both well-born and blessed with a nurture sheltered from the public eye, a woman who had not been unpractised in modesty, and had dwelt with chastity, who was not only surpassingly beautiful but also still a maiden' (x.2–3). The Theodora portrayed by Prokopios was, in contrast, the daughter of a bear-keeper (ix.2), in the public eye from an early age (ix.6–8), immodest, shameless, short and sallow (x.11), and no longer a virgin.

Beyond these biographic details, Prokopios' criticisms of Theodora are predictable and gender-based. They focus on the domesticised female arenas of sex, family, marriage, emotions and decorum.[33] In all cases, Theodora inverts normative behaviour, a pattern Prokopios continues when discussing her attitude towards church and state.

Rather than a modest and self-effacing Roman matron, Theodora is a 'slave to pleasure' (ix.16), a woman of unnatural lusts from whom respectable people flee (ix.25).[34] The sexual activities that Prokopios ascribes to Theodora are well known. According to him, as a child, she appropriated male behaviour and had anal intercourse with slaves, the lowest level of Roman society (ix.10); she then became an unskilled courtesan (ix.11–12) with 'not a particle of modesty, nor did any man ever see her embarrassed' (ix.14). Prokopios paints these sexual activities as a perversion of

---

[33] As noted above, the familiar *topos* of female characterisation, secrecy, also plays here. In Theodora's case, this is primarily invoked by her secret punishments that no one ever hears about (e.g. xvi.12–17).

[34] On the well-worn trope of the *meretrix augusta* (empress-whore), see, e.g., A. Richlin, 'Julia's jokes, Galla Placidia, and the Roman use of women as political icons', in B. Garlick, S. Dixon and P. Allen (eds.), *Stereotypes of Women in Power: Historical Perspectives and Revisionist Views* (New York, 1992), pp. 65–91, at p. 66; M. Vinson, 'Domitia Longina, Julia Titi, and the literary tradition', *Historia* 38 (1989), pp. 431–50; and the articles cited in note 15 above.

Roman ideals: her Leda and the swan imitation (ix.20–1) is a burlesque where even the swan becomes a gaggle of geese; her stage act, in which Theodora performs 'with pride the exercises of the only wrestling school to which she was accustomed' (ix.23), is a parody on the theme of the noble athlete.

To this mix Prokopios adds a number of other sex-related sins. As we have seen, his Theodora makes false accusations against men of sodomy (xvi.18–21) and homosexuality (xvi.23–8),[35] and she also forces Belisarios' only daughter to lose her virginity in order to guarantee her grandson's marriage to the girl, and thus ensure imperial control of the general's fortune (v.21).

Female status was largely dependent on marriage and kinship groupings, so Prokopios' Theodora destroys both. As anticipated by the tale of Belisarios' daughter, a theme of the *Secret History* is Theodora's 'unwomanly' disregard of the sanctity and honour of marriage. Prokopios merges actual changes in legislation – Justinian revised certain laws concerning marriage, in part to allow him to marry Theodora[36] – with social disruption to portray Theodora as usurping paternal authority by regulating all people's marriages (xvii.28–37) and forcing daughters with a 'lineage from men who were of the foremost blood of the whole Senate' to marry common 'beggars and outcasts' (xvii.7–15). Her practice of infanticide (x.3, ix.19) and the murder of her son (xvii.16–23) were noted above, and, in Prokopios' story, Theodora's inversion of gender norms polluted all women and destroyed the ideal of the Roman family: 'all the women had become corrupt in character' and, with her encouragement, became adulteresses and treated their husbands 'outrageously' (xvii.24–6).[37]

Prokopios plays on the Byzantine view of woman as vehicles of emotion (as opposed to rational men) in his picture of Theodora's inability to control her passions.[38] His Theodora is wilful, prone to anger, and self-indulgent. The empress 'never did anything at any time as the result of persuasion or compulsion by another person, but she herself, applying a stubborn

---

[35] See also xvi.11, where Areobindos is 'disappeared' to counter suspicions that Theodora loved him.

[36] See D. French, 'Maintaining boundaries: the status of actresses in early Christian society', *Vigiliae Christianae* 52 (1998), pp. 293–318, which now largely supersedes D. Daube, 'The marriage of Justinian and Theodora, legal and theological reflections', *Catholic University of America Law Review* 16 (1967), pp. 380–99. Prokopios notes the changed legislation at ix.51.

[37] Though Theodora herself is never unfaithful to her husband, a ploy that would have isolated her too much from Justinian to suit Prokopios' aims.

[38] The best general overview of assumptions about women in late antiquity remains G. Clark, *Women in Late Antiquity: Pagan and Christian Lifestyles* (Oxford, 1993); on women as emotional beings, see esp. pp. 120–6.

will, carried out her decisions with all her might' (xv.2); she was consumed by a passion beyond power to assuage (xv.5); and 'whenever this hussy became excited' she allowed nothing to stand in her way (xvi.22). She shows her teeth (i.14)[39] and becomes 'beside herself' (v.8–12) in anger, and she never forgave a perceived slight (xv.3–4). Her self-indulgence surfaces in a propensity for long baths, lots of sleep, and eating and drinking too much (xv.6–9). Here Theodora is the opposite of Justinian. But, in a conceit that is repeated throughout the *Secret History*, Prokopios uses this contrast not to highlight positive qualities in the emperor, but to suggest that Justinian's ability to cope without much sleep or food is evidence of his demonic nature (xii.27),[40] and it is put in the service of ruining his empire: 'he made it his task to be constantly awake and to undergo hardships and to labour for no other purpose than to contrive constantly and every day more grievous calamities for his subjects' (xiii.28–32).

By now it comes as no surprise that Prokopios' Theodora also betrays the rules of female decorum. She 'burst into a loud laugh' on inappropriate occasions (ix.14) and treated everything, even the most serious, as a joke 'as though she were on the stage in the theatre' (xv.24); she ridiculed patricians (xv.25–35), and mocked law courts into forgiving her favourites (xv.23). She was 'unusually clever and full of gibes', and before marrying Justinian had been 'admired' by the licentious for her banter and her new devices for intercourse (ix.13–14). At that point in her life, too, she flew in the face of convention by pursuing men 'with clownish posturing with her hips' (ix.15), thus once again appropriating a male role. Theodora is also 'envious and spiteful' of other women, both those with whom she performed on stage (ix.26) and those of noble blood whom she meets later in her career (xvi.1–5).

Theodora's sins against Byzantine social convention are also used to cast doubt on her piety, an imperial requisite. Prokopios' Theodora is as shameless about violating church sanctuary and desecrating sacred places as she is about abusing her own body and polluting others through her brazen sexuality. He describes her having Photios dragged away from the sanctuary of the church, and adds: 'For no inviolable spot ever remained inaccessible to her, but it seemed nothing to her to do violence to any and all sacred things' (iii.25); later in the narrative, Prokopios has her pull aristocratic widows away from the font of Hagia Sophia, thus demonstrating that 'for her no place remained undefiled or inviolate' (xvii.10–11).[41]

---

[39] So too Justinian (xiii.3).   [40] On this theme, see p. 97 below.
[41] Prokopios also describes Theodora violating sanctuary without sexual overtones at xvi.22.

The Theodora of the *Secret History* inverted the normative power relations of the state as well. Prokopios calls her a 'slave-instructor' of the government (xv.16–17), who 'claimed the right to administer everything in the state by her own arbitrary judgement' (xvii.27). Senators 'were all to do obeisance to the woman as though she were a god' (x.6) and no one – priest, populace or soldier – opposed her (x.6–9) 'because, I suppose . . . Fortune had made an exhibition of her power' (x.9). It goes without saying that Theodora perverted justice, particularly against patricians (e.g. xv.20–3).

The Theodora created by Prokopios destroys all that he holds dear. She is an ideal type, the perfect anti-woman, with all qualities that late Roman culture valued in a woman inverted. Prokopios' portrait of Justinian provides an equally consistent reversal of the good late Roman male and emperor.

JUSTINIAN

Prokopios' Justinian is as gender-bound and predictable as his image of Theodora. His secular rather than his military role is stressed, but the domestic arena within which the empress exercises power in the *Secret History* has been banished: Justinian's sexual appetite is mentioned only once (xii.27), and we hear nothing of his response to family values or marriage. Instead, Prokopios' characterisation of Justinian focuses on the male virtues of justice, wisdom, piety, philanthropy, temperance, self-control and pursuit of the common good.[42] In all, Justinian is found wanting. For Menander, under the good emperor 'piety is increased' and 'laws are more legal, contracts between men are more just'.[43] For Prokopios, 'while Justinian ruled over the Romans, neither good faith nor belief in God remained secure, no law remained fixed, no transaction safe, no contract valid' (xiii.24).

Prokopios' Justinian is a weak and foolish man, driven by greed. He perverts justice, is inconsistent and capricious, intemperate and reckless, and brings confusion to all he touches. He fails to uphold the principles of the church, has no sense of proper imperial behaviour, and his only consistency is in bringing evil and ruin to the Roman world. Everyone suffers, for, as Prokopios' reaction to Justinian's ability to do without sleep intimated, it is the emperor's fatal flaw that he can do no right: 'in the end even his natural good qualities resulted in the undoing of his subjects' (xiii.33).

---

[42] See p. 86 above.   [43] Ed. Russell and Wilson, 92–3, 90–1 (377 line 14; 375, lines 27–8).

In the Justinian of the *Secret History*, justice is overruled by 'base greed' (xiv.5). The emperor seizes property illegally,[44] fabricating wills and forging documents in order to do so (xii.5–10, xxvii.1–15); he establishes monopolies and appoints shady administrators to bleed the public, with all monies flowing to him.[45] Justinian accepts bribes,[46] and sells justice: 'without any hesitation he shattered the laws when money was in sight' (xxvii.33).[47] He is 'eager to squander public funds with complete recklessness' (viii.4), and throws money senselessly at the barbarians,[48] who manipulate him for peace money and so 'enslave the Roman empire' (xi.5–11). Thus, with 'unreasoning generosity' (xi.9), Justinian 'lightly banished wealth from the Roman world and became the creator of poverty for all' (viii.33).[49] His lack of wisdom thus established, Prokopios adds that Justinian is a mixture of 'folly and wickedness' (viii.23), who is sufficiently idiotic to attempt 'to rival the power of the sea by the sheer power of wealth' (viii.7–8). Similarly, Justinian's religious beliefs were destructively naïve – priests prevailed even when unjust (xiii.4–6) and 'in his eagerness to gather all men into one belief as to Christ, he kept destroying the rest of mankind in senseless fashion' (xiii.7) – and so 'while he seemed to have a firm belief as regards Christ, yet even this was for the ruin of his subjects' (xiii.4).[50] As portrayed by Prokopios, in Justinian the imperial virtues of justice, wisdom and piety are overwhelmed by greed, foolish and naïve behaviour, misplaced benevolence, and insufficient respect for *romanitas*. Far from exercising wise statecraft, Justinian's 'commonwealth resembled a kingdom of children at play' (xiv.14).

Prokopios' catalogue of Justinian's imperial flaws continues. During Justinian's rule, Roman peace was shattered (xi.5) and 'the whole Roman empire was filled with murder and exiled men' (xi.21–3). Prokopios claims 'a greater slaughter of human beings to have been perpetrated by this man than has come to pass in all the preceding time' (viii.31).[51] Thus, 'during his reign the whole earth was constantly drenched with human blood' (xviii.30).[52]

---

[44] See, e.g., viii.9, xi.3, xii.1–3, xix.11–12, xxi.15. Prokopios also condemns Justinian's confiscation of the property of heretics: xi.14–20, 31–3.

[45] See, e.g. xx.1–23, xxi.1–6, 20–1.   [46] See, e.g., xiii.24–5, xiv.6, xxvii.26–33.

[47] See also, e.g., viii.10–11, xiii.21–2, xiv.8, 10, 15–23.

[48] See, e.g., viii.31–2, xi.3, 12, xix.6, 10, 13–16 (and see also xxi.26–9).

[49] See further viii.31–2, xii.12–13, xiii.20, xix.1–6, xxvii.1–2, xxix.1–38.

[50] Other church irregularities at, e.g., xiii.6–7 and xxvii.3–25.

[51] More of the same at, e.g., xi.3, 13, 29–30, xiii.8–9, xviii.2–21, xviii.31–5.

[52] The theme is invoked repeatedly, even in the midst of other topics. E.g., Prokopios exploits the circumstances of Justinian's elevation as co-ruler on 1 April 527 (three days before Easter) to claim that the accession coincided with the period when one was forbidden to greet others with the phrase 'peace be unto you' (Luke 24.36; ix.53–4). Prokopios thus implicitly connects Justinian's rise with

Roman male virtues are also absent from Prokopios' Justinian. Like Theodora, Justinian does not understand Roman social codes. He learns nothing from past errors of judgement, and does not mind appearing loathsome (x.5); his speech is uncouth (xiv.3). Moderation and balance are not part of his character: the emperor is portrayed as intemperate, reckless and listening happily to slander; he 'never paused for a thorough investigation before reaching a decision' (viii.28–9).[53] Instead of preserving the *status quo* and respecting tradition, he 'kept doing everything out of season' (xviii.29), ignored established custom, and 'in speech and in dress and in thinking played the barbarian' (xiv.1–2). Prokopios' Justinian excels at 'throwing everything into confusion' (viii.4, ix.50, xviii.12) and at 'tearing down all existing institutions and those made familiar by custom' (xi.1). In the *Secret History*, even Justinian's measures against heresy are condemned as attacks against 'ancestral faith' (xi.14–23) and 'the beliefs of their fathers' (xi.26).[54] He is portrayed as capricious and mutable (viii.30); he reversed his position for no real reason, but only so 'that everything might be new' (xi.2), and was 'like a cloud of dust in instability' (xxii.30–1).[55]

This Justinian is dishonest – 'insincere, crafty, hypocritical, dissembling his anger, double-dealing, clever' – and an actor 'always playing false', with fake tears and the like; 'he departed straightway from his agreements and his oaths, just like the vilest slaves' (viii.24–5).[56] His thinking was always the opposite of what it appeared (xiii.13–14); he was 'wilfully forgetful' (xiii.28) and 'untrustworthy in all things' (xiii.16, 18).

The Justinian of the *Secret History* protects the evil and harms the good.[57] He promotes 'outrageous' men, and 'traffics in human lives' (xxii.1–10).[58] Far from advancing the common good, he ruins everyone: peasants and land-owners (xxii.40, xxiii.1–22, xxxiii.24), the army (xxiv.1–29), and the bureaucracy and merchants (xxiv.30–3, xxv.1–19); so that 'practically the whole population found itself suddenly reduced to beggary' (xxv.25). Culture is destroyed (xxvi.1–44): one of the most poignant lines of the *Secret History* is 'there was no laughter in life for anyone' (xxvi.10).

Christ's death, a conceit that plays into his characterisation of the emperor as Antichrist (on which see pp. 97, 99 below). For the date of accession, Martindale, *Prosopography*, vol. II, 647–8; for the date of Easter, V. Grumel, *La Chronologie traité d'études byzantines* (Paris, 1958), p. 310.

[53] For another 'reckless' prosecution, see xi.34–6.

[54] Prokopios also accuses Justinian of harassing the Jews (xxvii.16–19).

[55] More innovations at, e.g., xxx.21–6.   [56] See further, e.g., xxvii.1–2.

[57] See, e.g., vii.41–2, xxi.6–15, 22–4; Prokopios also paints Justinian's opposition to astrologers as attacks on 'respectable' men (xi.37).

[58] For Prokopios' story of Justinian's involvement in the grain scandals, see xxii.14–19.

No free Roman man could sustain this catalogue of flaws, and, as we have seen, Prokopios duly likens Justinian to barbarians and slaves. But Justinian was more besides: he was a demon, indeed the 'Lord of the Demons in the palace sitting on the throne' (xii.24–7). Prokopios spends much of chapter twelve on this theme, beginning with a joint condemnation of both Justinian and Theodora: 'these two persons never seemed to be human beings, but rather a kind of avenging demons' (xii.14). The total destruction they have engendered demonstrates that 'they performed their fearful acts, not by human strength, but by another kind' (xii.15–17).

Soon, however, it becomes only the emperor who is the demon: in an inversion of Menander's recommended maternal dreams of greatness before the birth of an emperor, Justinian's mother claims he was son of a demon (xii.18–19); 'men whose souls were pure' have visions of a headless emperor (xii.20–3), and his energy, which in Prokopios' other works is praised, is here evidence of the emperor's unnatural strength: 'And how could this man fail to be some wicked demon, he who never had a sufficiency of food or drink or sleep . . . [and] walked about the palace at unseasonable hours of the night' (xii.27).

Theodora is made to concur. Even before she met Justinian, he claimed her: her lovers say that a demon descended on them 'at night and drove them from the room in which they were spending the night with her' (xii.28), and, in another perverse twist to Menander's instructions to invent miraculous birth stories,[59] she tells a friend about her dream that 'as soon as she should come to Byzantium [Constantinople], she would lie with the Lord of the Demons, and would quite certainly live with him as his married wife, and he would cause her to be the mistress of money without limit' (xii.30–2).

Later in the narrative, Justinian's demonic nature is simply assumed: he is 'some manner of demon in human form' (xviii.1); and the 'demon who had become incarnate in Justinian' caused extraordinary calamities and natural disasters (xviii.36–44). The *Secret History* ends with the promise that 'when Justinian either, if he is a man, departs this life, or, as being the Lord of evil spirits, lays his life aside, all who have the fortune to have survived to that time will know the truth' (xxx.34).

Prokopios' Justinian, like his Theodora, is an inverted ideal type.[60] He is the anti-emperor, the anti-Roman and, beyond that, the Lord of the Demons – the Antichrist – to Theodora's anti-woman. At the same time,

---

[59] See p. 86 above.   [60] Cameron, *Procopius*, p. 229: 'Justinian is a caricature.'

however, both portraits respect conventional Byzantine gender boundaries, in the sense that Theodora's sphere of malfeasance is domesticated while Justinian's extends across the empire. When acting as a unit with Justinian, however, Theodora's remit can extend outside the palace compound.

JUSTINIAN AND THEODORA

While Prokopios keeps Justinian away from Theodora's domestic sphere, he implicates Theodora in Justinian's public actions. Prokopios often links the imperial couple generically, as in 'they ruined the Roman empire' (vi.1, ix.32–3, xv.17–20), but he also accuses them more specifically of setting Christians against one another (x.15), dividing the Factions (x.16–18) and seizing money (xi.40). His favourite double-act has the couple pretending to disagree while in reality they are acting together to ruin their subjects.[61] In this way, the couple 'succeeded in dividing their subjects and in fortifying their tyranny' (x.23). So Theodora's influence can move into the public arena, but, when it does, the empress is never acting on her own: she works with and through Justinian.[62] In the *Secret History*, Theodora's role is to buttress Prokopios' picture of Justinian.

Working within the domestic confines of the palace, in a series of actions that become metaphors for her relationship with Justinian, Prokopios has Theodora throw men into darkness and reduce them to a bestial state. Photios, Belisarios' stepson, is placed in 'concealed rooms which were completely hidden, being dark and isolated, where no indication of night or day could be observed' (iii.21–2); a senator is stripped of his property and confined 'like an ass' in an underground chamber (iii.8–9); and Bouzes, 'a man sprung from a line of consuls', is thrown into a 'suite of rooms in the palace, below ground level, secure and a veritable labyrinth, so that it seemed to resemble Tartarus . . . he could not distinguish whether it was day or night, nor could he communicate with any other person. For the man who threw him his food for each day met him in silence, one as dumb as the other, as one beast meets another' (iv.7–11). Photios, the senator and Bouzes were innocent victims, seized by the empress's servants. Justinian does not have this excuse; he has chosen to marry Theodora, to live in darkness

---

[61] See, e.g., x.14–18, xiv.8, xvi.6–10, xvii.1–4. Sometimes this ploy failed: e.g., xvii.38–45.

[62] From a completely different perspective, Foss, 'Theodora', comes to the same conclusion. P. Allen, 'Contemporary portrayals of the Byzantine empress Theodora (AD 527–548)', in Garlick, Dixon and Allen (eds.), *Stereotypes of Women in Power*, pp. 92–103, however, believes that Prokopios was not attempting to damn Justinian but was driven by fear of Theodora.

(working the night through) and to behave like a creature rather than like a Roman. Justinian's decision to marry Theodora reveals his character flaws.

Throughout the *Secret History*, Theodora is used to point out Justinian's failures, especially his bad judgement and his weak character. Prokopios opens his description of Justinian with a comparison between him and the Roman emperor Domitian, reviled as an Antichrist figure in the Byzantine period (viii.13–21).[63] This is yet another obvious inversion of the standard patter of Byzantine panegyric, where emperors were habitually linked with former glorious rulers. But what is significant to us here is that Prokopios also mentions Domitian's wife, a woman 'of noble character and discreet, and neither had she herself ever harmed any man in the world nor was she pleased at all with any of the actions of her husband' (viii.15).[64] By implication, even Domitian had better sense in his marriage arrangements than Justinian, whose marriage to Theodora is ample indication of the emperor's lack of judgement and foul nature, worse even than Domitian's.

Prokopios also uses Theodora to underscore Justinian's feeble character.[65] Running alongside and constantly underscoring Justinian's failures as an emperor and as a man is his personal weakness. The emperor is 'both an evil-doer and easily led into evil'; and while he is a 'moral pervert' and 'deceitful and crafty', he is also 'an easy prey, to those who wished to deceive him' (viii.22).[66] It is his weakness that allows Theodora to manipulate him; often by playing on his greed, 'she could win over her husband quite against his will to the action she desired' (xiii.19). Justinian's lack of self-control and moral frailty is brought out in his 'overpowering' and 'extravagant' love for Theodora (ix.30–1). In the story of the *Secret History*, the entire state falls before his infatuation for Theodora: 'And the state became the fuel for this love' (ix.32).

As these examples suggest, the characterisation of Theodora in the *Secret History* is less about her than about her husband. Prokopios himself makes this explicit. Immediately after his recital of the qualities of a perfect wife, he wrote: 'And I think that I need make mention of nothing else whatever in regard to the character of this man. For this marriage would be

---

[63] Rubin, *Iustinian*, pp. 478–9; Cameron, *Procopius*, p. 57.

[64] That Domitia Longina was herself the target of sexual slander resembling that which Prokopios throws at Theodora makes the use of her in this context (unintentionally?) ironic: see Vinson, 'Domitia'.

[65] See also Cameron, *Procopius*, p. 71 ('one of the chief charges levelled against both Belisarius and Justinian is precisely their subjection to their wives').

[66] For similar but even more damning sentiments, see viii.26; further parallels in, e.g., xiii.10, xiv.11–12.

amply sufficient to show full well all the maladies of his soul, since it serves as both an interpreter and a witness and recorder of his character' (x.3–5).

GENRE AND GENDER

The existence of invective as a discrete genre has been questioned;[67] and parallels between the *Secret History* and Prokopios' other works have been invoked in an attempt to blur the distinction between a text constructed as an invective and one constructed as reportage, thus allowing the *Secret History* to be read as factually accurate – exaggerated and distorted perhaps, but not invented.[68] The gendered and formalised patternings set out in this chapter are the main reason why I consider this approach fundamentally ill advised. Whether or not Prokopios criticises Justinian (and Belisarios) in his other two works, the *Wars* and the *Buildings*, neither of these is the same type of text as the *Secret History*, which has as its sole aim the discredit of the emperor Justinian through a series of carefully structured inversions of imperial and male virtues. In the *Secret History*, Theodora's role is not simply to damn Justinian by association, though she certainly achieves that goal through Prokopios' variant on the tried and tested *topos* of the empress-whore.[69] More importantly, however, Theodora is used by Prokopios to demonstrate Justinian's weakness – for as portrayed in the *Secret History*, he is not able to control his wife – and his lack of good judgement in selecting this anti-woman as his wife in the first place.

In the *Secret History*, Justinian is painted as a barbarian, and Prokopios draws on, and inverts, the entire arsenal of late Roman attitudes towards masculinity and imperial virtues to discredit the emperor. Theodora's depiction is also gender-based, and Prokopios has turned her into a powerful and enduring example of everything a late Roman woman should not be. If, as Amy Richlin has argued for the Roman period, women are used in literature as representatives of class purity,[70] Prokopios' inversion of the ideal woman in Theodora suggests that the fear of class disintegration that permeates the *Secret History* was one of its driving forces. Theodora's main role in the *Secret History* is to support Prokopios' condemnation of Justinian by exemplifying, vividly, his lack of judgement, weakness of will and moral decrepitude – his lack of *romanitas*, in fact. But she also exemplifies at least

---

[67] See references in note 8, above.   [68] Greatrex, 'Procopius the outsider?'; Foss, 'Theodora'.
[69] See note 34, above.
[70] Richlin, 'Julia's jokes', p. 67; Richlin extrapolates from a theory developed in S. Ortner, 'The virgin and the state', *Feminist Studies* 4 (1978), pp. 19–35.

one of the reasons why Prokopios was so determined to blacken Justinian's name in the first place: fear of change. Roger Scott argued that Prokopios' antipathy towards Justinian was based largely on his resistance to the innovations that he – and others of his conservative and patrician class – believed the emperor was imposing on Roman society.[71] Prokopios' Theodora, the inversion of the good Roman matron, exemplifies Justinian's pollution of the ideals of the old Roman senatorial elite. Her mockery of the great and the good shows the emperor's true colours.

The *Secret History* is a successful piece of fiction, a brilliant parody on the imperial panegyric. It tells us next to nothing about Justinian and Theodora. It does, however, tell us a great deal about how gender was constructed, and how those constructs could be subverted for use as social commentary, in sixth-century Byzantium.[72]

---

[71] R. Scott, 'Malalas, the Secret History, and Justinian's propaganda', *DOP* 39 (1985), pp. 99–109. See also Cameron, *Procopius*, p. 239; and compare Angold, 'Procopius', esp. pp. 32–3. On antiquarianism as an 'idiom of resistance' under Justinian, see further M. Maas, *John Lydus and the Roman Past* (London, 1992).

[72] I thank Liz James and Chris Wickham for comments on an earlier draft of this text.

CHAPTER 6

Romance and reality in the Byzantine bride shows

Martha Vinson

'By incidents resembling truth, truth is exhibited.' So ends the story, 'Pride and love', a work of American popular fiction published in the November 1840 issue of *Godey's Lady's Book*, a magazine combining fashion news with special features such as poetry and short stories.[1] 'Pride and love', like many stories in this and more recent publications, is essentially a courtship tale. It opens when the wealthy and aristocratic Edward Clavering meets the new girl in town, the equally aristocratic but impoverished Margaret Vassal, and concludes when she accepts his proposal of marriage. The story has been stripped of all non-essential elements to focus on the young lovers: his parents are conspicuous by their absence and Mrs Vassal makes a mute appearance merely to establish that her daughter is not a streetwalker when she encounters Mr Clavering outside her home. That theirs is truly a love match becomes clear when Edward comes to call and the two engage in a detailed discussion of the literary merits of Byron and Wordsworth. Their progress towards the altar, however, comes to a dead halt when Miss Vassal mistakenly believes that Edward wants to sever their incipient relationship because of her poverty. Clavering, of course, is able to see past her lack of material goods and recognises that her richness of character can recall him from his downward spiral into cynicism and self-absorption. After months of mutual misery, the two reconcile: 'And in that hour of unveiled and unshadowed emotion, there was established a perfectness of confidence and an entirety of love, which no future conduct could disturb by one danger – no misunderstanding could darken with one doubt.'

Such is the fictional ideal of courtship and marriage in nineteenth-century America. Real life, on the other hand, was a different matter altogether, as we learn from *The Glitter and the Gold*, the autobiography of

---

[1] W. Landor, 'Pride and love', *Godey's Lady's Book*, November 1840, pp. 225–30. The quotations are on p. 230.

Consuelo Vanderbilt Balsan.[2] Although Mme Balsan eventually found happiness with a French aviator, her first marriage to the Duke of Marlborough in 1895 was a nightmare, or to use her own term, a 'sacrifice', engineered by her socially ambitious mother.[3] In fact, both parties could be described as victims in that each was in love with someone else and had to give up this relationship in order for the marriage to take place. The bride, however, put up more of a fight than did the groom and for her trouble was placed under virtual house arrest. She eventually gave in, but it was only after her mother faked a heart attack and threatened to shoot her fiancé that she broke off her secret engagement with 'X'. No effort is made to present the match with Marlborough as anything other than a marriage of convenience. Even the bride's baby brother knew the score: 'He is only marrying you for your money.' To her husband, on the other hand, she was merely a 'link in the chain'.[4] Unfortunately, submission to her mother's 'towering ambition' did not lead to an improvement in the relationship. The bride was completely excluded from all preparations for the wedding; Mrs Vanderbilt unilaterally selected the trousseau, 'not troubling to consult the taste she claimed I did not possess', and similarly choosing the bridesmaids 'from among her friends for her own reasons'. During the actual service, the bride glanced at the groom only to find that 'his eyes were fixed in space'. Having thus exchanged 'one bondage for another', the new duchess did what was expected of her – providing 'an heir and a spare', mastering the duties of her position, using American money to subsidise the aristocratic lifestyle of a man who despised America and everything connected with it – before leaving him in 1906 and finally obtaining a divorce in 1920.[5]

These two texts, one romantic fiction, the other autobiography, illustrate how difficult it is to understand the actual process by which elite marriages are made, particularly in periods like classical antiquity and Byzantium

[2] Consuelo Vanderbilt Balsan, *The Glitter and the Gold* (New York, 1952), especially ch. 2, 'A debutante of the '90's', pp. 29–54 and ch. 3, 'A marriage of convenience', pp. 55–89.

[3] *Ibid.*, p. 25: 'It was here that Marlborough later proposed to me, and that I accepted a sacrifice that, in obeisance to the dictates of my upbringing, I felt was ordained'; *ibid.*, p. 45: 'It was that afternoon that he must have made up his mind to marry me and to give up the girl he loved, as he told me so tragically soon after our marriage. For to live at Blenheim in the pomp and circumstance he considered essential needed money, and a sense of duty to his family and to his traditions indicated the sacrifice of personal desires.'

[4] *Ibid.*, p. 66: 'At the age of 18, I was beginning to chafe at the impersonal role I had so far played in my own life – first a pawn in my mother's game and now, as my husband expressed it, "a link in the chain" . . . the fact that our happiness as individuals was as nothing in this unbroken chain of succeeding generations was a corroding thought.'

[5] Interestingly, Mme Balsan (*ibid.*, pp. 55–6) claims that she received her 'first lesson in class consciousness' from her husband on their honeymoon, and 'in time I learned that snobbishness was an enthroned fetish which spreads its tentacles into every stratum of British national life'.

where we lack the sort of brutally honest – one is tempted to say typically American – insider account provided by Consuelo Vanderbilt Balsan. Yet such sources can be used to repair the deficiencies in both the quantity and the quality of evidence for the pre-modern period and help us to make the most of the information that we do have.[6] A comparison of the similarities and differences can shed light on which kinds of things were considered negotiable and which were not, even in the realm of romantic fantasy. To begin with, both the Claverings and the Marlboroughs share a common language, religion and cultural background, and similar, or rather comparable, social standing. Again, with both couples, there is a vast disparity in economic status; poverty is seen as an impediment to marriage, but one that can be overcome by aristocratic birth. The differences, on the other hand, are equally informative. The most striking is in the area of personal compatibility; the fictional Claverings exhibit an intellectual and emotional harmony that bodes well for their future, while 'oil and water' does not begin to describe the deep personal antipathy between the Duke and Duchess of Marlborough. An equally significant and not unrelated factor is the process by which the couples were brought together. In the fictional world of a lady's magazine, young people are free to pair off, work out their differences and come to an understanding all by themselves; of course, there is adult supervision in the form of chaperones and parents, but these grown-ups do not intrude or interfere in the lives of the young. In real life, on the other hand, Consuelo Vanderbilt was merely a 'pawn' in the game played by her 'born dictator' of a mother.[7] Indeed, one may speculate that her marriage to the Duke of Marlborough was made even more miserable by the fact that, having found the man of her dreams on her own, she was not allowed to live out her romantic ideal like a fictional heroine.

This heart-wrenching disparity between the fictionalised ideal of courtship and the lived reality of elite women should instil in us a healthy sense of caution as we approach the problem of Byzantine bride shows.[8] As described in Byzantine sources, a bride show was essentially an empire-wide

[6] For another approach to the problems posed by Byzantine sources, see J. Herrin, *Women in Purple: Rulers of Medieval Byzantium* (Princeton, 2001).

[7] Balsan, *The Glitter and the Gold*, p. 6.

[8] See M. Vinson, 'The life of Theodora and the rhetoric of the Byzantine bride show', *JÖB* 49 (1999), pp. 31–60, for a survey of the problem with previous bibliography, to which should now be added the discussion in Herrin, *Women in Purple*, pp. 132–8, 190–1, 222–6, and M. Vinson, 'Rhetoric and writing strategies in the ninth century', in E. Jeffreys (ed.), *Rhetoric in Byzantium* (Aldershot, 2003), pp. 9–22. See also the important study by L. Rydén, 'The bride shows at the Byzantine court – history or fiction?', *Eranos* (1985), pp. 175–91, who provides a translation of the primary sources (except for the *Lives* of Theodora and Eirene of Chrysobalanton) as well as useful tables of the relevant data. For

beauty contest in which attractive young women came to Constantinople from throughout the realm in order to compete against one another for the privilege of being chosen as the emperor's wife. The contest was organised along the lines of the Miss Universe rather than the Miss America pageant, that is, the winner was chosen solely on the basis of physical appearance. While there might be the equivalent of the swimsuit competition when the groom's mother inspected the contestants at bath-time, there was no 'talent' component or any process to determine whether the bride and groom shared any common interests or likes and dislikes. This method of choosing the Byzantine empress is attested only in the eighth and ninth centuries, and during that time five marriages are said to have been arranged by means of bride shows: Constantine VI and Maria of Amnia in 788, Staurakios and Theophano in 807, Theophilos and Theodora in 830, Michael III and Eudokia Dekapolitissa in 855, and Leo VI and Theophano in 882.[9]

Unfortunately, our only sources of information for this phenomenon are literary accounts; 'hard' evidence such as contemporary archival, autobiographical, epigraphic or numismatic documentation is entirely lacking.[10] In other words, there is no Consuelo Vanderbilt for Byzantium. By far the largest category of source material is hagiography or saints' lives; the *vitae* of Sts Philaretos, Theodora, Theophano and Eirene of Chrysobalanton all contain accounts of bride shows. Historiography is also represented by the *Chronographia* of Theophanes and the *Chronicle* of Symeon the Logothete and there is one eulogy, the *Funeral Oration for Basil I* by his son Leo VI. A further complication is that all of these texts were written by men with an agenda that was often at odds with the events they were describing. Because of the nature of the evidence, the accounts of the Byzantine bride shows provide very little information about the actual process of choosing an imperial consort and even less about the women themselves. Indeed, literary analysis of these accounts has shown that they reflect objective reality only to the extent that the emperor's selection of a wife does at least theoretically represent a choice made over every other woman in the empire.

the *vitae* of Theodora and Irene, see M. Vinson, 'Life of St. Theodora the Empress', in A.-M. Talbot (ed.), *Byzantine Defenders of Images* (Washington, DC, 1998), pp. 353–82, and J. O. Rosenqvist, *The Life of St. Irene Abbess of Chrysobalanton: A Critical Edition with Introduction, Translation, Notes and Indices* (Uppsala, 1986). For more information about particular emperors or topics such as marriage or Iconoclasm, the interested reader is referred to the *Oxford Dictionary of Byzantium*, 3 vols. (New York, 1991).

9 For a parallel analysis of the western bride show tradition, see Mayke de Jong's chapter 14 below.

10 Cf. P. Speck, 'Eine Brautschau für Staurakios?', *JÖB* 49 (1999), pp. 25–30, who argues that one of the sources, the account of Theophano's marriage to Staurakios in Theophanes' *Chronographia*, contains a fragment of an official document.

Yet because they represent a wide variety of genres, perspectives and time periods, they are none the less very useful indicators of cultural values and ideals about gender during the middle Byzantine period.

When we speak of Byzantine values and ideals, it is important to remember that Byzantium was a society deeply indebted to the classical tradition of Greece as well as Rome. That the Byzantines called themselves *Rhomaioi*, the Greek term for Roman, rather than the Latin *Romani* illustrates very clearly the hybrid nature of this society. Despite the modern tendency to lump ancient Greece and Rome together under the rubric of Greco-Roman antiquity, these represent two different cultural traditions, each of which made its influence felt in Byzantium. From Rome, the Byzantines took the legal and political institutions that served as the nuts and bolts of empire. From Greece, the debt was less tangible but no less important: language and culture.

Culture of course is a broad term that includes social practices and artistic achievements. Both are important for understanding the Byzantine bride show. Yet because this phenomenon was a textual event rather than an actual one, the aspect of Greek culture that is most useful for understanding Byzantine bride shows is the literary tradition. Indeed, it would be difficult to overestimate the importance of the Greek language and literary heritage in Byzantine society. Even after the introduction of Christianity, educational curricula, at least for the social elite, continued to emphasise the study of classical authors like Homer and Plato as well as training in rhetoric. The high value placed on all things Greek cut across religious boundaries and could manifest itself as cultural chauvinism and snobbery. For example, the pagan rhetorician Themistios had no qualms about making the Roman emperor Valens sit through an oration in Greek that he could not possibly have understood while the Christian Gregory of Nazianzos practically boasted about his ignorance of Latin in a letter to a public official.[11] Nor was this disdain for the Latin west mere posturing on the part of the eastern intellectual elite. How deeply the Hellenic tradition could be internalised is illustrated by Gregory of Nazianzos, who, in the darkest hour of his stormy tenure as bishop of Constantinople (379–381), preached a sermon in which he identified himself not with Christ or Job or any other Judaeo-Christian victim of unjust persecution but rather with

---

[11] John Vanderspoel, *Themistius and the Imperial Court: Oratory, Civic Duty, and Paideia from Constantius to Theodosius* (Ann Arbor, MI, 1995), p. 157; Gregory of Nazianzos, *Ep.* 173.1 to Postumianus the Pretorian Prefect from summer 383, ed. and trans. P. Gallay, *Saint Grégoire de Nazianze: Lettres*, vol. II (Paris, 1967), pp. 61–2.

the fifth-century Athenian philosopher Socrates.[12] That Gregory communicated this by imbedding allusions to Plato's early or Socratic dialogues in the sermon illustrates one of the difficulties in evaluating Byzantine texts. References to classical literature are often seamlessly integrated into these texts without attribution and as a result it is easy for the unwary reader to mistake a literary allusion for a piece of authentic contemporary information.

The problem of disentangling fact from fiction is made even more difficult in the case of the bride shows because of the issue of gender. Although the male authors responsible for the accounts of the bride shows may have thought they were living in classical Athens, in reality they were citizens not of a democracy or even a republic but rather of an empire which, beginning with the first Roman emperor Augustus, had a long history of exploiting the women of the imperial family in political propaganda.[13] Of course, the use of women as icons of virtue and vice was not invented by Augustus or even the Romans. In one of the earliest works of western literature, Homer's *Odyssey*, we find the characters of Penelope and Clytemnestra used to establish models of feminine behaviour that persist, with only slight modifications, to the present day. In the person of Penelope, womanly virtue is defined in terms of chastity and childbearing, with her sexual fidelity to her husband ensuring the legitimacy of his male heir. To the extent that such a woman has any talent independent of her sexual and reproductive capacity, it is valued only in so far as it advances her husband's interests, as when Penelope uses her knowledge of weaving to postpone a decision on remarriage during Odysseus' absence. By contrast, Penelope's antithesis Clytemnestra is both a bad wife because she commits adultery and a bad mother because she rejects her son and his claim to the throne in favour of her new lover.

Today we are all familiar with the devastating emotional impact of divorce and remarriage on families. In the pre-modern era, on the other hand, when the wife of a king or emperor engaged in an extra-marital affair, the results could go far beyond hurt feelings and wounded pride. A queen's adultery was at the same time an act of treason with the potential to affect the political and economic well-being of the state. This is why the private behaviour of imperial women, both good and bad, could serve as an indicator of the quality of the emperor's leadership skills and administration of the empire.

---

[12] M. Vinson, 'Gregory Nazianzen's Homily 36: a Socratic response to Christian persecution', *Classica et Mediaevalia* 44 (1993), pp. 255–66.

[13] On this topic, see the important book by Susan E. Wood, *Imperial Women: A Study in Public Images, 40 B.C.–A.D. 68* (Leiden, 1999).

Here it is important to remember that these public images of elite women were carefully constructed to place their male kinsmen in a positive or negative light and for this reason may have very little in common with the real people they represent. To cite a contemporary example, the public persona of Barbara Bush as the kindly grandmother who bakes cookies and teaches underprivileged children how to read is sharply at odds with the tough-as-nails political operative she is behind the scenes.[14] Similarly, the public image of Nancy Reagan as a devoted and doting wife was undercut by the allegation that she engaged in an adulterous affair with Frank Sinatra in the White House, in order to discredit her husband, the 'Teflon President', Ronald Reagan.[15] But whether or not these public images accurately reflect the private persona, they are none the less useful indicators of cultural values, in the case of the examples just cited, that motherhood and marital fidelity are female virtues in twentieth-century America no less than in Homeric times.

The Byzantine bride shows functioned in a similar way to create a positive or negative image of the reigning emperor and his regime. The concept itself was not without precedent; the stories of the biblical queen Esther and Athenais/Eudokia, who became the wife of the emperor Theodosius in the fifth century, represent essentially the same phenomenon. What is new is that the selection of a wife assumed the properties of a rhetorical *topos* or commonplace of imperial panegyric and invective, that is, praise and blame. The question that then arises is, why did this particular activity, the process of choosing an empress, become a criterion of political worth at this particular time in the history of Byzantium?

Marriage continued to play an important role even after the introduction of Christianity, although the emphasis on celibacy in recent scholarship might lead one to suspect otherwise. One of the factors ensuring the survival of family life was the prominence of dualist heresies such as Gnosticism and Manicheanism during the early Christian period.[16] These heresies challenged the supremacy of the Christian deity by positing equal and opposing forces of good and evil which were identified with spirit and matter, soul and body, male and female. This is why Christians, both individuals and members of the ecclesiastical hierarchy, were more or less

---

[14] Kati Marton, *Hidden Power: Presidential Marriages That Shaped Our Recent History* (New York, 2001), pp. 274–305.
[15] Kitty Kelley, *Nancy Reagan: The Unauthorized Biography* (New York, 1991), pp. 188, 311–12.
[16] See, for example, G. Clark, 'The old Adam: the Fathers and the unmaking of masculinity', in L. Foxhall and J. Salmon (eds.), *Thinking Men: Masculinity and Its Self-Representation in the Classical Tradition* (London, 1998), p. 176.

forced into accepting the legitimacy of sexuality and procreation, however great the inclination to reject the body and all things connected with it. This ambiguity expressed itself in strange ways. For example, the author of a famous treatise on virginity, Gregory of Nyssa, was himself a married man.[17] Similarly, the celibate Gregory of Nazianzos declined a wedding invitation, not because he disapproved or thought that marriage was nothing to celebrate, but rather because in his view he was so old and sick and cranky that he would have been a wet blanket at what should be a festive occasion.[18]

Marriage thus remained a feature of the Christian as well as the pagan empire and women continued to perform their time-honoured role as 'links in the chain' advancing the political and economic interests of the family. Yet if the institution of marriage itself did not experience significant change with the advent of Christianity, the same could not be said of the related issues of divorce and remarriage.[19] Here, the difficulty lay in the discrepancy between what was thought to be morally or socially acceptable and what was legally permissible under civil and canon, i.e. church, law. Generally speaking, it was felt that the marriage bond once made was inviolable and indissoluble even though it was not actually against the law to remarry after divorce or the death of a spouse. The lack of a uniform standard of conduct created many difficulties, and resolution of the problem came only in the tenth century as a consequence of the affair of the tetragamy, that is, the fourth marriage of Leo VI (emperor 886–912).

In the meantime, the gap between the law and popular morality profoundly affected the way that sexual transgression was defined and reported. One of the consequences of the more restrictive view of marriage was that sexual misconduct was pushed to the margins in order to preserve the sanctity of the marital relationship itself. For example, adultery, which was a common form of sexual slander in classical antiquity, fell out of use in the early and middle Byzantine periods and was replaced by remarriage as in the case of Constantine VI (780–797), whose second marriage instigated what is popularly known as the 'Moechian Controversy', that is, the controversy over adultery. Even more importantly for the present discussion, the premarital period assumed a significance it did not have in classical

---

[17] For an English translation of *On Virginity*, see *Saint Gregory of Nyssa: Ascetical Works*, trans. Virginia Woods Callahan (Washington, DC, 1967), pp. 6–75.

[18] Gregory of Nazianzos, *Epp.* 193 and 194 to Vitalianos near the end of his life; Gallay (ed.), *Lettres*, vol. II, pp. 84–5.

[19] On the shift in sexual values, see Martha P. Vinson, 'The Christianization of sexual slander. Some preliminary observations', in C. Sode and S. Takács (eds.), *Novum Millennium: Studies on Byzantine History and Culture Dedicated to Paul Speck* (Aldershot, 2001), pp. 415–24.

antiquity when serial marriages were quite common. For example, women of the Julio-Claudian dynasty were remarried, or rather bred, as soon as they became available through death or divorce in order to ensure the survival of the *domus Augusta* through the transmission of legitimacy.[20] In an environment where so many women were entering second and third marriages, often with children from prior unions, it would have been counterproductive to make an issue of virginity. The situation was different in the Christian era, when both men and women essentially had only one chance to get it right where marriage was concerned. With women, on the one hand, we find an intense interest in the bride's premarital sexual history, with a special interest in the question of virginity. For example, in Prokopios' *Secret History*, the sixth-century empress Theodora is alleged to have engaged in sexual relationships with an assortment of human beings and animals prior to her marriage, even giving birth to an illegitimate child, but once she married Justinian she remained faithful to him for the duration of their marriage.[21] With men, on the other hand, since adultery was off limits even in the literary realm of invective, the emphasis shifted from control of the wife's sexuality to the husband's decision-making ability in choosing a wife. In faulting Justinian for marrying Theodora, Prokopios is unusually explicit on the connection between the choice of a wife and a man's leadership skills.

> It never even occurred to her husband that his conduct was shocking, though he was in a position to take his pick of the Roman Empire and select for his bride the most nobly born woman in the world, who had enjoyed the most exclusive upbringing, and was thoroughly acquainted with the claims of modesty, and had lived in an atmosphere of chastity, and in addition was superbly beautiful and still a virgin . . . No: he must needs make the common bane of all mankind his very own . . . and consort with a woman double-dyed with every kind of horrible pollution, and guilty over and over again of infanticide by wilful abortion. Not one more thing need be mentioned . . . regarding the character of this man: this marriage would be quite enough to reveal only too clearly all his moral sickness; it was both interpreter, witness, and chronicler of the course he followed. For when a man cares nothing for the infamy of his actions, and does not hesitate to be known to all and sundry as a revolting character, no path of

---

[20] M. Corbier, 'Male power and legitimacy through women: the *Domus Augusta* under the Julio-Claudians', in R. Hawley and B. Levick (eds.), *Women in Antiquity: New Assessments* (London, 1995), pp. 178–93.

[21] For detailed discussion of Prokopios' presentation of Justinian and his marriage to Theodora, see Leslie Brubaker, chapter 5 above.

lawlessness is closed to him, but armed with the shamelessness visible at every moment in his face, he advances cheerfully and without any misgivings to the most loathsome deeds.[22]

As Leslie Brubaker argues in the preceding chapter, Prokopios' criticism of Justinian is characteristic of a particular literary form called invective, or *psogos* in Greek. Its positive counterpart is praise or *epainos*. Each type was employed as both a genre and a tactic. That is, an entire work could be devoted to the praise or blame of an individual, as in an encomium for example, or one may find elements of praise or blame within a different genre such as historiography. Each type contains traditional qualities such as greed and generosity, cruelty and kindness, which were used to illuminate individual character. But while the general kind of thing said in praise or blame remained more or less constant, historical circumstances could result in a shift in focus or a change in the particular example of a general class of behaviour, as we have just seen in the case of sexuality. These deviations from the norm are especially important for the historian because they help to identify the issues and concerns of a given period.

This is particularly true of the eighth and ninth centuries. Theologically, the age was dominated by Iconoclasm, a bitter theological dispute involving the proper role and use of sacred images in Christian worship. Byzantine Iconoclasm took place in two phases, from *c.* 730 until 787, when the veneration of icons was restored by Eirene and Constantine VI, and from 815 until the Triumph of Orthodoxy under Theodora and Michael III in 843. As often happened with religious controversies in Byzantium, Iconoclasm went far beyond the simple question of whether or not icons should be venerated and came to involve issues of gender, education and lifestyle.[23] Further complicating this mix of difficult social and religious questions, the empire faced extremely serious political problems from both within and without. For example, during the period in question, that is, 730–842, there were eleven different emperors from five different families.[24] The frequent turnover in leadership created questions of legitimacy which

---

[22] Prokopios, *Secret History* 10.2–5; English translation by G. A. Williamson, *Procopius: The Secret History* (Baltimore, 1966), pp. 89–90.

[23] For a discussion of these issues, see Martha P. Vinson, 'Gender and politics in the post-iconoclastic period: the *Lives* of Antony the Younger, the empress Theodora, and the patriarch Ignatios', *Byzantion* 68 (1998), pp. 469–515.

[24] Isaurian dynasty: Leo III (717–741), Constantine V (741–775), Leo IV the Khazar (775–780), Constantine VI (780–797), Irene (797–802), Nikephoros I (802–811), Staurakios (811), Michael I Rangabe, the son-in-law of Nikephoros I (811–813), Leo V the Armenian (813–820); Amorian dynasty: Michael II (820–829), Theophilos (829–842).

could be resolved by a strategic marital alliance. Foreign enemies were less easily dealt with. Although the early iconoclast emperors seemed to enjoy the divine favour because of their victories over the Arabs, this perception was seriously challenged by the defeat of the emperor Theophilos at his hometown of Amorion in 838. To the north, hostilities with the Bulgarians resulted in the deaths of the emperor Nikephoros and his son Staurakios in 811. Nikephoros' skull was allegedly made into a drinking cup for the khan Krum.

History is written by the winners and those emperors like Nikephoros who died violently in battle were particularly vulnerable to a revisionist assessment of their regime that would account for their ignominious ends. This was certainly the case with Theophanes' *Chronographia*, where Nikephoros is portrayed as a man who could not do anything right, including something so simple as finding a suitable wife for his son. According to Theophanes,

On 20 December, after making an extensive selection of maidens from all the domains subject to him with a view to marrying his son Staurakios, Nikephoros chose the Athenian Theophano, a kinswoman of the blessed Eirene, although she was betrothed to another man and had lain with him many times. Acting in this respect with the same unlawful impudence as in all others, he separated her from her man and wed her to the wretched Staurakios. He also selected along with her another two maidens who were more beautiful than she and openly violated them during the very days of the wedding, while everyone ridiculed the detestable man.[25]

Because of Theophanes' overt hostility to his subject ('unlawful impudence', 'everyone ridiculed'), it is easy to see that the bride show performed a function much like Nancy Reagan's alleged adultery and in fact was just one of many invective elements such as mismanagement of state finances and heresy used to portray Nikephoros as a complete and abject failure. Let us note at the outset that the match between Staurakios and Theophano was clearly a dynastic one: like a Julio-Claudian princess, the bride's role was to transmit legitimacy to the new regime through her kinship with the iconophile empress Eirene. Unfortunately, Nikephoros derived no advantage from this relationship, as he is elsewhere characterised as an iconoclast, nor did he get any credit for marrying the young woman to his son when he might have taken her for himself. Even more unfortunately, the poor bride was dragged through the mud in order to attack her father-in-law. The fact that she was not only already engaged and

---

[25] C. Mango and R. Scott, *The Chronicle of Theophanes the Confessor: Byzantine and Near Eastern History AD 284–813* (Oxford, 1997), pp. 663–4, and for a discussion of the date of the *Chronographia*, see pp. lii–lxiii.

had lost her virginity but was also relatively unattractive underscores the emperor's bad judgement and tyrannical character. In ancient Rome, it was not uncommon for a fertile and even happy marriage to be broken up for political reasons, and both Augustus and Domitian, for example, married women who already had husbands.[26] With the more restrictive attitude towards marriage, however, such behaviour became unacceptable and we find that fiancée-stealing replaces wife-stealing as a metaphor for the abuse of power. By the same token, Nikephoros' seduction of the other contestants represents a departure from classical invective where respectable married women rather than unmarried girls figure more commonly as the victims of imperial lust. Finally, Theophano's lack of virginity reflects a new concern in elite match-making, which further set the evil and incompetent Nikephoros apart from God-fearing and effective emperors like Theodosios I (378–395), who insisted that his wife be a virgin.[27]

Unlike other forms of sexual slander such as adultery and the defloration of virgins, the selection of a wife was morally neutral and could be used in a positive way to praise as well as blame. This soon happened in the *Life of Philaretos*, written in 821–822 by the monk Niketas in the hope of being recalled from exile. The bride show described in this saint's life is the one which resulted in the marriage of Philaretos' granddaughter, Maria of Amnia, to Constantine VI, the son of the empress Eirene, in 788. Constantine VI divorced Maria and his remarriage became the occasion of the 'Moechian Controversy' noted above. But the surviving daughter of his first marriage, Euphrosyne, was extracted from the convent to which she had been consigned with her mother after her divorce to become the wife of Michael II (820–829), the founder of the Amorian dynasty. Like Theophano, Euphrosyne brought legitimacy to the new regime through her relationship with Eirene and Constantine VI. The problem was that Maria of Amnia was neither Constantine's first choice nor his last, his mother having broken up his earlier engagement to Rotrud, the daughter of the Frankish king, Charlemagne. In presenting Maria as Constantine's own enthusiastic choice, the bride show in the *Life of Philaretos* validates their marriage and thus Euphrosyne's value as a dynastic link.

In comparison to Theophanes' *Chronographia*, the account of the bride show in the *Life of Philaretos* is quite elaborate. Dispatched by the empress

---

[26] M. Flory, 'Abducta Neroni Uxor: the historiographical tradition on the marriage of Octavian and Livia', *Transactions of the American Philological Association* 118 (1988), pp. 342–59; M. P. Vinson, 'Domitia Longina, Julia Titi, and the literary tradition', *Historia* 38 (1988), p. 438.

[27] John Malalas, *Chronicle*, Book 14.3, trans. E. Jeffreys, M. Jeffreys and R. Scott *et al.* (Melbourne, 1986), pp. 191–2.

Eirene to find a suitable bride for her son, imperial agents scoured the whole empire without success until they came to the little town of Amnia. They accepted the saint's hospitality and, with the neighbours' help, he entertained his guests at a banquet. The next day, Philaretos allowed the agents to examine his granddaughters after first proclaiming, 'We may be poor, but our girls have never left their bedroom.' All of the women in the family were so beautiful that the saint had to help the agents tell the daughters from the granddaughters. After measuring the eldest girl's height and shoe size and comparing her with an ideal portrait, the agents found that she fitted the imperial specifications perfectly. Once in Constantinople, Maria urged the ten other contestants to make a sisterly agreement among themselves so that whoever became empress would help the others. To this proposal, one of the girls haughtily replied that she was sure to be chosen because she was richer, nobler and prettier. The young women were brought before the emperor and his mother, but all were rejected, beginning with the boastful one. The granddaughters of Philaretos appeared last and were so impressive that the emperor instantly proposed to the eldest while her two younger sisters were snapped up by other noblemen.

Unlike the bride show in the *Chronographia*, where Theophano's negative qualities were emphasised in order to condemn Nikephoros' judgement in choosing her, here the bride and her family are presented in a positive light to achieve the opposite effect. What is interesting is that in the present example the Greek tradition dominates at the expense of the Roman. To begin with, the elaborate banquet at which St Philaretos entertained the imperial agents is an all-male affair, which reflects Greek rather than Roman custom in dining, a distinction of which the Romans themselves were aware.[28] Again, the saint's claim that his girls have never left their bedroom establishes their sexual purity, but the practice of female seclusion is Greek, or rather Athenian, as illustrated by the claim of a litigant in the fourth century BC that his sister and nieces lived such respectable lives that they were ashamed to be seen even by their own relatives.[29] Finally, in the scene that resulted in her selection as a candidate, Maria is not singled out by name but is identified merely as the eldest of the saint's three granddaughters, which recalls the Greek reluctance to mention women by name, evidenced by Thucydides 2.45, where we are told that a woman's greatest glory is to be least talked about by men whether in praise or blame.[30] All of these details help to make the point that Maria is a nice girl from a good Greek family,

---

[28] Cornelius Nepos, *Vitae* praef. 6–7.   [29] Lysias, *Against Simon* 3.6.
[30] Additional references and discussion in D. Schaps, 'The woman least mentioned: etiquette and women's names', *Classical Quarterly* 27 (1977), pp. 323–30.

thus affirming Constantine VI's good judgement and the validity of their union.

These two texts from the early ninth century, Theophanes' *Chronographia* and the *Life of Philaretos*, reveal that the Byzantine bride show originated during the second iconoclast period as a way of legitimising or discrediting a regime through the emperor's selection of a wife. After this promising beginning, however, we hear no more of bride shows until well after the official end of the iconoclast controversy when the motif reappears in two works from the very end of the ninth century, the *Funeral Oration for Basil I* and the *Life of Theodora*, the widow of the last iconoclast emperor Theophilos, who restored the veneration of icons after her husband's death.[31] Both works follow the pattern of using the bride show as a form of imperial propaganda, but of the two, the saint's life was by far the more influential. Not only are all subsequent accounts of bride shows dependent on it for both form and content, but this *vita* also had a lasting effect on the hagiographical tradition with profound consequences for the lives of real women.

The *Life of Theodora* belongs to a rhetorical genre called a *basilikos logos* or imperial oration. This was a special kind of speech used to praise an emperor, or in this case, an empress. The instructions for composing an imperial oration as well as a funeral oration are found in a late antique rhetorical handbook by Menander Rhetor.[32] Because the format of an imperial oration is so distinctive, it is easy to establish the dependent relationship between the *Life of Theodora* and the *Lives* of Sts Theophano, Eirene of Chrysobalanton and Mary the Younger. Although the shared rhetorical form played a crucial role in identifying the literary and chronological relationship between these works, even without this critical piece of information one may discern a thematic connection between them: with the exception of the *Life of Mary the Younger*, all contain bride shows and, with the exception of the *Life of Eirene of Chrysobalanton*, all concern married women.

The concepts of the married saint, the bride show and Iconoclasm were intimately connected with one another and with the *Life of Theodora*. Although marriage and sainthood may at first appear to be an odd combination, married female saints emerged in Byzantium during the

---

[31] The bride show involving Theodora and Theophilos also figures in the tenth-century *Chronicle of Symeon the Logothete*, but because this work is dependent on the *Life of Theodora*, it has no independent value and is therefore omitted from the present discussion; see Vinson, 'Rhetoric of the Byzantine bride show', pp. 38–41.

[32] *Menander Rhetor*, ed. with trans. and comm. D. A. Russell and N. G. Wilson (Oxford, 1981), pp. 76–95 and 170–9. For the details of Menander's guidelines for the *basilikos logos*, see the comments of Leslie Brubaker, above, p. 86.

post-iconoclast era, replacing a more independent and assertive type of saint such as Thekla or the cross-dressing Matrona. This reversion to a secular rather than a monastic model of feminine virtue was part of a larger programme of secularisation which included such things as using the format of an imperial oration to compose hagiography. As social engineering, however, this policy had a disproportionate impact on women and evidence such as the steep decline in female literacy indicates a tremendous step backward from the status women appear to have enjoyed during the iconoclast period.[33] As a diversionary tactic, the repression of women is a well-documented phenomenon in human history, and the emperor Augustus, for example, attempted to consolidate power after a long and bitter civil war by expanding opportunities for men, particularly those who had previously been excluded from power-sharing, while at the same time restricting women, especially among the elite, to the functions of marriage and motherhood. Yet, as even the Taliban realised, such a policy will work only if there is a carrot on the stick of repression. In the early Roman empire, restrictive social legislation was accompanied by a sophisticated propaganda campaign employing art and literature to promote family values. Not surprisingly, the women of the imperial family played a critical role in the success of this campaign, which could include the elevation of the empress to superhuman status in furtherance of what Mary Beard has called the 'cult of conjugality' and I have termed the 'cult of domesticity'.[34]

The bride show in the *Life of Theodora* should be seen as part of a similar policy implemented by the early Macedonian emperors in the aftermath of the iconoclastic controversy. But where in pagan Rome an empress such as Livia might be deified as a reward for her faithful service as a wife and mother, in Christian Byzantium canonisation replaced apotheosis as the pinnacle of human achievement. Because Theodora's sainthood was a product of her marital status, the process by which she became empress thus assumes a critical importance. According to the *Life of Theodora*, the future empress was born in Paphlagonia to god-fearing, that is, iconophile, parents. When she reached marriageable age, she was so beautiful that she was summoned to Constantinople by the emperor along with a number of

---

[33] For example, the mother of Theodore Studite, a prominent monastic defender of icon veneration, decided that family life was not for her and abandoned her husband and small children for a convent. See Theodore Studite, *Laudatio funebris in matrem suam*, PG 99, col. 892C.

[34] Mary Beard and John Henderson, 'The emperor's new body: ascension from Rome', in M. Wyke (ed.), *Parchments of Gender: Deciphering the Body in Antiquity* (Oxford, 1998), pp. 191–219; M. P. Vinson, 'The empress Theodora and the cult of domesticity in Byzantine hagiography', Twenty-Second Annual Byzantine Studies Conference, October 24–27, 1996, The University of North Carolina at Chapel Hill, *Abstracts of Papers*, p. 70.

attractive young women. On the way, Theodora was mercilessly tormented by the other contestants but she bravely endured their abuse; she stopped at Nikomedia to visit a holy man, who gave her an apple together with a prophecy of her selection as empress. Once in the capital, Theophilos selected seven finalists, gave each an apple, and sent them off to their rooms. The next day, the emperor assembled the girls and asked for their apples, but only Theodora was able to produce hers. As she handed over the apples given to her by the emperor and the holy man, she explained that they symbolised her virginity and the son she would bear to him. The emperor then presented her with an engagement ring and she went off with her future mother-in-law and her ladies-in-waiting until the wedding, which was celebrated with great pomp and ceremony.

What appeared to be a marriage made in heaven became a nightmare when Theophilos turned into the husband from hell. In fact, until the day he died, marrying Theodora was the only decent thing this emperor did in his entire life. His poor wife lived in terror of his violent mood swings and temper tantrums and angry shouting. Even more offensive than these revolting personal qualities were the emperor's religious beliefs, for almost immediately after the wedding Theophilos revived Iconoclasm, to the great distress of the iconophile Theodora. Yet in a radical departure from the tradition of saints like Thekla and Matrona who defied male authority in defence of their faith, the Theodora of her *vita* not only failed to challenge her husband on the question of icon veneration but even refused to defy his policy by worshipping images in the privacy of her quarters in the palace. It was this quality of submissiveness under the most difficult circumstances imaginable that made Theodora a saint. The implicit message was that if the most beautiful and powerful woman in the empire could patiently submit to her heretical brute of a husband, her subjects should do no less. The example set by Theodora paved the way for a saint like Mary the Younger, whose husband beat her to death after her malicious sister-in-law falsely accused her of adultery with a slave.[35]

The *Life of Theodora* thus marks a turning point in the hagiographical tradition and helps to explain the decline and eventual disappearance of female saints in Byzantium. The bride show eventually outlived its usefulness as well, but it still had a role to play until the Macedonian dynasty became

---

[35] She defended herself on the charge of adultery by saying: 'O sweetest husband . . . with whom I alone have had intercourse. I would happily have abstained even from that if it had been possible and if divine law permitted it.' See the *Life of St. Mary the Younger*, trans. A. E. Laiou, in A.-M. Talbot (ed.), *Holy Women of Byzantium: Ten Saints' Lives in English Translation* (Washington, DC, 1996), p. 263.

firmly entrenched. For example, in his *Funeral Oration* for his father Basil I, Leo VI used the motif of the bride show to justify his father's assassination of his predecessor Michael III, the son of Theodora and Theophilos. In this case, Michael III, like Nikephoros I before him, is politically discredited by his preference for an inferior candidate while his successor gives a hint of his future greatness by choosing the 'ineffably superior woman' that Michael III passed over. This same bride show also appears in the last work to feature this motif, the *Life of Eirene of Chrysobalanton*, written sometime after the late tenth century, where it figures as one of many elements used in an elaborate form of antiquarian name-dropping designed to enhance the stature of Eirene's convent.

The *Life of Theophano*, which describes the bride show resulting in the marriage of Theophano and Leo VI, represents an intermediate stage between the *Lives* of Theodora and Eirene of Chrysobalanton. Like the *Life of Theodora*, it is political propaganda but instead of being generated by the imperial court it is the work of a private citizen who hoped to exploit a slight relationship with the royal family for personal gain. Interestingly, in this account both parents, Basil I and Eudokia, were involved in the process that brought twelve young women to the Magnaura palace in Constantinople to compete for the hand of their son. Among them was Theophano, who was born in the capital of noble blood. As in the *Life of Philaretos*, the girls made a pact among themselves, in this case that the first one to get up, put on her shoes and bow to the emperor when he came to inspect them would become empress. Theophano performed the required tasks before the rest and the empress chose her along with two others as finalists. After examining the girls in the bath, Eudokia selected Theophano because of her superior beauty and presented her to her husband. The emperor thereupon gave her a ring and, as in the *Life of Theodora*, the future empress went off with her mother-in-law to await the wedding.

Although, as noted above, the *Life of Theophano* made use of the same rhetorical form as the *Life of Theodora*, it is even more deeply indebted to the *Life of Philaretos* for its content, as can be seen quite clearly for example in the scene where the contestants make a pact among themselves. This similarity can be accounted for by the fact that the marriages of both Constantine VI and Leo VI were unsuccessful. In fact, faced with her husband's infidelity with the woman who would become the second of his four wives, Theophano is said to have offered him a divorce before leaving him to live as a nun. Of course, the *vita* contains no hint of these marital difficulties but on the contrary portrays the couple as so perfectly matched that they actually have the same dream. In real life, however, Theophano's royal birth indicates that she was chosen to serve as yet another 'link in the chain' of a dynastic marriage. Yet unlike her namesake and predecessor, the bride of Leo VI was unquestionably a virgin for we are explicitly informed that she never left her father's house except to bathe, and then only at the crack of dawn accompanied by 'very many male and female servants'. Nevertheless, despite Theophano's beauty, piety and virginity, her marriage failed and, while personal incompatibility may have been a factor, the real reason can only have been her failure to produce a male heir. Indeed, it was this need for a son that led Leo VI to precipitate a crisis of church and state with his fourth marriage in 906, a crisis that was resolved only in 920, eight years after his death. The resolution of this crisis by establishing a uniform policy on the issue of remarriage paved the way for the return of adultery as a form of sexual slander, while the longevity of the Macedonian dynasty resulted in the creation of a new *topos* of imperial legitimacy, the *porphyrogennetos*, or prince 'born in the purple'.

But until the longevity of the Macedonian dynasty rendered the bride show obsolete as a tool of political propaganda, the selection of an emperor's wife retained its viability as a means of legitimising or discrediting a regime. A survey of the marriages alleged to be so arranged has shown that the actual process and criteria by which imperial brides were chosen in the eighth and ninth centuries remain obscure. Yet in those cases where a glimpse of the true picture emerges, we find that the truth is sharply at odds with the romantic image put before us. For example, the noble origin of the two Theophanos shows that theirs were dynastic marriages and they themselves merely 'links in the chain' transmitting legitimacy from one regime to another. What is significant, however, is that the bride shows conceal this crass reality and create the illusion that the empresses of Byzantium were chosen strictly on the basis of their own merit, regardless of their families' social, political or economic status. This, after all, is the logical consequence of Prokopios' moral: if the emperor can choose any woman in the empire, then it follows that any woman in the empire can be chosen.

No less than the process itself, however, the criterion of beauty is a two-edged sword.[36] Unlike her family's wealth or position, a woman's physical appearance is inalienably her own to make of what she will. In defining beauty as the sole measure of a woman's worth, the bride show treats women as independent individuals, effectively isolating them from their families. It is thus no accident that in the accounts of the Byzantine bride shows the bride's parents play no role in the proceedings, if indeed they are even

[36] Cf. de Jong, below, pp. 263, 269–70, 275.

mentioned at all. While some women no doubt viewed the separation from their natal families as a form of liberation, there might well come a time when they would welcome access to the resources that can only be provided by blood kin, and their *amici* (friends) and *clientes* (associates).

In creating the illusion of romance and equality, the accounts of the Byzantine bride shows conceal the darker truth that their focus on female beauty serves as a means of disempowering the bride and her family and placing the wife under the exclusive control of her husband. The marriages arranged in this manner can thus be seen as a reversion to a type of wedlock common in the old Roman republic in which the wife was said to be *in manu viri*, that is, in her husband's power or control (literally, 'hand').[37] How the women themselves felt about this, we simply do not know. Did Theophano, for example, resent the break-up of her engagement like Consuelo Vanderbilt or did she view her marriage to Staurakios as the opportunity of a lifetime? The fact of the matter is that no one in Byzantium cared enough to find out or transmit this information to posterity. And in this one important respect, we find that the Roman tradition remains untransformed and unreconstructed.

[37] S. Treggiari, *Roman Marriage: Iusti Coniuges from the Time of Cicero to the Time of Ulpian* (Oxford, 1991), pp. 16–17, 442–3.

CHAPTER 7

Men, women and slaves in Abbasid society

Julia Bray

I

[C]ompetition played a major part but in a different fashion from that found in agonistic societies; in the form of revocable offices which depended, often quite directly, on the pleasure of the prince; and nearly always in an intermediary position between a higher power whose orders must be conveyed or carried out, and individuals or groups whose obedience must be obtained . . . And if one wishes to understand the interest that was directed in these elites to personal ethics . . . it is not all that pertinent to speak of decadence, frustration, and sullen retreat. Instead one should see in this interest the search for a new way of conceiving the relationship that one ought to have with one's status, one's functions, one's activities and one's obligations . . . the new rules of the political game made it more difficult to define the relations between what one was, what one could do, and what one was expected to accomplish. The formation of oneself as the ethical subject of one's own actions became more problematic.[1]

Gender roles, it can be argued, have played a crucial part in the shaping of Islamic history. As Michel Foucault describes them, the changed roles of men under the early Roman empire bear more than a passing similarity to the position in which Muslim men found themselves in the ninth to mid-tenth centuries AD, the period between the consolidation of the Abbasid imperial state and its breakup as a political entity. The parallel, as we shall see, is a useful one for Islamicists; but it may be coincidental. The question of whether early Islam – the Islam of the conquests and of Umayyad rule – was a successor to the late Roman world in any except the geographical sense has been vigorously reopened of recent years, and the fragmentary picture that is emerging from new sources and approaches is, as might be expected, far from simple.

---

[1] Michel Foucault, *The Care of the Self* (*The History of Sexuality*, vol. III, first published as *Le Souci de soi*, Paris, 1984), trans. Robert Hurley (London, 1990), p. 84.

It may be useful to give examples of some of the types of evidence available for this earlier period, and of the gaps in it and in the questions that
have been asked of it, in order to explain why I shall adopt a tenuously
late Roman, i.e. Abbasid, point of vantage from which to discuss changes
in Muslim men's roles following the Islamic conquests, and how, over a
period of time, they are bound up with changes in those of women (and in
those of slaves and converts). The majority of modern discussions overlook
the ways in which the Abbasids – the main chroniclers of early Islam –
identified patterns of social and gender relationships in their own society
and contrasted them with those of the Arab past. Yet Abbasid analyses,
though far from transparent or innocent, are worth bringing into the equation, because they offer the possibility of negotiating an impasse which
has developed in some areas of the fledgling discipline of Islamic gender
studies. The first generations of modern scholars to concern themselves
with the sexes in pre-Islam and Islam were unselfconsciously progressive
and set their sights on retrieving positive or powerful images of women.[2]
Then, for several decades, women barely figured as a topic of research.
Now that they have re-emerged, some recent feminist scholars have abandoned the optimism of their predecessors and set up as a polemical target
what they identify as a crudely polarised Islamic male discourse which oblit-
erates female agency and can readily be made to serve repressive modern
agendas. The presumption of simple sexual polarity is based on readings
of the sources which often leave much to be desired,[3] and which derive in

[2] See Ruth Roded (ed.), *Women in Islam and the Middle East: A Reader* (London and New York,
1999), pp. 11, 22: 'From 1928 (corresponding roughly to the high-point of the Western women's
rights movement) until 1946, five scholarly books (and numerous articles) were published by female
classical orientalists . . . Margaret Smith, *Rabi'a the Mystic and Her Fellow Saints in Islam* (Cambridge:
Cambridge University Press, 1928); Ilse Lichtenstädter, *Women in the Aiyam al-'Arab: A Study of
Female Life during Warfare in Pre-Islamic Arabia* (London: Royal Asiatic Society, 1935); Gertrude
Stern, *Marriage in Early Islam* (London: Royal Asiatic Society, 1939); Nabia Abbott, *Aishah: The
Beloved of Muhammad* (Chicago: Arno Press, 1942); *Two Queens of Baghdad: Mother and Wife of
Harun al-Rashid* (Chicago: Chicago University Press, 1946) . . . These studies are serious works of
scholarship that have withstood the test of time, but they are not lacking an explicit ideological
message.'
[3] Roded, *Women in Islam*, pp. 14–15, surveys the effects of recent feminism on scholarship. For a
detailed critique of reductive textual analyses, see Julie Scott Meisami, 'Writing medieval Muslim
women: representations and misrepresentations', in Julia Bray (ed.), *Muslim Horizons: Writing and
Representation in Medieval Islam* (forthcoming). Ghassan Ascha, 'The "Mothers of the Believers".
Stereotypes of the Prophet Muhammad's wives', in Ria Kloppenborg and Wouter J. Hanegraff (eds.),
Female Stereotypes in Religious Traditions (Leiden, 1995), pp. 89–107, cites modern polemical writing
supporting or directed against tradition-based stereotypes but without quoting the primary sources.
Examples of these are translated in Roded, *Women in Islam*, and in her *Women in Islamic Biographical
Collections: From Ibn Sa'd to Who's Who* (Boulder, Co and London, 1994); see also Wilferd Madelung,
The Succession to Muhammad: A Study in the Early Caliphate (Cambridge, 1997), pp. 363–70, 380–7.

the first instance from Abbasid materials, since these are felt to establish a, if not the, normative image (and programme) of Islam.

Polemical approaches often hinge on the question of whether Islam was a break with the past, and whether previous Middle Eastern societies had been more (or less) favourable to women.[4] One angle from which this question can be approached is obviously that of cultural influence: was pre-Islamic Arab culture self-contained, or might Arabs have absorbed traits from surrounding cultures before Islam? To what extent did the cultures of the conquered peoples shape that of the Arab conquerors? It is undeniable that Islamic society underwent major changes in the course of its first two centuries. Are we looking at entirely new processes or, in some cases, at the prolongation of existing ones? Later in this chapter, we will consider the question in retrospect, from internal, Abbasid viewpoints. As regards the evidence in pre-Abbasid sources, which are for a large part external, the issue of whether the inhabitants of Roman Arabia were in fact Arabs is debated,[5] as is the importance of subsequent Byzantine relations with pre-Islamic diaspora Arabs[6] and the volume of cultural exchange between peninsular and diaspora Arabs in the period surrounding the emergence of primitive Islam. Moving inwards from the Arab diaspora of Syria and Mesopotamia and from the border and coastal regions of the Arabian peninsula which are known, to a degree the significance of which is disputed, to have been in contact with the late Roman and Sasanian worlds, inner Arabian society immediately before Islam and during the Prophet's career has been variously reconstructed, always sketchily and speculatively because of the paucity of sources. For post-conquest Islam, as for cultural influences in the immediately preceding period, the only substantial contemporary Arabic record is poetry. Among other things, this yields an idea of the terms in which the new Arab rulers in Syria proclaimed their public titles to authority,[7] which in part may reflect previous Arab dealings with imperial cultures as well as a more direct and complex engagement between

[4] Eleanor Doumato has usefully questioned the assumption that there is a normative 'woman' independent of status and circumstances, and the presupposition of 'an entity called Islam against which change may be measured', in 'Hearing other voices: Christian women and the coming of Islam', *International Journal of Middle East Studies* 23 (1991), pp. 177–99 at p. 178; see also pp. 187–9.

[5] Franz Altheim and Ruth Stiehl (eds.), *Die Araber in der Alten Welt* (Berlin, 1964–69) provide an interdisciplinary source survey of the Arabs of Arabia and the diaspora; see also Robert G. Hoyland, *Arabia and the Arabs from the Bronze Age to the Coming of Islam* (London and New York, 2001), and G. W. Bowersock, *Roman Arabia* (Cambridge, MA, 1983).

[6] Irfan Shahîd, *Byzantium and the Arabs in the Fourth/Fifth/Sixth Century* (Washington, DC, 1984, 1989, 1995), maximises the importance of Arab–Byzantine relations.

[7] See Patricia Crone and Martin Hinds, *God's Caliph: Religious Authority in the First Centuries of Islam* (Cambridge, 1986).

persisting elements of a pre-Islamic Arab world-view and the simultaneous demands laid on it by Islam and by the caliphate's challenge to Byzantine authority.[8] Poetry remains a difficult and underused source; but some attention has been paid to the ways in which the roles that the male poetry of this period assigns to women express, albeit symbolically, the anxieties of Arabs lower down the social scale forced to adjust to new geographical and political horizons.[9] The interplay between imperfectly synthesised cultural allegiances has been noted but not probed in the case of poets such as al-Akhṭal, the Christian Arab panegyrist of the early Umayyads;[10] but what such configurations of old and new loyalties may have meant on any wider social scale in the newly conquered territories remains open to question. On the other hand, the non-literary, archaeological and documentary record, once meagre, is now expanding enough to afford some sense both of continuity in late antique communities living under Muslim rule and – perhaps as importantly, for this has been contested by revisionists chiefly on later textual evidence – of the Muslim Arab incomers' cultural distinctiveness.[11] There are non-Muslim sources too which enable us to to glimpse the responses of the conquered populations to the emergence of Islam, and which a recent survey has made more widely accessible; an earlier survey examined the internal development of non-Muslim communities in Iraq following the conquest.[12] But for the shaping of Muslim communities – a thin and uneven veneer on the conquered populations – what remains the

---

[8] See Nadia Jamil, 'Caliph and Quṭb. Poetry as a source for interpreting the transformation of the Byzantine cross on steps on Umayyad coinage', in Jeremy Johns (ed.), *Bayt al-Maqdis, Jerusalem and Early Islam*, Oxford Studies in Islamic Art 9 (ii) (Oxford, 1999), pp. 11–57.

[9] E.g. A. F. L. Beeston, T. M. Johnstone *et al.* (eds.), *The Cambridge History of Arabic Literature: Arabic Literature to the End of the Umayyad Period* (Cambridge, 1983), pp. 419–27; see also Régis Blachère, 'Regards sur l'"acculturation" des Arabo-Musulmans jusque vers 40/661', *Arabica* 3 (1956), pp. 255–7.

[10] See *The Encyclopaedia of Islam*, new edition (hereafter *EI²*), ed. H. A. R. Gibb *et al.* (Leiden, 1960–2002), vol. 1, p. 331, article 'al-Akhṭal' (R. Blachère). Al Akhṭal (*c.* 20–92 AH/*c.* 640–710 AD) belonged to the north Syrian Monophysite tribe of Taghlib and, through his mother, to the Christian tribe of Iyād; both tribes, famously, refused to convert after the conquests. So too did al-Akhṭal, in spite of his close ties with the early Umayyad caliphs as panegyrist and boon companion: 'In his poetry, certain features prove his zeal for his faith and even indicate a certain ostentation in asserting it . . . His moral standards, however, do not seem to have differed markedly from those of the society in which he lived [they included divorce, drink, and poetic vituperation] . . . his poetry attacked all opponents of the [Umayyad] dynasty.' For Abbasid readings of the anomalies of al-Akhṭal's position, see Hilary Kilpatrick, 'Representations of social intercourse between Muslims and non-Muslims in some medieval *Adab* sources', in Jacques Waardenburg (ed.), *Muslim Perceptions of other Religions: A Historical Survey* (New York and Oxford, 1999), pp. 216–17.

[11] For the latter, see Robert G. Hoyland, 'The content and context of early Arabic inscriptions', *Jerusalem Studies in Arabic and Islam* 21 (1997), pp. 77–102.

[12] Robert G. Hoyland, *Seeing Islam as Others Saw It: A Survey and Evaluation of Christian, Jewish and Zoroastrian Writings on Early Islam* (Princeton, 1997); M. G. Morony, *Iraq after the Muslim Conquest* (Princeton, 1984).

most used source, Islamic historiography, makes its appearance only in the ninth century AD (the third Islamic century). This was a generation after the Abbasid revolution (132/750), and by this time the capital of the Islamic empire had been moved from the former Byzantine territory of Syria to the former Sasanian territory of Iraq, with what are generally accepted as profound changes in Muslim social, political and intellectual culture alike.

What any previous levels of casual or deliberate cultural exchange between the Arab incomers and the local populations may have added up to is much debated.[13] In this period, however – the period when caliphs were prepared to take lessons in statecraft from bureaucrats quoting what they claimed to be age-old Persian political wisdom; the period also of the scholarly recovery of elements of Greek and late antique thought under high political patronage – Islamic thought itself achieved a sophistication comparable to that of the conquered peoples and became an intellectual magnet. Having gained cultural as well as political supremacy, Abbasid Muslims were reluctant to acknowledge that any sort of historical learning process could have been at work; and if Abbasid historiography is taken as the main source for understanding what went before, then all pre-Abbasid transitions and transformations, whether in the Arabian, the post-Byzantine or the post-Sasanian domain, whether political or social, and including those in the conception of gender and roles of men and women, can only – according to the most pessimistic view – be perceived through an Islamised, triumphalist Abbasid optic. It is true that Abbasid Muslims were little concerned with the conquered peoples either as such or as converts, but rather with the manifest destiny of Muslims and Islam, and that they treated Islam normatively[14] and Muslims as if they had always been a virtual majority in the conquered territories, which was far from

---

[13] Louise Marlow, *Hierarchy and Egalitarianism in Islamic Thought* (Cambridge, 1997), discusses Syrian and Egyptian Christianity and how they may have 'stimulated developments that in some ways anticipated the collision between hierarchical and egalitarian sentiments that would accompany the rise of Islam' (pp. 44–5). The general view is that such intellectual continuity with late antiquity as there may have been in post-conquest Alexandria and Damascus is of less direct significance than the rediscovery of Greek thought which took place later in Iraq (pp. 46–7).

[14] Differences within the early Muslim community are usually presented in terms of sectarianism. However, this is not the only perspective afforded by the sources. On the beginnings of socio-political change within early Muslim Arab society brought about by inter-tribal marriages (a subject that has still hardly been researched), see Blachère, 'Regards', pp. 247–65 and cf. note 50 below. On early Arab settlements and the social patterns arising out of them, some detailed case studies are now available, e.g. Peter von Sivers, 'Taxes and trade in the 'Abbāsid Thughūr, 750–962/133–352', *JESHO* 25 (1982), pp. 71–111, and Paul M. Cobb, 'Scholars and society in early Islamic Ayla', *JESHO* 38 (1995), pp. 417–28. On aristocratic Arab land-holding in Iraq, including that by women, see note 63 below.

being the case even in their own time.[15] By this time, however, at least in the urban centres, conversion was beginning to have a noticeable impact, and there is a tension between the ideas of 'Arab' and 'Muslim'. Arabs had been the primary and privileged bearers of Islam, but also the bearers of pre- and non-Islamic values that were felt to be equally essential to the conquerors' identity. Now that Arabs no longer formed the majority of Muslims, ways had to be found of transmuting Arab particularism into more generally useful concepts of how the Arab heritage underwrote Islam. 'Arabness' in the sense of an automatic title to privilege and its progressive marginalisation as an operative social reality is one of the measures of change implicit in the sources discussed below.

A good example of the extent to which transition could be telescoped and digested by a normative Abbasid view of earlier social processes is the following extract from an entry in the 'History of Baghdad' (*Ta'rīkh Baghdād*) of al-Khaṭīb al-Baghdādī,[16] which, despite its name, is not a chronological study of the Abbasid capital, but essentially a biographical dictionary of all the noteworthy Muslims known to have been in some way connected with it. For all its lack of chronological continuity, or perhaps because of it, its compiler's method of information-gathering sometimes allows elements of individual historical perspective to persist within the common formats he applies to the entries. Thus our chosen entry[17] was put together in the eleventh century AD from tenth-century informants who claim to be transmitting family history in an unbroken chain, and refers to a sequence of events framed by approximate dates from early in the eighth century, when the Umayyads regained control of Iraq after a major revolt, to the beginning of the 750s, when the first Abbasid caliph was establishing his hold on the region. What is noteworthy about it is the way in which it handles the ideas of 'Arab' and 'Muslim', and the fact that 'Arab' here means an urbanised civilian rather than a tribal warrior. The subject of the biography, Ḥassān ibn Sinān, was a land-owner and a member of an Arab tribe, Tanūkh, which had settled in Sasanian Iraq long before Islam and which was Christian. The single most important

---

[15] The rate and volume of early conversion remain highly speculative; A. N. Poliak, 'L'arabisation de l'Orient sémitique', *Revue des Etudes Islamiques* 12 (1938), pp. 1–34, still provides a basic framework. For detailed case studies, see Milka Levy-Reuben, 'New evidence relating to the process of Islamization in Palestine in the early Muslim period – the case of Samaria', *JESHO* 43 (2000), pp. 257–76, which uses a non-Muslim source and shows, for the single decade 820–830, how different the factors leading communities to convert could be.

[16] For the author, or more accurately compiler, see Julie Scott Meisami and Paul Starkey (eds.), *Encyclopedia of Arabic Literature* (London, 1998), vol. II, pp. 438–9, article 'Al-Khaṭīb al-Baghdādī (393–463/1002–1071)' (W. Al-Qāḍī).

[17] Which is anomalous, since its subject was not connected with Baghdad, though his son, his grandson and most of his descendants were.

fact in Ḥassān's life is that he converted to Islam, though quite late in life, at an uncertain date and in unclear circumstances. The speaker reporting his biography – typically, the entry is written as if it reproduced a series of oral communications verbatim – is a respected Muslim scholar and a descendant of Ḥassān. Looking back at the patriarch of a family which had given five generations of service to Islam, as judges and civil servants within the Abbasid state apparatus and as religious and literary scholars outside it, he does not suppress the possibility that his ancestor's conversion might have owed something to expediency, but stresses that its sincerity was the cause of the family's subsequent successes. Unusually, he emphasises Ḥassān's non-Muslim antecedents, and even mentions that his daughter was a recusant. This sort of detail is rare enough for the history of Muslim conversion to have remained extremely speculative; and how conversion affected women in the conquered territories is almost totally obscure.

> Our ancestor Ḥassān ibn Sinān . . . was born a Christian, in [the city/region of] al-Anbār in the year 60 of the Hijra [679 AD]. Christianity had been his faith and that of his fathers before him; but he converted and became a good Muslim. At the time of his conversion he had a daughter of marriageable age who remained a Christian, and when she died, she willed all her property to the convent of Tanūkh in al-Anbār. Ḥassān could speak, read and write Arabic, and also Persian and Syriac. He was born under the Umayyads but lived on into Abbasid times, and when [the first Abbasid caliph] al-Saffāḥ made Rabī'a al-Ra'ī *qāḍī* of al-Anbār, which was his capital at that time, and he was brought some documents written in Persian that he could not read, he asked for some pious and trustworthy man who would be able to do so. He was told of Ḥassān ibn Sinān, and had him fetched. Thereafter Ḥassān read his Persian documents, and once he had got to know him and found him to be of good morals, he made him his secretary (*kātib*), putting him in charge of all his business. Previous to this [*in fact some forty years earlier*], Ḥassān had seen Anas ibn Mālik, the servant of the Prophet – may God bless him and keep him – and transmitted [a tradition (*ḥadīth*)] from him. It is not known whether he met any other Companions of the Prophet. Our ancestor Ḥassān died at the age of a hundred and twenty [lunar years, i.e. in 796 AD].[18]

It would be tempting to dwell on the glimpse of family tension afforded by the unnamed daughter's refusal to convert, on her presumably unmarried state at her death, on her command of her own property, and on the varied evidence this short passage offers of how un-Islamised and ethnically

---

[18] Al-Khaṭīb al-Baghdādī, *Ta'rīkh Baghdād aw Madīnat al-Salām* (Cairo, 1931; repr. Beirut, 1968), vol. VIII, pp. 258–60. The family history of Ḥassān ibn Sinān is discussed fully in my forthcoming study of the family.

and linguistically heterogeneous this part of Iraq remained even in the early 750s – over a century after the Muslim conquest – when al-Saffāḥ chose it as his capital. But because details as suggestive as these are comparatively rare (and laborious to track down in the voluminous Arabic sources), a framework for critical discussion is largely lacking.[19] Clearly, though, the raw materials of Ḥassān's life story have been selected and structured according to Abbasid codes of value. In this case, a code of Muslim piety[20] is uppermost – elsewhere in the biographical entry Ḥassān's longevity is directly attributed to his having acquired *baraka* thanks to his personal contact with 'someone who had seen [the Prophet]';[21] but we can also discern the template of a typical success story of the secretarial (*kātib*) class, those state administrators who, from father to son, served the Abbasids as they had served their Umayyad and pre-Muslim predecessors irrespective of origin or religion. The joint emphasis is on continuity: continuity of place and status. Ḥassān, as preceding versions of his life story made clear, had been prominent in his local community when a Christian; and as an Arab, by becoming a Muslim, he retained and added to his advantages without having to go through the intermediate stage of clientship as did non-Arabs.[22] Continuity of cultural tradition seems to be equally important: Ḥassān assimilated not only to Islam but also to a pre-Islamic service ethic, both of which were to be hallmarks of his family for generations to come. The notion of transformation is also adumbrated elsewhere in the entry: in his descendants, Ḥassān's literacy and skills in the local languages instead took the form of Muslim scholarship and skill in Arabic language and literature; and whereas he had been only *kātib* to a judge, they became distinguished judges and civil servants in their own right. The Christian daughter seems

[19] For the communal development of Christians and Jews in Iraq under the Sasanians and after the Muslim conquest and some aspects of their interactions with Muslims, see M. G. Morony, 'Religious communities in late Sasanian and early Muslim Iraq', *JESHO* 17 (1974), pp. 113–35, and Morony, *Iraq after the Muslim Conquest*.

[20] Marshall G. S. Hodgson used the term 'piety-minded' of those who 'worked out what we may call the "Sharīʿah-minded" programme for private and public living . . . They exercised a wide sway . . . in Muslim speculative and theological thought [and] effective – but never decisive – pressure in the realms of public order and government, and controlled the theoretical development of Muslim law', *The Venture of Islam: Conscience and History in a World Civilization*, vol. 1: *The Classical Age of Islam* (Chicago and London, 1974), p. 238; i.e. their place in the structure of authority was fluid, self-made and self-defining. I shall use the term 'pious' to express this complex.

[21] As two of his descendants attest: '[By virtue of this encounter between my grandfather and a Companion of the Prophet] I am included in the blessing of the Prophet, may God bless him and keep him, which he gave when he said: "Blessed is he who has seen me, and he who has seen one who has seen me, and he who has seen one who has seen one who has seen me . . ."'; "It was because of the *baraka* of the blessing that Anas gave to Ḥassān that he lived to be a hundred and twenty years old, and that among his issue were many jurisprudents, judges, men who held high positions (*ru'asā*), righteous men (*ṣulaḥā*), *kātib*s and ascetics"', al-Khaṭīb al-Baghdādī, *Ta'rīkh Baghdād*, pp. 258–60.

[22] On clientship and conversion, see *EI²*, vol. VI (1991), pp. 874–82, article 'Mawlā' (P. Crone).

to play a dual, and ambivalent role: she serves both as a moral foil to her exemplary father, and as a reminder, through her bequest to the convent of Tanūkh, of her family's wealth and standing (they maintained an influential presence in al-Anbār well into the next centuries as well as becoming prominent residents of Baghdad).[23]

This brief passage is homogenised by a mature Muslim outlook; nevertheless, by retaining the archaeological nuggets of the daughter's non-conversion and Ḥassān's linguistic versatility, it also suggests the persistence of a certain plurality of values. This sort of latent plurality is, however, something that has yet to be widely exploited as an index of change, or of the culture's own acknowledgement of change.[24] One reason for this is that different types of Abbasid discourse – for example, historical, legal or literary – are often treated as unconnected and lacking a common frame of reference (despite the fact that they are frequently products of the same milieu, family or even author).[25] As a result, neighbouring discourses may be ignored in the interpretation of a source belonging to a given genre, and too much credence given to the perspective of a single genre. A related factor is that women, and until recently even families, have been considered so poorly visible in the sources for our period that their importance to social change (or social resistance) has been played down.[26] Despite their much greater prominence in biographical sources from around the thirteenth century onwards and in documentary sources from the Mamluk and Ottoman

---

[23] One can only speculate what the effect of the landlord's conversion would have been on his peasants; see *ibid.*, p. 879: 'In the Umayyad period . . . no villager converted without leaving his village and thus also such land as he might possess . . . because the attraction of conversion lay in its promise of access to the ranks of the conquerors: converting without joining these ranks would have been pointless and, locally, extremely unpleasant.' But as Kilpatrick notes, 'Some *adab* [literary] texts reflect the fact that [at other social levels] religious differences could exist within families without conversion or separation ensuing', 'Representations', p. 216; this was still true in the vizieral family of the Banū al-Jarrāḥ at the end of the third/ninth century, see Harold Bowen, *The Life and Times of ʿAlī ibn ʿĪsà, 'The Good Vizier'* (Cambridge, 1928), pp. 36–7.

[24] Chase F. Robinson, *Empire and Elites after the Muslim Conquest: The Transformation of Northern Mesopotamia* (Cambridge, 2000), combines Syriac and Arabic sources and provincial and metropolitan viewpoints in an attempt to interpret expressions of the response to change.

[25] Al-Khaṭīb al-Baghdādī and his informant for the lives of Ḥassān ibn Sinān and his descendants, who was a judge by profession, are well-known cases in point: both were men of letters and transmitters of historico-biographical materials as well as being learned in the religious sciences, as was the informant's father, who was one of the sources which will be cited here, see notes 44, 45, 49, 57, 71, 72, 75, 76.

[26] Thus R. Stephen Humphreys, *Islamic History: A Framework for Inquiry*, revised edn (London and New York; Princeton, 1991), which is intended as 'a comprehensive (though far from exhaustive) survey of . . . reference tools and sources [and an overview of] research problem[s]' (p. x), does not list one single work directly concerned with the Muslim family. A basic bibliography for the early periods is provided in A. L. Udovitch, 'Scenes from eleventh-century family life: cousins and partners – Nahray ben Nissim and Israel ben Natan', in C. E. Bosworth *et al.* (eds.), *Essays in Honor of Bernard Lewis: The Islamic World, from Classical to Modern Times* (Princeton, NJ, 1989).

periods, and the greater attention that both families and women of these
later periods are now receiving,[27] women – though no longer families – still
tend to be seen as objects, rather than as agents, of social development.[28]
To some extent, this reflects the outlook of the sources; but not entirely.

II

While Abbasid historical sources in fact pay great attention to family –
though they do not always present the information in convenient formats –
the literary sources are attentive both to women and to family,[29] and give
considerable prominence to gender roles. What I mean by 'literature' should
be briefly defined. Abbasid literature consists broadly of two components:
poetry, which has a primarily symbolic function; and story-telling, which
pretends to report reality, and therefore almost always passes itself off as
history and adopts the formats of historiography. A convenient distinction
between Abbasid history and story-telling would be to say that story-telling
foregrounds the individual, and looks for meaning in experiences that affect
the individual rather than in the events which have shaped the whole
Muslim community, as does historiography, or what modern historians
recognise as historiography. This fragile distinction was never formulated
or rigidly observed by the Abbasids, and masks a multitude of gradations,
but is useful for present purposes. For reasons of moral convenience, many
medieval theorists categorise poetry as a form of make-believe; but it is
often appropriated by story-telling and given a historiographical narrative
setting which supplies a social context and interprets the poetry itself as
autobiography. Poetry is much concerned with what 'straight' Abbasid
histories tend to dismiss as marginal or immoral gender roles. The poetry-
cum-story-telling formula, however, treats them not only as normative and
ethically important but as historically significant.

Combining these elements, one of the most frequent formats in Abbasid
literature is that of the biography which tells the story of a career. This
may be structured around emotional episodes (often illustrated by poetry),
but is shaped overall by the notion of professional success or failure; and

[27] See Ruth Roded, 'Mainstreaming Middle East gender research: promise or pitfall?', *Middle East
Studies Association Bulletin* 35 (1) (2001), pp. 15–23, whose bibliography illustrates the much greater
volume of work that exists on the late medieval to early modern Middle East in the areas of the
economic, political and ideological analysis of gender roles.

[28] The recognition of the family as a social force owes much to Richard W. Bulliet, *The Patricians of
Nishapur: A Study in Medieval Islamic Social History* (Cambridge, MA, 1972).

[29] The pioneering studies of family in literary sources are those published in the 1970s by J. E. Bencheikh,
in which he traces the relationships between political patronage and literary dynasties.

opportunities for success are shown as being conditioned, in their turn, either by factors (such as talent) which override the givens of the individual's social situation, or, conversely, by social inheritance: family support or the lack of it, an individual's gender and the spectrum of roles available to each sex, and his or her discretion in observing appropriate demeanours or boldness in overstepping them. In other words, there is an implicit awareness of how social rules and roles are exploited or stretched.

This kind of implicit sociological analysis can be set alongside that found in sources like the 'History of Baghdad', where, despite its format, the emphasis is not so much on the individual subjects of biographies as on the professional and family networks to which the subjects belong. Each is defined primarily in terms of his (occasionally her) teachers and pupils and often family, and cross-reference between entries allows a reader to trace how families fare over the generations and how communities and micro-communities of men of learning and religion establish an identity. Our major literary source, the 'Book of Songs' (*Kitāb al-Aghānī*) of Abū al-Faraj al-Iṣfahānī, has some structural features which are similar and can be similarly exploited.[30] Although the individual entries are not arranged chronologically, the compiler pays great attention to historical context, and cross-reference between entries enables the changes in the themes and data characteristic of successive periods to be traced.[31]

The 'History of Baghdad' is, of course, concerned solely with Baghdad and its hinterland. The 'Book of Songs' is a major source for pre-Islamic and early Islamic Arabia and Umayyad Syria, and thereafter for the courts of the Abbasid caliphs up to a generation or so before the compiler's own time (he settled in Baghdad and had had family connections with the court). The fact that the caliphal court looms large contributes an important factor to the analysis: Abū al-Faraj al-Iṣfahānī is able to trace the opportunities for self-advancement that could be seized by talented individuals, whether or not they could claim an Arab lineage, thanks to the unravelling, under the Abbasids, of the Arab exclusivity which had characterised Umayyad politics and society. In parallel, sources such as the 'History of Baghdad' show families pursuing a similar path and taking advantage of an expansion of

---

[30] For the author/compiler, see *Encyclopedia of Arabic Literature*, vol. I, pp. 30–2, article 'Abū al-Faraj al-Iṣbahānī (284–*c*.363/897–*c*.972)' (H. Kilpatrick).

[31] All modern *Aghānī* studies are indebted to Hilary Kilpatrick; see now her *Making the Great Book of Songs: Compilation and the Author's Craft in Abū l-Faraj al-Isbahānī's Kitāb al-aghānī* (London and New York, 2003). Of her many articles, the following provides a brief guide to how the work's biographical content is structured and motivated: 'Modernity in a classical Arabic *Adab* work, the *Kitāb al-Aghānī*', in J. R. Smart (ed.), *Tradition and Modernity in Arabic Language and Literature* (Richmond, Surrey, 1996), pp. 242–56.

the public and private professions to gain a place in Muslim society, indeed
to become its architects – in fact, this is how al-Khaṭīb al-Baghdādī sees
Baghdad's role. Taken in conjunction with the historical sources, the 'Book
of Songs' and other literary sources with a wider social range also highlight fundamental configurations which run through the whole of urban
Abbasid society from the political apex downwards: structures of political
absolutism which are opposed by growing communitarian consciousness
and self-confidence; structures of legalistic social regulation which are interwoven with an increased awareness of the value of the self derived in large
part from the civility of court culture. Last but not least, the literary sources
more than any others highlight the importance of domestic, that is, non-
military, slavery in shaping the *mores* of Abbasid society,[32] and of female
slavery in reshaping the Abbasid family.

Because they are so largely a product of Abbasid Baghdad, these sources
should not be taken as representing a general pattern.[33] They do, though,
supply grounds for arguing that a family and gender-inclusive perspective
is, or should be, central to interpreting metropolitan Abbasid society; and
if we bear their local stamp in mind, we will be better placed to get specific
information out of the stereotypes they offer.

III

Abbasid Muslims conceived personal and legal status – basically a matter
of gender and of degrees of personal freedom and competence, particularly
with regard to property – pluralistically and relativistically. Legal theory, still
developing at this time, recognised varying positions on the scale between
free male and free female and between freedom and slavehood.[34] The

---

[32] For military slaves and their role in the early Abbasid state, see Patricia Crone, *Slaves on Horses: The Evolution of the Islamic Polity* (Cambridge, 1980). It is military slavery that has attracted the most attention in modern scholarship.

[33] For conditions in different regions, the picture is as patchy and controversial as it is for the Abbasid heartlands, not least in the case of Spain/al-Andalus, where modern scholarship has been divided over the question of whether the Muslim incomers assimilated to Hispanic, 'western' patterns of kinship or imposed 'oriental' patterns of gender relations on the Hispanic population. An authoritative survey is Pierre Guichard, 'The social history of Muslim Spain from the conquest to the end of the Almohad régime (early 2nd/8th–early 7th/13th centuries', in Salma Khadra Jayyusi (ed.), *The Legacy of Muslim Spain* (Leiden, 1992), vol. II, pp. 679–708. On the other side of the Islamic world, in the highlands of Daylam by the Caspian, where Islam had penetrated little and previous social structures had survived and contributed to the play of political forces, 'Marriage links were an important way of consolidating alliances and links through the female line were more important than in much of Islamic society': Hugh Kennedy, *The Prophet and The age of the Caliphates: The Islamic Near East from the Sixth to the Eleventh Century* (London and New York, 1986), p. 213.

[34] Bernard Lewis, *Race and Slavery in the Middle East: A Historical Enquiry* (New York and Oxford, 1990), pp. 3–11, 13–15 and notes on pp. 103–9, gives a brief comparative survey of previous conditions

positions of free women and of slaves, male or female, are analogous in that both vary according to circumstance, whereas the legal status of the free Muslim male is invariable. Thus slaves might pass through several changes or combinations of status in the course of a lifetime. Male slaves in particular might purchase their freedom in stages, as in earlier Mediterranean societies, and enjoy some of the competence and authority of a free person either in conducting their own business or as agents for their owners.[35] A female slave might go from being at the opposite end of the scale to a free Muslim woman – that is, sexually available without criminality and without a legal right to recompense for her services – to occupying a similar position to that of a free Muslim wife if she bore her master a child which he acknowledged. (The technical term for such a woman is *umm (al-)walad*. The fact that there is some fuzziness in the disagreements of the early schools of law over the details of the status of slave 'mothers of children' may indicate that here the jurists were tackling a fluid social reality rather than constructing an ideal.)[36]

Both women and slaves are envisaged legally as a combination of financial asset and liability. What distinguishes a free woman in law from a slave is that she is considered exclusively in the context of family. However, the family, in law, is an inherently unstable entity, easily dissolved by divorce and reduced to a matter of simple paternity and rights to maintenance and inheritance. Here it is highly probable that the law frequently parted company with reality. Under the Umayyads, an exclusive, tribal conception of family seems to have persisted among the great Arab aristocrats, but even the law faintly recognises that exclusivity was not always maintained, a recognition which must cover a multitude of different social realities.[37] Under the Abbasids, a more broadly based type of family begins to emerge as the vehicle through which a steadily growing and diversifying body of non-aristocrats, and indeed non-Arabs, establish their participation in

---

of slavery in the conquered territories and of legal conditions of enslavement, sources of supply, legal and personal status, and types of slave employment in medieval Islam.

[35] Although outside our timeframe, an outstanding instance is the great historian of Abbasid men of letters, Yāqūt (575–626/1179–1229). Born a Byzantine Christian and taken captive as a child, he worked in partnership with his master, a Baghdad merchant, until freed at the age of about twenty, when he went into business on his own account as a copyist-bookseller and author.

[36] See *EI*[2], vol. x, pp. 857–9, article 'Umm al-walad' (J. Schacht); vol. i, pp. 24–34, article ''Abd' (R. Brunschvig); Reuben Levy, *The Social Structure of Islam*, being the second edition of the *Sociology of Islam* (Cambridge, 1957), pp. 79, 111–14; Joseph R. Strayer (ed.), *Dictionary of the Middle Ages* (New York, 1982–89), vol. iii, pp. 527–9, article 'Concubinage, Islamic' (S. E. Marmon); S. D. Goitein, *A Mediterranean Society: The Jewish Communities of the Arab World as Portrayed in the Documents of the Cairo Geniza*, vol. i: *Economic Foundations* (Berkeley, 1967): 'Slaves and slave girls'.

[37] See Marlow, *Hierarchy and Egalitarianism*, pp. 32–4, Blachère, 'Regards' and Crone, 'Mawlā', p. 879.

public life. These families often develop into dynasties, and seem to owe at least some of their long-term stability to their ability to make slaves 'part of the family', a dimension not reflected in legal theory. In some ways, the absorption of slaves into the family parallels the way in which non-Arab converts had previously integrated themselves into Islamic society by becoming clients of an Arab patron; but the new process is more intimate, and more immediately cohesive, like the process by which converts had already begun to assimilate by marriage, though with obvious structural differences in so far as most (though not all) slaves lacked the baggage of family. Notorious examples of female slaves who brought family with them and insinuated them into key positions by virtue of their own status as concubines are documented for the Abbasid caliphal family; for example, al-Khayzurān, concubine of al-Mahdī, together with her sister Salsal, who was concubine to al-Mahdī's half-brother, virtually colonised the caliphal family during the last decades of the second/eighth century. Al-Mahdī passed over his sons by his wife in favour of al-Khayzurān's children, the future caliphs Mūsā al-Hādī and Hārūn al-Rashīd; al-Khayzurān also bore his favourite daughter. Salsal's daughter Zubayda married al-Rashīd and bore his heir al-Amīn, while two daughters of Giṭrīf, the brother of al-Khayzurān and Salsal, married al-Hādī and al-Rashīd respectively.[38] We do not know how widely this sort of pattern occurred in other families.

As far as we can tell from our sources, it was only under the Abbasids that slavery began to be perceived as a social force, although huge numbers of captives are estimated to have been taken during the Muslim conquests. Abbasid slaves were conspicuous emblems of both change and assimilation. In contrast to the previous dynasty, all but three of the Abbasid caliphs were born of foreign slave mothers and therefore lacked a maternal lineage, something which became common in well-to-do sections of society. Lower down the scale, as domestics, slaves, Islamised from birth or infancy and lacking any pedigree or identity but that of Islam and their host family, swelled the Muslim community at all levels from the small urban household upwards. This may have contributed to the feeling of confessional homogeneity and numerical ascendancy mentioned earlier.

Besides bulking out the Muslim community, the presence of slaves now began visibly to alter the structure of family and personal relations. In the domestic or small-scale business context, slaves could contribute to the

---

[38] Abbott, *Two Queens of Baghdad*, pp. 25, 29–30, 32–3. On Giṭrīf's political career, cf. *ibid.*, pp. 31, 127. Al-Khayzurān's family apparently came from Yemen but may have been Berbers, which would explain their servile status.

gaining and conserving of family wealth and to the sense of family solidarity. Islamic inheritance law divides the wealth of blood relatives according to fixed portions, instead of concentrating it; slavery to some extent counter-balanced this situation. A skilled male slave might not only increase the value of his owner's business but also accumulate wealth of his own, in which case his owner's family became his heirs when he died. He on the other hand had no claim on his owner's estate. Female domestic slaves may have been less directly profitable;[39] but a female slave who gave birth to her master's children usually became an inalienable part of his household – a position at least as secure as that of a free wife, who could be divorced – and her children were heirs. (Their potential to contribute to the family's human wealth may be guessed at from the outstanding abilities of many of the Abbasid princes born to slave mothers.) As against this, unlike a free co-wife, she herself was not a statutory heir and posed no threat to the inheritance and other rights of the mistress of the household.

Both kinds of slavery enabled families to reinforce or diversify their strengths without forming potentially compromising alliances, as a low-cost, low-risk alternative or complement to marriage and business partner-ships,[40] though in the ruling family there are prominent instances of slave alliances carrying as much commitment and risk as free marriages. Shaghab, the Greek (former) slave mother[41] of al-Muqtadir (r. 295–320/908–932), who was put on the throne at the age of thirteen and was notoriously under his mother's thumb, had a brother, Gharīb, who used his influence to help depose one vizier, Ibn al-Furāt, and to support another, 'Alī ibn 'Īsā, and took part in high councils of state.[42] His son, Hārūn ibn Gharīb, was a soldier and built on his father's position in the caliphal family; at one point, he commanded the caliphal army, briefly becoming 'all-powerful'. After al-Muqtadir's murder, al-Qāhir, his half-brother, gave 'the son of the Maternal Uncle' a governorship. He died while marching against his great-nephew, al-Muqtadir's son and al-Qāhir's successor, al-Rāḍī: 'he reckoned that his relationship entitled him once more to a place at court. Ar-Rádhí,

---

[39] Though not necessarily so. We know little about the organisation of manufacturing activities, as opposed to trade (in which male slaves are reasonably visible); but by far the most important of these, textile production in its various forms and stages, is likely to have been domestically based to some extent and to have involved the participation of household slaves. For women and textile production, see Jean-Claude Garcin *et al.*, *Etats, sociétés et cultures du monde muslman médiéval Xe–XVe siècle* (Paris, 1995–2000), vol. II, p. 213.

[40] See Strayer (ed.), *Dictionary of the Middle Ages*, vol. III, pp. 527–9, and *ibid.*, vol. XI, pp. 330–3, article 'Slavery, Islamic world' (Shaun E. Marmon).

[41] Concubine mothers became free at their master's death.

[42] Bowen, '*The Good Vizier*', pp. 106, 115, 147–8. On Shaghab, see also Nadia Maria El Cheikh, chapter 8 below.

however, had borne a grudge against the Lady his grandmother [Shaghab] that embraced her relations as well'; these had included a sister at court.[43]

IV

The middling to wealthy Abbasid household, which usually included a proportion of slaves who were functionally part of the family or family business and the offspring of slaves who were an integral part of it, was clearly a socioeconomic entity of some complexity. We do not know, partly because no one has asked, how the development of this type of mixed-status family came about and gained acceptance. Whatever its early history, it achieved its full potential only in the commercial, property-owning and career-orientated conditions of Abbasid urban life. For all its advantages, the mixed-status Abbasid family was probably far from being a uniformly efficient machine in economic terms. The higher up the social scale a family was, the more expensive and less profitable the slave component would be. In rich and powerful families, there would be a contingent of domestic slaves who were expected to contribute chiefly, perhaps solely, to the family's prestige rather than to its earning power, by being objects of ostentatious expenditure, displaying the family's wealth in their numbers and dress.

The relationship between cost and real or anticipated gain is highly problematic throughout Abbasid society, in which gestures of deliberate extravagance figure largely, in both literary sources and chronicles, as a way of trying to buy status and loyalty. What lies behind the clichés in terms of rational strategies is problematic. For the questions which concern us, the main analysts of the risks and perceived gains from such gestures are the literary sources. Thus, at the higher end of the Abbasid social scale, as badges of conspicuous consumption, female slaves (*jāriya*, pl. *jawārī*) occupied a unique position. The hired female entertainer – the heroine, or sometimes villain, of countless romantic stories, who is nearly always a slave or an ex-slave (unlike her male counterpart) – was a notorious drain on wealth, and a source of instability, perhaps even a threat to family identity, in so far as she distracted young men from marriage. This is the

---

[43] Bowen, 'The Good Vizier', pp. 180–1, 241–3, 280–2, 309, 311, 313–15, 345–6. On Gharīb and his daughters, see also El Cheikh, chapter 8 below, pp. 149 and 156. A maternal link between the military and the caliphate was not a new phenomenon. The important Turkish commander, Mūsā ibn Bughā, who may have been implicated in the murder of the caliph al-Mutawakkil in 247/861, was the son of al-Mutawakkil's maternal aunt. He was the cousin of al-Mu'tamid, the son who succeeded al-Mutawakkil in 256/870, and became the right-hand man of the effective ruler, the new caliph's brother, al-Muwaffaq; see Hugh Kennedy, *The Armies of the Caliphs: Military and Society in the Early Islamic State* (London and New York, 2001), pp. 149 and 164 n. 6.

side of her which is seen in Abbasid satirical literature (where her role as a skilled earner, with functional parallels to that of male slaves who took part in business, is also acknowledged).[44] But in romantic literature, the luxury female slave plays a more complex role which is cultural, ethical even, rather than economic. She is not a courtesan but a soul-mate, who educates her lover in monogamous love. At the same time, she may train him in the arts, making him a fit companion for princes and eligible for patronage and advancement. In this fictional context, the normal relations between slave and free are turned upside down: the master (in one of the most hackneyed themes of Abbasid literature) is dominated by the slave; overcoming the legal obstacles, the pair may even marry, and in their union, aristocratic and bourgeois values are symbolically fused.[45]

Arguably, this literary *topos* is less a fantasy than a gloss applied to the commercialisation of gender relations and the vulgarisation of aristocratic culture. The luxury female slave is a cultural intermediary. She brings an accessible, feminised (and therefore purchasable) form of court culture to the urban household,[46] as part of a process of social levelling-up in which leisure and pleasure have become ceremonialised, providing a common language and protocol for all ranks of an expanding polite society.[47] But, as Abbasid literary sources recognise, this role is paradoxical, and marks a

---

[44] See A. F. L. Beeston (ed. and trans.), *Risālat al-qiyān: The Epistle on Singing-Girls of Jāḥiz* (Warminster, 1980). Al-Jāḥiz (*c.* 160–255/776–868), with his modest background and powerful court connections, was a uniquely acute and well-placed observer of society. He was also a leading participant in a sophisticated debate on cultural and intellectual identity, and his realism should not be mistaken for naive reportage. Both men and women dealt in female slaves; for women of good family, training them for resale seems to have been a long-term home-based investment. For a fictional example, see al-Muḥassin ibn ʿAlī al-Tanūkhī (327–384/939–994), *al-Faraj baʿd al-shidda*, ed. ʿA. al-Shāljī (Beirut, 1398/1978), vol. IV, pp. 331–8; for examples in biographical sources, see Roded, *Women in Islamic Biographical Collections*, p. 126. Shaghab, the mother of al-Muqtadir, may be a case in point. Before becoming the concubine of al-Muʿtaḍid, she had belonged to a woman called Umm Qāsim, daughter of Muḥammad ibn ʿAbdallāh [ibn Ṭāhir], a member of one of the most powerful families in Baghdad; see Franz Rosenthal (trans.), *The History of al-Tabarī*, vol. xxxviii: *The Return of the Caliphate to Baghdad* (Albany, NY, 1985), p. 25 n. 139. For vignettes of the careers of women singers, see Jacques Berque (trans.), *Musiques sur le fleuve: les plus belles pages du Kitâb al-Aghâni* (Paris, 1995), pp. 178–97.

[45] See Julia Ashtiany Bray, 'Isnāds and models of heroes: Abū Zubayd al-Ṭāʾī, Tanūkhī's sundered lovers and Abū al-ʿAnbas al-Ṣaymarī', *Arabic and Middle Eastern Literatures* I (1998), pp. 12–15, and cf. Thomas Bauer, *Liebe und Liebesdichtung in der arabischen Welt des 9. und 10. Jahrhunderts* (Wiesbaden, 1998).

[46] Male courtiers and entertainers were free men. For our period, there is little evidence of male slaves being trained to court standards but available for hire or purchase by urban customers, as were the most sought-after female slaves; and in literature, the male (boy) slave lovers of male masters do not play the role of educators. On romantic love of women as a courtly reality and its dissemination, cf. Julie Scott Meisami, 'Masʿūdī on love and the fall of the Barmakids', *Journal of the Royal Asiatic Society* (1989), p. 265.

[47] Cf. Ashtiany Bray, 'Isnāds', pp. 14–15, and her 'Third and fourth century bleeding poetry', *Arabic and Middle Eastern Literatures* 2 (1999), pp. 75–92.

profound change in cultural self-perception. As an artist, the female entertainer is a mouthpiece of Arabic culture, for she sings and even composes
Arabic poetry; but she is a non-Arab. Her lack of memory of her own
cultural past[48] and the fact that she is a standardised commercial article,
sexually available and unmarriageable, obviously make her a symbol of her
customers' supremacy; yet unlike a wife, she has to be courted as well as
paid for, and since free women of good family are invisible on the wider
social scene, she is the only available female object of romantic attachment:
a necessary emotional ideal, and an outlet for male individualism.

Literary convention asserts that individualism can find fulfilment only
if the normal pattern of male–female authority is altered so that power and
legal entitlement do not become the sole guides to conduct. Examples given
above suggest that, not only in romance, but also in legal discourse and in
real life, individualism could be stabilised by the elasticity of the law, and the
female slave and her offspring integrated into the family. Within the realm
of literary imaginings, some stories dwell particularly on the male fantasy
of being able to combine emotional self-fulfilment with social acceptance
and success in a career.[49] Others mark the change from what was, or what
the Abbasids believed to be, the sharper polarities of earlier, Arab society
by producing, in contrast to the urban Abbasid slave-heroine, two types of
female romantic heroine who could exist only in the past and in a purely
Arab, tribal context: the Umayyad bedouin heroine, forbidden to marry her
suitor and forever chaste and unattainable, and the aristocratic Umayyad
virago, who goes unveiled, taunts her admirers, and marries and divorces
her way through the ranks of the nobility at her own pleasure.[50]

In the Abbasid analysis – or at any rate, the romantic literary analysis –
it is the post-Umayyad detribalisation of society, and of masculinity and
femininity, as much as Islamisation, that has brought about a fundamental
change in male needs and demeanours. From the same literary viewpoint,
before this change took place, Arab male and female lives both had a
similar outline, dictated by lineage and character. In those more heroic
times, romantic fulfilment had nothing to do with finding one's feet on the

[48] The writings of Yāqūt (see note 35) are an example of such assimilation; they show no consciousness
of non-Muslim cultural memory. However, the early Abbasid poetry written by (free, male) poets
of mixed origin often does show cultural memory, even cultural aggression.

[49] See al-Tanūkhī, *Faraj*, chapter 14, where the love-and-success nexus is particularly well illustrated.

[50] Both are well illustrated in Abū al-Faraj al-Iṣfahānī's 'Book of Songs'; for examples, see Berque
(trans.), *Musiques sur le fleuve*, pp. 311–15, 327–9. The much-married noblewomen had historical as
well as romantic significance, since their alliances and offspring contributed to the politics of early
and Umayyad Islam; these received considerable attention from third/ninth-century genealogists
and anecdotal historians; see, e.g., al-Madā'inī (d. 225/840), *Kitāb al-Murdifāt min Quraysh*, in 'Abd
al-Salām Hārūn (ed.), *Nawādir al-Makhṭūtāt* (repr. Beirut, 1411/1991), vol. I, pp. 67–87.

career ladder or with undergoing a sentimental education; love was a test of essential virtue, symbolising non-urban, non-domestic, non-prudential and hence Arab values. This viewpoint is a poetic telescoping of over a century of social restructuring, and of changes in the roles of Muslim men, of which the most significant was their demilitarisation. Unlike his Arab Umayyad forefathers, who were fighters or pioneer settlers as occasion demanded, or pensioners of a military machine, the typical, ethnically mixed Abbasid male is a civilian, and, if literate, his ambitions are purposefully harnessed to the pursuit of a career.[51]

v

Commenting on 'a cluster of rudimentary descriptions of society' attributable to early Abbasid milieux, Louise Marlow notes that

> they seek to identify the occupations and activities [religion, the learned and literate professions] suitable for Muslims in an urban environment. It is noteworthy that the soldiery are absent in almost all of these examples, a feature that may suggest the emergence of civilian élites and an increasing alienation of the urban population from the state . . . [though] none of these social imaginings is ever likely to have corresponded very closely to historical realities.[52]

The soldiery was, of course, very much present as a social reality; but educated Baghdadis of the ninth and tenth centuries – as the literary and biographical sources show – had no desire to make their career in the army, except if seconded to it as administrators or judges. Richard Bulliet argues, more sweepingly and from a slightly later, provincial perspective, that

> conversion to Islam leads almost inevitably, after it has passed its half-way point, to the weakening or dissolution of centralized government . . . from the very beginning of Islam, there were inherent reservations about the scope and function of political leadership . . . the importance of a central political institution diminished as the community's need for it diminished [and it diminished] most sharply by the spread, through conversion, of the confident feeling that Islam was a permanent way of life and not endangered by other local religions.[53]

---

[51] For more detailed views of the composition of the military from Umayyad to mid-Abbasid times, see *EI* [2], vol. II, pp. 504–9, article 'Djaysh. (i) – Classical' (Cl. Cahen), and Kennedy, *The Armies of the Caliphs*, esp. pp. 119, 196–7.

[52] Marlow, *Hierarchy and Egalitarianism*, pp. 39, 174.

[53] Richard W. Bulliet, *Conversion to Islam in the Medieval Period: An Essay in Quantitative History* (Cambridge, MA, 1979), pp. 128–9.

This organicist view of the tranquil civilian growth of Muslim community and communities reflects the self-depiction of the religious classes and
their wish to promote the ideal of godly self-government by an overarch-
ing community (i.e. themselves) uncontaminated by power and violence.
The view that Islam means community, not polity, has been influential in
modern scholarship, given the disjunction between state and community
structures; but in the Abbasid caliphate, the social processes which gave rise
to the concept can ultimately be grasped only in relation to central political
institutions, ill-defined as they were.

If we turn to another early Abbasid social self-description – this time
less a rudimentary one than one deliberately oversimplified for polemical
purposes, and situated in some dim, unspecified past – we find the mid-
ninth-century writer al-Jāḥiẓ asserting that the Arabs had previously been
innocent of urban trades, crafts and professions.[54] In the post-conquest
period, these, we may gather from other sources, had been exercised mainly
by non-Muslims and converts; but on the contemporary social scene, the
situation was different; 'Arabs' as such have disappeared from view, and all
urban Muslims are craftsmen, traders or professionals: they have assimilated
the roles established by earlier generations of converts.[55] One of the most
important of these was that of state bureaucrat (kātib), the ultimate career
goal for many Baghdadi or Iraqi families since it not only led to rich pickings
and the possibility of placing family and friends in similar posts but was also
the route to the vizierate. (There are tantalising glimpses of how marriage
might function in this context, as when we are told of a woman who was
'the daughter, the wife, the sister, the daughter-in-law and the mother of
a vizier',[56] a kind of description which had once been applied to Arab
aristocrats as the wives and mothers of caliphs.) The Abbasid family also
gave its members the chance to diversify (for example, by placing one son in
the bureaucracy and another in the judiciary), to move between professions,
or to combine them. The descendants of Ḥassān ibn Sinān offer a good
example of such a family strategy. As importantly, they have left us two

---

[54] 'So waren die Araber keine Händler, keine Handwerker, keine Ärtze, keine Buchhalter, und sie übten
keine Gewerbe aus', quoted in J. Juda, 'Die sozialen und wirtschaftlichen Aspekte der Mawālī in
frühislamischer Zeit' (PhD thesis, Eberhard-Karls-Universität Tübingen, 1983), p. 112, from al-Jāḥiẓ,
Manāqib al-Turk ('The merits of the Turks') in Rasāʾil, ed. ʿAbd al-Salām Hārūn (Cairo, 1384–
85/1964–65), vol. 1, pp. 69–70. The epistle has been translated by William H. Hutchins, Nine Essays
of al-Jāḥiẓ (New York, 1989), pp. 175–218.

[55] See Juda, 'Die sozialen und wirtschaftliche Aspekte', pp. 109–50, for the trades and professions
exercised by converts in late Umayyad and early Abbasid times, and especially pp. 111–12 for their
employment of slaves as business associates; see also Crone, Slaves on Horses, pp. 49–51.

[56] Bowen, 'The Good Vizier', p. 293 n. 1.

different images of themselves. One is the 'pious' image afforded by the biographical entries in the 'History of Baghdad', which stress the organic growth in the family of religious standing exercised publicly through the judiciary and semi-privately through teaching and rooted economically in the family's land in al-Anbār. This is an image deliberately tailored to the ideal of apolitical Muslim community-building. The other image, however, shows the extent to which the family's success depended on being able to seize the opportunities offered for direct and indirect dealings with the sources of political power through service in the bureaucracy. This image, retailed by another of Ḥassān ibn Sinān's descendants (in fact the father of the man who transmits their 'pious' image in the 'History of Baghdad'), is particularly important as showing the different demeanours, the different perceptions of the self and deployments of the personality and persona, that it was necessary for an individual to exercise in different contexts.[57]

The diversification of male roles, and of the self, in response to the diversification of career opportunities, involved a sliding scale of authority and autonomy in the different areas of a male individual's life, and is one of the most significant developments of metropolitan Abbasid society compared to earlier Muslim societies. Abbasid analysts saw it as the last phase in the digestion of the conquests and of a process of social transformation which had begun some two centuries before. Debarred from the exercise of physical force by the increasing professionalisation of the caliph's army since the Abbasid revolution, and especially since the reforms of al-Muʿtaṣim some eighty years later in the 830s, the competence of the metropolitan Abbasid male, as a male, was effectually limited, and the parallel with slavery is inescapable, not least because military power was now largely being devolved upon slaves, who received pay, and were therefore in some respects difficult to distinguish from free agents in spite of their legal status. (Al-Jāḥiẓ, in his epistle on 'The merits of the Turks', which was written for the caliph al-Muʿtaṣim,[58] not only argues that the predominantly non-Arab contingents in the caliph's army are, in fact, 'Arab' by virtue of their historical mission, etc., but also manages to avoid mentioning the key distinction of the Turkish troops: the fact that most of them were slaves.)[59] In turn, the roles of male civilians within the power structure had to be

---

[57] See al-Tanūkhī, *Nishwār al-Muḥāḍara*, trans. D. S. Margoliouth, *The Table-Talk of a Mesopotamian Judge* (London, 1922) (= part I) and 'The table-talk of a Mesopotamian judge', *Islamic Culture*, 3–6 (1929–32) (= parts VIII and II).

[58] Though never actually presented to him, al-Jāḥiẓ, *Manāqib al-Turk*, in *Rasāʾil*, vol. I, p. 36.

[59] On the question of what proportion of the Turks may have been slaves, see Kennedy, *The Armies of the Caliphs*, pp. 121–2.

reinvented; *kātib*s had to seek ways not only of ingratiating themselves with their superiors but, in relation to the caliph himself, of imposing a psychological ascendancy – a parallel this time with feminine demeanours as illustrated in romantic literature – to counterbalance that of ever-present armed force and guarantee continued rewards for themselves, and their expanding caste and families. The notions of entitlement and dominance, therefore, although they could be polarised by legal theorists, could not in practice provide ready-made roles for anyone who dealt with the power system, or be neatly gendered on a regular scale from freedom to slavehood outside the ideal legalistic concept of the family. In order to understand what being a 'free male' meant or came to mean, in the course of the first two centuries of Abbasid rule, in metropolitan Iraq, the spectrum of gender needs to be reappraised. In particular, the images which literature promotes of women and slaves, of the precariousness of male roles, and of how the relatively weak (women, male civilians) bargain for authority within the power structure, need to be read as a subtext to the images of timeless piety, patriarchal authority and organic communitarian growth promoted by 'pious' sources. The scramble for power at the centre of the system was a complex process which underwent rapid mutations, and even the 'pious' classes were more closely implicated in it than their self-descriptions like to allow.

Men of any ambition had to make difficult, compromising choices if they were to extract advantages from the power structure and perpetuate them through their families. The result of their choices was a sharpened sense of selfhood and of human complexity and vulnerability, and this is reflected above all in the literary sources, but becomes most apparent when we are able to compare the images of a subject afforded by different genres, and even by a given subject's own writings about the present and the past, as we can for some of the descendants of Ḥassān ibn Sinān. When we are able to see one and the same Abbasid subject through different facets of the prism, this in turn gives a new dimension to the problematics of using Abbasid sources to reconstruct the earlier Muslim past. Among the many, often conflicting agendas applied by Abbasid Muslims to reading their own past, modern scholarship has focused on religious and dynastic polemic almost to the exclusion of social identity. If we can recover a more rounded sense of Abbasid selfhood, we have a better chance of interpreting gainfully what Abbasid sources choose to tell us about the historical processes which led to its creation.

That regularising the role of women in these processes was essential to achieving some sense of moral stability can be seen by the way in which 'pious' Abbasid biographical sources relegate early Muslim women to 'pious' and often marginal roles, safely inscribed within the collectivity.[60] Literary sources, on the other hand, give many early Muslim women a transformative role in the development of a sense of male (and female) selfhood which finds itself in conflict with the values of the moral majority. It is rare, though, for us to be able to see one and the same woman from both angles, and it remains rare in sources dealing with Abbasid women. Shaghab, the mother of al-Muqtadir, is, however, an exception, and her case is particularly interesting since a number of the varying images we have of her hinge ultimately not on her femininity as such, but on her economic power as a land-owner, giving prominence to another factor in the Abbasid social equation, the independent property rights of Muslim women, that modern historians have tended to neglect.[61] Her and her female allies' roles in public affairs are part of the slash-and-burn vizieral politics of the period.[62] However, the basis of her wealth represents the last gasp of a system established since the conquests. Prominent women had long received grants of agricultural land in Iraq,[63] but there had been changes in land use in the years before al-Muqtadir's accession ('commercial interests encouraged the expansion of a market-orientated form of agriculture, especially industrial crops'),[64] and the court itself was in financial crisis, forcing the caliph and his mother to sell or invite bids for tax-farming their estates. Local land-owners were eager to buy. The ways in which Shaghab used this income can be represented in 'pious', providential or simply realistic terms.[65] Let us end by looking briefly at the webs of ethical, cultural and historical Muslim self-definition that each of these images implies.

In her obituary in al-Ṣafadī's (d. 764/1362) *al-Wāfī bi al-Wafayāt*, compiled after the watershed of the Mongol sacking of Baghdad in 1258 which ended the Abbasid caliphate, the image given of Shaghab is entirely 'pious', virtually ahistorical, and carries little more than a few literary echoes of

---

[60] For the development of 'pious' counter-images of women as a source of disorder, see Walid Saleh, 'The woman as a locus of apocalyptic anxiety in medieval Sunnī Islam', in Angelika Neuwirth, Birgit Embaló *et al.* (eds.), *Myths, Historical Archetypes and Symbolic Figures in Arabic Literature: Towards a New Hermeneutic Approach* (Beirut, 1999), pp. 123–45.

[61] An exception is Abbott, *Two Queens of Baghdad*.

[62] For an overview of al-Muqtadir's controversial reign, see Richard W. Bulliet's article 'Muqtadir, al', in Strayer (ed.), *Dictionary of the Middle Ages*, vol. VIII, pp. 534–6. Court politics are illustrated in detail in Bowen, 'The Good Vizier'.

[63] Michael G. Morony, 'Land holding and social change: lower 'Irāq in the early Islamic period', in Tarif Khalidi (ed.), *Land Tenure and Social Transformation in the Middle East* (Beirut, 1984), 209–22, and esp. pp. 211, 212, 214, 217, for land grants to women and client converts.

[64] Morony, 'Land holding', p. 220.

[65] El Cheikh emphasises the political uses to which Shaghab put her wealth, chapter 8 below.

whatever Abbasid sources al-Ṣafadī may have used.[66] These, however, are of interest. Her annual income from her agricultural estates is put at one million dinārs, 'most of which she gave away in charity', notably on supplying water and medical help to pilgrims. Her role here is calqued on that of her great predecessors, al-Khayzurān, concubine of al-Mahdī, and above all Zubayda, consort of Hārūn al-Rashīd, in the glory days of the Abbasid caliphate.[67] The second part of the entry casts her in a martyr's role as a guardian of the values of the community. After her son's murder, his successor tries to make her revoke her religious endowments so that he can seize her assets, which are tied up in them. Even under torture, she refuses to disavow 'any trust that I have made for God'. This hagiography, surely, carries the message that Islam is not polity but the common enterprise of pious individuals under the law.

Ibn al-Jawzī (c. 511–597/1116–1201), the great Baghdadi scholar and preacher, tells the story in a more overtly dramatic and historically engaged style, which he owes to a source whose family had had political and financial dealings with Shaghab (the same source to whom we owe the account of Ḥassān ibn Sinān's conversion quoted earlier in this chapter).[68] Her charities are mentioned briefly, but her torture is described in detail. Here it is not a question of a refusal to cancel a religious trust, and a different image of martyrdom, or rather tragedy, is evoked when she tells the new caliph (her son's half-brother): 'I am your mother [too] according to the Book of God.' This recalls how the mother of Jaʿfar the Barmakī, who was also Hārūn al-Rashīd's wet-nurse and foster-mother, pleaded with him in vain to show mercy to her menfolk.[69] Ibn al-Jawzī then adds a slightly different version of events told by an eyewitness. The new caliph has extorted (so we infer) from Shaghab a power of attorney enabling him to sell her property. (Like a disgraced vizier of the period, she is made to disgorge her wealth to finance the new regime.) In order to legalise it, he summons two members of the judiciary as witnesses. The narrator has been selected for this task by his uncle, a judge whose father had played a profitable political role under

---

[66] Al-Ṣafadī, al-Wāfī bi al-Wafayāt, ed. Helmut Ritter et al. (Istanbul and Wiesbaden, 1931–83), vol. XVI, pp. 167–8 (year 321/933). The entry is paraphrased in Roded, Women in Islamic Biographical Collections, p. 124.

[67] For their income, expenditure and charities, see Abbott, Two Queens of Baghdad, pp. 124–5, 237–47, 251–4.

[68] Ibn al-Jawzī, al-Muntaẓam fī Taʾrīkh al-Mulūk wa al-Umam, ed. Muḥammad and Muṣṭafā ʿAbd al-Qādir ʿAṭā and Naʿīm Zarzūr (Beirut, 1413/1993), vol. XIII, pp. 321–9.

[69] Two versions of this famous story are discussed in András Hamori, 'Going down in style: the Pseudo-Ibn Qutayba's story of the fall of the Barmakīs', Princeton Papers in Near Eastern Studies 3 (1994), pp. 89–125.

al-Muqtadir. Although he and his companion insist on observing the legal formalities, they are obliged to register the document as valid.

For anyone acquainted with the dynastic history of the Baghdad judiciary – which produced 'pious' histories of itself frequently cited in the 'History of Baghdad', from which in turn Ibn al-Jawzī quotes heavily – there would have been food for thought in what this anecdote suggests about the relations between polity and community, or the more worldly of its self-appointed guardians. Shaghab stands as a pathetic symbol of how the interface functioned. 'For the rest of the day', says the narrator, 'we could not concentrate on our own business for thinking of the mutability of events and the reversals wrought by time – but we registered the document with [my uncle].'[70] Quite so: the 'pious' were good survivors.

But for Ibn al-Jawzī, Shaghab in her heyday had been an agent of kindly providence. Immediately after the cue provided by the words 'mutability and reversal', he quotes an example which derives from the selfsame 'pious' milieu, once again by way of the biographer of Ḥassān ibn Sinān. This folk tale, or fairy tale as one might almost call it – for in it Shaghab plays the role of fairy godmother – occupies the whole of the remainder of the biographical notice.[71] There is a bundle of such stories in which, by virtue of her wealth and her discreet manipulation of her son, she brings fortune to the humble, happiness to lovers and honour to her dependants.[72] Some contemporaries blamed Shaghab and her female protégées for the disasters of al-Muqtadir's reign.[73] Others, with only a few decades' retrospect, saw it as a golden age,[74] rationalising the seemingly haphazard dependency culture that aristocratic largesse promoted and casting Shaghab in the role of redistributor of wealth and mediator to the people of the acceptable face of power.

[70] Ibn al-Jawzī, *Muntaẓam*, vol. XIII, p. 322. An earlier version of the story is at al-Tanūkhī, *Nishwār al-Muḥāḍara*, vol. II, pp. 77–9.

[71] Ibn al-Jawzī, *Muntaẓam*, vol. XIII, pp. 322–9. For the original of the story quoted by Ibn al-Jawzī from al-Tanūkhī, see Julia Ashtiany [Bray], 'Tanūkhī's *al-Faraj baʿd al-shidda* as a literary source', in Alan Jones (ed.), *Arabicus Felix: Luminosus Britannicus, Essays in Honour of A. F. L. Beeston on his Eightieth Birthday* (Reading, 1991), pp. 111–13. (By the time this story reappears in the fourteenth-century version of the *Arabian Nights* as 'The Steward's Tale', Shaghab has become Zubayda, consort of Hārūn al-Rashīd, see Husain Haddawy (trans.), *The Arabian Nights* (London: Everyman's Library, 1990), pp. 228–237.)

[72] For a story of a tradesman saved from ruin by Shaghab's lady-in-waiting, see al-Tanūkhī, *Faraj*, vol. III, p. 99; for the story of a courtier who wins Shaghab's support through his wet-nurse, see Julia Ashtiany Bray, 'Figures in a landscape: the inhabitants of the Silver Village', in Stefan Leder (ed.), *Story-Telling in the Framework of Non-fictional Arabic Literature* (Wiesbaden, 1998), pp. 92–3.

[73] Notably the historian al-Masʿūdī (c. 283–345/896–956), *Kitāb al-Tanbīh wa al-Ishrāf*, trans. B. Carra de Vaux, *Le Livre de l'avertissement et de la révision* (Paris, 1897), pp. 482–3.

[74] See Bowen, 'The Good Vizier', p. 390. See pp. 321–87 for the events following al-Muqtadir's death which shaped this view.

That the same milieu and sources should be capable of providing yet a third, pragmatic perspective on Shaghab bears oblique witness to their own sense of the complexities of social and moral identity. In our last bundle of stories, Shaghab and the 'pious' are equal contenders in the power game, in which she is sometimes an opponent and sometimes an unwitting ally: an opponent when she tries to rob God and the community of their due by cancelling a religious trust[75] (contrast her martyr's legend in al-Ṣafadī's *al-Wāfī bi al-Wafayāt*); a providential, and above all material, accomplice when winning the management or tax-farming of one of her landed estates gives a 'pious' member of the provincial Iraqi *kātib* elite the chance to torture and finally eliminate a rival and achieve a modest local ascendancy in tactics worthy of a mini-vizier.[76]

As such examples suggest, the roles of Abbasid women were relational not absolute. Despite their legal disabilities, they might participate in more than one sort of power structure. Like those of slaves, the roles of women, both active and passive, were part of the evolving deep structure of urban society. In particular, women, as either property owners or chattels – or sometimes both at the same time – were involved in the investment and deployment of wealth. No less important than the roles played by women in real life were the images of women that were developed in literature, romantic or historical. These imaginative models were one of the means through which free men could reflect on their own moral identity and on what constituted tolerable relations with power.

---

[75] Al-Tanūkhī, trans. Margoliouth, *Table-Talk*, pp. 129–31.
[76] Al-Tanūkhī, trans. Margoliouth, *Table-Talk*, pp. 110–17. (This is a different estate from those run by al-Barīdī, see El Cheikh, chapter 8 below.)

Gender and politics in the harem of al-Muqtadir

Nadia Maria El Cheikh

The debate in Islamic medieval sources over the relationship of all women to Islamic government dates back to the political involvement of 'A'isha, wife of Prophet Muḥammad, in the first Islamic civil war in the seventh century. 'A'isha's political legacy was transformed into a convenient component of the medieval cultural construct which defined all women as threats to the maintenance of the Islamic political order. Her subsequent retreat from public life was perceived as representative of the future limited role of women in the community.[1] Zubayda, wife of Hārūn al-Rashīd (170–193/786–809), was also criticised in the sources for trying to have her son al-Amīn assume the position of first succession to the caliphate, thus acting with little regard for the long-term good of the Abbasid state and the Muslim community.[2] Muslim historians have tended to pass over such 'unsavory' references to women's political involvement as briefly as possible and have usually reported such influence negatively, making it synonymous with decadence and decline.

In an article published in 1979 entitled the 'Problems in the study of Middle Eastern women', Nikki Keddie argued that in certain periods a few women were extremely powerful politically. Keddie stressed that 'it is time to look again at some of these powerful women and see what they actually accomplished and what the circumstances were that might have impeded them'.[3] Some serious research had already been done anticipating the lines Keddie suggested.[4] Most recently, an edited collection entitled *Women in*

---

[1] Denise A. Spellberg, 'Political action and public example: 'A'isha and the battle of the camel', in Nikki Keddie and Beth Baron (eds.), *Women in Middle Eastern History: Shifting Boundaries in Sex and Gender* (New Haven and London, 1991), pp. 45–57, and Spellberg, *Politics, Gender and the Islamic Past: The Legacy of 'A'isha bint Abi Bakr* (New York, 1994), pp. 101–49.

[2] Tayeb El-Hibri, *Reinterpreting Islamic Historiography* (Cambridge, 1999), pp. 42–4, and Nabia Abbott, *Two Queens of Baghdad* (London, 1986), p. 218.

[3] Nikki Keddie, 'Problems in the study of Middle Eastern women', *International Journal of Middle Eastern Studies* 10 (1979), pp. 225–40.

[4] Nabia Abbott, *Aishah the Beloved of Mohammed* (Chicago, 1942). The Fatimid Sitt al-Mulk has been the focus of a number of modern studies, for instance, Yaacov Lev, 'The Fatimid Princess Sitt al-Mulk',

the Medieval Islamic World: Power, Patronage and Piety included studies of a number of women who wielded political power.[5] In this chapter I will review historical evidence of importance in understanding the role that Shaghab, the mother of the Abbasid caliph al-Muqtadir (295–320/908–932), played in state affairs. The main discussion will deal with the specific influence of Umm al-Muqtadir as well as with the broad topic of women's participation in the public sphere. More particularly, it will explore Shaghab's sources of authority, her networks and other channels of influence which allowed her and her female retinue to exercise an extraordinary degree of political influence.

Lady Shaghab's description in the texts fits the frame of a prevalent medieval Islamic model of women as dangerous and destructive to the political order. Abū al-Fidā' (d. 723/1331) states that 'al-Muqtadir used to behave according to the indication of women and referred to their utterances and advice. The kingdoms seceded and the governors of the provinces became covetous.'[6] Ibn al-Ṭiqṭaqā (d. 701/1302) also mentions the negative influence of al-Muqtadir's mother, women and servants: 'It was an empire whose affairs turned around the management of women and servants while he [al-Muqtadir] was distracted with his pleasures. In his days, rebellions took place, the treasury was empty and there were conflicts of opinion.'[7]

Modern Arab historians have, by and large, adhered to this assessment. Muṣṭafā Jawād repeats almost verbatim the criticisms which occur in the medieval historical works. He stresses the all-important role of the caliph's mother and her harem stewardesses, the *qahramānas*, leading to confusion in the administration, and to bad consequences.[8] 'Alī Ibrāhīm Ḥasan singles out the increasing involvement of women in political matters and the absence of competent viziers to explain the general context behind the decline of the Abbasid caliphate. In his view, this situation reached a climax during the reign of al-Muqtadir when supreme authority passed to his mother.[9] In discussing the conditions that played a role in the breaking up of the Abbasid empire, A. al-Dūrī mentions first 'the weakness of al-Muqtadir and his fall under the influence of the *ḥarīm*'. He points out

Journal of Semitic Studies 32 (1987), pp. 319–28. Another important harem woman who emerged at a critical moment in Islamic history to play a highly public role was Shajar al-Durr, the wife of the Ayyubid sultan who reigned in mid-thirteenth-century Cairo. See Judith Tucker, 'Gender and Islamic history', in Michael Adas (ed.), *Islamic and European Expansion* (Philadephia, 1993), pp. 37–73.

[5] Gavin Hambly (ed.), *Women in the Medieval Islamic World: Power, Patronage and Piety* (New York, 1998), pp. 3–27.
[6] Abū al-Fidā', *Mukhtaṣar akhbār al-bashar* (Beirut, 1348), vol. III, p. 84.
[7] Ibn al-Ṭiqṭaqā, *al-Fakhrī fī al-adāb al-sulṭāniyya wa al-duwal al-islāmiyya* (Beirut, 1966), p. 262.
[8] Muṣṭafā Jawād, *Sayyidāt al-balāṭ al-'abbāsī* (Beirut, 1950), p. 81.
[9] 'Alī Ibrāhīm Ḥasan, *Nisā' lahunna fī al-tārīkh al-islāmī naṣīb* (Cairo, 1950), p. 96.

that Shaghab's influence was generally damaging, for 'she spoiled her son by encouraging him to abandon himself to the pleasures and to squander money'. Al-Dūrī, however, also points to other long-term and decisive factors leading to the effective decline of the caliphate, namely, the divisions within the bureaucracy, the interference of the army in politics, and the actions of the Qarāmiṭa.[10]

In fact, the court was alive with intrigue and competition for favour, and the situation was made particularly dangerous by the financial crisis of the reign. The problem, in the words of Hugh Kennedy, was that 'the great consumers of public wealth, the palace and the military, were in a very strong position'.[11] Indeed, the process of decline of the Abbasid caliphate, which became evident in the early tenth century, had started early on in the ninth century. The political fragmentation of the Abbasid domains affecting the resources of the imperial treasury, the decline in agricultural production and developments among the rural population in Iraq during the second half of the ninth century, all contributed to the collapse of the Abbasid caliphate.[12] Nevertheless, the judgement of the Abbasid, Mamluk and modern authors is essentially the same: women overstepping boundaries and capturing authority were the symptom of collapse and the principal cause of corruption and general decline of the state. How women wielded power in a society deeply suspicious of their intrusion in public affairs is crucial to uncover. A rereading of the sources is therefore necessary in order to fathom the mechanisms women used to exercise authority and power and to understand how the rhetorical stereotypes were established.

The death of the Abbasid caliph al-Muktafī in 295/908 led to a period of crisis, especially since he had made no provisions for the succession. It was Jaʿfar, the thirteen-year-old brother of al-Muktafī, who was proclaimed caliph despite objections raised on account of his age. He was the youngest of the Abbasid caliphs to achieve rule and reigned for the long period of twenty-four years. His caliphate, a period of unstable government, started out with the appointment of a sort of regency council composed of his mother Shaghab, his maternal uncle Gharīb, Muʾnis the treasurer, Muʾnis al-Muẓaffar, leader of the Baghdad forces, Ṣāfī the chief of Eunuchs and the chamberlain Sawsan.[13] This situation allowed members of

---

[10] ʿAbd al-ʿAzīz al-Dūrī, *Dirāsāt fī al-ʿuṣūr al-ʿabbāsiyya al-mutaʾakhira* (Baghdad, 1945), pp. 193–7. The Qarāmiṭa were adherents of a branch of *the Ismāʿiliyya* who, in the early tenth century, began a series of devastating campaigns in southern Iraq during which they sacked Basra and Kūfa and raided pilgrims' caravans.

[11] Hugh Kennedy, *The Prophet and the Age of the Caliphates* (London and New York, 1986), p. 190.

[12] David Waines, 'The third century internal crisis of the Abbasids', *JESHO* 20 (1977), pp. 282–306.

[13] Dominique Sourdel, *Le Vizirat abbaside de 749 à 936* (Damascus, 1960), vol. ii, p. 387.

the administration, servants in the palace, viziers and relatives of the caliph
to negotiate the realities of political power among themselves. Indeed, it
seems that the ambitious courtiers preferred to raise to the throne a boy
who would be weak and manageable rather than to promote the more
independent candidate, Ibn al-Muʿtazz.[14] One of his foremost opponents
was Abū al-Ḥasan ibn al-Furāt, who was to serve repeatedly as vizier to
al-Muqtadir. Ibn al-Furāt told the vizier ʿAbbās ibn Ḥasan who consulted
him about who should succeed the dying caliph:

> For God's sake, do not appoint to the post a man who knows the house
> of one, the fortune of another, the gardens of a third, the slave-girl of
> a fourth . . . Not one who has mixed with people, has had experience
> of affairs, has gone through his apprenticeship, and made calculations
> of people's fortunes.[15]

Instead of a caliph well versed in finance and statesmanship, Ibn al-Furāt
preferred a caliph who could be manipulated and who would do what he
would be told. Thus, the choice fell on the young al-Muqtadir.

Al-Muqtadir's reign has been described as 'one of the most disastrous
reigns in the whole of Abbasid history',[16] as the young caliph was manipulated, exploited and deceived by his advisors and courtiers. His reign
inaugurated a period of unparalleled weakness for the caliphate which contrasted with the strength that the state had already partially regained. The
two main factions among the bureaucrats were the Banū al-Furāt, led by
Abū al-Ḥasan ʿAlī, and the Banū al-Jarrāḥ, led by ʿAlī ibn ʿIsā. Another
important player was the powerful military leader of the Baghdad forces,
Muʾnis al-Muẓaffar. Groups of supporters formed around these figures. It
was this power struggle between the various factions that allowed Umm al-
Muqtadir, along with a number of qahramānas, to exercise political power
and influence.

Known in our texts as Shaghab or as al-Sayyida (the Lady), the caliph's
mother played a remarkably important role in the history of the period.
Al-Tanūkhī lists Shaghab, along with the qahramāna Umm Mūsā, al-
Muqtadir's aunt Khāṭif and Dastanbuwayh (umm walad[17] of al-Muʿtaḍid)
as al-sāda who were conducting affairs during the youth of al-Muqtadir.[18]

---

[14] See Ibn al-Athīr, al-Kāmil fī al-tārīkh, ed. C. J. Tornberg (Beirut, 1979), vol. VIII, p. 10, and Ibn
Khaldūn, Kitāb al-ʿibar (Beirut, 1977), vol. III, pp. 752–3.

[15] Miskawayh, The Eclipse of the Abbasid Caliphate, ed. and trans. H. I. Amedroz and D. S. Margoliouth
(London, 1921), vol. I, p. 2.

[16] Kennedy, The Prophet, p. 188.

[17] A concubine who bore her master a child achieved the status of umm al-walad and could no longer
be sold, pawned or given away. Most jurists agreed that the umm al-walad was automatically freed
on her master's death.

A Byzantine by birth, Umm al-Muqtadir was bought by the caliph al-Muʿtaḍid (279–289/892–902). She was called then Nāʿim. In 282/895, Nāʿim gave birth to a son, Jaʿfar. At that point the caliph changed her name to Shaghab.[19] Her bringing forth of a male son was felt to be troublesome (*shaghab*) for the other wives of the caliph, hence her name. She was freed as *umm walad* on al-Muʿtaḍid's death, becoming the most influential person at the court.[20] Operating within the harem, Shaghab and her retinue were not able to cross the threshold that separated private from public sphere. But this restriction had little impact for, in reality, major politics was conducted from the private rooms of the caliphal palace.[21]

As an issue of public versus private and its role in the reading of gender in Islamic history, it has been assumed that the segregation of the sexes, a prevalent feature of the urban upper-class Muslim society, created a gender-based dichotomy between easily discernible public and private spheres. Women have been identified exclusively with the harem and denied any influence beyond its physical boundaries. Conversely, the harem has been seen as a woman's world, domestic, private and parochial. L. Peirce has pointed to a misunderstanding of the nature and function of the harem institution. In contrast to the image of a group of concubines existing solely for the sexual convenience of their master, the harem of a household included women related to the male head of the household and to each other in an often complex set of relationships, many of which did not include a sexual component.[22] Recent research has similarly attempted to challenge the notion of rigidly demarcated and mutually impenetrable territories, showing that the private and public spheres were anything but bipolar, that the two shared many points of contact with the other in varying historical circumstances.[23]

Umm al-Muqtadir surrounded herself with the trappings of authority. She behaved as a professional, establishing a bureau with secretaries who

---

[18] Al-Tanūkhī, *al-Faraj baʿda al-shidda*, ed. ʿAbbūd al-Shaljī (Beirut, 1978), vol. II, pp. 44–5.

[19] Al-Ṭabarī, *Tārīkh al-umam wa al-mulūk* (Beirut, 1988), vol. V, p. 612.

[20] Harold Bowen, *The Life and Times of Ali b. Isa, 'The Good Vizier'* (Cambridge, 1928), p. 100, note 2.

[21] If the palace of the Abbasid caliphs at Samarrāʾ is any indication, we are dealing with huge compounds with endless successions of apartments, courts, rooms, halls and passageways. The palace at Samarrāʾ consisted of two major structures: a public palace with official administrative functions and another unit which consisted almost entirely of residential accommodations and functioned as the private residence of the caliph and his women. Alastair Northedge, 'An interpretation of the palace of the Caliph at Samarra (Dar al-Khilafa or Jawsaq al-Khaqani)', *Ars Orientalis* 23 (1993), pp. 143–70.

[22] Leslie Peirce, 'Beyond harem walls: Ottoman royal women and the exercise of power', in Dorothy O. Helly and Susan M. Reverby (eds.), *Gendered Domains: Rethinking Public and Private in Women's History* (Ithaca, 1992), pp. 4–55.

[23] Asma Afsaruddin, 'Introduction: the hermeneutics of gendered space and discourse', *Hermeneutics and Honor: Negotiating Female Public Space in Islamicate Societies* (Cambridge, MA, 1999), pp. 1–28.

handled political and military affairs. The first such secretary was Aḥmad ibn al-ʿAbbās ibn al-Ḥasan.[24] Later, she took on Aḥmad al-Khaṣībī as her *kātib*, secretary. When he became vizier and grew busy with his new duties, she appointed a new *kātib*, ʿAbd al-Raḥmān ibn Muḥammad ibn Sahl. One source states that upon hearing of his new appointment as vizier, al-Khaṣībī 'wished that he had not taken charge of the vizierate', realising that being a *kātib* for Umm al-Muqtadir was more beneficial to him than being the caliph's vizier.[25] Al-Khaṣībī's appointment as vizier was related to his closeness to Umm al-Muqtadir. It was she, together with her sister Khāṭif, who suggested that Abū al-ʿAbbās al-Khaṣībī be appointed vizier in 313/925.[26] According to the *Ṣilat tārīkh al-Ṭabarī*, he used to be the *kātib* of the *qahramāna* Thumal. Thus, his political career owed a great deal to harem women.

The position of vizier was extremely important after 296/903 since viziers had great resources at their disposal and were able to apply their individual political programme. Indeed, Dominique Sourdel calls this period 'the great epoch' of the institution of the vizierate.[27] Umm al-Muqtadir intervened on behalf of many viziers, administrators or courtiers. Her influence was so great, fear of her was such, that any negative mention of her, even in her absence, had sinister consequences. The vizier Ibn al-Furāt, during his third term in office, once disclaimed being in fear of any woman. The reference was meant to be to Umm al-Muqtadir. Those present perceived that his fall was now near at hand.[28] On another occasion, fearing that he would be dismissed from his office of vizier, he consulted with the secretary of Umm al-Muqtadir on how to pacify her and avert loss of his office.[29] Conciliating her was, evidently, essential for his political survival.

The power of Umm al-Muqtadir and her retinue was manifested in the success of their plots against viziers and in their ability to aid their own candidates to achieve such influential positions. Attempting to bring about the dismissal of Ibn al-Furāt in 298/9, Muḥammad ibn Khāqān wrote a letter to the *qahramāna* Umm Mūsā implicating Ibn al-Furāt in a conspiracy against the caliph. He asked her to inform the caliph and his mother of this matter. Moreover, al-Khāqānī enlisted the help of al-Muʿtaḍid's *umm walad*, Dastanbuwayh. In return for the large sum of 100,000 dinārs, she was to promote his cause with al-Muqtadir and his mother.[30] Ibn al-Furāt was arrested. Umm Mūsā and Dastanbuwayh were thus the crucial link in the

[24] ʿArīb, *Ṣilat tārīkh al-Ṭabarī*, ed. M. J. De Goeje (Leiden, 1897), p. 23.   [25] ʿArīb, *Ṣilat*, p. 128.
[26] Miskawayh, *Eclipse*, vol. I, p. 158.   [27] Sourdel, *Le Vizirat*, vol. I, p. xvii.
[28] Hilāl al-Ṣābī, *Tuḥfat al-umarāʾ fī tārīkh al-wuzarāʾ*, ed. H. F. Amedroz (Beirut, 1904), p. 67.
[29] Hilāl al-Ṣābī, *Tuḥfat al-umarāʾ*, p. 97.   [30] ʿArīb, *Ṣilat*, p. 37. Al-Ṣābī, *Tuḥfat al-umarāʾ*, pp. 66–7.

dismissal of Ibn al-Furāt and the appointment of al-Khāqānī. The brother of Abū Ḥusayn ibn Abī Baghl intrigued, however, to obtain the vizierate for him as soon as he was able to interview Umm Mūsā, offering her a large sum of money. Hearing that Umm Mūsa had turned against him in favour of Ibn Abī Baghl, al-Khāqānī got in touch once again with Dastanbuwayh and promised her 50,000 dinārs. She invalidated the instructions concerning Ibn Abī Baghl.[31] The replacement of viziers in this particular instance was the result of the manipulation and interference of Umm al-Muqtadir's retinue.

The most influential among them was undoubtedly Umm Mūsā. Shaghab had appointed Umm Mūsā in 299/911 as *qahramāna* upon the death of the *qahramāna* Fāṭima. For the years to come and until her dismissal from office on the accusation of disloyalty, Umm Mūsā's influence intensified. The story concerning the dismissal from office of the powerful vizier ʿAlī ibn ʿIsa was related to an angry Umm Mūsā who was refused an audience. She had come to see the vizier with a list of requirements, since many of the arrangements for the harem were in her hands. Despite his belated excuses, she managed to remove the vizier from office by setting the queen-mother and her son against him.[32]

Umm al-Muqtadir's involvement in making political appointments, whether direct or indirect, through her *qahramānas* or through other loyal officials, has been estimated to have been all negative. If one emphasises different aspects of her involvement though, the picture that emerges is far more nuanced. Indeed, from the outset, Umm al-Muqtadir devoted herself in supporting the reign of her son, the legitimate Abbasid caliph. Very shortly after his accession, al-Muqtadir was deposed in 296/908 because 'of his youth, his inability to administer the caliphate and the taking over of affairs by his mother and the *qahramāna*'.[33] The plot aimed at replacing the inexperienced young caliph with the older and more experienced Ibn al-Muʿtazz. Sensing the danger, the queen-mother ordered that Muʾnis, the loyal commander of the army, be brought back from Mecca. The intervention of Muʾnis on behalf of al-Muqtadir, coupled with the loyalty of the young caliph's palace retinue, saved the reign. Upon the failure of the conspiracy and the reinstatement of al-Muqtadir, generous gifts were made by Umm al-Muqtadir to the army, the public officials and others.[34]

---

[31] Miskawayh, *Eclipse*, vol. I, p. 23; Al-Ṣābi', *Tuḥfat al-umarā'*, p. 271 and ʿArīb, *Ṣilat*, p. 40.

[32] Miskawayh, *Eclipse*, vol. I, p. 45, and al-Ṣābi', *Tuḥfat al-umarā'*, p. 285.

[33] Jamāl al-Dīn ibn Taghrībardī, *al-Nujūm al-zāhira fī mulūk miṣr wa al-qāhira* (Beirut, 1992), vol. III, p. 182.

[34] Louis Massignon, *The Passion of al-Hallaj: Mystic and Martyr*, trans. Herbert Mason (Princeton, 1982), vol. I, p. 336.

In various major instances, Umm al-Muqtadir reassessed the political situation of her son and intervened on his behalf. One such incident happened in the year 311/923 when the vizier Ibn al-Furāt attempted to arrest Naṣr the chamberlain. Al-Muqtadir almost acquiesced when the intervention of *al-Sayyida* not only saved Naṣr but, more importantly, redressed the balance of power among the caliph's courtiers. Umm al-Muqtadir reminded her son that Ibn al-Furāt had already removed Mu'nis al-Muẓaffar from his entourage. His current wish to ruin Naṣr the chamberlain was 'in order to get you under his power'. She then asked him: 'On whom, I should like to know, will you call for aid if he means mischief and plots your dethronement?'[35]

Unlike her son, she came to understand the dangers of the excessive taxation imposed by Ibn al-Furāt and the need for equitable economic policies recommended by 'Alī ibn 'Isa. She increasingly supported the latter and defended him until the end in 316/928.[36] As early as 304/916, feeling himself threatened, 'Alī ibn 'Isa wrote an apology to Umm al-Muqtadir reminding her of his merits and of the fact that, unlike his predecessors, he had never taken one dirham from the private treasury of the caliph.[37] When 'Alī ibn 'Isa was accused in 316/928 of being in communication with the Qarāmiṭa and was near to being tortured, it was *al-Sayyida* who found the means of getting at the facts behind the accusation and was able to convince her son of its falsity.[38] Following 'Alī ibn 'Isa's fall from power, Ibn al-Furāt's vindictive son al-Muḥassin besought the caliph to deliver 'Alī ibn 'Isa into his hands. One more time, Umm al-Muqtadir took the 'good vizier's'[39] side, reminding the caliph of his long service and piety.

In addition to providing sound judgement to guard her son's position, *al-Sayyida* used her wealth to buttress his reign. The dominant problem of this period was the bankruptcy of the treasury. Historians have blamed al-Muqtadir's close female circle for being indirectly responsible for this state of affairs. Without minimising the financial profligacy of the reign, one ought to point out that Umm al-Muqtadir used her private money to support the state. In 311/923 the Qarāmiṭa of Bahrain began raiding Iraq. Under Abū Ṭahir al-Jannābī they sacked Basra. The following year the *ḥajj* caravan was attacked. The raids of the Qarāmiṭa continued until they attacked Baghdad in 315/927 and, for a while, it seemed that the capital would fall. During these critical circumstances, Umm al-Muqtadir supported the treasury with her own private wealth. 'Alī ibn 'Isa addressed al-Muqtadir in the following

---

[35] Miskawayh, *Eclipse*, vol. I, p. 130.   [36] Massignon, *The Passion*, p. 402.
[37] Hilāl al-Ṣābī, *Tuḥfat al-umarā*, pp. 283–5.   [38] Miskawayh, *Eclipse*, vol. I, pp. 107 and 270.
[39] In reference to the title of the book by Bowen, mentioned above, note 20.

terms: 'Fear God, O Commander of the Faithful, and speak to the Queen-Mother, who is a pious, excellent woman and if she has any hoard she has amassed against any necessity that may overtake her or the empire, then, this is the time to bring it out.'[40] *Al-Sayyida* ordered the transference of half a million dinārs of her own to the public treasury to be spent on the troops fighting the Qarāmiṭa. Her act was momentous for, in the words of the vizier, 'since the demise of the Blessed Prophet no more serious disaster has befallen the Moslems than this'.[41]

Her generosity also supported the state in its holy war against Byzantium. The largest lodging complex for Muslim volunteers in the war against Byzantium in the whole of the *thughūr* – the lines of fortifications protecting the gaps along the Arab–Byzantine frontiers – was founded by Umm al-Muqtadir in Ṭarsūs. It housed 150 slave warriors; it had attached to it blacksmiths and armourers for the repairs of equipment and weapons. Shaghab was emulating one of her forerunners, a caliphal consort, Qabīḥa, the slave concubine of al-Mutawakkil (232–247/847–861) and mother of al-Muʿtazz, who had founded such a complex in the street of Bāb al-Ṣafṣāf.[42]

In addition to supporting the reign financially on various critical occasions, Shaghab was described as the most generous woman since Zubayda in her concern for the welfare of pilgrims and holy places. The sources praised Zubayda for her philanthropic deeds in the early ninth century and, in particular, for funding the building of water stations on the pilgrim road between Iraq and Mecca. Zubayda set important precedents in both patronage and public display of authority. Religious and charitable works were the dominant forms of women's philanthropy. Such pious gestures, the sources hint, exemplify the role that a woman can and perhaps should have in the public sphere. Julia Bray confirms that the image of Shaghab as pious and charitable is calqued on that of her predecessors, most notably Zubayda.[43] Umm al-Muqtadir was thus following a patronage tradition established by Abbasid women. The earlier female patrons determined, to some extent, the patterns by which the representation of Umm al-Muqtadir's patronage was formulated. Umm al-Muqtadir's energies focused on pious deeds and on means to provide comfort for those Muslims attempting to accomplish

---

[40] Miskawayh, *Eclipse*, vol. 1, p. 204.   [41] Miskawayh, *Eclipse*, vol. 1, p. 203.

[42] Iḥsān ʿAbbās, *Shadharāt min kutub mafqūda fī al-tārīkh* (Beirut, 1988), pp. 37–8 and 439–59. Volunteers from various parts of the Muslim world came to the frontier regions to serve the cause of Islam. The volunteers were put up at houses in Ṭarsūs maintained by *awqāf* endowed for this purpose. See J. F. Haldon and H. Kennedy, 'The Arab–Byzantine frontier in the eighth and ninth centuries: military organization and society in the borderlands', *Receuil des Travaux de l'Institut d'Etudes Byzantines* 19 (1980), pp. 79–114.

[43] See in this volume, Julia Bray, chapter 7.

their religious duties. While the lavishness served political and public relations ends, it was also part of a devotional demonstration. Ibn al-Jawzī
(d. 597/1201) states that: 'Shaghab is said to have devoted one million
dinārs each year from her private estates to the pilgrimage. She was devoted
to the pilgrims' welfare sending water tanks and doctors and ordering that
the reservoirs be fixed.'[44] Ibn Kathīr (d. 774/1373) specifies that she used to
spend more than this sum to provide for water, provisions and doctors for
the pilgrims and to facilitate the roads and the food supply lines.[45]

The third holiest place in Islam, the Ḥaram of Jerusalem, profited
also from her generosity. She had the roof of the sanctuary repaired and
endowed it with four beautifully worked doors of pine wood.[46] Moreover, she endowed pious endowments, awqāf, at Mecca and Medina. She
also founded a hospital in Baghdad that was inaugurated by the physician Sinān ibn Thābit. The monthly expenditure for this hospital totalled
600 dinārs.[47]

Shaghab's enhanced status was thus made manifest to the population of
the empire through her munificence and numerous endowments. Engaging
in philanthropy was one of the few ways in which women were permitted to
assert their power openly. Umm al-Muqtadir took full advantage of it, using
it towards a variety of ends, political, social and religious. As the texts make
clear, she was a visible patron and gained prestige through philanthropic
deeds. Her work mainly served to assert the political authority of the dynasty
through religious benefaction. In addition to legitimising her power and
that of her son by funding the pilgrimage and by taking care of Islam's holy
places, the numerous endowments for public welfare testified to the ruling
family's piety and its concern for the welfare of their subjects.

Umm al-Muqtadir saved the reign financially on critical occasions. She
promoted the state, enhancing its prestige through her religious endowments and donations. Her wealth became almost proverbial and was manifested in a spectacular way in the gifts that she sent on behalf of her nieces,
the daughters of Gharīb, to their husbands. Umm Mūsā transported the gift
in a magnificent procession including twelve horses carrying luxury cloths
and 100,000 dinārs.[48] Moreover, when al-Muqtadir was overthrown a second time, Ibn Nafīs went to the mausoleum of Umm al-Muqtadir, where

[44] Ibn al-Jawzī, al-Muntaẓam fī tārīkh al-umam wa al-mulūk, ed. Muḥammad ʿAṭā and Muṣṭafā ʿAṭā
    (Beirut, 1992), vol. XIII, p. 321.
[45] Ibn Kathīr, al-Bidāya wa al-nihāya (Beirut, 1966), vol. XI, p. 175.
[46] Christel Kessler, 'Above the ceiling of the outer ambulatory in the Dome of the Rock in Jerusalem',
    Journal of the Royal Asiatic Society (1964), pp. 83–103.
[47] Ibn al-Jawzī, al-Muntaẓam, vol. XIII, p. 178; and Ibn Tagrībardī, al-Nujūm, vol. III, p. 216.
[48] ʿArīb, Ṣilat, p. 78.

he found 600,000 dinārs which he carried to al-Qāhir.[49] Umm al-Muqtadir clearly had access to important resources. Al-Tanūkhī (d. 384/994) wrote: 'Shaghab, mother of al-Muqtadir . . . enjoyed a life of luxury like no one else and played with the fortunes of this world in ways that have been related abundantly.'[50]

The economic basis of power is crucial to our understanding of Umm al-Muqtadir's status and authority. Ibn al-Jawzī has an entry on Umm al-Muqtadir at the end of his chapter on the year 321, in the section entitled 'Mention of the eminent personalities who died this year.' 'She had great amounts of money, beyond calculation. She raised from her estates on a yearly basis one thousand thousand dinārs. She used to donate in alms more than that.'[51] Thus, an important portion of her income came from her estates. Umm al-Muqtadir was an extensive property owner. The sources mention a bureau of the queen-mother's estate and a bureau of the queen-mother's sister's estate.[52] Ibn al-Athīr (d. 630/1232) talks about a *qahramāna* who was in charge of the income and expenditures of Umm al-Muqtadir's vast property.[53] Shaghab had also private property in Ahwāz. Its overseer was Abū Yūsuf ibn al-Barīdī.[54] Her income from al-Ahwāz must have been significant since, from the fiscal standpoint, Ahwāz was the granary of the empire.

She also accumulated income by exercising her influence. In return for exerting her sway in appointing high officials, Umm al-Muqtadir was compensated by payments. 'Ubaydallāh al-Khāqānī guaranteed her 100,000 dinārs as a reward for conferring upon him the vizierate in 299/911.[55] Ibn al-Furāt, having been reappointed vizier for a second time in 304/916, fulfilled his promise towards the caliph and his mother, ensuring the significant daily payment of 1500 dinārs. Of this, 1000 dinārs went to al-Muqtadir; 333⅓ to the queen-mother; and the rest to al-Muqtadir's two sons.[56]

Umm al-Muqtadir accumulated some of her wealth through confiscating the money of her own retinue. In 307/919 her secretary Muḥammad ibn 'Abd al-Ḥamīd passed away. She took of his legacy 100,000 dinārs.[57] A few years later, she seized the resources of the vizier Abū al-'Abbās Aḥmad ibn 'Ubaydallāh, who had previously been her secretary.[58] More spectacular was the confiscation of the wealth of Umm Mūsā. This indicates the vast

[49] Ibn Khaldūn, *Kitāb al-'ibar*, vol. III, p. 797.
[50] Al-Tanūkhī, *Nishwār al-muḥāḍara wa akhbār al-mudhākara*, ed. 'Abbūd al-Shaljī (Beirut, 1971), vol. II, p. 76.
[51] Ibn al-Jawzī, *al-Muntaẓam*, vol. XIII, p. 321.　　[52] Miskawayh, *Eclipse*, vol. II, pp. 160 and 184.
[53] Ibn al-Athīr, *al-Kāmil*, vol. V, p. 138.　　[54] Massignon, *The Passion*, vol. I, p. 148.
[55] Ibn al-Jawzi, *al-Muntaẓam*, vol. VI, p. 109.　　[56] Miskawayh, *Eclipse*, vol. I, p. 47.
[57] 'Arīb, *Ṣilat*, p. 80.　　[58] Ibn al-Ṭiqṭaqā, *al-Fakhrī*, p. 270.

amounts of money that the *qahramāna* had managed to amass because of the power which her closeness to Umm al-Muqtadir had brought. Umm Mūsā's wealth, her connections with both the bureaucracy and the military establishment, and her influential role at the court, all conferred upon her an impressive amount of power. In the words of Ibn Khaldūn, 'she managed to amass vast amounts of money and won the loyalty of the military leaders'.[59] In 310/922 Umm al-Muqtadir handed her over to the *qahramāna* Thumal, who was famous for her cruelty. Thumal tortured Umm Mūsā, her sister and her brother, extorting from them money, clothing, furniture, perfume and jewels.[60] The vizier 'Alī ibn 'Isa even created a special bureau to deal with the property confiscated from Umm Mūsā and her dependants. It was said that about a million dinārs were obtained from them.[61]

When al-Muqtadir was killed in 320/932, his mother became desperate upon hearing that he had been put to death and had not been properly buried. In the words of Miskawayh (d. 420/1030), 'she bruised her face and head and would neither eat or drink until she nearly died'.[62] Al-Qāhir (320–322/932–934) had Shaghab arrested and inflicted upon her all types of torture in attempting to seize her wealth. She is reported to have said: 'Had I possessed any money I should not have delivered my son to his death.'[63] In al-Tanūkhī's *Nishwār* she is said to have uttered these slightly different words: 'Oh you, if we had money, we would not be suffering and you would not be in a position to chastise me in such a manner.'[64] Al-Qāhir wanted her to testify that she had dissolved her *awqāf* in order to sell them. While she acquiesced in selling her property she refused to abolish the *awqāf* saying: 'They were pious foundations set up in Mecca, Madina and the *thughūr* in order to please God and for the sake of the poor and the weak. I will not allow their abolition but I will allow the selling of my property.'[65] The establishment of endowments in addition to bringing her fame and perpetuating her name was now used to protect her property from confiscation.

The sources describe in horrid detail the torture inflicted on Umm al-Muqtadir, after her son's death. The new caliph 'had her suspended by one foot and beat her mercilessly on the soft parts of her body'. He himself related how with his own hands 'he had scourged her a hundred times on

[59] Ibn Khaldūn, *Kitāb al-'ibar*, vol. III, p. 814.
[60] Ibn Tagrībardī, *al-Nujūm*, vol. III, p. 229, and Miskawayh, *Eclipse*, vol. I, p. 93.
[61] Miskawayh, *Eclipse*, vol. I, p. 93.   [62] Miskawayh, *Eclipse*, vol. I, p. 274.
[63] Miskawayh, *Eclipse*, vol. I, p. 274, and Ibn al-Athīr, *al-Kāmil*, vol. VIII, p. 245.
[64] *Nishwār*, vol. II, p. 76.
[65] Ibn al-Athīr, *al-Kāmil*, vol. VIII, p. 245, and al-Ṣafadī, *al-Wāfī bi al-wafayāt*, ed. Wadād al-Qāḍī (Stuttgart, 1994), vol. XVI, pp. 167–8.

the soft parts of her body with intent to make her confess and how she had not confessed to the possession of a single *dirham'*. She died owing to her increasing illness and to the tortures which al-Qāhir made her suffer.[66] The texts hint at his ungratefulness. 'He showed no gratitude for the kindness she had done him when he was imprisoned by Muqtadir.'[67] She herself told him: 'I am your mother according to the Book of God . . . I am the one who saved you from my son the first time thus enabling you to get to this position.'[68] Indeed, following the second revolt against al-Muqtadir in 317/929, al-Qāhir had been imprisoned in the quarters of Umm al-Muqtadir. She was extremely kind and generous to him, lodging him magnificently and buying him slave-girls to serve him.[69]

She was last seen by the witnesses who were brought into the palace. They were to confirm the appointment of an agent for the sale of her possessions. One of them said:

> I heard weeping and lamentation behind the curtain which was then removed. I asked her, are you Shaghab? . . She cried for a while and answered yes. When I saw her I found her an old woman, with a delicate face, a complexion verging towards paleness and manifesting varying marks [on her body] and dressed in shabby clothes.[70]

The witnesses went away remembering her past glory and pondering on the fickleness of destiny.

Umm al-Muqtadir's role as a focus of court politics and intrigues was so bitter that the courtiers and top administrators based their choice of the next caliph on the fact that his mother was dead at the time of his accession. Ibn al-Athīr relates how initially Mu'nis suggested that al-Muqtadir's son Abū al-ʿAbbās succeed. Abū Yaʿqūb Isḥaq al-Nawbakhtī rejected this suggestion saying: 'After all this work we have finally been delivered of a caliph who has a mother, a maternal uncle and a harem who manage him. And we would choose to get back to such a situation!'[71] Abū Yaʿqūb and others aimed to avoid a government in which women would interfere. Choosing Abū al-ʿAbbās would have allowed Shaghab, the grandmother, to intervene, and, more generally, it meant perpetuating the existing order.[72]

---

[66] Miskawayh, *Eclipse*, vol. I, pp. 274–5.
[67] Miskawayh, *Eclipse*, vol. I, p. 274. See analysis of this and other such episodes on torture in Fedwa Malti-Douglas, 'Texts and tortures: the reign of al-Muʿtaḍid and the construction of historical meaning', *Arabica* 46 (1999), pp. 313–36.
[68] Al-Tanūkhī, *Nishwār*, vol. II, p. 76.   [69] Ibn al-Athīr, *al-Kāmil*, vol. VIII, p. 206.
[70] Al-Tanūkhī, *Nishwār*, vol. II, pp. 77–9.   [71] Ibn al-Athīr, *al-Kāmil*, vol. VIII, p. 244.
[72] Bowen, '*The Good Vizier*', pp. 321–2.

CONCLUSION

This chapter has examined the evidence for Shaghab and her harem, inquiring how much power they were able to exercise and in what spheres. Although it has been difficult to assess whether Shaghab's influence affected the overall decline of the caliphate, specific incidents, such as her sound political advice to her son as well as her financial contribution towards the thwarting of the threat of the Qarāmiṭa, and her wide philanthropic activities, do illustrate some aspects of her positive influence and power.

The figure of the forceful queen-mother who, in seeking to advance the interests of her son, found herself intervening in affairs of state, is of course not limited to the example of Umm al-Muqtadir. Her example is significant in that it provides a spectrum of the possibilities open to such indirect exercise of authority. Studying Shaghab and her retinue has allowed us to see some alternative channels of female political participation and influence. Although women did not hold actual political positions, they were well placed to influence public affairs, even if inconspicuously. It is of course true that the reign of al-Muqtadir was particularly propitious for the harem women to exert strong influence in public affairs. But it is also true that they were never very far from the court and were well placed to come to the fore whenever the opportunity allowed for it.

Female roles and ideologies of femininity do not exist in a social vacuum. Women and ideas about women's roles existed and interacted with male roles and notions of masculinity.[73] The criticisms with respect to Umm al-Muqtadir fit neatly within the general critical attitude that the sources hold towards female intervention in politics. Criticisms against her echoed those made with respect to Zubayda, a century earlier, because she insisted on having her son al-Amīn assume the position of first succession. Umm al-Muqtadir's greater involvement made her the target of more vehement attacks in the sources. While our texts disclosed the reality of women's presence in the political arena in early tenth-century Abbasid Baghdad, the implicit ideology as well as the explicit comments continued to stress what was expected of women in that sphere. Thus, 'Arīb (d. c. 370/980), in a partial defence of al-Muqtadir states: 'Had he not been dominated in most affairs, people would have lived comfortably. But his mother and others of his retinue thwarted his plans.'[74]

---

[73] Julia Smith, 'Did women have a transformation of the Roman world?', *Gender and History* 12 (2000), pp. 552–71.
[74] 'Arīb, *Ṣilat*, p. 24.

Rather than presenting an assessment of the actual actions of these women, the sources concentrated on the general negative stereotypes linked with women crossing over to the public political realm. Women striding across conventional social boundaries called upon themselves the vitriolic condemnation of the men who recorded their activities. Such writers organised the experiences of these women and represented them within a particular perceptual framework, one which firmly upheld the paradigm of public versus private spheres, a paradigm which 'prevents the actions of women from being considered according to the same criteria as those of males'.[75] Adopting the well-entrenched public–private dichotomy, the medieval authors could not incorporate women's public activities. For their interpretations to be consistent with this worldview, they had to explain this particular transgression away by insisting that it was a sign of deterioration of the community and thus a dangerous event. Thus, these explanations are part of rhetorical strategies that reflect, to some extent, the style of the Arabic texts as well as the assumptions, mentalities and ideologies of the medieval authors. In their assessment of Umm al-Muqtadir, the texts revealed, therefore, much about politics, gender and the interpretation of the past as presented exclusively by men.

[75] Arlene W. Saxonhouse, 'Introduction – public and private: the paradigm's power', in Barbara Garlick *et al.* (eds.), *Stereotypes of Women in Power: Historical Perspectives and Revisionist Views* (New York, 1992), pp. 1–9.

PART II

Gender in Germanic societies

CHAPTER 9

Dressing conservatively: women's brooches as markers of ethnic identity?

Bonnie Effros

CHARTING THE GERMANIC MIGRATIONS

Among the basic tools used in introducing students to medieval history are the maps featuring arrows that track the migrations of Germanic groups from the steppes to the Roman provinces ringing the Mediterranean Sea during the fourth and fifth centuries AD. This longstanding tradition of graphically arranging colourful lines to depict the movement of tribes began in the eighteenth century, and became especially popular in the nineteenth century because of its successful conceptualisation of the transfer of people and the strategies of military campaigns over the course of hundreds of years.[1] Yet, the appeal of these maps' simplification of complex historical developments should not be seen as a measure of their historical accuracy; even today, aesthetic considerations often play a more influential role than the contemporary sources from which they were drawn.[2] Besides smoothing over the fact that the nature of these migrations has long been disputed, for example in debates over the magnitude of Frankish presence in Gaul,[3] these maps imply a uniformity of experience that never existed.[4]

With the growing influence of archaeological remains on historical debates in the twentieth century, the design of maps has increasingly come to rely upon physical artefacts linked by scholars to various Germanic groups, since these prolific finds supplement the deficiencies of historical sources. In Gaul, the majority of the archaeological evidence derives

[1] Walter Goffart, 'What's wrong with the map of the Barbarian invasions?', in Susan I. Ridyard and Robert G. Benson (eds.), *Minorities and Barbarians in Medieval Life and Thought* (Sewanee, 1996), pp. 159–77.

[2] Walter Goffart, 'The map of the Barbarian invasions: a longer look', in Marc Anthony Meyer (ed.), *The Culture of Christendom: Essays in Commemoration of Denis L. T. Bethell* (London, 1993), p. 21.

[3] Karl Ferdinand Werner, 'La "conquête franque" de la Gaule: itinéraires historiographiques d'une erreur', *Bibliothèque de l'Ecole des Chartes* 154 (1996), pp. 7–45.

[4] Walter Goffart, 'The theme of "the Barbarian invasions" in late antique and modern historiography', in Evangelos Chrysos and Andreas Schwarcz (eds.), *Das Reich und die Barbaren*, Veröffentlichungen des Instituts für Österreichische Geschichtsforschung 29 (Vienna, 1989), pp. 87–107.

not from settlements but rather from graves, which from the fifth to late seventh centuries commonly included deposits of clothing, personal possessions and tableware, despite the progressive decline of this rite during the latter part of this period.[5] While many discoveries of early medieval cemeterial remains in France and Germany resulted from the construction of railways in the second half of the nineteenth century, and were hence poorly documented if recorded at all,[6] improved methodologies in modern excavations mean that the quantity of mortuary artefacts available for study should continue to increase over the coming decades. By enabling us to challenge many interpretations derived from early medieval written sources, mortuary evidence allows for the creation of a more complex picture of the migration, assimilation and social *mores* of the inhabitants of western Europe in late antiquity and the early Middle Ages.

None the less, the archaeological evidence used to design cartographic models of the migration is itself not lacking in controversy. The link between ethnicity and grave goods is highly tenuous, since it relies on few contemporary written sources but rather is based primarily upon distribution patterns of particular burial artefacts. Regional distinctions in burial dress may have resulted in part from the expression of ethnic identity, but local customs, gift-exchange, trade and the location of workshops where these goods were produced also represented contributing factors.[7] Yet, only recently has this more complex approach won out over more positivistic interpretations of the one-to-one correspondence between particular cemeterial artefacts and specific ethnic groups. Part of the eagerness to relinquish the use of ethnic typologies of grave goods has stemmed from archaeologists' desire to distance themselves from the Nazis' abuse of these theoretical approaches for political objectives.[8] Because ethnic associations of the material evidence of late antiquity and the early Middle Ages have for so long been the basis of conceptual images of the migrations,[9] however, it will be a long time until their hold on the popular imagination is diminished. The ubiquity of

---

[5] For an introduction to the archaeological evidence, see Bonnie Effros, *Merovingian Mortuary Archaeology and the Making of the Early Middle Ages* (Berkeley, 2003).

[6] Claude Seillier, 'L'époque des migrations en Gaule du Nord dans les collections publiques et privées', in *Trésors archéologiques du nord de la France* (Valenciennes, 1997), pp. 108–14.

[7] For a discussion of the distribution of sword burials, for instance, see Frans Theuws and Monica Alkemade, 'A kind of mirror for men: sword depositions in late antique northern Gaul', in Frans Theuws and Janet L. Nelson (eds.), *Rituals of Power from Late Antiquity to the Early Middle Ages*, Transformation of the Roman World 8 (Leiden, 2000), pp. 401–76.

[8] Bettina Arnold, 'The past as propaganda: totalitarian archaeology in Nazi Germany', *Antiquity* 64 (1990), pp. 464–7.

[9] See, for instance, Richard H. Randall, Jr., 'Migration jewelry', in *Jewelry: Ancient to Modern* (New York, 1979), p. 128.

such maps in textbooks and surveys indicates just how deeply ingrained this interpretation of the material evidence is and how much it has influenced our perceptions of the migration period.

This volume on gender, however, provides an important opportunity to question more rigorously the methodological basis which scholars have used to distinguish the graves of Romans from various Germanic groups. The exploration is relevant because the objects most frequently and confidently applied to ethnic interpretations of grave goods are brooches associated with female dress.[10] Nevertheless, while ethnic interpretations have relied upon artefacts thought to have been buried with women, scholarly attention has instead focused on the armies which women allegedly accompanied.[11] Rather than addressing the population as a whole, analysis has concentrated on the male members of these groups, since it is they who are perceived as actively involved in shaping their communities' identity and future. Consequently, as advances have been made in debates on the ethnic significance of various forms of personal adornment and weaponry buried with the dead, they have not affected the understanding of the *mores* of women in an ethnic context. Throughout the twentieth century, preconceptions about gender relied upon the assumption that, from the standpoint of archaeology, women were passive icons of group identity; hence their brooches were taken to represent the most reliable markers of ethnicity. Our general understanding of the migration period thus rests upon gender stereotypes which deny women's ability to play an active role in ethnic expression. This chapter contests such premises.

In order to measure the impact of brooches on discussions of migrations, I have chosen a number of exceptional cases in which artefactual finds normally uncommon to a particular region have come to light in a cemeterial context. Because these graves defy general customs in their locality, they offer archaeologists particularly broad latitude in explaining how such 'foreign' goods arrived at these isolated sites in larger cemeteries. They also provide an excuse to re-examine women's contribution to the construction

---

[10] Frank Siegmund, *Alemannen und Franken*, Ergänzungsbande zum Reallexikon der Germanischen Altertumskunde 23 (Berlin, 2000), pp. 218–20. Hence, some, such as Hans Zeiß, resisted giving greater weight to ethnic symbolism of these brooches, since he believed that armament of soldiers should play a larger role in these discussions than the jewellery worn by warriors' presumed wives. Mechthild Schulze-Dörrlamm, 'Romanisch oder germanisch? Untersuchungen zu den Armbrust- und Bügelknopffibeln des 5. und 6. Jahrhunderts n. Chr. aus den Gebieten westlich des Rheins und südlich der Donau', *Jahrbuch des Römisch-Germanischen Zentralmuseums Mainz* 33, 2 (1986), pp. 686–90.

[11] Alexander Koch, *Bügelfibeln der Merowingerzeit im westlichen Frankenreich,* Römisch-Germanisches Zentralmuseum, Forschungsinstitut für Vor- und Frühgeschichte, Monographien 41, 1 (Mainz, 1998), vol. II, pp. 515–17, 570–80.

of ethnic identities. The brooches on which the fourth section below will concentrate were typical of the Danube region but were found in early medieval cemeteries in north-western Gaul. They have therefore provoked much speculation, but as I shall demonstrate, the scope of interpretive possibilities has been kept unnecessarily narrow in those graves exhibiting features linked to female gender. Typical of the explanations of these objects are the views of Christian Pilet, who has asserted that such rare 'eastern' finds in sepulchres in the west arrived there when:

> From the end of the third century, the integration of the barbarian contingents occurred throughout the Roman army. They came as communities organized with women, children and baggage. In the second half of the fifth century, they had become the essence of this army. This process, without any doubt, is the source of the diffusion of objects testifying to Danubian customs of dress which one finds in the cemeteries [of Gaul].[12]

Archaeological evidence is thus used to confirm and supplement imprecise historical sources regarding the arrival of foreign warriors in Gaul. As wives or captives and thus passive participants, women are consistently grouped by scholars along with property as markers of their husband's ethnicity or their captor's prowess in battle. When discovered out of their usual geographical context, such as in Gaul, brooches of Danubian origin are hence more often than not assumed to have travelled with female bearers subjected to warrior males, or removed from their own communities by foreign marriages or abduction. While these interpretive options are certainly possibilities, we also need to take into consideration a much wider range of explanations for the presence of these artefacts in early medieval graves in Gaul.[13] Elite gift-exchange, trade or missionary activity are all well recognised ways of moving luxury objects over long distances.[14] This chapter thus also offers suggestions about women's participation in networks of exchange of various sorts.

---

[12] Comment by Christian Pilet in Jean-Yves Marin (ed.), *Attila, les influences danubiennes dans l'Ouest de l'Europe au Ve siècle. Exposition au Musée de Normandie, Caen, 23 juin – 1 octobre 1990* (Caen, 1990), p. 94.

[13] While in some instances she attributes the distribution of garnet jewellery exclusively to exogamy, Birgit Arrhenius also points to the possibility of other interpretations, depending upon the circumstances of particular finds. Birgit Arrhenius, *Merovingian Garnet Jewellery: Emergence and Social Implications* (Stockholm, 1985), pp. 193–8.

[14] Matthias Hardt, 'Silbergeschirr als Gabe im Frühmittelalter', *Ethnographisch-Archäologische Zeitschrift* 37 (1996), pp. 431–44. Matthias Hardt, 'Silverware in early medieval gift exchange: *imitatio imperii* and objects of memory', in Ian Wood (ed.), *Franks and Alamanni in the Merovingian Period: An Ethnographic Perspective*, Studies in Historical Archaeoethnology 3 (Woodbridge, 1998), pp. 317–26.

ETHNIC INTERPRETATIONS OF ARMAMENT

Because the relationship between material culture and ethnicity has turned primarily on study of the furnishings of male graves with specific types of weaponry and items of apparel, this reassessment of the ethnic symbolism of women's brooches requires a brief recapitulation of the development of these gendered arguments about men's burial goods. Scholarly dialogue on the concept of Culture-Provinces, the association of specific regions with ethnic groups on the basis of the remains of material culture, began over a century ago. The hypothesis was circulated most influentially in the works of the German linguist and theoretical archaeologist Gustaf Kossinna (d. 1931),[15] whose research was embraced in the first half of the twentieth century by a broad spectrum of scholars including both fascists and socialists.[16] Although some German scholars during the Second World War hesitated to view individual artefacts as anything more than signs of ethnic influence,[17] their caution was not long lasting. Moreover, this emphasis on the ethnic symbolism of archaeological finds was not confined to German scholarship: for instance, in 1951, the English archaeologist E. T. Leeds confidently used brooches bearing close resemblance to those manufactured in the Danube region to chart the Vandals' trajectory across western Europe.[18] While most Anglophone archaeologists have ignored debates in German and French circles over the ethnic significance of archaeological artefacts,[19] the pioneering scholarship of the British-domiciled archaeologist V. Gordon Childe was directly influenced by the work of Kossinna. His writings remain a part of the standard archaeological literature on migration.[20] Even if such ideas are no longer considered reliable, archaeologists in Britain and the United

---

[15] Gustaf Kossinna, *Die Herkunft der Germanen: zur Methode der Siedlungsarchäologie*, Mannus-Bibliothek 6 (Würzburg, 1911), p. 17. Guy Halsall, 'Archaeology and historiography', in Michael Bentley (ed.), *Companion to Historiography* (London, 1997), pp. 806–7. Sebastian Brather, 'Kossinna, Gustaf', in *Reallexikon der Germanischen Altertumskunde*, vol. XVII, new edition (Berlin, 2000), pp. 263–7.

[16] Ulrich Veit, 'Gustaf Kossinna and his concept of a national archaeology', in Heinrich Härke (ed.), *Archaeology, Ideology and Society: The German Experience*, Gesellschaften und Staaten im Epochenwandel 7 (Frankfurt, 2000), pp. 40–64. Henning Hassmann, 'Archaeology in the "Third Reich"', in Härke (ed.), *Archaeology, Ideology and Society*, pp. 65–139.

[17] Hans Zeiß, 'Die germanischen Grabfunde des frühen Mittelalters zwischen mittlerer Seine und Loiremündung', in *31. Bericht der Römisch-Germanischen Kommission 1941*, 1 Teil (Berlin, 1942), pp. 28–31.

[18] E. Thurlow Leeds, 'Visigoth or Vandal', *Archaeologia* 94 (1951), pp. 195–8, 205–7.

[19] Heinrich Härke, 'Die Anglo-Amerikanische Diskussion zur Gräberanalyse', *Archäologisches Korrespondenzblatt* 19 (1989), pp. 185–94. Heinrich Härke, 'Archaeologists and migrations: a problem of attitude?', *Current Anthropology* 39 (1998), pp. 19–24.

[20] V. Gordon Childe, *The Dawn of European Civilization* (London, 1925); *The Prehistory of European Society* (Harmondsworth, 1958).

States have at least been initially exposed to these ideas in the course of their training.[21]

The earliest challenges to ethnic interpretations of material culture were posed in the 1960s by historians who questioned the meaning of ethnic terminology in early medieval written sources.[22] Particularly since the late 1970s, consensus has also grown among early medieval archaeologists that distinct methodological problems exist in the identification of ethnic groups on the basis of dress-related artefacts found in a mortuary context.[23] This change is particularly relevant to discussions of the burial of clasps with men, the distribution of which was probably not regulated to any significant degree during the late Roman empire.[24] Challenges to Kossinna's identification of specific artefacts as markers of Germanic migration have resulted in the belief that presence of immigrants may no longer be reliably mapped on the basis of mortuary deposits of weaponry, buckles, brooches and other objects of personal adornment.[25] Yet, these important discussions have been implicitly gendered, for they have primarily advanced the interpretation of artefacts associated with men rather than the brooches that formed an essential part of female dress.[26]

Turning more specifically to the case of Merovingian Gaul, both Edward James and Patrick Périn agreed in the late 1970s that the 'mixed' population characteristic of regions conquered by the Franks made a direct link between particular grave goods and ethnicity anachronistic.[27] The polysemic nature of material artefacts meant that any object's symbolic role was far more complex than the one-to-one relationships supported by ethnic readings of the evidence.[28] Even the *francisca*, an axe long associated with the Franks,

---

[21] Ulrich Veit, 'Ethnic concepts in German prehistory: a case study on the relationship between cultural identity and archaeological objectivity', in Stephen Shennan (ed.), *Archaeological Approaches to Cultural Identity*, One World Archaeology 10 (London, 1989), pp. 39–40. Sebastian Brather, 'Ethnische Identitäten als Konstrukte der frühgeschichtlichen Archäologie', *Germania* 78 (2000), pp. 154–7.

[22] Reinhard Wenskus, *Stammesbildung und Verfassung: das Werden der frühmittelalterlichen Gentes* (Cologne, 1961), pp. 14–15, 33–4, 44–93.

[23] Stephen J. Shennan, 'Some current issues in the archaeological identification of past peoples', *Archaeologia Polona* 29 (1991), p. 30.

[24] Dominic Janes, 'The gold clasp of the late Roman state', *EME* 5 (1996), pp. 148–53.

[25] Stephen Shennan, 'Introduction: archaeological approaches to cultural identity', in Shennan (ed.), *Archaeological Approaches to Cultural Identity*, pp. 1–7.

[26] Koch, *Bügelfibeln*, vol. II, pp. 565–70.

[27] Edward James, 'Cemeteries and the problem of Frankish settlement in Gaul', in P. H. Sawyer (ed.), *Names, Words and Graves: Early Medieval Settlement* (Leeds, 1979), pp. 71–5. Patrick Périn, 'A propos de publications étrangères récentes concernant le peuplement en Gaule à l'époque mérovingienne: la "question franque"', *Francia* 8 (1980), pp. 537–52. Patrick Périn, 'Quelques remarques sur la "question franque" en Gaule du Nord', *Bulletin de Liaison: Association Française d'Archéologie Mérovingienne* 2 (1980), pp. 79–85.

[28] Christopher Tilley, 'Interpreting material culture', in Ian Hodder (ed.), *The Meanings of Things: Material Culture and Symbolic Expression*, One World Archaeology 6 (London, 1989), pp. 188–93.

appeared first in the seventh century in Isidore's *Etymologiae*. Nor did Isidore identify it as double-bladed (*bipennis*), an allusion made no earlier than the early eighth century in the *Liber Historiae Francorum*. The weapon thus did not represent an exclusive symbol of Frankish male identity during much of the Merovingian period.[29] In the fifth century in particular, the deposition of weaponry in the Merovingian kingdoms may have constituted an expression of warrior status and identity rather than allegiance to a particular ethnic group.[30] Hence, Guy Halsall has argued that funerary deposits and ceremonial highlighted the level of competition and instability among military elites,[31] and varied regionally in their application as social strategies in early medieval Gaul.[32]

Despite these new interpretive paradigms, reluctance to renounce a migrationist interpretation of material culture has remained common-place in some circles on the Continent.[33] A number of scholars have drawn attention to influential European archaeologists who have resisted abandoning direct associations between material culture and ethnic categories.[34] With respect to fifth- to seventh-century Gaul, these archaeologists have regarded the Frankish conquest as a mass movement of population whose adherents were clearly distinguishable by their appearance. In recent years, ethnic interpretations of mortuary artefacts have even gained ground owing to their 'confirmation' with statistics of alleged skeletal character-istics attributed by some scholars to ethnic groups.[35] These reactionary approaches are symptomatic of general rejection or in some cases igno-rance of archaeological and anthropological models formulated in Britain

[29] Walter Pohl, 'Telling the difference: signs of ethnic identity', in Walter Pohl with Helmut Reimitz (eds.), *Strategies of Distinction: The Construction of Ethnic Communities, 300–800*, Transformation of the Roman World 2 (Leiden, 1998), pp. 32–40.

[30] Heiko Steuer, 'Archaeology and history: proposals on the social structure of the Merovingian king-dom', in Klavs Randsborg (ed.), *The Birth of Europe: Archaeology and Social Development in the First Millenium A.D.*, Series Analecta Romana Instituti Danici Supplementum 16 (Rome, 1989), pp. 105–9. Walter Pohl, 'Alemannen und Franken: Schlußbetrachtung aus historischer Sicht', in Dieter Geuenich (ed.), *Die Franken und die Alemannen bis zur 'Schlacht bei Zülpich' 496/97* (Berlin, 1998), pp. 644–50.

[31] Guy Halsall, *Settlement and Social Organization: The Merovingian Region of Metz* (Cambridge, 1995), pp. 9–21.

[32] Guy Halsall, 'Social identities and social relationships in early Merovingian Gaul', in Wood (ed.), *Franks and Alamanni in the Merovingian Period*, pp. 151–2.

[33] Härke, 'Archaeologists and migrations', pp. 19–21. Werner, 'La "conquête franque" de la Gaule', pp. 7–19.

[34] Veit, 'Ethnic concepts in German prehistory', pp. 35–41. Bettina Arnold and Henning Hassmann, 'Archaeology in Nazi Germany: the legacy of the Faustian bargain', in Philip L. Kohl and Clare Fawcett (eds.), *Nationalism, Politics and the Practice of Archaeology* (Cambridge, 1995), pp. 70–81. Falko Daim, 'Gedanken zum Ethnosbegriff', *Mitteilungen der Anthropologischen Gesellschaft Wien* 112 (1982), pp. 63–4.

[35] Walter Goffart, 'Two notes on Germanic antiquity today', *Traditio* 50 (1995), pp. 14–19; Effros, *Merovingian Mortuary Archaeology*, pp. 100–10.

and the United States in the past two decades.[36] Interdisciplinarity, with its eclectic and sometimes indiscriminate borrowing from a variety of fields, has resulted in historians', archaeologists' and anthropologists' uncritical use of written and material sources to create a model for early medieval ethnicity.[37]

In Merovingian mortuary archaeology in France in recent years, physical anthropologists have contributed to the development of a model of morphological characteristics of skulls which they purport allows them to distinguish between Germanic and indigenous populations in early medieval cemeteries in Normandy and northern France, even when the skeletal remains are poorly preserved.[38] Because they acknowledge that weaponry and clothing may be insufficient to identify the deceased as a part of such a clearly defined group,[39] proponents of this anthropological methodology believe that skull remains allow them to do it with greater certainty. Yet, rather than classify morphological differences as regional,[40] they have equated these characteristics with historically derived ethnic distinctions. In essence, this approach ties detailed statistics on skeletal dimensions to ethnic identity on the basis of the grave goods that accompany the bones, and the data derived in this fashion have been used in turn to support circular arguments in favour of the specific ethnic characteristics of certain types of grave goods.[41] Such confidence in the cultural and biological homogeneity

[36] Jan Vansina, 'Historians, are archaeologists your siblings?', *History of Africa* 22 (1995), p. 377. English-speaking archaeologists are likewise guilty of ignoring major archaeological developments published in German. Härke, 'Die anglo-amerikanische Diskussion', pp. 185–91.

[37] Walter Pohl, 'Ethnizität des Frühmittelalters als interdisziplinäres Problem', *Das Mittelalter* 4 (1999), pp. 69–75.

[38] J. Dastugue and S. Torre, 'Le cimetière de'Hérouvillette (vie –viie siècles): étude anthropologique', *Archéologie Médiévale* 1 (1971), pp. 127–41. Luc Buchet, 'La nécropole gallo-romaine et mérovingienne de Frénouville (Calvados): étude anthropologique', *Archéologie Médiévale* 8 (1978), pp. 11–18, 26–7. Joël Blondiaux, 'Evolution d'une population d'immigrés en Gaule du Nord de la fin du IVe siècle à la fin du VIIe siècle: Vron (Somme)', in Luc Buchet (ed.), *Homme et milieu: approches paléoanthropologiques. Actes des Quatrièmes journées anthropologiques de Valbonne, 25–26–27 mai 1988*, Dossier de Documentation Archéologique 13 (Paris, 1989), pp. 60–71.

[39] Patrick Périn, 'Les conséquences ethniques de l'expansion franque: état de la question', in *Le Phénomene des grandes 'invasions': réalité ethnique ou échanges culturels? L'anthropologie au secours de l'histoire. Actes des Premières journées anthropologiques de Valbonne (16–18 avril 1981)* (Valbonne, 1983), p. 88.

[40] A regional as opposed to ethnic interpretation has recently been put forward at the sixth- and seventh-century cemetery of Doubs, where the skeletal remains of women indicated tendencies rather different from those of their male counterparts. Jean-Pierre Urlacher, Françoise Passard and Sophie Manfredi-Gizard, *La Nécropole mérovingienne de la Grand Oye à Doubs (Département de Doubs) VI–VII siècles après J.-C.*, Mémoires de l'Association Française d'Archéologie Mérovingienne 10 (Saint-Germain-en-Laye, 1998), pp. 35–45.

[41] Luc Buchet, 'Les habitants de la Gaule rurale, société des morts, société des vivants: apports de l'anthropologie', in Alain Ferdière (ed.), *Monde des morts, monde des vivants en Gaule rurale. Actes du*

of ethnic groups contrasts markedly with widespread acknowledgement among historians of the highly flexible use of ethnic terminology by early medieval authors. These methodologies thus reveal a widening gap between scholars working in the disciplines of history on the one hand, and archaeology and physical anthropology on the other.[42] These trends, however, are far from absolute,[43] but parallel similarly gendered arguments regarding the sexing of skeletons on the basis of grave goods.[44] Such interpretive tendencies result from the desire to see the deceased buried in cemeteries as members of unified groups rather than as individuals and social agents.[45]

WOMEN'S BURIAL AND ETHNIC IDENTITY IN THE ARCHAEOLOGICAL RECORD

How have discussions of early medieval ethnicity affected research on early medieval women? Theories positing links between ethnicity and female adornment have been a comparatively recent development. They centre mainly on the third through sixth centuries and are largely confined to technical pieces aimed at an audience of specialists. Beyond general neglect of the importance of understanding the roles of women, this reticence stems from disputed interpretations of the *fibulae* (brooches) on which ethnoarchaeological arguments have hinged. For instance, it is usually thought that distinctive cross-bow brooches (*Zwiebelkopffibeln*) were male possessions. They probably fastened military and civilian officials' garments in the late Roman period, in this case with a single brooch closing a cloak on the right shoulder.[46] Only in the second half of the twentieth century were graves with more than one brooch but lacking armament viewed as relevant to discussions of women, and thus female graves also attributed with

colloque ARCHEA/AGER (Orléans, 7–9 février 1992), 6e Supplément de la Revue Archéologique du Centre de la France (Région Centre, 1993), pp. 17–19.

[42] For the historical view, see Patrick J. Geary, 'Ethnic identity as a situational construct in the early Middle Ages', *Mitteilungen der Anthropologischen Gesellschaft Wien* 113 (1983), pp. 15–26. Pohl, 'Telling the Difference', pp. 40–51.

[43] Brather, 'Ethnische Identitäten', pp. 139–77. Sebastian Brather, 'Kulturgruppe und Kulturkreis', in *Reallexikon der Germanischen Altertumskunde*, vol. XVII, new edition (Berlin, 2000), pp. 442–52.

[44] For more on this topic, see Bonnie Effros, 'Skeletal sex and gender in Merovingian mortuary archaeology', *Antiquity* 74 (2000), pp. 632–9.

[45] Roberta Gilchrist, 'Ambivalent bodies: gender and medieval archaeology', in Jenny Moore and Eleanor Scott (eds.), *Invisible People and Processes: Writing Gender and Childhood into European Archaeology* (London, 1997), pp. 46–50. D. M. Hadley and J. M. Moore, '"Death makes the man"? Burial rites and the construction of masculinity in the early Middle Ages', in D. M. Hadley (ed.), *Masculinity in Medieval Europe* (London, 1999), pp. 24–6.

[46] See for example, Joachim Werner, 'Römische Fibeln des 5. Jahrhunderts von der Gurina im Gailtal und vom Grepault bei Truns (Graubünden)', *Der Schlern* 32 (1958), pp. 109–12.

ethnic symbols.[47] Since little actual clothing survives from early medieval graves, studies of women's garments have relied extensively on brooches and brooch positions. Reconstructions of the original appearance of early medieval clothing have rested upon a limited number of mosaics and other images of high-status women in this general period.[48]

Analysis of graves presumed to contain the remains of women on the basis of accompanying 'feminine' artefacts is usually based upon the premise that authorities were far more interested in regulating male than female appearance, since women could not hold administrative offices.[49] As noted by Mary Harlow in this volume (chapter 3 above), male garments such as the toga and trousers received more extensive attention in the written sources; officials' main concern was that men should not appear effeminate. By contrast, owing to extensive dependence upon brooches found in cemeteries for the determination of that population's identity, scholars have long persisted in the idea that, before the late seventh century, women wore the clothing of a single ethnic heritage from birth to death with few exceptions.[50] Such a view assumes that the inability to alter personal markers of identity in late antiquity and the early Merovingian era, even in burial, applied to all women regardless of their ethnic affiliation. Scholars normally presume, therefore, that so-called foreign brooches belonged to women who travelled with transitory minority populations such as bands of Germanic soldiers (*foederati*), or who came to reside far from their birthplaces as a consequence of exogamous relationships with members of other Germanic groups or with Romans.[51] Although marriages between Romans and 'barbarians' or Franks and Visigoths in Gaul were certainly conceivable in the fourth, fifth and sixth centuries,[52] and brooches may have passed from one community

[47] Ute Haimerl, 'Die Vogelfibeln der älteren Merowingerzeit. Bemerkungen zur Chronologie und zur Herleitung der Fibelgattung', *Acta Praehistorica et Archaeologica* 30 (1998), pp. 99–103.

[48] Max Martin, 'Schmuck und Tracht des frühen Mittelalters', in Max Martin and Johannes Prammer (eds.), *Frühe Baiern im Straubinger Land. Gaudemuseum Straubing* (Straubing, 1995), pp. 40–7.

[49] 'Excepting empresses who might sport male badges, since women did not hold office, their baubles were not of political significance.' Janes, 'The golden clasp', p. 146.

[50] Max Martin suggests that the only reason a woman might change her brooch was if it were broken. Max Martin, 'Fibel und Fibeltracht: Späte Völkerwanderungszeit und Merowingerzeit auf dem Kontinent', in *Reallexikon der Germanischen Altertumskunde*, vol. VIII, new edition (Berlin, 1994), pp. 574–7.

[51] Koch, *Bügelfibeln*, vol. II, pp. 515–25.

[52] On the CT 3.14.1 and its ineffective ban on marriages between provincials and barbarians, see Hagith Sivan, 'Why not marry a barbarian? Marital frontiers in late antiquity (the example of *CTh* 3.14.1)', in Ralph W. Mathisen and Hagith Sivan (eds.), *Shifting Frontiers in Late Antiquity* (Aldershot, 1996), pp. 136–45. Hagith Sivan, 'The appropriation of Roman law in barbarian hands: "Roman–barbarian" marriage in Visigothic Gaul and Spain', in Pohl and Reimitz (eds.), *Strategies of Distinction*, pp. 189–203.

to another through a bride's possessions, this proposal should not constitute the only interpretive possibility explored by archaeologists, since it rests on a long series of gender assumptions.

The weakness of existing models of female bodily display is their implication that women were without exception passive agents; the assumed stability of a woman's costume none the less contributes to archaeologists' confidence in the accuracy of their typological markers. Yet such approaches do not take into account the manner in which grave goods conveyed multiple meanings regarding the identity of the deceased, their significance not being limited to ethnicity and gender.[53] Certain types of personal adornment such as bracelets and beads seem to have been used across the late Roman empire, whereas others were limited to particular regions. These distinctions are better characterised as regional preferences, since it is impossible to know whether they correlated with those individuals' personal identification with specific ethnic groups.[54] Traditional models, moreover, assume that women were incapable of initiating or activating the expression of ethnicity, and that the style of women's dress, beyond that affected by age, remained unchanged throughout their lifetimes. Methodological bias of this sort has affected the interpretation of early medieval graves throughout the western Roman empire.[55]

We must therefore re-evaluate existing assumptions, keeping in mind the ways in which these views may be contingent upon modern sensibilities.[56] Early medieval women are too seldom conceived as viable contributors to gift-giving or trade networks in their communities. Another issue of importance is the role of cultural imitation most commonly discussed in conjunction with the influence of Byzantine jewellery and ceremonial on the Franks. Other Germanic peoples, including Scandinavians, may have deliberately sought to mimic prestigious foreign styles.[57] Current studies thus give too little weight to the symbolism of the adornment of hair, face

---

[53] Michelle I. Marcus, 'Incorporating the body: adornment, gender and social identity in ancient Iran', *Cambridge Archaeological Journal* 3 (1993), pp. 157–9. I thank Allison Karmel Thomason for kindly referring me to this piece.

[54] Ellen Swift, *Regionality in Dress Accessories in the Late Roman West*, Monographies Instrumentum 11 (Montagnac, 2000), pp. 228–30.

[55] See, for instance, Max Martin, 'Die Gräberfelder von Straubing-Bajuwarenstraße und Straßkirchen: Zwei erstrangige Quellen zur Geschichte der frühen Baiern im Straubinger Land', in Martin and Prammer (eds.), *Frühe Baiern im Straubinger Land*, pp. 18–27.

[56] S. J. Lucy, 'Housewives, warriors and slaves? Sex and gender in Anglo-Saxon burials', in Moore and Scott (eds.), *Invisible People and Processes*, pp. 150–68.

[57] Mechthild Schulze, 'Einflüsse byzantischer Prunkgewänder auf die fränkische Frauentracht', *Archäologisches Korrespondenzblatt* 6 (1976), pp. 149–50, 157–8. Hayo Vierck, '*Imitatio imperii* und *interpretatio germanica* vor der Wikingerzeit', in Rudolf Zeitler (ed.), *Les Pays du nord et Byzance (Scandinavie et Byzance): Actes du Colloque d'Upsal, 20–22 avril 1979*, Acta Universitatis Upsaliensis,

and body as affected by age and other factors such as marital and social status.[58] We need to consider the likelihood that both women and men had some degree of control over their garments within a range of artefacts available to them and their families.

Now that we have addressed the general shortcomings of ethnoarchaeological approaches to grave goods associated with female skeletons, it is helpful to demonstrate their application in individual cases. Of particular interest for our purposes are the significant numbers of Danube-style brooches which have been found in cemeterial contexts in Gaul. They are labelled most frequently as 'Visigothic', but sometimes also as 'Alan', 'Vandal', 'Hunnic' or more generally typical of the Danube and Black Sea regions (Fig. 8). At more than forty cemeteries in Frankish, Burgundian and Alamannic regions, for instance, Volker Bierbrauer has catalogued what he believes to have been the graves of fifth-century Visigothic women. As he posits that Visigothic women were distinguished from their contemporaries through the use of tunics fastened at the shoulders, Bierbrauer has identified these tombs as female on the basis of the brooches with which the bodies were buried. However, the *peplos*, a Greek term used to designate this style of dress, had been abandoned at least three centuries earlier by the Roman population.[59] In contrast, Max Martin suggests that fifth-century Frankish, Alamannic, Thuringian and Lombard women probably wore four brooches on their upper body to fasten their clothing whereas Roman women typically closed draped cloaks with a single large round brooch just below the neck.[60] Yet, finds in Frankish regions of *fibulae* identified as Visigothic brooches have surprisingly few parallels in regions which the Visigoths are known from written sources to have inhabited at the same

---

Figura, Nova Series 19 (Uppsala, 1981), pp. 65–70, 83–92. Michael McCormick, 'Clovis at Tours, Byzantine public ritual and the origins of medieval ruler symbolism', in Chrysos and Schwarcz (eds.), *Das Reich und die Barbaren*, pp. 163–4.

[58] Gabriella Schubert, *Kleidung als Zeichen: Kopfbedeckungen im Donau-Balkan-Raum*, Osteuropa-Institut an der Freien Universität Berlin, Balkanologische Veröffentlichungen 20 (Wiesbaden and Berlin, 1993), pp. 31–68. I thank Guy Halsall for allowing me to read his very relevant but as yet unpublished manuscript: 'Material culture, sex, gender and transgression in sixth-century Gaul: some reflections in the light of recent archaeological debate'.

[59] Volker Bierbrauer, 'Les Wisigoths dans le royaume franc', in Françoise Vallet, Michel Kazanski and Patrick Périn (eds.), *Des Royaumes barbares au 'regnum francorum': l'Occident à l'époque de Childéric et de Clovis (vers 450 – vers 530). Actes des XVIIIes Journées internationales d'archéologie mérovingienne, Saint-Germain-en-Laye, Musée des antiquités nationales, 23–24 avril 1997*, Mémoires publiés par l'Association Française d'Archéologie Mérovingienne 11 (Saint-Germain-en-Laye, 1998), pp. 167–75.

[60] Max Martin, 'Tradition und Wandel der fibelgeschmückten frühmittelalterlichen Frauenkleidung', *Jahrbuch des Römisch-Germanischen Zentralmuseums Mainz* 38, 2 (1991), pp. 629–34.

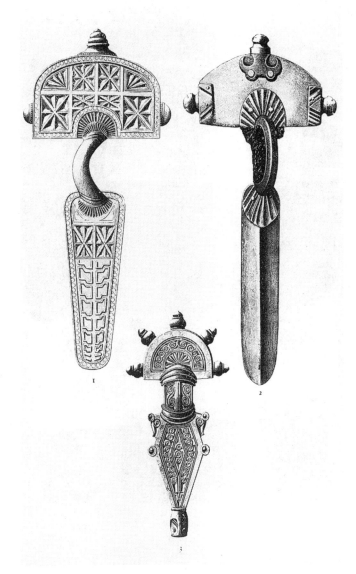

8   Danube-style brooches from fifth-century cemeteries in Gaul. The three brooches in
this image were all discovered in the cemetery of Marchélepot (Somme). The one depicted
on the upper right (2) was one of a pair of silver *fibulae* described by C. Boulanger as
Gothic in style and typical of the regions of Hungary and the Crimea.

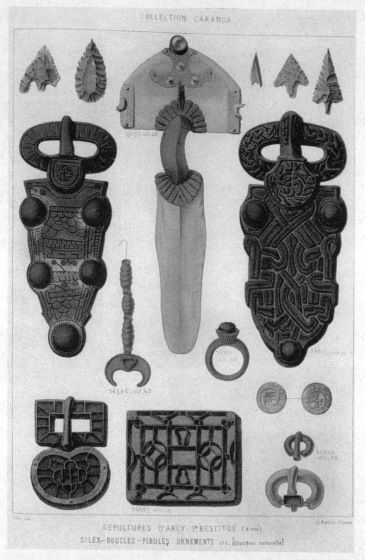

9 Grave goods from Arcy-Sainte-Restitue (Aisne), as published by the excavator in 1879. The large 'Danubian-style' brooch at the top centre of this plate was discovered in a richly appointed sepulchre at this cemetery by Frédéric Moreau. The same grave also contained a bronze coin, a silver ring with a monogram, two large silver earrings and a small amphora of red clay.

period.[61] While differences in dress between individual graves are nearly always linked to the presence of adherents of other ethnic groups, explanations for the appearance of 'foreign' brooches in random graves in Gaul must be more complex than those individuals' expression of ethnic identity.

THE ASSUMED PASSIVITY OF EARLY MEDIEVAL WOMEN:
A CRITIQUE

A few specific cases will help to explain the implications of current ethnic interpretations of female burials. One of the most well known is a fifth-century grave uncovered at Airan (Calvados) during road construction in 1876. Workers found there a single skeleton of unidentified sex accompanied by a pair of polychrome brooches connected by a chain, as well as an engraved silver belt buckle, a gold necklace and other assorted pieces of jewellery. Since skeletal remains were scant, the rich assemblage of jewellery, which antiquaries deemed Danubian in appearance, contributed to the identification of the grave as that of a 'foreign' woman. Owing to the lack of a broader cemeterial context, Edouard Salin and Albert France-Lanord's reassessment of the solitary Airan grave goods in 1949 was inconclusive: they tentatively suggested that the objects belonged to the wife of an Alan chieftain or perhaps represented the acquisitions by trade of a Saxon princess in Normandy.[62] Recent studies of the Airan artefacts have been less cautious. Michel Kazanski has unquestioningly identified the deceased as an elite female member of a migrating band from the Danube region.[63] Seeing the expression of ethnicity as the primary or sole objective of mortuary display has thus restricted the interpretive potential of the symbolic functions of brooches associated with female burials.

Knowledge of many additional fourth and fifth-century cemeterial sites in Gaul containing so-called foreign artefacts is unfortunately limited, owing to the survival of only brief descriptions of the artefacts and almost no information about their original context. This is the case, for example, for brooches uncovered in the late 1870s and 1880s by Frédéric Moreau at Arcy-Sainte-Restitue and Chassemy (Aisne) (Figs. 9 and 10). Despite painstaking reconstruction of Moreau's excavation by Françoise Vallet, it is

[61] Patrick Périn, 'La progression des Francs en Gaule du Nord au Ve siècle: histoire et archéologie', in Geuenich (ed.), *Die Franken und die Alemannen bis zur 'Schlacht bei Zülpich' 496/97*, pp. 76–9.
[62] Edouard Salin and Albert France-Lanord, 'Le trésor d'Airan en Calvados', *Monuments et Mémoires* 43 (1949), pp. 119–35.
[63] Michel Kazanski, 'Deux riches tombes de l'époque des grandes invasions au Nord de la Gaule (Airan et Pouan)', *Archéologie Médiévale* 12 (1982), pp. 17–24.

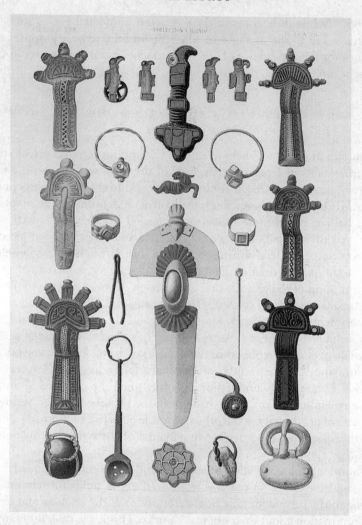

10 Grave goods from the cemetery at Chassemy (Aisne), as published by the excavator
Frédéric Moreau in 1889. The large silver brooch portrayed at the centre of this plate is
decorated with gilded ornaments in the pattern of a shell and closely resembles the single
brooch found at Arcy-Sainte-Restitue in 1878. It was originally part of a pair of matching
pieces discovered at a depth of more than 1 metre and resting on the chest of a female
skeleton. Besides the two brooches, two iron rings, thought by Moreau to have formed
part of the coffin, were the only artefacts found in this grave.

impossible to re-establish in which graves these objects once lay and with what sorts of assemblages. Poor documentation thus greatly hinders discussion of the type of garments worn by the deceased.[64] The significance of the exact placement of brooches in a burial may be illustrated with an example from the cemetery of Saint-Martin-de-Fontenay (Calvados), at which archaeologists unearthed nine graves containing alleged Visigothic artifacts. In the case of grave no. 741, Merovingian-style *fibulae* were deposited at chest level in the presumed style of the Visigoths. Bierbrauer has interpreted this practice as evidence of gradual Gothic acculturation to customs of the majority following their forced displacement in Frankish regions.[65] Other interpretations are equally possible, however, for indigenous women might well have acquired other types of clothing over the course of their lives through trade, gift-exchange or the desire to imitate 'foreign' styles of dress.

Where the archaeological context of 'foreign' artefacts is better known, explanations have become increasingly sophisticated. At the cemetery of Vicq (Yvelines), for instance, tomb no. 756 yielded a pair of gilded silver bird-shaped brooches with eyes made of garnets, two silver brooches with a rounded head and three knobs, a large gilded bronze plaque-buckle with inlaid glass, and a silver ring. As noted by Edmond Servat, however, the first set of brooches were worn in a 'Frankish' manner near the neck (*au niveau de cou*), whereas the style and apparent use of the latter set of brooches was more analogous to customs in Visigothic regions.[66] In the early sixth century, according to Servat's interpretation, this Visigothic woman still retained garments from her land of origin while assimilating some elements of her dress to the *mores* of her new land by marriage. Alexander Koch has proposed a similar explanation for the roughly contemporary grave no. 140 at Nouvion-en-Ponthieu (Somme), in which some of the so-called Visigothic additions to the grave were actually manufactured locally in the north of Gaul in the Visigothic style.[67] Despite the complexity of these assemblages, it is apparently inconceivable to Servat and Koch that

---

[64] Françoise Vallet, 'Parures féminines étrangères du début de l'époque mérovingienne, trouvées dans le Soissonnais', *Studien zur Sachsenforschung* 8 (1993), pp. 109–21; Vallet, 'Tombe de femme d'Arcy-Sainte-Restitue (Aisne)', in Marin (ed.), *Attila, les influences danubiennes dans l'Ouest de l'Europe au Ve siècle*, pp. 95–6.

[65] Bierbrauer, 'Les Wisigoths', pp. 169–75.

[66] Edmond Servat, 'Exemple d'exogamie dans la nécropole de Vicq (Yvelines)', *Bulletin de Liaison: Association Française d'Archéologie Mérovingienne* 1 (1979), pp. 40–4.

[67] Alexander Koch, 'Fremde Fibeln im Frankenreich. Ein Beitrag zur Frage nichtfränkischer germanischer Ethnien in Nordgallien', *Acta Praehistorica et Archaeologica* 30 (1998), pp. 78–82.

these brooches might have conveyed anything other than ethnic symbolism or that they might have acquired different or multiple meanings in this geographical context.

An additional issue that complicates the discussion of Visigothic or Danube region grave goods in Merovingian cemeteries is the occasional discovery of limited numbers of artificially heightened skulls, attributed most frequently to female skeletons. Depending upon the location of their discovery, they have been linked by anthropologists to Alamannic peoples,[68] Hunnic inhabitants of the Burgundian kingdom,[69] and more generally to steppe populations that migrated to Gaul. When they are found in early medieval graves with distinctive archaeological artefacts, Luc Buchet has argued that there are sufficient grounds for their identification with specific ethnic groups.[70] In the case of Saint-Martin-de-Fontenay (Calvados), for instance, Buchet has used seven examples of voluntary skull deformation among female, and in one case male, inhabitants to support his hypothesis of the burial of a Visigothic minority at this cemetery, despite the fact that the Visigothic grave goods were not in the same sepulchres as this anthropological evidence.[71] As has been argued by Eric Crubézy, however, the ritual of artificial deformation of infants' and children's skulls may have been practised among indigenous inhabitants who assimilated to the customs of those hailing from further abroad, since no means exist to identify individual members of ethnic populations. Such skull shapes could have also resulted in individual cases from a headband or headdress worn tightly at an early age.[72] It seems likely that voluntary skull deformation represents no more reliable an ethnic marker than brooches, belts or weapon sets.

---

[68] Neil M. Huber, *Anthropologische Untersuchungen an den Skeletten aus dem alamannischen Reihengräberfeld von Weingarten, Kr. Ravensburg*, Naturwissenschaftliche Untersuchungen zur Vor- und Frühgeschichte in Württemberg und Hohenzollern 3 (Stuttgart, 1967), p. 7.

[69] H. Gaillard de Sémainville, 'Aux origines de la Bourgogne: Burgondes, Francs et Gallo-Romains', in *Bourgogne médiévale, la mémoire du sol: 20 ans de recherches archéologiques* (Mâcon, 1987), pp. 42–3, 59. Marc-Rodolphe Sauter, 'Sur des crânes déformés de la nécropole de Saint-Prex, Vaud (VIe siècle)', *Bulletin der Schweizerischen Gesellschaft für Anthropologie und Ethnologie* 32 (1955–56), pp. 6–7.

[70] Luc Buchet, 'La déformation crânienne en Gaule et dans les régions limitrophes pendant le haut moyen âge, son origine – sa valeur historique', *Archéologie Médiévale* 18 (1988), p. 65.

[71] Luc Buchet and Christian Pilet, 'Les femmes orientales en Basse Normandie au Ve siècle', in Luc Buchet (ed.), *La Femme pendant le moyen âge et l'époque moderne. Actes des Sixièmes journées anthropologiques de Valbonne, 9-10-11 juin 1992*, Dossier de Documentation Archéologique 17 (Paris, 1994), pp. 114–23.

[72] Eric Crubézy, 'Merovingian skull deformations in the southwest of France', in David Austin and Leslie Alcock (eds.), *From the Baltic to the Black Sea: Studies in Medieval Archaeology*, One World Archaeology 18 (London, 1990), pp. 189–208.

CONCLUSIONS

Current methodological dictates hold that fourth- and fifth-century arte-facts in the typical style of the Danube basin and identified as 'Visigothic' which have been found in regions occupied by the Franks are a sign of Germanic military presence displayed on the garments of soldiers' wives. By contrast, archaeologists suggest that, by the sixth century, these minor-ity populations had become assimilated to the majority of inhabitants, an explanation neatly in accord with the pattern of mixed goods observed in a limited number of sepulchres in Merovingian cemeteries of this period. While the bearers of the so-called Visigothic brooches have been described as participants in exogamous marriages, Roman or Germanic military wives, or even kidnap victims taken to distant regions,[73] these romantic theories share in common the assumed passivity of their female bearers. They also rest on the problematic determination that certain artefacts were forever associated with the expression of a specific ethnic identity regardless of the manner in which they were used or by whom. While certain brooches may well have conveyed ethnic symbolism in certain situations and places, this interpretation cannot replace a broad range of other possibilities as to how individual 'foreign' objects came to rest in early medieval graves in Gaul. The fact remains that these *fibulae* may have been viewed not as alien by contemporaries but rather as unique and therefore highly desirable symbols in the expression of social, religious and gender identity.

Of broader significance than the interpretation of individual brooches is the way in which archaeological evidence has been assumed sufficient to ascertain the ethnicity of deceased individuals in late antique and early medieval graves. In the desire for straightforward answers regarding the identity of the populations of early medieval cemeteries, scholars have tended not to question the suitability for this purpose of brooches that had both practical and symbolic functions. This chapter has identified some of the dangers of the analysis of early medieval grave goods exclusively for the purpose of determining the deceased's ethnicity, and, especially, the error of assuming that women were passive bearers of ethnic identity. The uneven handling and interpretation of artefacts found in graves based on the pre-sumed gender of their bearers has had serious repercussions and has skewed our understanding of the transformation of the Roman world into the early medieval one. Aside from influencing the reading of individual graves, such

[73] For the last proposition, see Koch, 'Fremde Fibeln', pp. 70–4.

gender-biased assumptions have affected our cartographic representations of the Germanic migrations and the distribution of their settlements. And, through this medium, our students inherit these ill-considered stereotypes of passive women. A more nuanced approach, one that admits that we do not have all of the answers and that leaves more room for the uncertainty of our interpretations of burial goods, will help us to teach them in the long run to be more critical thinkers and better scholars.[74]

[74] I thank Nina Caputo, Heinrich Härke, Jörg Jarnut, Frans Theuws and the anonymous reviewers of this volume for their comments on the above discussion. Patrick Périn and Chantal Dulos kindly offered their assistance in procuring photographs for this piece. Research on and revision of this chapter were made possible by a Faculty Development Fund stipend from the College of Arts and Sciences and two Summer Research Fellowships (2000–1) from the Graduate School, Southern Illinois University at Edwardsville. Final adaptations were made during a Sylvan C. Coleman and Pamela Coleman Memorial Fund Fellowship at the Metropolitan Museum of Art (2001–2), taken with the assistance of Title F leave from the State University of New York at Binghamton.

CHAPTER 10

Gendering courts in the early medieval west

Janet L. Nelson

The sociologist's question, what makes a court society, is inseparable from the historian's, who, when and where? For early modernists, the time of the court society's appearance was the long Renaissance, from the fifteenth to the seventeenth century; and the place was France. Norbert Elias focused on changes in the social utilisation of space, that is, the removal of the nobility from the countryside and from nature, and in aristocratic psychology, that is, the noble's acquisition of artifice, his internalisation of restraint, and in particular his abandonment of such 'feudal' virtues as 'impetuous lust for battle'. The king, or rather the monarchic state, set about taming the nobility – the essence of Elias's civilising process – not by force, but by guile. Uprooted, drawn into the ambit of the palace, nobles pursued honour and status at court, where they danced to the king's tune.[1] At the same time, and this is Foucault's gloss on Elias, the monarchic state perfected techniques of disciplining not just elites but the population at large.[2] Both Elias and especially Foucault managed to write a lot about control, and self-control, of the body. Both tended to write as if the world consisted of men only.[3]

More recently, the origins of a court society have been investigated by medievalists. Stephen Jaeger stressed the role of clergy at courts, German as well as French, from the tenth century to the twelfth, and clerical inculcation

---

[1] N. Elias, *Über den Prozess der Zivilisation: soziogenetische und psychogenetische Untersuchungen* (Berne, 1939, repr. 1969), English trans. E. Jephcott, *The Civilising Process* (Oxford, 1994); Elias, *Die höfische Gesellschaft* (Berlin, 1973), English trans. E. Jephcott, *The Court Society* (Oxford, 1983). Cf. G. Klaniczay, 'Everyday life and elites in the later Middle Ages', in P. Linehan and J. L. Nelson (eds.), *The Medieval World* (London, 2001), pp. 671–90.

[2] M. Foucault, *Histoire de la folie à l'âge classique* (Paris, 1961), English trans. R. Howard, *Madness and Civilisation* (London, 1967); Foucault, *Discipline and Punish*, extracts in P. Rabinow (ed.), *The Foucault Reader* (London, 1991).

[3] To be fair, Elias did occasionally mention women, e.g. *Court Society*, pp. 243–4. For Foucault, see L. Foxhall, 'Pandora unbound: a feminist critique of Foucault's *History of Sexuality*', in A. Cornwall and N. Lindisfarne (eds.), *Dislocating Masculinity: Comparative Ethnographies* (London, 1994), pp. 133–46.

of civilised virtues of mildness, equanimity and humour.[4] John Gillingham's twelfth-century renaissance saw the birth of chivalry, of rules of war, and (it must be said, taking a rather minor place) love, generally from the perspective of the married man.[5] Scholars of vernacular languages and literatures have kept the chronological focus in the central and later Middle Ages, with a geographical span across what I would call the post-Carolingian world.[6] The court society remains, with honourable exceptions, overwhelmingly male-dominated.

A third tack is possible as well, and it is the one I intend to take here, taking a leaf from a not-so-recent book, vol. 1 of Reno Radwolf Bezzola's *Les Origines et la formation de la littérature courtoise*.[7] Courtliness, I shall argue, was made in the earlier Middle Ages, in the courts of so-called barbarian kings culminating in those of Carolingians, and among its makers and diffusers, alongside and no less important than clergy or kings and knights, were women. The inclusion of women has implications for the reproduction as well as the formation of courtliness, for the gendering of space, and for a remodelling of aristocratic male psychology.

Even as the Middle Ages dawned, a barbarian king's Roman-educated bride was represented as a one-woman civilising process. When Theoderic, king of the Goths, sent his niece (she is not named – this is every-princess) to King Hermenfrid of the Thuringians in 506/512, Cassiodorus penned the accompanying letter on Theoderic's behalf:

> I send you the glory of a court and home, the increase of a kindred, a loyal and comforting counsellor, a most sweet and charming wife. With you, she will lawfully play a ruler's part, and she will discipline your nation with a better way of life. Fortunate Thuringia will possess what Italy has reared, a woman learned in letters, schooled in moral character, glorious not only for her lineage, but equally for her feminine dignity. So your country will be famous for her character, no less than for its victories.[8]

---

[4] C. S. Jaeger, *The Origins of Courtliness: Civilizing Trends and the Formation of Courtly Ideals* (Philadelphia, 1985).

[5] J. Gillingham, 'Love, marriage and politics in the twelfth century', *Forum for Modern Language Studies* 25 (1989), pp. 292–303, repr. in Gillingham, *Richard Cœur de Lion* (London, 1994), pp. 243–4; Gillingham, 'Kingship, chivalry and love. Political and cultural values in the earliest history written in French', in C. W. Hollister (ed.), *Anglo-Norman Political Culture and the Twelfth Century Renaissance* (Woodbridge, 1997), pp. 33–58, repr. in Gillingham, *The English in the Twelfth Century* (Woodbridge, 2000), pp. 233–58.

[6] For penetrating discussion of the range of just some of this material in Old French, Occitan and Anglo-Norman French, see L. Paterson, 'Gender negotiations in France during the central Middle Ages: the literary evidence', in Linehan and Nelson (eds.), *The Medieval World*, pp. 246–66.

[7] R. R. Bezzola, *Les Origines et la formation de la littérature courtoise*, 2 vols. (Paris, 1944, 1963).

[8] Cassiodorus, *Variae epistulae* IV.1, ed. T. Mommsen, *MGH AA* XII (Berlin, 1894), p. 114, part-trans. S. J. B. Barnish, *Cassiodorus: Variae* (Liverpool, 1992), p. 74. For the context and significance

The letter continued by describing the exceptionally fine horses sent in return by the Thuringian king, and concluded by comparing gift and counter-gift: 'the herd for all its nobility is surpassed, since the woman outdoes them all'. Cassiodorus' claims for similar intellectual and moral endowments on the part of Theoderic's daughter Amalasuntha strengthen the impression that a royal woman could actually be, and was indeed deployed as, a cultural agent.[9] Curiously, although Gregory of Tours was extremely critical of Hermenfrid's wife as queen ('a wicked and cruel woman'), he supplies information that suggests she performed as advertised.[10] Keen to foment rivalry between Hermenfrid and his brother, she coded the message thus: 'one day when her husband came in for dinner, he found that the table was only half-laid, and when he asked his wife what she meant by this, she replied: "a king deprived of half his kingdom deserves to find half his table bare"'. The king acted as cued, attacked his brother and seized his half of the kingdom. Later, after the Franks attacked and defeated Hermenfrid, among the war-captives was the king's niece, Radegund. She had apparently been brought up at the court of her uncle and aunt. Now the victorious Merovingian Chlothar I claimed her as bride. Radegund, after a period of trial, famously rejected married life, but her subsequent career as abbess of the convent of the Holy Cross at Poitiers, and her interest in the latest Roman piety, may have owed something to her aunt's schooling in character and certainly offered occasions for continuing contact with Chlothar's and other Merovingians' courts. A royally patronised convent, with a woman like Radegund in charge, could itself become an ancillary form of courtly society.[11] In other words, the gendered rhetoric of Roman Christian

---

of Cassiodorus' work, the best short *entrées* are provided by P. Heather, 'The historical culture of Ostrogothic Italy', in *Teoderico il grande e I Goti d'Italia*, Atti del XIII Congresso internazionale di studi sull' Alto Medioevo (Spoleto, 1993), pp. 317–53; Heather, 'Theoderic, king of the Goths', *EME* 4 (1995), pp. 145–73; and C. La Rocca, 'Perceptions of an early medieval urban landscape', in Linehan and Nelson (eds.), *The Medieval World*, pp. 416–31. The significance of gendered cultural roles in inter-dynastic marriages deserves more discussion.

9 Cassiodorus, *Variae* XI.I, pp. 327–30, trans. Barnish, pp. 145–50.

10 Gregory of Tours, *Decem libri historiarum* III.4, 7, ed. B. Krusch and W. Levison, *MGH SRM* I, I (Berlin, 1951), pp. 99–100, 103–5.

11 For Radegund, her convent, and her connections, see J. George, *Venantius Fortunatus: A Latin Poet in Merovingian Gaul* (Oxford, 1992), pp. 161–78; I. Wood, *The Merovingian Kingdoms* (London, 1994), pp. 136–9; I. Moreira, 'Provisatrix optima: St. Radegond of Poitiers' relic petitions to the East', *Journal of Medieval History* 19 (1993), pp. 285–306; and for insights on the convent's local exclusivity co-existing with high-level political contacts, B. Rosenwein, 'Gregory of Tours and episcopal exemption', in K. Mitchell and I. Wood (eds.), *The World of Gregory of Tours* (Leiden, 2002), pp. 181–98 at pp. 189–95. For Anglo-Saxon convents, see S. Foot, *Veiled Women I* (Aldershot, 2000), pp. 35–61. On convents and courts more generally, see the path-breaking discussion of K. J. Leyser, *Rule and Conflict in an Early Medieval Society* (Oxford, 1979), pp. 63–73; further, M. A. Meyer, 'Patronage of the West Saxon royal nunneries in late Anglo-Saxon England', *Revue Bénédictine* 91 (1981), pp. 332–58; S. Airlie, 'The palace of memory: the Carolingian court as political centre', in S. Rees Jones *et al.* (eds.),

rulership could affect the way educated barbarian royal women lived out
their roles, allotted and/or chosen, in more ways than the well-known converting of pagan husbands.[12]

Two further examples support that idea, and amplify the social and spatial
contexts in which royal women worked, to include other women and also
other men. The first is Queen Balthild, wife then widow of the Frankish
king Clovis II, and subsequently venerated as a saint at her convent of
Chelles.[13] Her care of the young men and youths at her husband's court 'as
the best of nurturers', and her 'exhorting of the young to religious studies',
were celebrated by the author of her *Life*.[14] In the same source, she was
presented as a captive slave, 'bought at a low price' by the Frankish mayor
of the palace Erchinoald, and 'raised from the dunghill' by her royal marriage.[15] I wholeheartedly accept the rereading of Balthild's origins offered by
Paul Fouracre and Dick Gerberding. No low-born Merovingian queen she,
but a high-born Anglo-Saxon, whose connections did Erchinoald and the
Merovingians a power of good.[16] Her 'chemise', in fact a kind of tabard or
overall, amazingly rediscovered in the 1980s in a reliquary at Chelles where

   Courts and Regions in Medieval Europe (York, 2000), pp. 1–20 at pp. 18–20; and B. Yorke, *Nunneries
   and the Anglo-Saxon Royal Houses* (London, 2003.) Gender issues here would merit exploration in
   a broader comparative context, on lines fruitfully pursued by P. Stafford, 'Queens, nunneries and
   reforming churchmen: gender, religious status and reform in tenth- and eleventh-century England',
   Past and Present 163 (1999), pp. 3–35, and S. MacLean, 'Queenship, nunneries and royal widowhood
   in Carolingian Europe', *Past and Present* 178 (2003), pp. 3–38.

[12] Some implications of conversion through queens in Anglo-Saxon England are examined by S. Hollis,
   Anglo-Saxon Women and the Church (Cambridge, 1992), pp. 208–42; A. Scharer, 'La conversion des
   rois anglo-saxons', in M. Rouche (ed.), *Clovis: Histoire et Mémoire I* (Paris, 1997), pp. 881–98; M. A.
   Meyer, 'Queens, convents, and conversion in early Anglo-Saxon England', *Revue Bénédictine* 109
   (1999), pp. 90–116; and I. Wood, 'Augustine and Gaul', in R. Gameson (ed.), St. *Augustine and the
   Conversion of England* (Stroud, 1999), pp. 68–82.

[13] See J. L. Nelson, 'Queens as Jezebels: Brunhild and Balthild in Merovingian history', in D. Baker
   (ed.), *Medieval Women* (Oxford, 1978), pp. 31–77, repr. in Nelson, *Politics and Ritual in Early
   Medieval Europe* (London, 1986), pp. 1–48 esp. pp. 16–23, 31–44; Wood, *The Merovingian Kingdoms*,
   pp. 197–202.

[14] *Vita Balthildis* c. 4, ed. B. Krusch, *MGH SRM* II, p. 485, trans. in P. Fouracre and R. Gerberding,
   Late Merovingian France: History and Hagiography 640–720 (Manchester, 1996), p. 121.

[15] *Vita Balthildis*, c. 2, p. 483, trans. p. 119, with important commentary at pp. 97–104.

[16] Fouracre and Gerberding, as preceding note, draw on the wider context sketched by Wood, 'Frankish
   hegemony in England', in M. Carver (ed.), *The Age of Sutton Hoo* (Woodbridge, 1992), pp. 235–41.
   In my 1978 paper, I accepted the 'information' of the *Vita Balthildis* unreflectively. Thanks to a
   symposium organised in July 2002 by the Norwich Museum and the University of East Anglia, the
   recent discovery at Postwick near Norwich of a seal-ring matrix inscribed with the name 'Baldehildis'
   has prompted new debate, without so far any firm new conclusions. My paper on that occasion,
   where I argued that the *Vita* included a version of Balthild's life based on her own recollections at
   Chelles, may be published in the proceedings of the symposium. See also my article, 'Balthild', in
   The Oxford Dictionary of National Biography, forthcoming.

it remains to this very day, has also inspired some new thinking in the light of both material and textual evidence.[17] The chemise, a piece of linen some 117 × 84 cm, is embroidered with brightly coloured silk thread to suggest three necklaces, from the second of which hangs an embroidered pectoral cross. The silken necklaces reproduce, in another medium, the heavy necklaces of jewels and precious metals worn by Byzantine empresses, early medieval queens, and the ladies of their courts. The first hypothesis, then, is that Queen Balthild, in her life at court, had actually worn necklaces, reminiscent of those that her exact Anglo-Saxon contemporary Æthelthryth of Ely had worn as an East Anglian princess and then as a Northumbrian queen. Æthelthryth renounced these when she became an abbess, but when dying from a tumour of the neck, she cheerfully (and unforgettably) recalled that 'when I was a young girl I used to wear an unnecessary weight of necklaces, [but] I believe that God in his goodness would have me endure this pain in my neck in order that I may thus be absolved from the guilt of my needless vanity – so, instead of gold and pearls, a fiery red tumour now stands out upon my neck'.[18] The chemise preserves the shadowy image of a gendered display culture at early medieval Frankish and Anglo-Saxon courts where women's conspicuous consumption, mimicking the splendours of Byzantium, showed off the status of queens and noble ladies in waiting, and, by reflected glory, their kin. These women acted in gender-specific ways, then: as agents of *romanitas*, and as exemplars of rank, deploying their own strategies of distinction.[19] On a second and related hypothesis, the shadow itself offers substantial testimony to the religious culture of a court in which holy persons were venerated, and from which royal and noble persons could move into a religious life which, far from being remote from the court, remained in close contact with it, as recalled in Balthild's *Life* written at Chelles shortly after her death, in the early 690s by a member of the community, probably a woman.[20] Balthild's spiritual adviser Eligius had told her to sacrifice her jewels as a sign of humility, evidently in

---

[17] What follows owes much to J.-P. Laporte, *Le Trésor des saints de Chelles* (Chelles, 1988), pp. 1–3, 55–61, 71–101; J.-P. Laporte and J. Boyer (eds.), *Trésor de Chelles: sépultures et reliques de la reine Bathilde et de l'abbesse Bertille*, Catalogue de l'exposition organisée au Musée Alfred Bonno (Chelles, 1991), pp. 22–31, 42–5.

[18] Bede, *Historia ecclesiastica gentis Anglorum* IV.19, ed. C. Plummer (Oxford, 1896), p. 246, trans. B. Colgrave revd J. McClure and R. Collins (Oxford, 1994), pp. 204–5.

[19] I borrow this apt phrase from Walter Pohl, who in turn entitled *Strategies of Distinction* (Leiden 1998) under the inspiration of Pierre Bourdieu, *La Distinction* (Paris, 1979), trans. R. Nice, *Distinction: A Social Critique of the Judgement of Taste* (Cambridge, MA, 1984).

[20] *Vita Balthildis* c. 12, p. 498, trans. p. 128 (where I assume that the plural subjects of 'visit [the court]' are the abbess and Balthild herself).

imitation of Radegund.[21] The embroidered jewels were made precisely in order to commemorate Balthild's sacrifice and its authenticity to an audience of high-status visitors to Chelles (for instance, on the occasion of the burial there of Balthild's son King Clothar III in 673), and to the high-status nuns of the community themselves, both during the queen's life and, as a secondary relic, after her death.[22] A royal convent could function, then, as an outpost of courtliness, displaying, and inverting, the symbolism of the queenly regalia.

Evidence from the eighth century, again from both sides of the Channel, shows that a woman's religious life could even be lived out *at* the court, through specifically female forms of nurturing and networking. A letter of Alcuin's reveals the presence at the palace of King Offa of Mercia of 'a woman consecrated to God' named Hundrud, who was also a longstanding 'friend' of Alcuin.[23] She must live a life of sobriety in the palace environment, Alcuin enjoined her; and all she did must be in the honourable estate of chastity 'so that, by your example, younger people may be instructed, and older ones may rejoice, and all be edified, and so that the devotion of a life lived according to a Rule can be seen at the king's palace in your *conversatio*'. Alcuin asked Hundrud to greet the queen (Cynethryth) for him, and assure her that he, Alcuin, was most certainly *fidelis*, 'as far as I can be', to her 'lord' Offa. 'Let them do to me as they will: my faith to them shall never be breached.' Finally Alcuin asked his 'sweetest sister' to 'greet my son Ecgfrid', that is, the son of Offa and Cynethryth, and heir-apparent. Clearly Hundrud had the ear of all the right people. Whether we infer she was a nun or a veiled widow depends on how strictly the phrase *regularis vita* is interpreted.[24] Either way, Hundrud had apparently taken vows of chastity and devotion to the task of morally guiding young and old. The notable point is that this was a life that a woman could live at court.

---

[21] *Vita Eligii* c. 41, ed. Krusch, *MGH SRM* IV (Hanover, 1902), p. 724. I assume that this passage belongs to the seventh-century core of the *Vita*, rather than being the work of an eighth-century reviser. For Radegund's renunciation of her fine clothes, jewels and gold-encrusted belt, see Venantius, *Vita Radegundis* c. 2, ed. Krusch, *MGH SRM* II (Hanover, 1888), p. 365. For an explicit reference to Radegund as model, see *Vita Balthildis* c. 18, p. 506, trans. pp. 131–2.

[22] According to the collective memory recorded at Chelles in the seventeenth century, Balthild had worn the chemise as an overall while waiting on the nuns at table: Laporte, *Le Trésor*, 213. Laporte (pp. 89–90) surmises that Balthild may have made this garment herself as a sign and memento of humility. Its ultimate function as grave-shirt must have been, to judge from its state of preservation, a relatively late adaptation.

[23] Alcuin, *Ep.* 62 (datable 789 × 796), ed. E. Dümmler, *MGH Epp.* IV (Berlin, 1895), pp. 105–6.

[24] In otherwise helpful comments, Sarah Foot's translation 'religious life' begs the question: *Veiled Women I*, p. 57. Alcuin hints that Hundrud may have been associated with a minster community at *Inmercum* (unidentified) which the king and queen had somehow maltreated.

In a slightly later letter, Alcuin addressed Gundrada, Charlemagne's cousin.[25] She too was a consecrated woman (*sponsa deo dignissima*) living at court. Alcuin had a nickname for her, Eulalia (after the celebrated virgin-martyr of Merida), a sure sign of membership of the inner circle of those bound by *familiaritas* to each other and (in this context) to Charlemagne.[26] She had so much influence with Charlemagne, Alcuin thought, that he asked her to transmit his apologies for having to refuse a summons to court: 'speak to my lord David so that he's not angry with his servant'. Alcuin urged her to continue to be 'an exemplar for all the other young women in the palace, so that they'll be as noble in their conduct as they are in birth'. Alcuin's rating of Gundrada is borne out by Paschasius in his *Life* of Adalard, Gundrada's brother: she was 'a virgin more close to the king, [and] most noble of noble ones' (*virgo familiarior regi, nobilium nobilissima*). Paschasius added, reflecting the retrospective rubbishing of Charlemagne's court at that of his son, that Gundrada was unique in having managed to keep her virginity while living 'amidst the lustful heats of the palace'.[27] I am struck by the influence of these two exactly contemporary religious women at two different courts and the way that their gendered continence enabled them, in their educational and advisory roles, to act as conduits between persons at, or with valued contacts at, court, and between such persons and powerful rulers. The implications for spatial arrangements at these courts are intriguing. Where exactly did these chaste women live? Where did they conduct their exemplary *conversationes* with persons of both sexes? The noble girls at Charlemagne's court may have lived with their noble parents in the houses that Notker describes surrounding the palace.[28] But if they were members of a royal woman's retinue, whether of

---

[25] Alcuin, *Ep.* 241 (datable '*c.* 801'), pp. 386–7.

[26] M. Garrison, 'The social world of Alcuin: nicknames at York and at the Carolingian court', in L. A. J. R. Howen and A. MacDonald (eds.), *Alcuin of York: Scholar at the Carolingian Court*, Germania Latina 3 (Groningen, 1998), pp. 59–79, noting Alcuin's appeal to Christ in *Ep. 241* as a model-giver of nicknames (perhaps nicknaming a woman needed special justification?), and the choice of virgin-martyrs' names for women friends (chastity being not just an apt but a loaded trait for an influential royal woman at this court?).

[27] Paschasius, *Vita Adalhardi* c. 33, *PL* 120, col. 1526. This *Life* was written soon after Adalard's death in 826. For the retrospective view here, see Nelson, 'Women at the court of Charlemagne: a case of monstrous regiment?', in J. C. Parsons (ed.), *Medieval Queenship* (New York, 1993), pp. 43–61, repr. Janet L. Nelson, *The Frankish World, 750–900* (London 1996), pp. 223–42 at p. 240. I would now put more stress on the fact that Gundrada and Adalard (and their brother Bernar and sister Theodrada as well) were also siblings of Wala, and the whole sib-set's influence in Charlemagne's later years threatened the succession of Louis the Pious: this emerges fairly clearly if *Vita Adalardi* cc. 32, 33 and 34 are read in conjunction with Astronomer, *Vita Hludovici*, c. 21, ed. E. Tremp, *MGH SRG* LXIV (Hanover, 1995), pp. 346–7.

[28] Janet L. Nelson, 'Aachen as a place of power', in M. de Jong, F. Theuws and C. van Rhijn (eds.), *Topographies of Power in Early Medieval Europe* (Leiden, 2001), pp. 217–41.

a king's consort or a king's daughter, their quarters seem not to have been so secluded as was the *gynaikonitis* of Constantinople with its 1000 women and eunuchs.[29] The tale of Charlemagne's daughter Bertha, carrying her lover Angilbert piggyback across the snow-covered palace courtyard one dark night to evade paternal wrath, is undeniably *folklorique*, but there is contemporary evidence that Bertha was a well-built girl, that Angilbert was her lover, at court, and that the pair produced two boys.[30] Angilbert clearly knew his way to and around the *puellarum camerae* he evoked in a poem addressed to Charlemagne himself.[31]

My last example of a woman playing (in both senses) the rules of gender at court is the Empress Judith. The atmosphere of *this* court, the court of her husband Louis the Pious, was as devout as Balthild's but its style was different, showier, more self-consciously engaged in a renaissance of Christian-Roman imperial culture. Central elements in this were the translations of old saints to new shrines – one of the great ritual events Louis and Judith staged was the translation of Balthild's relics to a new and more splendid tomb[32] – and the importing of relics from Rome by means, yes, of some dark skullduggery in Roman cemeteries, but thereafter of highly lit *translationes*, strongly ritualised, public transfers of sacred power into Francia and Saxony.[33] *Ad palatium, regina quae plurimum valet evocante, promoveo* ('I'm moving up to the court, at the summons of the queen who counts for a lot there'): thus Lupus of Ferrières boasting to his brother in 837.[34] By then Judith had counted for a lot at court over nearly two decades, admittedly with brief interruptions. She had set the same tone

[29] L. Garland, *Byzantine Empresses: Women and Power in Byzantium, AD 527–1204* (London, 1999), p. 5.

[30] Nelson, 'La cour impériale de Charlemagne', pp. 186–8.

[31] Angilbert, *Verse epistle* to Charlemagne and his entourage, datable to 794–5, in P. Godman, *Poetry of the Carolingian Renaissance* (London, 1984), p. 116, line 79. Cf. Alcuin, *Ep.* 244, p. 392, on 'crowned doves', with allusion to Isaiah 60.8. On Carolingian courts, see Airlie, 'The palace of memory'; M. Innes, '"A place of discipline": Carolingian courts and aristocratic youth' and J. L. Nelson, 'Was Charlemagne's court a courtly society?' both in C. Cubitt (ed.), *Court Culture in the Early Middle Ages* (Turnhout, 2003), pp. 39–57, 59–76.

[32] *Translatio S. Balthechildis*, ed. O. Holder-Egger, *MGH SS* xv (i) (Hanover, 1887), pp. 284–5. The abbess of Chelles at this point was Judith's mother Heilwig, and the two women's initiative in the *translatio* seems likely.

[33] For the significance of these events, not least in affording women access to the sacred, see J. M. H. Smith, 'Old saints, new cults: Roman relics in Carolingian Francia', in J. M. H. Smith (ed.), *Early Medieval Rome and the Christian West* (Leiden, 2000), pp. 317–39.

[34] Servatus Lupus, *Epistolae* 6, ed. P. K. Marshall (Leipzig, 1984), p. 16. In a penetrating review, *Aevum* 77 (2003), pp. 483–7 at 484–5, of O. Münsch, *Der Liber Legum des Lupus von Ferrières* (Frankfurt, 2001), Veronika von Büren argues persuasively that Judith was behind the commission to Lupus to make the *Liber Legum* for Eberhard, and that the singling out of Eberhard in 836 as son-in-law, political ally and future provider of support for Charles the Bald as a whole 'scenario' in which Judith was 'l'acteur principal'. The invitation to Lupus to join the court in 837 was thus reward for work well done as well as solicitation of future service.

of literary patronage and moral concern that Cassiodorus evoked for the royal bride sent to Thuringia three centuries before. She was a patron of modern piety.[35] She could have acquired her own training in courtliness at Aachen, where her father, like his peers, may have had his town-house close by the palace. Like Balthild perhaps, Judith found inspiration for her own self-representation in the imperial court of Byzantium.[36] Like Balthild, she set patterns of conspicuous consumption and cultivated taste. Was it for her and her women that Louis the Pious protected and privileged Jewish merchants who purveyed oriental luxuries to the court?[37] And can the vicious propaganda attacks of Louis's rebellious sons on the court as brothel be seen in terms of back-handed tribute to the way Judith set the tone and called the tune?[38]

Two possible signs of Judith's influence will let me end where I began. One is about the geography of the court and the spatial settings of courtly communication.[39] Has anyone else wondered what happened to the baths at Aachen after Charlemagne had gone?[40] Louis the Pious's biographers say nothing about Louis's bathing or swimming. The serious conversations Charlemagne and his male *familiares et amici* had had in the baths were displaced, then – perhaps to the hunt, perhaps to the hall itself, perhaps to upper-floor rooms where people stood or sat about informally. In these locations, women could participate, as we can gather from Ermold's word-picture of the alfresco feast provided by Judith following Louis's hunt in

[35] E. Sears, 'Louis the Pious as *miles Christi*: the dedicatory image in Hrabanus Maurus's *De laudibus sanctae crucis*', in P. Godman and R. Collins (eds.), *Charlemagne's Heir: New Perspectives on the Reign of Louis the Pious* (Oxford, 1990), pp. 605–28 at pp. 620–1; Nelson, *Charles the Bald* (London, 1992), pp. 76–9, 82–7; M. de Jong, 'The empire as *ecclesia*: Hrabanus Maurus and biblical *historia* for rulers', in M. Innes and Y. Hen (eds.), *The Uses of the Past in the Early Middle Ages* (Cambridge, 2000), pp. 191–226 esp. pp. 206–7, 212–15; and see now E. Ward, 'The career of the empress Judith' (PhD dissertation, University of London, 2003).

[36] For relevant diplomatic contacts, see J. Fried, 'Ludwig der Fromme, das Papsttum und die fränkische Kirche', in Godman and Collins (eds.), *Charlemagne's Heir*, pp. 231–73 at pp. 260–1; J. Shepard, 'Byzantine relations with the outside world in the ninth century', and C. Wickham, 'Byzantium through western eyes', both in L. Brubaker (ed.), *Byzantium in the Ninth Century: Dead or Alive?* (Aldershot, 1998), pp. 167–80, 245–56. The questions of Judith's own selection as empress via a bride show, and the possibility that Judith was crowned and acclaimed, Byzantine-style, in 819, are illuminatingly discussed by Ward in 'The career of the empress Judith', ch. 2. For another interpretation of the so called 'bride show' of 819 and the style of Judith's courtliness, see Mayke de Jong, chapter 14 below.

[37] L. Weinrich, *Wala, Graf, Mönch und Rebell* (Hamburg, 1963), p. 58. On Judith in the 820s, see E. Ward, 'Caesar's wife: the career of the empress Judith, 819–29', in Godman and Collins (eds.), *Charlemagne's Heir*, pp. 205–27.

[38] E. Ward, 'Agobard of Lyons and Paschasius Radbertus as critics of the empress Judith', *Studies in Church History* 27 (1990), pp. 15–25.

[39] Cf. Airlie, 'The palace of memory', pp. 2–4, 9–10; S. Airlie, 'Bonds of power and bonds of association in the court circle of Louis the Pious', in Godman and Collins (eds.), *Charlemagne's Heir*, pp. 191–204.

[40] Nelson, 'Aachen as a place of power'.

826, or of court processions and banquets in which Judith prominently took part, or the exchanges with scholars whose works and visits she solicited.[41] If courtly space was gender-divided, I suggest Judith shifted some important activities into locations where both sexes could have agency, hence supplementing, or perhaps supplanting, the *ritus natandi* with a *ritus venandi* that found its apt conclusion in a *déjeuner sur l'herbe*. The Latin epic-poem *Waltharius*, with its affecting depiction of young lovers, including a woman with a voice of her own, could be just as well dated to the 820s or 830s, and linked with the audience of such a court, as it might be (and of course has been) to the twelfth century.[42] If the poem belongs in an Aquitanian context, the court could be King Pippin's and Queen Ringart's in the late 820s or early 830s.

Patronage of young scholars, and perhaps young lovers, may be linked with responsibility for instructing the young in courtliness, as Bezzola long ago surmised.[43] My second testimony to Judith's inspiration is indirect, no more than a hint. In her *Handbook* for her son William, Dhuoda assumed a teaching role that had more than William as its projected audience. Dhuoda envisaged her son, now at the court of Judith's son, showing her *Handbook* to other mothers' sons as well: she addressed not just William, 'as if I were with you', but 'all those to whom you may show this book and have them read it too'.[44] I think she saw William's *commilitones* in her mind's eye. And I think she saw them at the palace, perhaps a palace she herself had known: as she recalled for William and the others right at the beginning of her book, she had been married in 824 *in palatio*, that is, in the palace of Aachen, and very probably lived there for a while; and at the time she wrote the preface of her book, at the end of 841 or early in 842, William's lord, Charles the Bald, had some prospect of gaining control of Aachen in whatever division-agreement terminated the current war of the Frankish succession.[45] Equally Dhuoda may have imagined some other palace, or no particular palace at all. For 'the palace' was, as Hincmar put it a few years

---

[41] Ermold, *Poème sur Louis le Pieux*, lines 2168–503, ed. E. Faral (Paris, 1964), pp. 166–91; and for Judith's patronage, see above, notes 34 and 35.

[42] Godman, extracts from *Waltharius*, esp. lines 212–87, 324–57, in Godman, *Poetry of the Carolingian Renaissance*, pp. 332–9, with commentary, pp. 72–8. On the dating, see K. F. Werner, '*Hludovicus Augustus*: gouverner l'empire chrétien – idées et réalités', in Godman and Collins (eds.), *Charlemagne's Heir*, pp. 3–123 at pp. 101–23, arguing, not wholly persuasively, for Ermold's authorship.

[43] Bezzola, *Les Origines*, pp. 195–231.

[44] Dhuoda, *Liber Manualis* I, 1, ed. M. Thiébaux, *Dhuoda, Handbook for Her Warrior Son, Liber Manualis* (Cambridge, 1998), pp. 58–9 (the translation is mine). See further, Janet L. Nelson, 'Dhuoda', in P. Wormald (ed.), *Lay Intellectuals in the Carolingian World* (forthcoming).

[45] Dhuoda, *Liber Manualis*, preface, pp. 48–9. For the possibility that Dhuoda lived at Aachen after her marriage, see Nelson, 'Dhuoda'.

later, 'not a building but the people that dwelt in it'.[46] Dhuoda called it 'the king's big house (*domus magna*), where many conversations take place'.[47] Recalling her own young-womanhood as part of the court of Louis and Judith, and perhaps also the court of Pippin and Ringart for that too could have been very familiar to the wife of an Aquitanian magnate, Dhuoda saw herself as able, in the early 840s, to address another court, that of Charles, son of Louis and Judith, and to offer its denizens moral instruction in the conduct of a virtuous private and public life. In insisting on self-discipline and prayerfulness in the active life of young noblemen, Dhuoda met the needs of the *res publica* and found herself an audience.

Early medieval courts, then, were mental constructs as well as social microcosms.[48] They offered high-born women (as well as men) agency, a public, and cultural space. But, in addition, through predetermined and gender-specific roles as strategists of distinction, as negotiators, as emblems and purveyors of symbolic status, as nurturers and educators of the young of both sexes, such women could play a central part in the representation and transmission of courtly rules and values – hence, in the construction of the very idea of the court society. For the function of high-born women in this milieu transcended that of wife and mother in the noble household, hence was more than glorified domesticity. Surrounded in ritual displays by women who were also, in other contexts, her agents, the queen, pre-eminent among them, carried out political and administrative activities indispensable to the *status regni*: the reception and giving of gifts, the precisely organised provision of food and drink, the management of display, the supervision of conduct and speech.[49] In the palace, then, the queen's performance, active and enactive, maintained the well-functioning, stability and coherence of the realm.[50] Replicating queenly roles, whether, at a lesser level, in the palace, or in their own big houses in the provinces, noblewomen like Dhuoda reproduced court culture. In ways less susceptible to official definition, other women at court reinforced the lines of

---

[46] Hincmar, *Epistola* from the bishops at the Council of Quierzy to Louis the German, November 858, *MGH Conc.* iii, ed. W. Hartmann (Hanover, 1984), no. 41, c. (v), p. 412.

[47] Dhuoda, *Liber Manualis* iii, 9, pp. 108–9 (my translation, reading *domus . . . illa* to refer back to [the king's] *aula*).

[48] Janet L. Nelson, 'History-writing at the courts of Louis the Pious and Charles the Bald', in A. Scharer and G. Scheibelreiter (eds.), *Historiographie im frühen Mittelalter* (Vienna, 1994), pp. 435–42 at p. 439.

[49] Janet L. Nelson, 'La cour impériale de Charlemagne', in R. Le Jan (ed.), *La Royauté et les élites dans l'Europe carolingienne* (Lille, 1998), pp. 177–92; and Nelson, 'Les reines carolingiennes', pp. 121–32.

[50] I refer here to *De ordine palatii*, ed. T. Gross and R. Schieffer, *MGH Fontes iuris germanici* (Hanover, 1980), p. 80, generally attributed to Hincmar, but more likely the work of Adalard of Corbie, datable to c. 812: see Nelson, 'Aachen as a place of power'.

communication and also lines of demarcation within the palatine social world, while abbesses of major convents, not confined to the palace, yet in the Carolingian period able, indeed required, to move to and from it, maintained the court's outliers and partial replicas at key regnal cult-sites.[51] Courts, as well as being social spaces, thus transcended space – or rather combined concentrated spatial significance with multilocality and remote control.

An early medieval historian keen to understand how courts functioned in the sub-Roman world must be, like Autolycus in *A Winter's Tale*, 'a snapper-up of unconsidered trifles'. S/he faces methodological problems far more perplexing than do colleagues specialising in late antiquity or in later medieval or early modern periods. Earlier medieval evidential trifles are unconsidered because they are few, apparently unpromising, and seldom well advertised: witness the snippets on which this chapter has necessarily relied. They are, though, rather strongly gendered, and that trait must attract us early medievalists as irresistibly as Autolycus' wares did his clientele of shepherdesses on the coast of Bohemia. Giving gender due attention reveals a gap in the historiography, and one not filled, as other gaps have been recently, by attentive interdisciplinary reading. The eminent sociologists whose work has been so fruitful for historians in other respects had a blind spot, it seems, just where gender ought to have come into view. It may be no coincidence that those sociologists took their historical data from anywhere but the earlier Middle Ages.[52] Maybe the source-poor early medievalist's necessity can be turned into an advantage. Whenever sources do exist, and they are in fact of quite diverse kinds, from the epistolary, poetic and hagiographic to the artefactual, they show women not only present at the court as political centre, but active in gender-specific ways in the manufacture of courtliness.[53] These same sources also show women's

[51] For the link between royal convents and the court, see Airlie, 'The palace of memory', pp. 18–19, and further, P. Geary, *Phantoms of Remembrance: Memory and Oblivion at the End of the First Millennium* (Princeton, 1994), pp. 66–70.

[52] In addition to examples cited above, note 1, see M. Mann, *The Sources of Social Power*, vol. 1: *A History of Power from the Beginning to A.D. 1760* (Cambridge, 1986), where references to courts occur in chs. 5 (Mesopotamia), 8 (Assyria and Persia), 9 (Rome), and especially 13 and 14 (late medieval and early modern western Europe). The earlier medieval period receives little, and divided, attention. The few references to women cluster in two chapters (10 and 11) on Christianity and other world religions; and gender is simply unused as an analytical category. While Mann's work has the great (and, among sociologists, rare) merit of considering carefully periods earlier than the early modern, he was drawn (like Foucault) to antiquity. Cf., for relationships between sociologists' and historians' coverage of another important area, my comments in 'Medieval monasticism', in Linehan and Nelson (eds.), *The Medieval World*, pp. 576–604 at pp. 583–8.

[53] I have explored such sources in 'Women at the court of Charlemagne'; 'Making a difference in eighth-century politics: the daughters of Desiderius', in A. C. Murray (ed.), *After Rome's Fall: Narrators and*

occupation of sites that were spatially and culturally central. Activity gendered as female acquired social and political power when aligned with high class or social rank, and, at this level, it straddled the divides of ethnicity and religious status. The royal woman, however ethnically labelled, lent herself to Romanisation via the liberal arts, and once Romanised, voiced with book-learning, could become, as bride, the medium of civilisation to a barbarian court. Whether in secular or religious garb, women could act as exemplars and agents, edified and edifying, of Christian virtues that had ennobling political as well as personal consequences for men and women at court. Here, women could become active participants in the civilising process: older women could counsel younger men; women religious could counsel secular *potentes* (powerful men); royal wives and husbands could embark together on the inculcation of courtliness through gender difference enacted as gender complementarity. Thus, in these early medieval courts as compared with classical precursors, women acquired extended scope. Political changes supplied necessary conditions and contexts: the dynasticisation of politics and the replacement of republican political values by monarchic and regnal ones.[54] Interacting with these, though, and decisively, were religious changes including a type of Christianisation that conspicuously reinflected public life by crediting women, as well as men, with cultural authority, and women with authority that was in some respects gender-specific.[55] The sites of this interaction were the court and its convent outliers. In *conversationes* and *colloquia* in such settings, as never in Roman *contio* or early medieval *conventus*, men listened, sometimes, to women.[56] To explore the early medieval culture of courtliness is to retrieve subtle but critical changes in gender relations. More prosaically, it is to find, in new milieux, and in new and more varied ways, women at work.

Sources of Early Medieval History. Essays Presented to Walter Goffart (Toronto, 1998), pp. 171–90; and 'Was the court of Charlemagne a courtly society?'

[54] I use regnal in the sense pioneered by Susan Reynolds, *Kingdoms and Communities in Western Europe, 900–1300*, 2nd revd edn (Oxford, 1997), pp. 254–331, 'that which pertains to a kingdom'.

[55] On religious change, see M. Garrison, 'The Franks as the New Israel?', in Innes and Hen (eds.), *The Uses of the Past*, pp. 114–61 esp. pp. 120–3, 145–61; for some limits to the church's acknowledgement of female authority and even participation, see J. M. H. Smith, 'The problem of female sanctity in Carolingian Europe', *Past and Present* 146 (1995), pp. 3–37, and Smith, 'Women at the tomb: access to relic shrines in the early Middle Ages', in Mitchell and Wood (eds.), *World of Gregory of Tours*, pp. 163–80.

[56] Compare the institutions and structures evoked by P. Stafford, 'Powerful women in the early Middle Ages: queens and abbesses', in Linehan and Nelson (eds.), *The Medieval World*, pp. 398–415, and T. Reuter, 'Assembly politics', in the same volume, pp. 451–68.

CHAPTER II

Men, women and liturgical practice in the early medieval west

Gisela Muschiol

As celebrated and practised during the early Middle Ages, Christian liturgy had undergone a double transformation since the era of the early church. Liturgical texts had originally been spoken extempore, but the practice of committing them to writing began as early as the fourth century. This was the case with prayers for various occasions, but above all those which accompanied the Eucharist. Allan Bouley has aptly characterised this trend as 'from freedom to formula'.[1] The subsequent period, from the fifth to the seventh century, witnessed the formation in Rome of a type of liturgy which came to exert a decisive influence on worship throughout the medieval western church as a result of its promotion by the Carolingians.[2] Yet well into Carolingian times different regional traditions co-existed in western Europe: Gallican, Ambrosian and Mozarabic liturgies continued alongside the Roman, itself largely confined to Rome and the surrounding dioceses but also introduced into Anglo-Saxon regions. Moreover, Irish influences impinged on the liturgy of penance, as did, to name but one further example, influences of the eastern church on the liturgy of the hours. Amidst this pluralism, nineteenth- and twentieth-century liturgical scholarship deemed the most profound transformation to have been the adoption by the Carolingians of the Roman liturgy as normative.[3]

This shift has generally been construed within very narrow historical terms. Although scholars universally acknowledge the political stimulus of Carolingian rule, they nevertheless regard the change as one confined to the

---

[1] A. Bouley, *From Freedom to Formula: The Evolution of the Eucharistic Prayer from Oral Improvisation to Written Texts* (Washington, DC, 1981), pp. 159–215.

[2] For overviews, see A. Angenendt, *Das Frühmittelalter: Die abendländische Christenheit von 400 bis 900* (2nd edn, Stuttgart, 1995), pp. 245–9, 310–13, 327–48; D. A. Bullough, 'Roman books and Carolingian *renovatio*', *Studies in Church History* 14 (1977), pp. 23–50, repr. in his *Carolingian Renewal: Sources and Heritage* (Manchester, 1991), pp. 1–33.

[3] A. Angenendt, *Liturgik und Historik: Gab es eine organische Liturgieentwicklung?* (Freiburg, 2001), pp. 95–8.

internal specifics of worship. Whether, and how, this transformation might be seen as an aspect of what has famously been called the 'Decline and Fall of the Roman Empire' has seldom been discussed. Nor have historians of liturgy asked whether wider issues of cultural continuity and change might also apply to the history of Christian worship. This chapter begins the project by examining the role of gender difference in the western liturgy within the broad context of the transformation of the Roman world. It focuses on Merovingian Francia *c.* 500–750, when Roman and Frankish cultural influences co-existed and interacted over an extended period of time. A comparatively large number of sources from these centuries enables us to analyse the accommodations and adjustments which accompanied the gradual merging of cultures. Among the many aspects of life affected by these transformations were religious ideas and gender roles. This chapter argues that these changes rendered possible the development of liturgical functions which were, seen from a gendered perspective, more egalitarian than previously. As will be seen, the gendering of liturgical practice is never addressed directly by the extant liturgical handbooks of the period such as missals (only a few of which survive) but rather emerges from a range of indirect comments in other sources.

It must be borne in mind, however, that the liturgy only assumed more stable forms after the transition from antiquity to the Middle Ages. As a result there is no clearly defined starting point from which to trace change, since, at the close of antiquity, forms of worship remained fluid and open to improvisation. The stabilisation of liturgical texts and rites is without doubt closely linked to the changes of the Roman world, for the decomposition of late antique social structures prompted changes in knowledge and education, both preconditions of an improvisational liturgy.[4] To examine the liturgy is thus to examine only one strand in the complex web of Christian life and doctrine in late antiquity and the early Middle Ages. Nevertheless, focused attention on a single aspect is an appropriate starting point. Julia Smith has put it this way: 'If we wish to establish a gendered perspective on late antiquity and the Early Middle Ages, we have to start from a point of view which is not one of empire-wide grand narratives but one that is domestic and, by virtue of the poverty of documentation, often fragmented.'[5]

---

[4] Angenendt, *Frühmittelalter*, pp. 147–59, points out the changes in social structure and learning.
[5] J. M. H. Smith, 'Did women have a transformation of the Roman world?', in P. Stafford and A. B. Mulder-Bakker (eds.), *Gendering the Middle Ages* (Oxford, 2001), pp. 22–41 at p. 28.

GENDERING THE LITURGY

Rather than covering liturgical practice in its entirety, a gendered perspective must focus on selected aspects of difference.[6] It also requires a definition of liturgy broader than the conventional subjects of scholarship – the celebration of the Eucharist, the liturgy of the hours, baptisms and Masses for the dead. A more extensive definition includes coronations, baptismal sponsorships, allegiance ceremonies, the handing-over of keys in a monastery and a wide range of other para-liturgical activities. In addition, it is necessary to emphasise a seemingly trivial fact: in the Middle Ages, as in other periods, women and men did not constitute homogeneous social groups. Diversity is characteristic of both. The rural population, whether male or female, had far fewer opportunities for joining liturgical ceremonies than its urban counterpart. The aristocracy commonly worshipped in private chapels: elite men and women would thus have had a different experience of the liturgy from people of lower social status. In addition, peasants (male and female) normally had only limited access to learning and thus understood the liturgy differently.

In this context, the relationship between gender and language requires attention. As Christianity spread into areas of Germanic and Celtic speech, and as emerging Romance vernaculars increasingly diverged from formal, written Latin, the language of liturgy in the early medieval west – Latin – became a language of the learned elite. It should be reiterated here that the educated elite could include both men and women. Rules for women's religious communities, in particular, stressed that girls living in a convent were to learn at least how to read, and indeed nuns reading from the Bible, whether privately or aloud to others, were quite common in the early Middle Ages.[7] *Frequenter legere* (read frequently) was the injunction applied to the Scriptures. Besides reading, the art of writing was practised in convents, as the numerous nuns' scriptoria in the Frankish lands testify.[8]

As regards communities of men, scholars generally take it for granted that early medieval monks were literate. This assumption is still to be tested, and it remains unclear how widespread literacy as a precondition of liturgical practice really was. We certainly must not assume that the ability to read was

---

[6] T. Berger, *Women's Ways of Worship: Gender Analysis and Liturgical History* (Collegeville, MN, 1999) is fundamental here.

[7] See G. Muschiol, *Famula Dei: Zur Liturgie in merowingischen Frauenklöstern* (Münster, 1994), pp. 92–100.

[8] R. McKitterick, 'Frauen und Schriftlichkeit im Frühmittelalter', in Hans-Werner Goetz (ed.), *Weibliche Lebensgestaltung im frühen Mittelalter* (Cologne, 1991), pp. 65–118; R. McKitterick, 'Nuns' scriptoria in England and Francia in the eighth century', *Francia* 19 (1992), pp. 1–35.

a matter of course among male clerics. For example, one of the provisions of the Council of Narbonne (589) was that only those able to read were to be ordained deacons or priests. The council went on to stipulate that anyone who had already been ordained when illiterate and who refused to acquire reading skills was to be sent into a monastery.[9] In the latter case the monastery presumably served not only as a place of banishment but also as an institution in which male illiterate clerics were to learn how to read, and thus acquire the skill which was the basic prerequisite for the active participation in celebrating the liturgy.

A gendered perspective is not confined to literacy. It is also linked to the most fundamental precondition of liturgy, namely providing space for religious assembly. Involved in liturgical activity, therefore, were not just its leaders but also those men and women who cared for the fabric and the decoration of a church. There are frequent references to sixth-century married couples who used their combined assets for the benefit of the worship, the most noteworthy of whom consisted of a bishop and his wife. According to Gregory of Tours, the wife of Bishop Namatius of Clermont provided for the church of St Stephen to be built on the outskirts of the city, and while the work was in progress, she read to the painter from the life of St Stephen in order to specify the themes of the decoration.[10] While Bishop Namatius himself erected a new cathedral church, his spouse appears to have been in charge of the church in the suburbs. Even more concerned, it seems, with the interior decoration than with the building itself, Namatius' wife probably had an equivalent in Placidina, who was praised in poems by Venantius Fortunatus for the adornment of the church of St Martin in Bordeaux, where her husband, Leontius II, was bishop.[11] Whilst it seems that sometimes decorating churches tended to be the female role, and building them or supervising the construction process the male task, the assets used in order to finance both construction and decoration were the couple's combined assets. The establishment of nuns' convents by pious siblings followed a similar pattern. Once the religious houses were founded, however, a division of labour became apparent: the male founders, mostly bishops, assumed overall control of the convents whereas the female founders, mostly sisters or other relatives, were responsible for

[9] *Conc. Narbonense 589*, c. 11, *Concilia Galliae A. 511-A. 695*, ed. C. de Clercq, CCSL 148A (Turnhout, 1963), p. 256.

[10] Gregory of Tours, *Liber historiarum* 11, cc. 16–17, *MGH SRM* 1/1, ed. B. Krusch and W. Levison (Hanover, 1951), pp. 64–5.

[11] Venantius Fortunatus, *Carmina, Liber I*, no. 6, 14–16, *MGH AA* 1v/1, ed. F. Leo (Berlin, 1881), pp. 10–11, 16–19.

spirituality and liturgy within them.[12] Whether the foundation of male monastic communities was marked by a similar, gendered division of labour remains to be investigated.

This evidence concerning both married couples and siblings suggests that in sixth-century Gaul bishops were drawn from a social stratum in which status was more important than gender when it came to acts of public significance. By the close of the sixth century, however, married episcopal couples disappear from the sources because the office of the bishop had changed. It has been shown that it was liturgy itself which brought about this change. Whereas a bishop, together with his wife, had previously combined functions of urban leadership, commissioning and supervising the building of churches, administering alms and, last but not least, providing spiritual help and counselling, he became someone who was primarily concerned with liturgical tasks. This very fact rendered a bishop's wife not only unnecessary, but downright illicit.[13] This was why seventh-century founders of religious communities – women as well as men – acted not as part of a couple but on their own.[14]

While being comparable in terms of wealth, sixth-century bishops and their wives or female relatives were dissimilar in their access to ranks and positions within the church. Men could remain laymen, or they could become monks as well as clerics of all possible ranks, from deacon to bishop. Women could live as laywomen, consecrated virgins or nuns while being barred from the clergy. Whether in the western church female deacons were considered members of the clergy remains an open question.[15] Even though rendering a service to the local Christian community, the wife of a sixth-century bishop did not hold an office in the hierarchy of the church,

---

[12] See Muschiol, *Famula Dei*, pp. 63–71, for details.

[13] As argued by B. Jussen, 'Liturgie und Legitimation, oder: Wie die Gallo-Romanen das römische Reich beendeten', in R. Blänkner and B. Jussen (eds.), *Institution und Ereignis: Über historische Praktiken und Vorstellungen gesellschaftlichen Ordnens* (Göttingen, 1998), pp. 75–136. Available in English translation as 'Liturgy and legitimation: or how the Gallo-Romans ended the Roman empire', in B. Jussen (ed.) and P. Selwyn (trans.), *Ordering Medieval Society: Perspectives on Intellectual and Practical Modes of Shaping Social Relations* (Philadelphia, 2001), pp. 147–99.

[14] L. Ueding, *Geschichte der Klostergründungen der frühen Merowingerzeit* (Berlin, 1935); M. Hasdenteufel-Röding, 'Studien zur Gründung von Frauenklöstern im frühen Mittelalter: Ein Beitrag zum religiösen Ideal der Frau und seiner monastischen Umsetzung', PhD thesis, University of Freiburg, 1988, pp. 93–123; Muschiol, *Famula Dei*, pp. 70–1, 140–1.

[15] On this vexed issue see Muschiol, *Famula Dei*, pp. 295–300 (with literature); D. Ansorge, 'Der Diakonat der Frau: Zum gegenwärtigen Forschungsstand', in T. Berger and A. Gerhards (eds.), *Liturgie und Frauenfrage: Ein Beitrag zur Frauenforschung aus liturgiewissenschaftlicher Sicht* (St Ottilien, 1990), pp. 31–65; A.-A. Thiermeyer, 'Der Diakonat der Frau: Liturgiegeschichtliche Kontexte und Folgerungen', *Theologische Quartalschrift* 173 (1993), pp. 226–36; also the large omnibus volume, P. Hünermann (ed.), *Diakonat: Ein Amt für Frauen in der Kirche – ein frauengerechtes Amt?* (Ostfildern, 1997), esp. pp. 33–52, 172–91, 367–411.

however public her activities might be or however beneficial to the pious couple's reputation.

As this brief discussion has shown, the Christian liturgy was a dynamic and evolving system throughout late antiquity and the early Middle Ages. The men and women who participated in it were not a homogeneous group. Rather, it is appropriate to stress their diverse social status, varying regional traditions and the range of ways in which they manifested their Christian beliefs. Finally, as early as we have any evidence, functions within Christian liturgy were marked by gendered distinctions. With the different clerical ranks of consecration culminating in the episcopate being reserved for men, women wishing to lead an ascetic life received a non-clerical consecration. As to the laity, men and women seem to have been equal in ascribed status, but unequal in rights and obligations.[16]

LITURGY IN THE MEROVINGIAN KINGDOMS: SPACES, TIMES AND PLACES

The disparities characterising the period of transition from antiquity to the early Middle Ages have been summarised thus: 'Over the centuries from c. 300 to c. 800, the Roman World disaggregated into different regions, different polities, different economic networks, different religions (including different forms of Christianity), but also partially reintegrated as new links and identities emerged in altered geographical frameworks.'[17] The main focus of this chapter, the development of the liturgy in Merovingian Francia between the sixth and eighth centuries, was one aspect of this.[18] In what respects did gendered differences inform the practice of the liturgy of this period and region? What discontinuities and continuities are discernable across preceding and succeeding centuries? This discussion proceeds by considering spaces, times and places.

Spaces

Churches and chapels are the traditional spaces for Christian worship. Even in their simplest forms these places of assembly were divided into the chancel for the clergy and the area for the community. As early as the third

---

[16] A. Faivre, 'Une femme peut-elle devenir laïque?', *Revue des Sciences Religieuses* 58 (1984), pp. 242–50; cf. E. M. Synek, 'Ex utroque sexu fidelium tres ordines – The status of women in early medieval canon law', in Stafford and Mulder-Bakker (eds.), *Gendering*, pp. 65–91.

[17] Smith, 'Transformation', p. 554.

[18] Y. Hen, *Culture and Religion in Merovingian Gaul A.D. 481–751* (Leiden, 1995) for general background.

century, evidence from the eastern church points to further subdivisions within the community section.[19] The *Didascalia Apostolorum* placed the *cathedra*, the bishop's throne, in the east of the church. Moving westwards, spaces were assigned to priests, then laymen and, finally, women right at the western end, in an enactment of notions of social order. Within the female section of the congregation, too, there was a hierarchy: the first rank was reserved for women deacons, followed by virgins, widows and eventually younger, married women with small children.[20] Between 320 and 324 Emperor Licinius attempted to foist on the eastern churches a law banning men and women from attending divine worship at the same time.[21] He failed, but at the turn of the fifth century, John Chrysostom, bishop of Constantinople, insisted on a separation of men and women in church, even recommending a wall for this purpose.[22] Although the sources do not reveal which type of worship the measures championed by the emperor and by the bishop were meant to cover, we are entitled to presume that the separation of the sexes was aimed primarily at the celebration of the Eucharist on Sundays and at the sermon. Probably of less significance in this context was the liturgy of the hours, that is, the services comprising psalms accompanied by biblical readings and hymns which took place at specified times during the day. In the west, such a separation during the sermon was represented in numerous pictures dating from the high and the late Middle Ages,[23] and even in present-day rural parishes men and women may be allocated separate pews, the dividing line, however, running parallel, rather than perpendicular, to the east–west axis of the church. The habit of reserving the north of the nave for women and the south for men persisted throughout the Middle Ages and, in some places and on certain occasions, still survives today.[24] Apportioning the east to men and the west to women, however, also has a long tradition which finds its most visible expression in the western galleries of convent churches from the ninth century onwards.[25]

[19] E.g. L. Bouyer, *Liturgie und Architektur* (Einsiedeln, 1993).

[20] Details in G. Muschiol, 'Liturgie und Klausur: Zu den liturgischen Voraussetzungen von Nonnenemporen', in I. Crusius (ed.), *Studien zum Kanonissenstift* (Göttingen, 2001), pp. 129–48 at p. 142.

[21] G. Muschiol, 'Reinheit und Gefährdung? Frauen und Liturgie im Mittelalter', *Heiliger Dienst* 51 (1997), pp. 42–54 at p. 44 for further references.

[22] Muschiol, 'Liturgie und Klausur', p. 142; M. Aston, 'Segregation in church', in W. J. Sheils and D. Wood (eds.), *Women in the Church* (Oxford, 1990), pp. 237–94 at p. 240.

[23] E.g. the frontispiece in Sheils and Wood, *Women in the Church*, from the Piazza del Campo in Siena and illustrations in Margaret Aston's chapter.

[24] B. Maurmann, *Die Himmelsrichtungen im Weltbild des Mittelalters: Hildegard von Bingen, Honorius Augustodunensis und andere Autoren* (Munich, 1976), pp. 183–5.

[25] Maurmann, *Himmelsrichtungen*, pp. 135–46; Muschiol, 'Liturgie und Klausur', pp. 140–7; see also R. Gilchrist, *Gender and Material Culture: The Archaeology of Religious Women* (London, 1994).

In Merovingian Gaul, such forms of segregation during the celebration of the liturgy are not documented in the sources. Gallican synods do not lay down regulations requiring men and women to worship separately, nor does Gregory of Tours give an account of such a practice.[26] What has to be borne in mind is that both the early church and the post-Merovingian church were familiar with a separation of the sexes for worship. Whether this tradition lapsed in Merovingian times or whether the fragmentary extant documentation incompletely represents actual practice is an open question.

Nevertheless, in 567 the Council of Tours issued a ruling on the access to the altar of *laici et foeminae* (laity and women). It stipulated that the chancel of the church was to be separated by a partition (*cancelli*), but nevertheless allowed all members of the congregation to move forward to the altar for private prayer and for receiving Communion.[27] Merovingian texts therefore primarily characterised liturgical spaces by a functional rather than gendered difference. The chancel was normally reserved for the office bearers while the laity had access only in certain circumstances. The provision emphasised in several penitential books that women were not to sit between priests during Mass was likewise intended to establish a functional distinction between clerics and non-clerics.[28] This difference, however, had gendered implications simply by virtue of the fact that only men could join the clergy.

These seating and standing arrangements were, however, complemented by a set of regulations which dealt with receiving Communion. Even though conciliar decrees allowed all the laity to approach the altar for this purpose, they imposed gendered instructions about how this was to be done. According to the ruling of one sixth-century synod, married women were to cover their hands with a cloth rather than receiving Communion barehanded. Men, on the other hand, were required to wash their hands beforehand. Nuns were put on an equal footing with men, for they too must wash their hands prior to receiving the Eucharist.[29] Why nuns appear as 'honorary men' remains an open question. Together with the concept of the 'pure hands' of priests, these regulations about Communion reveal a notion of ritual purity which was completely absent from the New Testament and the early church.[30] The notion of ritual purity was thus present for men and

---

[26] Cf. G. de Nie, 'Is een vrouw een mens? Voorschrift, voorordeel en praktijk in zesde-eeuws Gallië', *Jaarboek voor Vrouwengeschiedenis* 10 (1989), pp. 51–74 at pp. 60–4.

[27] Muschiol, *Famula Dei*, p. 139.   [28] Muschiol, *Famula Dei*, p. 207.

[29] Muschiol, *Famula Dei*, pp. 195–208.

[30] A notion discussed by Muschiol, 'Reinheit und Gefährdung?', pp. 51–4; A. Angenendt, 'Mit reinen Händen: Das Motiv der kultischen Reinheit in der abendländischen Askese', in G. Jenal (ed.), *Herrschaft, Kirche, Kultur: Beiträge zur Geschichte des Mittelalters* (Stuttgart, 1993), pp. 297–316.

women alike, yet the manner of purification depended on gender. There is no evidence to link this to any notion of a hierarchy of the sexes, but it indicates one respect in which access to certain liturgical spaces did have a gendered component.

Times

The western liturgical year begins on the first Sunday in Advent and follows the events of Christ's life in an annual cycle. Its sequence of religious seasons and feasts such as Christmas, Easter and Pentecost were celebrated in the same manner by men and by women. In addition, the liturgical year contains a sequence of saints' feast days, spread unevenly throughout the year and varying from place to place according to local circumstances and custom, which will be considered below under the category of 'place'. The third main dimension of liturgical time was the daily cycle of the liturgy of the hours. Both male and female religious communities opened certain of their churches to the public during parts of the day so that all supplicants had access to the intercessory prayers of the communities.[31] To look for a gendering of time in either the annual or the daily cycles of time would thus be misplaced.

We find it instead in the liturgy surrounding the human lifecycle, particularly in matters of sexuality and reproduction. Especially striking are numerous stipulations concerning menstruation. The famous question put by Augustine of Canterbury to Pope Gregory I (590–604) about whether menstruating women were allowed to enter a church and receive Communion suggests that such a monthly banishment of women from liturgical practice not only lay within the purview of early medieval clerics but, because of its significance, had to be regulated by a papal reply. Gregory's answer conspicuously lacks a ban based on the menses.[32] None the less numerous early medieval books of penance did not transmit the papal decision to posterity, but instead stipulated its exact opposite.[33] Whether

---

[31] Muschiol, *Famula Dei*, pp. 114, 133–49.

[32] *Gregorii Papae Registrum Epistolarum* XI/56, *MGH Epp.* II, ed. L. Hartmann (Berlin, 1899), pp. 331–43 at pp. 339–40; see P. Meyvaert, 'Le Libellus Responsionum à Augustin de Cantórbery: une œuvre authentique de Saint Grégoire le Grand', in J. Fontaine, R. Gilet and S. Pelistrandi (eds.), *Grégoire le Grand* (Paris, 1986), pp. 543–50.

[33] Muschiol, *Famula Dei*, pp. 208–10; H. Lutterbach, *Sexualität im Mittelalter: Eine Kulturstudie anhand von Bußbüchern des 6. bis 12. Jahrhunderts* (Cologne, 1999), pp. 87–96; R. Meens, 'Questioning ritual purity: the influence of Gregory the Great's answers to Augustine's queries about childbirth, menstruation and sexuality', in R. Gameson (ed.), *St Augustine and the Conversion of England* (Stroud, 1999), pp. 174–86.

these pentitential provisions were really translated into liturgical practice is unclear. Nevertheless, the discussion about the ritual relevance of menstruation introduced an element into the reasoning of early medieval authors which recurs in numerous regulations. The *Institutio Sanctimonialium*, adopted at Aachen in 816, the treatise *De Institutione Laicali* by Jonas of Orleans from 828, the *Capitula* written by Haito of Basel (806–823) for his diocese, and several other ninth-century texts adduce the regular recurrence in women's lives of menstruation as justification for the temporary exclusion from the church and from the chancel, for the ban on touching the altar and altar vessels, and for similar restrictions. Nuns and other religious women, too, were subject to such regulations.[34]

Furthermore, another normal event in the lifetime of early medieval women led to a constraint on liturgical agency, for childbirth entailed a forty-day ban on setting foot in a church.[35] Indubitably this stipulation also reflected measures intended to protect women during and after their confinement. As Mary Douglas has shown, such protective measures appear not only in early medieval Christendom but in numerous other religions as well.[36] Whilst this ritual exclusion finds precedent in the Old Testament, it has no foundation in the New Testament, nor any roots in the liturgy of the early church. Only with the acculturation of Christianity to non-Roman mentalities did liturgical practice adopt this stipulation.

It is also noteworthy that penitential books include numerous provisions on the consequences of nocturnal emissions. These could lead to men being temporarily excluded from churches or banned from receiving Communion. The regulations on involuntary ejaculations, however, differed from those on masturbation.[37] Of course here, too, questions arise about how these liturgical provisions might have been applied in practice. Yet a comparison of the stipulations governing ejaculations and menstruation reveals that, although menstruation is never a voluntary act, it nevertheless carried stiffer penalties in the penitential books than even those ejaculations that were achieved deliberately. This amounts to the introduction of a gender hierarchy with respect to liturgical practice.

Married persons of both sexes, moreover, were affected by limitations arising from the intersection of the human reproductive cycle with the

---

[34] For references, see Muschiol, *Famula Dei*, pp. 207–8, and Muschiol, 'Liturgie und Klausur', p. 137.

[35] Lutterbach, *Sexualität*, p. 80.

[36] Mary Douglas, *Purity and Danger: An Analysis of Concepts of Pollution and Taboo* (London, 1969); Muschiol, 'Reinheit und Gefährdung?', pp. 52–4.

[37] Lutterbach, *Sexualität*, pp. 70–4, 86–7, 92–4; see also C. Leyser, 'Masculinity in flux: nocturnal emission and the limits of celibacy in the early Middle Ages', in D. M. Hadley (ed.), *Masculinity in Medieval Europe* (London, 1999), pp. 103–20.

course of the liturgical year. From the sixth century onwards penitential handbooks required married couples to observe specific periods of sexual abstinence, for instance the night preceding Sunday, three nights before receiving Communion, particular sections of the liturgical year such as Lent, times before the feasts of saints and times before other dates of liturgical significance.[38] In this case, however, neither the penalties for contraventions of the provisions nor general appeals for the bans to be heeded were gender-specific; responsibility for their own conduct lay with men and women alike.

Places

The places about whose liturgical practice we know most in the Merovingian period are the religious communities of men or women. Thanks to recent research, we are considerably better informed about practice in the women's convents than in the male religious houses of the Merovingian kingdoms. This is because liturgical celebrations by monks were traditionally regarded as so normative as not to require particular scrutiny, and because past scholars did not associate nuns with an independent way of celebrating liturgy. Recent studies have radically altered this assessment, and in particular have shown that it is equality rather than disparity of the sexes which predominated with regard to the liturgy of religious communities.[39] The following paragraphs therefore compare selected areas of liturgical practice in houses of female religious (convents) and male religious (monasteries).

One of the fundamental differences between the two types of institution seems to lie in the practice of enclosure. The standard notion is that nuns lived in very strict enclosure, men in less strict enclosure. Especially in Merovingian times, however, the practice of enclosure was much more varied than the standard interpretation suggests. Only the relatively small number of convents following the Rule of Caesarius observed a strict segregation of the community from outsiders. With this notable exception, nuns and monks abided by similar enclosure rules. Leaving the religious house

---

[38] H.-W. Goetz, 'Der kirchliche Festtag im frühmittelalterlichen Alltag', in D. Altenburg, J. Jarnut and H. Steinhoff (eds.), *Feste und Feiern im Mittelalter* (Sigmaringen, 1991), pp. 53–62 at p. 55; Lutterbach, *Sexualität*, pp. 77–9.

[39] See Hasdenteufel-Röding, 'Studien zur Gründung von Frauenklöstern'; Hen, *Culture and Religion in Merovingian Gaul*; F. Lifshitz, 'Des femmes missionnaires: l'exemple de la Gaule franque', *Revue d'Histoire Ecclésiastique* 83 (1988), pp. 5–33; Muschiol, *Famula Dei*; S. Wittern, *Frauen, Heiligkeit und Macht: Lateinische Frauenviten aus dem 4. bis 7. Jahrhundert* (Stuttgart, 1994).

was permissible subject to certain conditions, but it had to be accompanied by prayers of blessing which were shaped by liturgy. Visits to religious houses were also possible under certain defined circumstances.[40] The Council of Orleans of 549 offers an indication of how varied local practice could be, in its distinction between novitiate regulations in convents (but not in monasteries) with permanent enclosure and those with non-permanent enclosure.[41]

Enclosure practice indubitably impinged upon liturgical practice. In communities living according to the Rule of Caesarius, for instance, visits, even by clerics for liturgical purposes, were subject to strict conditions, with the result that Mass was celebrated at most once a week. These rules had the effect of leaving the nuns to celebrate the entire liturgy of the hours on their own without any priestly assistance. They also put the abbess in a position to preside over the convent's liturgy and herself say the concluding prayers (*collecta*) which in urban and local churches were reserved for the bishop or the local priest.[42] Hence stricter enclosure reduced the convent's dependence on male clergy for worship. In this context it must be stressed that the dependence of liturgical practice upon enclosure rules was not an issue in monasteries, which reinforced the fundamental gendered difference of liturgy, the prohibition on women from joining the clergy.

Although liturgical practice in convents was determined by enclosure practice, the liturgical prayers of female communities nevertheless tended to be more highly regarded than those of their male counterparts. Since nuns not only prayed for several hours a day but sanctified their entire daily routine through prayer, their suitability for intercessory prayer on behalf of the living and the dead was especially great. From the bishops of late antiquity through to the time of Boniface (d. 754) there was a continuous tradition of approaching nuns with requests for intercession. Sisterly prayer was deemed purer and thus more effective than men's.[43]

Nevertheless, a transformation in the appreciation of intercession is evident from the eighth century. This is closely linked to the prayer confraternity established by the bishops and abbots attending the Synod of Attigny (762) and to the growing importance of celebrating Mass.[44] Since the Mass was becoming the means of blessing and intercession *par excellence*, and since prayer confraternities required that the death of each of their members

---

[40] Muschiol, *Famula Dei*, pp. 72–80; on enclosure see also G. Muschiol, 'Klausurkonzepte. Mönche und Nonnen im 12. Jahrhundert', unpublished professorial thesis, Münster, 1999.

[41] *Conc. Aurelianense a. 549*, c. 19, *Concilia Galliae A.511–A.695*, p. 155.

[42] Details in Muschiol, *Famula Dei*, pp. 74–6, 101–6, 210–22, 367–71.

[43] Muschiol, *Famula Dei*, pp. 178–91.   [44] Angenendt, *Frühmittelalter*, pp. 290–1, 331–4, 338–9.

be celebrated by a large number of Masses, female convents could no longer compete on equal terms. In the amount of time which nuns needed to recite the complete Psalter for the benefit of a deceased person, a considerable number of Masses could be celebrated in monasteries. The sacrificial character of the Mass was now connected, above all, with intercession and blessing, and it promised much greater potency than the Psalter. Formerly held in high esteem, prayer by religious women succumbed to the Mass, always celebrated by men.

One of the consequences of this liturgical transformation was a decline in the spiritual influence of convents evident in the ninth and tenth centuries. Everywhere apart from Saxony, where numerous female communities were founded as late as the ninth and tenth centuries,[45] the number of religious houses for women shrank after the eighth century. Far fewer women had an alternative to wifehood and motherhood than in Merovingian times. At the same time, a clericalisation of the inhabitants of monasteries accompanied the increasing size and numbers of male houses. In effect, the balance between male and female communities shifted in favour of monks from the late eighth century onwards. This eventually resulted in the domination of monastic life by the liturgy, as at tenth- and eleventh-century Cluny.

In the life of religious communities in the early medieval west, penance was second only to the Eucharist in importance. Merovingian convents were characterised by a special form of conventual *confessio* and *reconciliatio*. Contrary to what might be expected, neither a priest nor a bishop nor a neighbouring abbot set foot in the convent in order to receive the *confessio* of the nuns and to administer the *reconciliatio* to them. Instead both tasks were left to the responsibility of the abbess and selected senior nuns, who used rituals in conformity with the established penitential rites in monasteries and urban or rural churches.[46] In other words, confession and reconciliation were performed by a woman for women, by the abbess for the nuns, in the same manner as the abbot acted as confessor to his monks. The similarity between monks and nuns in penitential terms is remarkable with respect to the powers of abbesses, since scholars writing on the early church emphasise that the powers of imposing penance and conferring reconciliation rested solely with the bishop.[47] Similarly, the system of tariffed penance which evolved in the early Middle Ages insisted in principle on the necessity for absolution to be performed by the members of the clergy.[48] In practice,

[45] K. J. Leyser, *Rule and Conflict in an Early Medieval Society: Ottonian Saxony* (London, 1979), pp. 63–73.
[46] Muschiol, *Famula Dei*, pp. 222–63.   [47] Bibliographical details in Muschiol, *Famula Dei*, p. 237.
[48] Muschiol, *Famula Dei*, p. 237.

however, a difference based on gender and legitimised by hierarchy did not exist between abbots and abbesses as far as their penitential powers for their respective communities were concerned. The hugely influential sixth-century Rule of Benedict compared the abbot in terms of his responsibility to a shepherd, thus putting him on an equivalent footing with a bishop.[49] With regard to her powers of binding and absolving, a Merovingian abbess thus held the same position *vis-à-vis* her flock as an abbot or a bishop.

Both in terms of directing penance and as leader of the liturgy of the hours, a Merovingian abbess performed a public and liturgical office in her own right. Such a role had been out of women's reach in late antiquity and once more became closed to women when Charlemagne's *Admonitio generalis* (789) and the Synod of Paris (829) took steps to contain and reduce the liturgical activity of abbesses.[50] The Merovingian period thus presented the heads of newly established convents with opportunities which were subsequently curtailed in the more restrictive climate of the Carolingian era. It must nevertheless be stressed that, despite its similarity with the penitential power of abbots and bishops, the penitential authority of Merovingian abbesses did have a gendered aspect. Unlike nuns, women who had not been consecrated lacked the opportunity of having the rite of penance administered to them by a woman, and instead had to confess to a cleric. The ensuing hierarchical relationship between confessing laywomen and absolving male cleric has a different quality from that between confessing nun and absolving abbess or between confessing layman and absolving male cleric.

Another transformation of gender roles in the early Middle Ages concerns male and female saints, in terms of both liturgical agency and post-mortem cult. The *Lives* of early medieval male saints characteristically followed the pattern of the 'man of God', the *vir dei*, familiar since antiquity.[51] Interestingly, the *Lives* of female saints depict a rather similar picture. These holy women, many of whom were termed *famula dei* (servant of God), gained their supernatural power from asceticism, enabling them to work miracles – exorcisms and socially beneficial deeds, but above all healings – by means of a quasi-standardised ritual sequence of prayer, laying on of hands, sign of the Cross and blessing.[52] Admittedly, it must be noted that the majority of

---

[49] *Benedicti Regula*, 2, 7–10, ed. R. Hanslik, CSEL 75 (2nd edn, Vienna, 1977), p. 22.

[50] *Admonitio generalis*, c. 76, *MGH Cap.* I, ed. A. Boretius (Hanover, 1883), p. 60; *Conc. Parisiense a. 829*, cc. 39, 43, *MGH Conc.* II/2, ed. A. Werminghoff (Hanover, 1908), pp. 637–8.

[51] Cf. P. Brown, 'The rise and function of the holy man in late antiquity', *JRS* 61 (1971), pp. 80–101.

[52] Muschiol, *Famula Dei*, pp. 353–66; see also, with a similar subject, L. L. Coon, *Sacred Fictions: Holy Women and Hagiography in Late Antiquity* (Philadelphia, 1997), esp. pp. 120–41.

the extant *Lives* were written by men and that it is therefore men who created this image of female sanctity. This makes it particularly remarkable that
asceticism and spiritual charisma produced an equality of the sexes which
was both intended by hagiographical authors and acceptable to those who
read or listened to the *Lives*. It is remarkable, too, that Merovingian holy
women were not represented like contemporary men, but that certain types
of holiness followed the model of Jesus, apparently irrespective of the sex
of the protagonists.[53] In effect, spiritual prowess remained independent of
early medieval notions of gender, despite the fact that the *Life of Martin*
written by Sulpicius Severus at the end of the fourth century was regarded
as the prototype of a life characterised by asceticism, political activity and
holiness. Early medieval hagiographers simply transferred this prototype to
numerous lives of sixth- and seventh-century women.[54]

In terms of their post-mortem cults, there was real competition between
the cults of St Martin and holy women such as Genovefa, Monegund and
Radegund, among others. Rather than resorting to Martin's healing powers,
a blind woman at his grave preferred to be healed by Monegund; Genovefa
exorcised demons in the immediate vicinity of Martin's grave; Radegund
raised a little girl from the dead 'in the manner of St Martin' (*more beati
Martini*).[55] Whether women in general tended to turn to a female saint (and
men to a male saint) when visiting graves in search of healing and help is a
question which is only beginning to receive attention. If first impressions
may be generalised, far more female than male pilgrims visited the graves
of women saints to venerate them and pray at their tombs. Certainly, by
the ninth century, some shrines of male saints were only visited by male
pilgrims. Part of the explanation for this lies in constraints upon access
imposed by both architectural layout and monastic tradition.[56] Furthermore, preliminary studies suggest that there may also have been gendered
patterns at work, attracting women to female saints' shrines and men to
male saints.[57] In effect, traditional notions of women's culturally ascribed

[53] Cf. J. Kitchen, *Saints' Lives and the Rhetoric of Gender: Male and Female in Merovingian Hagiography*
(New York, 1998). This study, in which the term 'gender' is applied to women only, is sometimes
problematic.
[54] G. Muschiol, 'Vorbild und Konkurrenz: Martin von Tours und die heiligen Frauen', *Rottenburger
Jahrbuch für Kirchengeschichte* 18 (1999), pp. 77–88.
[55] Muschiol, 'Vorbild und Konkurrenz', pp. 77, 81, 86 for references; for the issue of female holiness
in the Carolingian age see J. M. H. Smith, 'The problem of female sanctity in Carolingian Europe
c. 780–920', *Past and Present* 146 (1995), pp. 3–37.
[56] J. M. H. Smith, 'Women at the tomb: access to relic shrines in the early Middle Ages', in K. Mitchell
and I. Wood (eds.), *The World of Gregory of Tours* (Leiden, 2002), pp. 163–80.
[57] H.-W. Goetz, 'Heiligenkult und Geschlecht: Geschlechtsspezifisches Wunderwirken in
frühmittelalterlichen Mirakelberichten', *Das Mittelalter* 1 (1996), pp. 90–111.

weakness (their *imbecillitas sexus*) were challenged by the emergence of female saints in the early Middle Ages.[58] From the fifth century onwards, the reality of female asceticism and women's posthumous miracle-working ability could turn female weakness into strength and in this way transform gendered images of humanity.

SEARCHING FOR GENDERED RELIGIOUS MENTALITIES

This survey of Merovingian Francia has revealed that changes in religious practices and attitudes altered both women's and men's roles in cult and liturgy. In addition, it has suggested that the liturgy itself was also an agent of changing constructions of gender in this period. These conclusions themselves raise a host of other questions, which may be summarised under the headings 'public agency', 'hierarchy' and 'corporality'.

While the public celebration of the liturgy was an all-male affair in the late Roman world,[59] in the early Middle Ages women also assumed public liturgical roles. In the churches of their convents they said intercessory prayers on behalf of the living and the dead. As abbesses they administered penance to their conventuals and led the community's liturgy, most visibly during those parts of the liturgy of the hours to which the public had access. As renowned saints they attracted women and men thanks to their asceticism and miraculous powers. Yet questions about public agency remain. Miraculous powers and perceptions of holiness require further study in order to ascertain what types of cultic veneration were granted to male saints, what types to female saints, and by whom. Although holiness through asceticism transcended gender, we need to ask whether there were specific remits, for instance saints for pregnant women or saints for warriors. Who took over the tasks connected with the liturgy which had been the responsibility of the wives of bishops and priests in the sixth century? It is also desirable to investigate the role of enclosure in male monasteries. How did regulations about enclosure for monks affect their participation in confraternities of prayer? Last but not least, we also need a detailed gender-based study of why the celebration of Mass gained the upper hand over the intercessory prayers of female communities.

With regard to the ways in which gender established hierarchies of difference in liturgical contexts, the subdivision of liturgical space in buildings used for worship requires further research. How should we interpret the

---

[58] Cf. Smith, 'Transformation', p. 559.
[59] T. Berger, *Sei gesegnet, meine Schwester: Frauen feiern Liturgie* (Würzburg, 1999), pp. 66–75.

separation of the chancel, since laymen and laywomen alike were only in exceptional cases permitted to enter but only women were kept away from the altar in a particular manner? And should we regard nuns as part of the generality of womankind or stress their similarities with monks? Did nuns occupy a place somewhere between the sexes since they were required, like men, to wash their hands before receiving Communion instead of being obliged, like women, to receive Communion with their hands covered by a cloth? In view of the ascetic existence of monks and nuns alike and their intermediate position between laity and clergy, the concept of a third gender may be a fruitful one to apply, for the 'angelic life' (*angelikos bios*) led by male and female ascetics might well be the precondition for their particular liturgical roles.[60]

Furthermore, what are we to make of the lack of evidence for any separation of the sexes in Merovingian church buildings? Why was a gendered use of space within churches reintroduced in the Carolingian period? The second of three recently discovered fragments of Amalarius of Metz shows, on the one hand, the necessity to explain such a separation of the sexes, and its legitimation by quoting one of the epistles of Paul in the Bible.[61] On the other hand, the third fragment shows the problems of biblical legitimation for this separation: while interpreting the groups of clerics surrounding the altar as witnesses of the crucifixion, Amalarius found it hard to deal with the biblical story of the crucifixion because it mentions women standing next to the Cross.[62] Amalarius' laborious and slightly confused efforts to give reasons for the difference between the presence of women in the Gospel account and their absence from the altar during Mass suggests that their exclusion from the altar was in urgent need of explanation and defence.

A remaining question about differential hierarchy is that of the relative status of male and female religious communities in general, and of the intercessory value of their liturgy in particular. What would a gendered approach to monastic liturgy have to say about the role of liturgy in male monasteries within the socio-political fabric of the Merovingian kingdoms,

---

[60] Leyser, 'Masculinity in flux', p. 119, and, discussing the high and later Middle Ages, R. N. Swanson, 'Angels incarnate: clergy and masculinity from Gregorian reform to Reformation', in Hadley (ed.), *Masculinity*, pp. 160–77. For the *topos* of the *angelikos bios* see K. S. Frank, *Angelikos Bios: Begriffs-analytische und begriffsgeschichtliche Untersuchung zum 'Engelgleichen Leben' im frühen Mönchtum* (Münster, 1964); P. Brown, *The Body and Society: Men, Women, and Sexual Renunciation in Early Christianity* (New York, 1988).

[61] Edited by H. Schneider, 'Roman liturgy and Frankish allegory', in J. M. H. Smith (ed.), *Early Medieval Rome and the Christian West: Essays in Honour of Donald A. Bullough* (Leiden, 2000), pp. 341–79 at pp. 351 and 363.

[62] Schneider, 'Roman liturgy', pp. 353, 376–9.

given that convents were evidently credited with providing more effective prayer assistance?

Thirdly, the issue of 'corporality' suggests a changing understanding of the human body and its relation to liturgical celebrations. After childbirth a woman was considered blemished and unclean and thus temporarily ineligible to participate in worship. This in turn suggests further questions: were there also events in the course of a man's life which rendered him ineligible for the cult and required a special kind of purification? Were there purification rites for warriors who returned from military conflict or who had stained themselves with blood on other occasions? Were there rites for the purification of bishops who, contrary to ecclesiastical rules, still had sexual intercourse with their wives?

This exploration of the liturgy in Merovingian Francia thus extends the scope of research far beyond what has hitherto been undertaken. It suggests that there is a need to explore the gendered structure of all the various liturgical traditions of the early Middle Ages. Were there gendered differences and commonalities between, say, the Roman and the Ambrosian or the Gallican liturgy? How does gender difference interact with regional difference within the liturgy? All these questions serve to underscore the point made above, that liturgy did not take place in a social vacuum, but was intertwined with the social attitudes and political developments of the early Middle Ages. We must realise that the sign of the Cross made over a spoon in order to fend off demons was as important to the existence of individual Christians and as relevant a liturgical act as the intercessory prayers on behalf of king, people and country regularly said at Radegund's behest in her convent at Poitiers.[63]

Finally, the double transformation which characterised the western liturgy in the transition from antiquity to the early Middle Ages has to be grounded in a gendered perspective. The decline of traditional Roman learning on the one hand and the establishment of the Carolingian empire on the other marked the beginning and the end of a transformational process during which gendered roles in conducting the liturgy differed from those of the preceding and the subsequent periods. What is more, this Merovingian interlude appears to have permitted not only different gender roles, but generally more indeterminate ones. The encounter of the Roman and the Frankish worlds necessarily resulted in a phase of insecurity, fluidity and experimentation in the traditional distribution of liturgical roles. The attempts by the Carolingians to consolidate their hold over

---

[63] Muschiol, *Famula Dei*, pp. 176–7, 184.

the church, for example by introducing the Roman liturgy, replaced this period of creativity with an intensification of hierarchical structures and with attempts to increase ecclesiastical centralisation. The effect was to give new weight in politics and the church to persons of institutional authority, at the expense of the Merovingian acceptance of charismatic individuals. Thus the Carolingian liturgy became institutionalised in a way which hardly allowed any variability in gender roles.[64]

Inasmuch as the transformation of the Roman world was characterised by disintegration and reintegration, this chapter has shown how fruitfully these ideas can be applied to the liturgy. Further, it has demonstrated that a gendered approach reveals this with exceptional clarity. Out of the encounter between Gallo-Roman, Frankish and Irish traditions there emerged some identical roles for men and women, together with an appreciation of the intercessory potency of women's prayer. That is to say that, in the early Middle Ages, as in other times, liturgy was shaped by the sex of its participants, whether individual men and women or groups and communities. What is needed next is a much fuller exploration of the gendered nature of the liturgy than has yet been undertaken for the centuries in which the Roman world was transformed into the medieval one.[65]

---

[64] It is beyond the scope of this study to explore whether further changes in the ascription of liturgical roles followed the demise of the Carolingian empire or whether the gendered organisation of roles in the liturgy of the western church remained unaffected by the disintegration of the socio-political framework. For a preliminary discussion, see S. F. Wemple, *Women in Frankish Society: Marriage and the Cloister 500 to 900* (Philadelphia, 1981), pp. 194–6.

[65] Heartfelt thanks are due to my husband, Oliver Muschiol, for translating the text from German.

CHAPTER 12

Gender and the patronage of culture in Merovingian Gaul

Yitzhak Hen

The concept of 'gender' helps scholars to elucidate various social structures, developments and perceptions in a given society, and serves as a useful prism through which people, their beliefs and the motives behind their actions may be examined.[1] The following pages will focus on the sponsorship offered to artisans and writers, in an attempt to understand the extent to which gender differences influenced the patronage of culture in the Frankish kingdoms under the Merovingians.

Patronage of the arts is a universal phenomenon of western cultures – universal across time, space and civilisation. Throughout antiquity, the Middle Ages and the early modern era, rulers, clerics and wealthy aristocrats patronised artists and writers, and such acts of munificence were perceived as one of the obligations of a ruler or a rich person.[2] In this respect, Merovingian Gaul was no different. Yet, although there is substantial evidence of cultural patronage from the Merovingian period, no comprehensive study of this subject has been undertaken. The reasons for this neglect are clear. Not only is the relevant evidence from Merovingian Gaul widely scattered and unevenly distributed, it also presents difficult problems of interpretation. Moreover, the mechanisms through which cultural patronage operated in Merovingian Gaul are sometimes uncertain. No doubt the availability of material resources was a crucial prerequisite for the pursuit of patronage, and it was the privilege of those who possessed wealth to exercise patronage by commissioning works of art and literature. But it is only rarely that we are given any indication of the ways and circumstances by which such works were commissioned.

---

[1] See, for example, the various papers collected in the special issue of *Gender and History* 12, 3 (2000) (reprinted as P. Stafford and A. B. Mulder-Bakker (eds.), *Gendering the Middle Ages* (Oxford, 2001)).

[2] For a fuller discussion of this issue, see Y. Hen, *The Royal Patronage of Liturgy in Frankish Gaul to the Death of Charles the Bald (877)*, Henry Bradshaw Society Subsidia 3 (London, 2001), pp. 16–19, with further references.

An example from the Merovingian period is provided by the case of Eligius of Noyon. Born *c.* 588 in the area of Limoges, Eligius was sent by his father to the goldsmith and moneyer Abbo. After his apprenticeship period Eligius moved to Neustria (the north-western part of the Merovingian kingdom), where his talent as a goldsmith and jeweller was noticed by Bobo, King Chlothar II's treasurer. Subsequently, Eligius was commissioned by Chlothar II and his son, Dagobert I, to prepare several jewelled objects for the royal court, the most important of which was a golden throne.[3] Evidence such as this, however, is extremely rare, and in most cases we remain ignorant about who commissioned works of art, who produced them, and by what mechanisms patronage was exercised.

Let us take, for example, the jewellery of Arnegundis, who was buried in Saint-Denis. Whether we identify her with Queen Aregundis, wife of King Chlothar I (d. 561), or with Arnegundis, an otherwise unknown aristocrat, she was buried in a purple dress, covered with a red cloak decorated in gold thread embroidery, and adorned with two gold and garnet disc brooches, a long gold and garnet dress pin, two delicate gold earrings, two hairpins, a large gold filigree plaque-buckle, golden buckles and strap-ends from shoes and cross-garters, and a gold ring.[4] Were all these artefacts made especially for Arnegundis, or had she acquired them by purchase or as gifts or as inheritance? If she, her husband or her children commissioned them, are we to assume that they had an atelier of expert goldsmiths in their employment, or did they hire the services of a goldsmith who happened to have an independent workshop in the region? We simply do not know.

That wealthy Merovingian men and women invested much time and material resources in acquiring and commissioning precious artefacts is clear not only from the archaeological evidence, especially the grave goods,[5] but also from wills – for example, Bertramn of Le Mans and Burgundofara bequeathed the many precious objects they had collected throughout

---

[3] *Vita Eligii episcopi Noviomagensis* 1.1–5, ed. B. Krusch, *MGH SRM* IV (Hanover, 1902), pp. 669–73. On Eligius and his works, see H. Vierck, 'L'œuvre de saint Eloi, orfèvre, et son rayonnement', in P. Périn and L.-C. Feffer (eds.), *La Neustrie: les pays au nord de la Loire de Dagobert à Charles le Chauve (VIIe–IXe siècles)* (Créteil, 1985), pp. 403–9, and see the bibliography cited on p. 469. See also E. James, *The Franks* (Oxford, 1988), pp. 196–8; I. N. Wood, *The Merovingian Kingdoms, 450–751* (London and New York, 1994), pp. 150–1.

[4] On the tomb of Arnegundis, see P. Périn, 'Pour une révision de la datation de la tombe d'Arégonde, épouse de Clotaire Ier, découverte en 1959 dans la basilique de Saint-Denis', *Archéologie Médiévale* 21 (1991), pp. 21–50; G. Halsall, *Early Medieval Cemeteries: An Introduction to Burial Archaeology in the Post Roman World* (Glasgow, 1995), pp. 33–4. See also Bonnie Effros, chapter 9 above.

[5] See, for example, the lavishly illustrated volumes *Die Franken Wegbereiter Europas*, edited by A. Wieczorek *et al.*, 2 vols. (Mainz, 1996).

life to various churches and monasteries[6] – and from donation charters in which rich aristocrats donated jewels and other valuables to ecclesiastical institutions.[7] In addition, many gold and silver objects were commissioned by Merovingian kings, queens and nobles for donation to churches and monasteries throughout the Frankish realm, and these are frequently mentioned by the hagiographical sources from the seventh century onwards.[8] All these sources testify that a huge amount of wealth was spent in Merovingian Gaul on patronising artisans. This could only be expected in a society where there was court culture and aristocratic culture, with their ecclesiastical and monastic counterparts. The increasingly close links between secular and religious culture, and the growing dependency of churches and monasteries on the court that becomes apparent in the sources from the seventh century and later,[9] establish a framework for the patronage of culture in the Merovingian period.[10]

To understand the mechanism of cultural patronage in Merovingian Gaul, and the place of gender differences within it, we need to have before us all the relevant material. It is beyond the scope of this chapter to present a comprehensive survey, but what follows is a preliminary attempt to assemble some of the evidence. When we can determine the gender of the patron, my aim is to assess whether men's patronage and women's patronage differed in significant ways. I am interested, in other words, in the extent to which patronage of culture in Merovingian Gaul was divided along gender lines.

One of the main obstacles in understanding acts of patronage in Merovingian Gaul is the problem of matching the written evidence with surviving artefacts.[11] An exceptional case in point is provided, once again, by the work

---

[6] See Margarete Weidemann, *Das Testament des Bischof Bertramn von Les Mans vom 27 März 616* (Mainz, 1986); J. Guerout, 'Le testament de sainte Fare. Matériaux pour l'édition critique de ce document', *Revue d'Histoire Ecclésiastique* 60 (1965), pp. 761–821.

[7] See the various charters collected in *Diplomatae, chartae, epistulae, leges aliaque instrumenta ad res Gallo-Francicas spectantia*, ed. J. M. Pardessus, 2 vols. (Paris, 1843–49).

[8] This was also noted by Wood, *The Merovingian Kingdoms*, pp. 65–6.

[9] See, for example, Wood, *The Merovingian Kingdoms*, pp. 181–202 and 239–54. See also Y. Hen, *The Royal Court and the Patronage of Culture in the Barbarian Kingdoms* (forthcoming).

[10] Needless to say, this also remained the Carolingian frame of patronage, albeit on a much larger scale. See, for example, J. J. Contreni, 'The Carolingian renaissance: education and literary culture', in *The New Cambridge Medieval History*, vol. II: *c. 700–c. 900*, ed. R. McKitterick (Cambridge, 1995), pp. 709–57.

[11] On the methodological problems of how to deploy written and material evidence in tandem, see, for example, E. James, 'Burial and status in the early medieval West', *Transactions of the Royal Historical Society* 5th ser., 39 (1989), pp. 23–40; G. Halsall, 'Burial, ritual and Merovingian society', in J. Hill and M. Swan (eds.), *The Community, the Family and the Saint: Patterns of Power in Early Medieval Europe* (Turnhout, 1998), pp. 325–38.

of Eligius of Noyon. In 1940 B. de Montesquiou-Fezensac identified in the Cabinet des Médailles a small jewelled plaque thought to be part of the famous gold cross made by Eligius for Saint-Denis.[12] The ninth-century author of the *Gesta Dagoberti* describes in detail how King Dagobert I commissioned this jewelled cross from Eligius, the *summus aurifex* (chief goldsmith) in the entire Frankish kingdom.[13] But still it took much imagination, and a sixteenth-century painting by the master of Saint-Giles, to identify this piece with the famous cross commissioned by King Dagobert.[14] Precise information such as this is exceptional, and in most cases we have no contemporary evidence concerning who produced a certain work and who commissioned it.

Unless an artefact bears a notice naming the person who owned it or commissioned it, we usually remain ignorant about the circumstances which led to its production. Moreover, even when such a note exists, much of the information we are looking for is still missing. Let us take, for example, the so-called Chrismal of Mortain. This small case, designed originally to hold the host, is inscribed with a runic inscription that reads: 'May God help Eada who [made] this *kissmeel* [i.e. Chrismal].'[15] Thus we know the name of the goldsmith who made the case, but we know nothing else about him, nor is there any indication of who commissioned this work or in what circumstances. Similar queries surround the so-called Warnebertus Reliquary. At the bottom of this house-shaped reliquary the following note is inscribed: 'Bishop Warnebertus ordered [this reliquary] to be made in order to preserve relics. May the Saints Mary and Peter grant their support to the very same bishop. Amen.'[16] Although formal analysis suggests that this particular reliquary was produced in a Lombard atelier in the second half of the seventh century, we do not know the identity of the artisans who made it, or what mechanism of patronage was exercised by Warnebertus in

---

[12] B. de Montesquiou-Fezensac, 'Une épave de trésor de Saint-Denis: fragment retrouvé de la croix de Saint Eloi', in *Mélanges en hommage de F. Martroye* (Paris, 1940), pp. 288–301.

[13] *Gesta Dagoberti I regis Francorum*, c. 20, ed. B. Krusch, *MGH SRM* II (Hanover, 1888), p. 407: 'Crucem etiam magnam, quae retro altare aureum poneretur, ex auro puro et pretiosissimis gemmis insigni opere ac minutissima artis subtilitate fabricari iussit, quam beatus Eligius, eo quod in illo tempore summus aurifex ipse in regno haberetur, cum et alia, quae ad ipsius basilicae ornatum pertinebant, strenue prepararet, eliganti subtilitatis ingenio, sanctitate opitulante, mirifice exornavit.'

[14] See D. Gaborit-Chopin, 'Fragments de la croix de saint Eloi' and 'Les arts précieux', in Périn and Feffer (eds.), *La Neustrie*, pp. 125 and 287–289 respectively. See also B. de Montesquiou-Fezensac, *Le Trésor de Saint-Denis*, 3 vols. (Paris, 1973–77), vol. III, pp. 98–100.

[15] See P. Périn, 'Chrismale', in Périn and Feffer (eds.), *La Neustrie*, pp. 141–2, and the bibliography cited there. This is a standard formula, and therefore we assume that Eada was the artisan, not the patron.

[16] + VVARNEBERTUS P P FIERE / IUSSIT AD CONSERVANDO RELIQI / A SSCI MARIE PETRI OPE TRIBUANT / IPSIUS PONTEFICE AMEN +

commissioning the work.[17] We do not even know for sure who this Warnebertus was.[18] Similarly, we do not know who made the little gold reliquary known as the Reliquary of Mumma, or when and where it was crafted.[19] On its back a note reads: 'Mumma ordered [this reliquary] to be made for the love of Saint Mary and Saint Peter.'[20] Thus we know that Mumma commissioned the reliquary as an act of piety, but who made it and where it was made are not clear. The Reliquary of Mumma was found in 1642 under the main altar at the church of Fleury. Given that two churches, one dedicated to the Virgin Mary and the other to Saint Peter, were erected in Fleury in the mid-seventh century,[21] and given that the joint cult of Mary and Peter is attested at Fleury from a fairly early stage, it seems appropriate to suggest that the reliquary was commissioned by Mumma in order to be presented to the abbey of Fleury. But we still do not know who made it and, as in the case of Warnebertus, we do not even know who this Mumma was. Mumma can be an abridged form of the name Mummolus,[22] but it can also be the name of a woman. A certain woman named Mumma is mentioned in one of the charters from the abbey of Weisembourg,[23] and if our Mumma is indeed a woman, then we have in this reliquary evidence for the patronage of culture exercised by Merovingian women – but this is clearly tenuous.

The situation is not much better in the case of surviving manuscripts. Manuscripts, and especially those lavishly decorated, were not produced in a vacuum. They were very expensive, and many of them were especially commissioned by bishops, abbots and rich aristocrats.[24] Consequently, modern

---

[17] On this reliquary, see G. Haseloff, 'Das Warnebertus-Reliquiar im Stiftschaft von Beromünster', *Helvetica Archaeologica* 15 (1984), pp. 195–200; P. Périn, 'Reliquaire dit de Warenbertus', in Périn and Feffer (eds.), *La Neustrie*, p. 141, and see the bibliography cited there.

[18] It is impossible to ascertain whether the Warnebertus mentioned by this inscription is Abbot Warnebertus of Saint-Médard de Soissons (d. 676).

[19] On the reliquary of Mumma, see J.-M. Berland, 'Châsse de Mumma', in Périn and Feffer (eds.), *La Neustrie*, p. 142.

[20] MVMMA·FIERI·IVSSIT·I·AMORE / SCE·MARIE·ET·SCI·PETRI

[21] These two churches were destroyed by a fire in 974; see Aimoin, *Miracula sancti Benedicti* II.9, ed. E. de Certain (Paris, 1858), pp. 111–12. On the history of Fleury, see G. Chenesseau, *L'Abbaye de Fleury à Saint-Benoît-sur-Loire: son histoire, ses institutions, ses églises* (Paris, 1931); J. Laporte, 'Fleury', in *Dictionnaire d'histoire et de géographie ecclésiastique*, vol. XVII (Paris, 1969), cols. 441–76.

[22] Mummolus was the abbot of Fleury when the relics of St Benedict arrived there in 703.

[23] See Berland, 'Châsse de Mumma', p. 142.

[24] For a general survey, see R. McKitterick, 'The scriptoria of Merovingian Gaul: a survey of the evidence', in H. B. Clarke and M. Brennan (eds.), *Columbanus and Merovingian Monasticism*, BAR International Series 113 (Oxford, 1981), pp. 173–207 (repr. in her *Books, Scribes and Learning in the Frankish Kingdoms, 6th–9th Centuries* (Aldershot, 1994), chapter 1); J. Vezin, 'Les scriptoria de Neustrie, 650–850', in H. Atsma (ed.), *La Neustrie: Les pays au nord de la Loire de 650 à 850*, 2 vol., Beihefte der Francia 16 (Sigmaringen, 1989), vol. II, pp. 307–18.

scholars tend to associate such manuscripts with historically attested figures, but only on rare occasions do we find in a manuscript a contemporary
notice concerning who wrote it and who commissioned it. We know, for
example, that the large and handsome volume of canons, now in Toulouse,
was specially commissioned from the scribe Perpetuus.[25] The colophon at
the end of the manuscript did not survive, but a ninth-century copy of it,
now in Albi, states:

Here ends the book of canons. Amen. I Perpetuus, the ever unworthy presbyter,
was ordered by my lord Dido, the bishop of Albi, to copy this book of canons.
After the fire in the very same city, this book was recovered with the help of God
on 25 July in the fourth year of the reign of King Childeric [i.e. 666].[26]

Hence we know that the manuscript was commissioned by Bishop Dido of
Albi, and that the scribe Perpetuus, a *nimium indignus presbyter*, executed it.
Similarly, we know from a short note added to a copy of Isidore's *Synonyma*,
now in Fulda, that this codex – with which Boniface is supposed to have
defended himself – was commissioned by a woman called Ragyndrudis
(otherwise unknown) from the Burgundian scriptorium of Luxeuil at the
beginning of the eighth century.[27] A short notice on the last folio of this
manuscript states: 'I Ragyndrudis commissioned this book in honour of
our Lord Jesus Christ, and I bid everyone who reads it to find it appropriate
to pray to God on my behalf.'[28]

   Such precise statements are extremely rare, but there is considerable evidence that many manuscripts were commissioned and owned by
Merovingian women as well as men.[29] For example, a copy of Augustine's

[25] Toulouse, Bibliothèque Municipale, MS 364; *Codices Latini Antiquiores: A Palaeographical Guide to
Latin Manuscripts Prior to the Ninth Century*, 11 vols. with a supplement (Oxford, 1935–71; 2nd edn
of vol. 11, 1972) [hereafter cited as *CLA*], vii.836.

[26] Albi, Bibliothèque Municipale, MS 2, fol. 117v: 'Explicit liber canonum, amen. Ego Perpetuus
quamvis indignus presbyter iussus a domino meo Didone urbis Albigensium episcopum [*sic*] hunc
librum canonum scripsi. Post incendium civitatis ipsius hic liber recuperatus fuit Deo auxilliante
sub die viii Kal. Ag. ann. iiii regnant. domini nostri Childerici regis.' On these two manuscripts, see
C. H. Turner, 'Chapter in the history of Latin manuscripts, ii: a group of manuscripts of canons at
Toulouse, Albi and Paris', *Journal of Theological Studies* 2 (1900/1), pp. 266–73. See also McKitterick,
'The scriptoria of Merovingian Gaul', p. 176.

[27] On this codex, see L. E. von Padberg and H.-W. Stork, *Der Ragyndrudis-Codex des Hl. Bonifatius*
(Fulda, 1994); L. E. von Padberg, *Studien zur Bonifatiusverehrung: zur Geschichte des Codex Ragyndrudis und der Fulder Reliquien des Bonifatius* (Frankfurt, 1996), especially pp. 24–37.

[28] Fulda, Dommuseum, Codex Bonifatianus 2 (*CLA* viii.1197), fol. 143v: 'In honore domini nostri
Ihesu Christi ego Ragyndrudis ordinavi librum istum quicumque legerit coniuro per Deum vivum
ut pro me orare dignimini.'

[29] This, of course, has some serious implications (that cannot be discussed here) as far as female literacy
in Merovingian Gaul is concerned. On women and literacy in the early Middle Ages, see J. L. Nelson,
'Women and the word in the earlier Middle Ages', in D. Wood and W. J. Sheils (eds.), *Women in*

Enarrationes in Psalmos, now in Lyons, was owned by a certain Constantina, who wrote her name on two different folios of the manuscript,[30] and a copy of Augustine's sermons was read, and most probably owned, by a certain Juliana, who added on the margins of one of the folios: 'Iuliana legit lebrem estum [*sic*] Iuliana fecit.'[31] Who commissioned these books, we do not know, but it is enough to mention the book-collecting campaign of Abbess Geretrudis of Nivelles, who 'with God's inspiration . . . deservedly obtained through her envoys, men of good reputation, relics of the saints and holy books from Rome and from the regions across the sea';[32] or Abbess Bertila of Jouarre (and later of Chelles), who sent books and teachers to England to help establish monasteries there,[33] to realise that women in Merovingian Gaul took an active role in patronising culture by commissioning manuscripts for various purposes.[34] Rosamond McKitterick has also suggested that 'it might be deemed appropriate to associate the atelier or group of ateliers responsible for the production of a group of mid-eighth century sacramentaries, including the Gelasian, with Pippin III and Bertrada'.[35] Although one cannot assess the exact role of Bertrada in such an enterprise, the fact that these sacramentaries were commissioned from the nuns' scriptoria of the Seine basin indicates that whether or not a woman commissioned them, women certainly produced them.[36] Lastly, the colophon of the so-called Gundohinus Gospels states that these were commissioned in honour of Saint John and Saint Mary by Fausta and at

---

the Church, Studies in Church History 27 (Oxford, 1990), pp. 53–78 at pp. 65–6 (repr. in her *The Frankish World, 750–900* (London, 1996), pp. 199–221); R. McKitterick, 'Women and literacy in the early Middle Ages', in her *Books, Scribes and Learning*, chapter 13.

[30] Lyons, Bibliothèque Municipale, MS 426 (*CLA* vi.773), fols. 13v–14r and 19r. On this manuscript, see McKitterick, 'The scriptoria of Merovingian Gaul', pp. 180–2.

[31] Lyons, Bibliothèque Municipale, MS 604 (*CLA* vi.783), fol. 86r. On this manuscript, see McKitterick, 'The scriptoria of Merovingian Gaul', pp. 180–2.

[32] *Vita sanctae Geretrudis*, c. 2, ed. B. Krusch, *MGH SRM* ii, p. 457: 'et per suos nuntios, boni testimonii viros sanctorum patrocinia vel sancta volumina de urbe Roma et de transmarinis regionibus . . . meruisset habere'. I cite the translation of P. Fouracre and R. Gerberding, *Late Merovingian France: History and Hagiography, 640–720* (Manchester, 1996), p. 322.

[33] *Vita Bertilae abbatissae Calensis*, c. 6, ed. W. Levison, *MGH SRM* vi (Hanover, 1913), pp. 106–7. See also P. Sims-Williams, 'Continental influence at Bath monastery in the seventh century', *Anglo-Saxon England* 4 (1975), pp. 1–10.

[34] See also F. Lifshitz, 'Gender and exemplarity east of the middle Rhine: Jesus, Mary and the saints in manuscript context', *EME* 9 (2000), pp. 325–43.

[35] See R. McKitterick, 'Royal patronage of culture in the Frankish kingdoms under the Carolingians: motives and consequences', in *Committenti e produzione artistico-letteraria nell'alto medioevo occidentale*, Settimane di Studio sull'Alto Medioevo 39 (Spoleto, 1992), pp. 93–129 esp. pp. 100–3; the citation is from p. 100 (repr. in her *The Frankish Kings and Culture in the Early Middle Ages* (Aldershot, 1995), chapter 7).

[36] On these scriptoria, see R. McKitterick, '"Nuns" scriptoria in England and Francia in the eighth century', *Francia* 19 (1992), pp. 1–35 (repr. in her *Books, Scribes and Learning*, chapter 7).

the incentive of the monk Fulculfus.[37] This particular act of patronage occurred during the third year of the reign of King Pippin III (i.e. 754), and therefore is classified chronologically under the Carolingian period. But the phenomenon of cultural patronage which it represents did not emerge *ex nihilo*, and it evidently reflects tendencies which characterised the later Merovingian aristocracy.[38]

In the case of literary works, one might expect the evidence for patronage to stand out clearly and legibly. However, when we turn to the literature of Merovingian Gaul, the picture is less clear than one might hope. The best-known author who benefited from the generous patronage of Merovingian kings, queens and aristocrats was Venantius Fortunatus, the most obse-quious figure in Merovingian history.[39] He dedicated many poems and panegyrics to his patrons, among them King Sigibert and Queen Brunhild, King Chilperic and Queen Fredegund, King Charibert, Radegund, widow of King Chlothar I and abbess of Sainte-Croix in Poitiers, Gregory of Tours and the Austrasian *major domus* Gogo.[40] These poems and panegyrics are perhaps the best evidence for the patronage of culture exercised by the Merovingian court in the second half of the sixth century.[41] Although both his male and female patrons are depicted in terms derived almost entirely from the Roman past, Venantius describes the men mainly in terms of military prowess, justice and culture, while the women are praised for being pious, honourable and good wives.[42] This is undoubtedly a gendered response, structured mainly by the different roles which Venantius' protag-onists had in society, but which also goes straight back to Roman ideals and perceptions.[43] But gender was not the only motivating factor. While

---

[37] Autun, Bibliothèque Municipale, MS 3 (*CLA* VI.716), fol. 186r. On this manuscript, see L. Nees, *The Gundohinus Gospels*, Medieval Academy Books 95 (Cambridge, MA, 1987).

[38] In a series of papers and books Jeffrey Hamburger has suggested (with reference to the later Middle Ages) that books with illustrations were often produced for women (who were believed to need the prop, just like novice monks) while non-illustrated books were for men. See, for example, J. Hamburger, *Nuns as Artists: The Visual Culture of a Medieval Convent* (Berkeley, 1977); Hamburger, *The Visual and the Visionary: Art and Female Spirituality in Late Medieval Germany* (New York, 1998). It is far beyond the scope of this chapter to assess Hamburger's thesis with reference to early medieval Francia. It would suffice to note here that, as far as I can tell, this thesis receives no support from the manuscript evidence that survives from the Merovingian or the Carolingian period.

[39] On Venantius Fortunatus' career, see J. W. George, *Venantius Fortunatus: A Poet in Merovingian Gaul* (Oxford, 1992), pp. 18–34.

[40] See Venantius Fortunatus, *Carmina*, ed. M. Reydellet, 2 vols. (Paris, 1994).

[41] George, *Venantius Fortunatus*, pp. 35–61; M. Reydellet, *La Royauté dans la littérature latine de Sidoine Apollinaire à Isidore de Seville* (Rome, 1981), pp. 197–344.

[42] George, *Venantius Fortunatus*, pp. 40–57; Reydellet, *La Royauté dans la littérature latine*, pp. 321–2.

[43] For Venantius' use of classical poetic themes and tropes in his representation of women, see M. Roberts, 'Venantius Fortunatus' elegy on the death of Galswintha (*Carm.* 6.5)', in R. W. Mathisen

a substantial number of poems written for Radegund were devotional,[44] their subject matter responds to her monastic affiliation as much as to her gender. Some of Venantius' devotional works, including the verse version of the *Vita Martini*, were dedicated to Gregory of Tours,[45] while none was dedicated to either a man or a woman outside the ecclesiastical establishment.

Venantius Fortunatus is the best-documented protégé from the Merovingian period, but he was certainly not the only author to benefit from royal patronage. We know, for example, that Anthimius, a Byzantine physician, dedicated his short treatise *On the Observation of Food* to the Frankish King Theuderic I (d. 534),[46] and it has been argued that the early Carolingian attempt to sponsor the writing of history to justify its rulers' actions is a continuation of an even older Merovingian tradition.[47]

The clearest evidence for the patronage of literature exercised specifically by Merovingian women comes from hagiography. Baudonivia, a nun from Radegund's monastery in Poitiers, relates at the beginning of her version of the *Vita Radegundis* that Abbess Dedimia had imposed this task upon her.[48] The author of the *Vita Geretrudis* was commissioned by the abbess of Nivelles,[49] Florentius of Tricastina was commissioned to write the *Vita Rusticulae* by Abbess Celsa of Arles,[50] the *Vita Sadalbergae* was written for Omotarius and Abbess Anstrudis of Laon,[51] and the *Vita Austrebertae* was commissioned by Abbess Julia of Pavilly.[52]

But why? A fundamental problem in analysing any act of cultural patronage is tracing its motivation. Patronage of culture, as we are told, 'is

---

and D. Shanzer (eds.), *Society and Culture in Late Antique Gaul: Revisiting the Sources* (Aldershot, 2001), pp. 298–312.

[44] George, *Venantius Fortunatus*, pp. 32–4 and 161–77.

[45] See Venantius Fortunatus, *Vita sancti Martini*, ed. F. Leo, *MGH AA* IV.1 (Berlin, 1881), pp. 293–370, especially the *Epistulae ad Gregorium*, pp. 293–4.

[46] Anthimius, *De observatione ciborum*, ed. and trans. M. Grant (Chippenham, 1996), p. 46. The full title of Anthimius' treatise is *De observatione ciborum: qualiter omnes cibi comendantur ut bene digerantur et sanitatem praestare debeant, nam non infirmitatem stomachi nec anxietatem humani corporis* ('On the observation of food: how all food should be eaten so that it may be properly digested and promote health, rather than cause stomach problems and persistent infirmity of the body').

[47] See M. Innes and R. McKitterick, 'The writing of history', in R. McKitterick (ed.), *Carolingian Culture: Emulation and Innovation* (Cambridge, 1994), pp. 193–220 at p. 208.

[48] Baudonivia, *Vita sanctae Radegundis*, praef. ed. B. Krusch, *MGH SRM* II, pp. 377–8.

[49] *Vita sanctae Geretrudis*, praef., ed. Krusch, pp. 453–4. Fouracre and Gerberding identify the abbess who commissioned this work with Agnes, who also commissioned a church in honour of Gertrude at Nivelles; see Fouracre and Gerberding, *Late Merovingian France*, pp. 306–7.

[50] *Vita sanctae Rusticulae*, praef., ed. B. Krusch, *MGH SRM* IV, pp. 339–40.

[51] *Vita sanctae Sadalbergae*, praef., ed. B. Krusch, *MGH SRM* V (Hanover, 1910), pp. 49–50.

[52] *Vita sanctae Austreberta*, praef., *AASS Feb.* II, p. 419.

emphatically not random aesthetic pleasure or arcane intellectual curiosity, but an organised and determined assembly and deployment of resources to carry out what appears to be specific aims and objectives'.[53] In other words, patronage is an investment, and people patronise because they expect a return, either spiritual or temporal. Mumma, as we have seen, commissioned a reliquary 'for the love of Saint Mary and Saint Peter',[54] presumably in the expectation of Mary's and Peter's blessing, and Balthild invested vast amounts of landed property and granted privileges to various monasteries and churches 'so that she might better entice them to exhort the clemency of Christ, the highest king, for the king and for peace'.[55] Ragyndrudis commissioned a copy of Isidore's *Synonyma* 'in honore domini nostri Ihesu Christi',[56] and King Chilperic, we are told, commissioned a great gold salver encrusted with gems and which weighed fifty pounds 'for the greater glory and renown of the Frankish people'.[57] Thus, a great variety of motives – religious, reforming, commercial, vainglorious, aesthetic, altruistic and exhibitionist (not to mention rivalry, especially between honour-conscious aristocrats) – sustained the patronage of culture in the Merovingian period, and in terms of motivation there is little discernible difference between the men and the women. The problem is that the motives behind acts of patronage and sponsorship cannot always be firmly traced.

The evidence adduced above, undoubtedly only the tip of the iceberg, demonstrates clearly the complications of this type of research. Nevertheless, from the foregoing survey it seems clear that patronage of culture was exercised in Merovingian Gaul by men and women from the upper strata of society, both lay and ecclesiastical. Furthermore, it is also apparent that Merovingian women had a significant role in patronising culture. They commissioned works of art and literature just as men did and for many of the very same reasons.[58] Although at first glance Merovingian women appear to have patronised culture mainly for pious or devotional reasons – 'for the love of Saint Mary and Saint Peter', 'in honour of our Lord Jesus Christ', and so on – this is not necessarily always the case. Political and

---

[53] McKitterick, 'Royal patronage of culture', p. 112.   [54] See above, p. 221, with note 20.

[55] *Vita sanctae Balthildis*, c. 9, ed. B. Krusch, *MGH SRM* II, p. 494: 'ut melius eis delectaret pro rege et pace summi regis Christi clementiam exorare'. I cite the translation of Fouracre and Gerberding, *Late Merovingian France*, p. 125. On this particular act of patronage, see Hen, *The Royal Patronage of Liturgy*, pp. 37–41.

[56] See above, p. 222 with note 28.

[57] Gregory of Tours, *Libri historiarum X*, VI.2, ed. B. Krusch and W. Levison, *MGH SRM* I.1 (Hanover, 1951), p. 266: 'ad exornandam atque nobilitandam Francorum gentem'.

[58] See, for example, the patronage of liturgy exercised by Merovingian kings and queens, discussed in Hen, *The Royal Patronage of Liturgy*, pp. 33–41.

other reasons cannot be ruled out, as the examples of Balthild and Brunhild clearly elucidate. Balthild's patronage of liturgy, for example, was motivated by both devotional and political considerations,[59] and political incentives were almost certainly the impetus behind Brunhild's gifts to the king of Spain.[60] Such a use of patronage of culture accords well with the evidence on the involvement of Merovingian women in the politics of their time.

The central role played by women in Merovingian society is one of the most commonplace notions in the historiography of the period.[61] Although not all Merovingian queens made use of the opportunities to wield political power, many of them gained considerable access to the world of politics and control. This point was demonstrated by Janet Nelson in her classic paper 'Queens as Jezebels'.[62] But opportunities to wield power and influence are not *ipso facto* access to resources, and the extent to which Merovingian queens had control of the necessary material resources for the patronage of culture is not always clear. Modern scholars usually cite two incidents mentioned by Gregory of Tours which may suggest that Merovingian queens, like late antique empresses such as Helena,[63] had the royal *fiscus* at their disposal. In the first incident Gregory relates how King Chilperic came to Paris and took possession of the treasure which Brunhild had brought there.[64] In the second incident we are told that Fredegund took part of her treasure and secreted it within the city walls of Paris.[65] In both cases, however, the queen was a widow attempting to secure control over her late husband's treasure. Given the fact that treasure, as Régine Le Jan has clearly

---

[59] On Balthild's patronage of liturgy, see Hen, *The Royal Patronage of Liturgy*, pp. 37–41.

[60] On Brunhild's gifts to the king of Spain, see Gregory of Tours, *Libri historiarum* IX.28, ed. Krusch and Levison, p. 446: 'Brunechildis quoque regina iussit fabricari ex auro ac gemmis mirae magnitudinis clipeum ipsumque cum duabus pateris ligneis, quas vulgo bacchinon vocant, eisdem similiter ex gemmis fabricatis et auro, in Hispaniam regi mittit.' These gifts were sent by Brunhild to King Reccared, who was to marry King Childebert's daughter Chlodosind. King Guntram, however, regarded these gifts as part of a conspiracy against himself.

[61] For a general discussion, see S. F. Wemple, *Women in Frankish Society: Marriage and the Cloister, 500 to 900* (Philadelphia, 1981), esp. pp. 9–74.

[62] J. L. Nelson, 'Queens as Jezebels: the careers of Brunhild and Balthild in Merovingian history', in D. Baker (ed.), *Medieval Women*, Studies in Church History Subsidia 1 (Oxford, 1978), pp. 31–77 (repr. in her *Politics and Ritual in Early Medieval Europe* (London, 1986), pp. 1–48).

[63] On Helena, see the superb paper by L. Brubaker, 'Memories of Helena: patterns in imperial female matronage in the fourth and fifth centuries', in L. James (ed.), *Women, Men and Eunuchs: Gender in Byzantium* (London, 1997), pp. 52–75. See also J. Herrin, 'The imperial feminine in Byzantium', *Past and Present* 169 (2000), pp. 3–35.

[64] Gregory of Tours, *Libri historiarum* V.1, ed. Krusch and Levison, pp. 194–5.

[65] Gregory of Tours, *Libri historiarum* VII.4, ed. Krusch and Levison, p. 328.

and convincingly argued, was a constitutive element of royal power,[66] it is likely that queens, even queens as influential as Brunhild or Fredegund, had limited access to it, and could not simply spend it at will. This observation receives some substantial support from a third incident reported by Gregory of Tours:

> He [i.e. King Chilperic] invited the Frankish leaders and his loyal subjects to celebrate the engagement of his daughter. Then he handed her over to the Visigothic envoys, providing her with a tremendous dowry. Her mother added a vast weight of gold and silver, and many fine clothes. When he saw this, King Chilperic thought that he had nothing left at all. Queen Fredegund realised that he was upset. She turned to the Franks and said: 'Do not imagine, men, that any of this comes from the treasures amassed by your earlier kings. Everything you see belongs to me. Your most illustrious King has been very generous to me, and I have put aside quite a bit from my own resources, from the manors granted to me, and from revenues and taxes. You, too, have often given me gifts. From such sources come all the treasures which you see in front of you. None of it has been taken from the public treasury'. The king calmed down when he heard this.[67]

That Fredegund felt it necessary to explain that she did not use the royal *fiscus* for Rigunth's dowry, suggests that indeed she had some control over the *thesaurus publicus*. She could use it, but improper use caused friction: the king's disquiet indicates that she was not supposed to use it for her own good. This would not necessarily limit her powers of patronage, for Gregory's story also points to Fredegund's enormous independent wealth, carefully distinguished from public funds.

It seems likely therefore that, while married, Merovingian queens were dependent, to some extent, on the co-operation of their husbands in using public resources for patronising culture. Consequently, even in those clear cases in which the wife was the initiator and executor of a certain act of patronage, the entire enterprise is attributed by our sources to both her and

---

[66] R. Le Jan, *Famille et pouvoir dans le monde franc (VIIe–Xe siècle): essai d'anthropologie sociale* (Paris, 1995), pp. 60–71.

[67] Gregory of Tours, *Libri historiarum* VI.45, ed. Krusch and Levison, p. 318: 'convocatis melioribus Francis reliquisque fidelibus, nuptias celebravit filiae suae. Traditamque legatis Gothorum magus ei thesaurus dedit. Sed et mater eius immensum pondus auri argentive sive vestimentorum protulit, ita ut videns haec rex nihil sibi remanisse potaret. Quem cernens regina commotum, conversa ad Francus, ita ait: "Ne potitis, viri, quicquam hic de thesauris anteriorem regum habere; omnia enim quae cernetis de mea proprietate oblata sunt, quia mihi gloriosissimus rex multa largitus est, et ego nonnula de proprio congregavi labore et de domibus mei concessis tam de fructibus quam tributis plurima reparavi. Sed et vos plerumque me muneribus vestris ditastis, de quibus sunt ista quae nunc coram videtis; nam hic de thesauris publicis nihil habetur". Et sic animus regis dilusus est.' I cite the translation of L. Thorpe, *Gregory of Tours: History of the Franks* (Harmondsworth, 1974), p. 378.

her husband. Thus, we are told, Clovis built and decorated the basilica of St Peter in Paris at the instigation of Queen Clothild,[68] Ultrogotha and her husband, King Childebert I, founded together the monastery of St Peter in Arles,[69] and Venantius Fortunatus wrote his poems to Sigibert and Brunhild, and to Chilperic and Fredegund.[70] This, however, cannot be taken to imply that Merovingian women did not have their own independent resources for the patronage of culture. As we have just seen, Fredegund had managed to accumulate an impressive amount of silver and gold, enough to astound the Frankish magnates, and it is probable that other aristocratic women had private wealth of their own for the patronage of culture.[71]

Nevertheless, women appear in our sources as clearly independent patrons only after becoming widows, or as nuns. Once widowed, Merovingian queens, and most probably aristocratic women as well, received part of their husbands' treasure.[72] For example, Fredegar relates how on her husband's death, 'Queen Nantechildis had one-third of all that Dagobert has amassed.'[73] She could then do with her treasure whatever she liked – sponsor ecclesiastical institutions, use it in order to retain her political influence, or patronise artisans and authors. Similarly, nuns could use the material resources at their disposal.[74] Those nuns whom we find patronising culture in the Merovingian kingdom were either widows who already received their share of their husband's assets, or inherited part of their family's fortune on their father's death.[75] They were not enveloped within the bonds of

---

[68] *Vita sanctae Chrothildis*, c. 7, ed. B. Krusch, *MGH SRM* ii, pp. 344–5.

[69] Aurelianus of Arles, *Regula ad monachos*, praef., *PL* 68, col. 385.

[70] See above, p. 224. Similar characteristics can be found in the references to wives of sixth-century bishops; see Gisela Muschiol, chapter 11 above.

[71] See, for example, the case of Tetradia reported by Gregory of Tours, *Libri historiarum* x.8, ed. Krusch and Levison, pp. 489–91; see also Y. Hen, 'Marriage, property and the law: some reflections of the case of Tetradia' (forthcoming).

[72] On widowhood in the early Middle Ages, see B. Jussen, 'On church organisation and definition of a state. The idea of widowhood in late antique and early medieval Christianity', *Tel Aviver Jahrbuch für Deutsche Geschichte* 22 (1993), pp. 25–42; Jussen, 'Der "Name" der Witwe. Zur "Konstruktion" eines Standes in Spätantike und Frühmittelalter', in M. Parisse (ed.), *Veuves et veuvage dans le haut moyen âge* (Paris, 1993), pp. 139–75. See also J. L. Nelson, 'The wary widow', in W. Davies and P. Fouracre (eds.), *Property and Power in the Early Middle Ages* (Cambridge, 1994), pp. 81–113.

[73] Fredegar, *Chronicarum libri IV* iv.85, ed. J. M. Wallace-Hadrill, *The Fourth Book of the Chronicle of Fredegar with its Continuations* (London, 1960), pp. 71–2.

[74] On nuns in Merovingian Gaul, see Wemple, *Women in Frankish Society*, pp. 150–65; G. Muschiol, *Famula Dei: Zur Liturgie in merowingischen Frauenklöstern*, Beiträge zur Geschichte des Alten Mönchtums und des Benediktinertums 41 (Münster, 1994), especially pp. 41–80.

[75] See the case of Burgundofara, cited above, note 6. It may be useful to distinguish access to and inheritance of movable vs. immovable property, for there were different legal norms at work in each of these cases; see J. M. H. Smith, 'Did women have a transformation of the Roman world?', in Stafford and Mulder-Bakker (eds.), *Gendering*, pp. 29–30.

family and kinship, and therefore could patronise culture as independent individuals.[76]

But this is not the whole story, for equating patronage with a specific commission or a specific literary piece written at request is too narrow and inadequate a definition. Patronage of culture did not necessarily involve commissioning particular objects or works. It could also be an encouraging, supporting or initiating force which gave rise to artistic and literary creativity. This kind of 'passive' patronage was also exercised by Merovingian women – wives, widows and nuns alike. This could be identified in the phenomenon of women as dedicatees rather than commissioners,[77] although one must constantly bear in mind that dedicatees are not always 'passive patrons'.

Similarly, one must also consider the issue of gift giving. The importance of gifts in the creation, maintenance and transformation of social and political ties throughout the Middle Ages has long been acknowledged by scholars.[78] The inherent reciprocity of gift exchange forged dependencies and loyalties, that were part and parcel of the delicate social structure of early medieval society, secular as well as ecclesiastical. The *Vita Balthildis* relates how Balthild

> often suggested to the mother of the monastery that they [i.e. she and the abbess] should constantly visit the king and queen and the palace nobles in befitting honour with gifts, as was the custom, so that the house of God would not lose the good reputation with which it had begun, but would always remain more fully in the affection of love with all its friends and more strongly in the name of God in love.[79]

---

[76] On this issue, see the chapter by J. M. H. Smith, 'Gender and ideology in the early Middle Ages', in R. N. Swanson (ed.), *Gender and Christian Religion*, Studies in Church History 34 (Woodbridge, 1998), pp. 51–73.

[77] See the example of Radegund and Agnes in the case of Venantius Fortunatus; George, *Venantius Fortunatus*, pp. 32–4 and 161–77.

[78] For a useful summary on gifts and their implications in the Middle Ages, see A.-J. Bijsterveld, 'The medieval gift as agent of social bonding and political power: a comparative approach', in E. Cohen and M. de Jong (eds.), *Medieval Transformations: Texts, Power, and Gifts in Context* (Leiden, 2001), pp. 123–56. See also I. F. Silber, 'Gift-giving and the great traditions: the case of donations to monasteries in the medieval West', *Archives Européennes de Sociologie* 36 (1995), pp. 209–43; and see the various papers collected in Davies and Fouracre (eds.), *Property and Power in the Early Middle Ages*.

[79] *Vita sanctae Balthildis*, c. 12, ed. Krusch, p. 498: 'Et conferens sepe cum matre monsaterii, ut et regem et reginam et proceres cum digno honore cum eulogias semper visitarent, ut erat consuetudo, ut ipsa domus Dei bonam famam, quam coeperat, non amitteret, sed amplius semper in affectu caritatis cum omnibus amicis atque validius in Dei nomine permaneret in dilectione.' I cite the translation of Fouracre and Gerberding, *Late Merovingian France*, p. 128.

Balthild, it seems, had lost none of her political acumen, and when the honour of the nunnery was at stake, she knew exactly what to do. So, what were these gifts? Certainly not vegetables from the monastery's garden.[80]

Gift giving, one should stress, does not necessarily imply patronage of culture, but it does point to the fact that Balthild, the queen who had retreated to Chelles in a political predicament, and the mother-superior of Chelles were both, in a sense, potential patrons of the arts. Moreover, their gifts were sent to the king, the queen and the court nobles, themselves potential patrons. Bearing in mind that a scriptorium specialising in the production of *deluxe* manuscripts was located at Chelles,[81] Balthild's advice suggests that she hoped to attract the attention of the richest potential patrons. Patronage in the sense of commissioning, giving, then attracting in return sponsorship and prestigious gifts, meant friends, relations, networks, bases of power and, more than anything else, access to the court. Our evidence suggests that Merovingian queens like Brunhild and, especially, Balthild developed networking into art,[82] and it is against this background that one should understand the decisions of the Council of Ver in 755, according to which abbesses were forbidden to travel to the court unless they were requested to do so by the king.[83] This was undoubtedly an attempt to curtail an atmosphere in which female influence, with all its political implications, might have flourished.

To sum up, the fragmentary evidence adduced above points to the fact that almost no 'gendered' differences distinguished male from female acts of patronage in the Merovingian kingdoms. Merovingian women, just like Merovingian men, commissioned works of art, built and decorated churches, and sponsored poets and writers. Given the completely different self-presentation (and representations) of each gender in all other aspects, the lack of any 'gendered' differences as far as the patronage of culture is

---

[80] On the kinds of gifts brought to the court, see Gregory of Tours, *Libri historiarum* VI.45, ed. Krusch and Levison, p. 318: 'Franci vero multa munera obtulerunt, alii aureum, alli argentum, nonnulli equites, plerique vestimenta, et unusquisque ut potuit donativum dedit.'

[81] See B. Bischoff, 'Die Kölner Nonnenhandschriften und das Skriptorium von Chelles', in Bischoff, *Mittelalterliche Studien*, vol. 1 (Stuttgart, 1966), pp. 16–34; See also McKitterick, 'Nuns' scriptoria in England and Francia', pp. 1–35.

[82] On Brunhild's networking, see J. L. Nelson, 'A propos de femmes royales dans les rapports entre le monde wisigothique et le monde franc à l'époque de Reccared', in *El Concilio III de Toledo XIV Centenario (589–1989)* (Madrid, 1991), pp. 465–76 (repr. in J. L. Nelson, *Rulers and Ruling Families in Early Medieval Europe* (Aldershot, 1999), chapter 11).

[83] *Concilium Vernense* (755, Jul. 11), c. 6, ed. A. Boretius, *MGH Cap.* 1 (Hanover, 1883), p. 34. On the purpose and implications of the Council of Ver, see M. de Jong, *In Samuel's Image: Child Oblation in the Early Medieval West* (Leiden, New York and Cologne, 1996), pp. 249–51.

concerned is not self-evident. Yet, one must constantly bear in mind that the different self-presentations and representations of women and men in the early Middle Ages were a direct result of the different roles each gender had in society. The social, and to some extent religious, stances of women were distinct from those of men, and this distinction is quite accurately reflected in our sources.[84] But are we to assume that different social and religious roles also created a distinct culture for women in the Merovingian period? I would submit that such an assumption is anachronistic, and it is certainly at odds with the evidence. If we check, for example, what sort of books were produced by the nuns in Chelles, it appears that no major differences distinguished the scriptorium of Chelles from male scriptoria in Merovingian Francia. The Bible, Sacramentaries, patristic texts by Augustine, Jerome and Gregory the Great, Eusebius-Rufinus' *Historia ecclesiastica*, as well as some works by Isidore of Seville, were all copied there, and thus reflect, more or less, the standard repertoire of texts copied in Merovingian Gaul.[85] Moreover, a brief inspection of the literary works written by Merovingian women yields a similar impression. Like men, we find them corresponding with relatives and friends,[86] composing poetry,[87] and writing hagiography[88] and, perhaps, history.[89] Hence, women in Merovingian Gaul shared the culture of their male counterparts, and consequently patronised culture in the same way men did. The material resources available to women, which in most cases were less than those available to men, must have influenced the volume and frequency of female commissions and sponsorships. Yet, there can be no doubt that women in Merovingian Gaul had a central role in patronising cultural activity, and it seems

---

[84] See, for example, Wemple, *Women in Frankish Society*; Le Jan, *Famille et pouvoir dans le monde franc*; L. M. Bitel, *Women in Early Medieval Europe, 400–1000* (Cambridge, 2002).

[85] See Bischoff, 'Die Kölner Nonnenhandschriften und das Skriptorium von Chelles', pp. 21–2; McKitterick, 'Nuns' scriptoria in England and Francia', pp. 1–35; and compare with McKitterick, 'The scriptoria of Merovingian Gaul', pp. 173–207; D. Ganz, 'The Merovingian library of Corbie', in Clarke and Brennan (eds.), *Columbanus and Merovingian Monasticism*, pp. 153–72; Ganz, 'Texts and scripts in surviving manuscripts in the script of Luxeuil', in P. Ní Chatháin and M. Richter (eds.), *Ireland and Europe in the Early Middle Ages: Texts and Transmission* (Dublin, 2000), pp. 186–204.

[86] See, for example, the letters of Herchenfreda to her son, Bishop Desiderius of Cahors, in *Vita Desiderii episcopis Cadurcensis*, ed. B. Krusch, *MGH SRM* IV, pp. 547–602 (repr. in CCSL 117 (Turnhout, 1957), pp. 344–401).

[87] See, for example, the poem by Eucheria, the wife of Dynamius of Marseilles, in H. Homeyer (ed.), *Dichterinnen des Altertums und frühen Mittelalters* (Paderborn, 1979), pp. 185–7.

[88] See Nelson, 'Women and the word in the earlier Middle Ages'; McKitterick, 'Women and literacy in the early Middle Ages'.

[89] See the comments by Janet Nelson on the authorship of the *Liber historiae Francorum*, in her 'Gender and genre in women historians of the early Middle Ages', in J.-P. Genet (ed.), *L'Historiographie médiévale en Europe* (Paris, 1991), pp. 149–63 (repr. in her *The Frankish World*, pp. 183–97).

that they had more scope for this than their Carolingian successors. If one compares the great Merovingian queens and abbesses with their Carolingian counterparts, the difference becomes even clearer. One looks in vain for any Merovingian-like protagonists among Carolingian women. How pale seem Hildegard, Fastrada and Irmingard compared with Brunhild, Fredegund and Balthild![90]

[90] I should like to thank Rob Meens for his comments on an earlier draft of this chapter. This chapter was prepared during a sabbatical year at the Netherlands Institute for Advanced Study in the Humanities and Social Sciences (NIAS). I would like to express my gratitude to the Rector, staff and fellows of NIAS for providing an ideal environment for research.

CHAPTER 13

Genealogy defined by women: the case of the Pippinids

Ian Wood

In the European Judaeo-Christian tradition genealogies tend to be patrilineal, thus emphasising the male line. The most famous genealogical list, for instance, that which opens the Gospel according to St Matthew, is almost exclusively male. Only five women appear: Thamar, Rachab, Ruth, Bathsheba (unnamed, but quaintly referred to as 'her that had been the wife of Urias'), and finally Mary. Most modern counterparts of this genealogy, the reconstructed family trees beloved of historians, are not dissimilar. Underlying these genealogies and family trees is a tacit assumption that men are the dominant players in power structures and patterns of inheritance – an assumption that the lists and charts themselves serve to reinforce. Although there have been a number of studies of early medieval families which do give space to the women, it is rare to find a genealogical table which boasts positive discrimination.[1] There are, of course, reasons for presenting genealogies as patrilineal.[2] The inheritance of male offspring tended to be greater than that of females.[3] Indeed, early medieval families were usually defined by the male, rather than the female, line.

It is not surprising, then, that the Carolingian genealogies published by Waitz rarely emphasise the importance of women in the constitution of families: the *Commemoratio genealogiae domni Karoli gloriossimi imperatoris* (*Commemoration of the genealogy of the most glorious emperor, the lord Charles*), or better the *Genealogia domni Arnulfi* (*Genealogy of the lord Arnulf*), a Metz text which has been dated to the period between 800

---

[1] An exception is the chart of 'Plectrudis, her sisters and their descendants', in P. Fouracre, *The Age of Charles Martel* (London, 2000), p. 197.

[2] On the question of agnatic (i.e. patrilineal) and cognatic kinship groupings see the debate of D. Bullough, 'Early medieval social groupings: the terminology of kinship', *Past and Present* 45 (1969), pp. 3–17, and K. Leyser, 'Maternal kin in early medieval Germany: a reply', *Past and Present* 49 (1970), pp. 126–38.

[3] *Pactus legis Salicae*, 108 = Cap. IV, ed. K. A. Eckhardt, *MGH Leges* IV, 1 (Hanover, 1962).

and 814,[4] mentions only Blithildis, supposed daughter of Chlothar II, and wife of Anspert, and their equally legendary daughter, the virgin Tarsicia:[5] that is two women in eight generations, both of them arguably fictional. The ninth-century *Genealogia regum Francorum* (*Genealogy of the kings of the Franks*) again mentions Blithildis, and adds Fredegund, the wife of Chilperic I and mother of Chlothar II, Begga, the wife of Ansegisus, and Louis the Pious's wives, Irmingard and Judith:[6] that is, six women in fourteen generations. A slightly earlier genealogy of Arnulf and his descendants, from the end of the eighth century, forms part of Paul the Deacon's *Libellus de ordine episcoporum* (*Booklet on the order of bishops*) of Metz. Paul has nothing to say of the women in the Arnulfing family – the descendants of Bishop Arnulf – until he reaches the wives of Charlemagne. In describing Arnulf himself he does, however, talk of the offspring *juventutis suae tempore ex legitimi matrimonii copula* ('from the time of his youth from the bond of legitimate marriage'), presumably to allay fears about the saint having been sexually active while a bishop.[7]

Nevertheless, there were exceptions to this male emphasis, and even in the most well-known of kin-groups. Modern historians (though not early medieval writers) refer to the ancestors of Charlemagne as Pippinids (the descendants of Pippin I), and as Arnulfings (the descendants of Arnulf), and as Carolingians (the descendants of Charles Martel). The first dynastic

---

[4] For the chronology of the genealogies: O. G. Oexle, 'Die Karolinger und die Stadt des heiligen Arnulf', *Frühmittelalterliche Studien* 1 (1967), pp. 252–79; K.-U. Jäschke, 'Die Karolingergenealogien aus Metz und Paulus Diaconus', *Rheinische Vierteljahresblätter* 34 (1970), pp. 190–218; E. Tremp, *Studien zu den Gesta Hludowici imperatoris des Trierer Chorbischofs Thegan*, MGH Schriften 32 (Hanover, 1988), pp. 26–44; H. Reimitz, 'Anleitung zur Interpretation. Schrift und Geneaologie zur Karolingerzeit', in W. Pohl and P. Herold, *Vom Nutzen des Schreibens: soziales Gedächtnis, Herrschaft und Besitz*, Forschungen zur Geschichte des Mittelalters 4 (Vienna, 2002), pp. 167–81, with references to older literature; and most recently H. Reimitz, 'Networks and identities in Frankish historiography. New aspects of the textual history of Gregory of Tours' *Historiae*', in R. Corradini, M. Diesenberger and H. Reimitz (eds.), *The Construction of Communities in the Early Middle Ages* (Leiden, 2002), pp. 265–7. See also E. Friese, 'Die *Genealogia Arnulfi comitis* des Priesters Witger', *Frühmittelalterliche Studien* 23 (1989), pp. 203–43.

[5] G. Waitz, *Genealogia Karolorum* II, MGH SS XIII (Hanover, 1871), pp. 245–6. The text is included in Vienna ÖNB MS 473. See also J. M. Wallace-Hadrill, 'History in the mind of Archbishop Hincmar', in R. H. C. Davies and J. M. Wallace-Hadrill (eds.), *The Writing of History in the Middle Ages* (Oxford, 1981), p. 55, where he notes that Hincmar's *Ordo* for Charles' Metz coronation (869) mentions that the Carolingians were descended from the Merovingians through Arnulf of Metz, and suggests that Hincmar may have been thinking of the anonymous *Origo et exordium gentis Francorum* (ed. E. Dümmler, *MGH Poet.* II (Berlin, 1884), pp. 141–5), addressed to Charles the Bald, where Ansbert, grandfather of Arnulf, was the husband of Blithildis, daughter of Chlothar I. Wallace-Hadrill notes that there is no supporting evidence for the claim, citing E. Hlawitschka, 'Merowingerblut bei den Karolingern', in J. Fleckenstein and K. Schmid (eds.), *Adel und Kirche* (Freiburg, 1968), pp. 68–91.

[6] Waitz, *Genealogia* IV, pp. 246–7.

[7] Paul, *Libellus de ordine episcoporum*, PL 95, cols. 705–6. Also ed. G. H. Pertz, *MGH SS* II (Hanover, 1829), pp. 260–8. On Paul's genealogical account, Jäschke, 'Die Karolingergenealogien'.

name privileges the three Pippins in the family, all of whom held high secular office; the second privileges Arnulf, bishop of Metz, and one of the chief saints in the family; the last should only be used to refer to the descendants of Charlemagne's grandfather, Charles Martel. At one crucial point the Pippinid (although not the Arnulfing) line was not patrilineal, for Pippin II was the son of Pippin I's daughter, Begga, and Arnulf's supposed son, Ansegisus. Moreover, much of the landed wealth of the dynasty seems to have been brought into the family by women. It is worth pausing on these two points, before looking at the presentation of Pippinid women in our genealogical sources, in an attempt to say something about their position in the traditions relating to that one family (see Fig. 11).

BEGGA AND THE PIPPINIDS

The first point is obvious, but perhaps underappreciated. The Pippinid line runs through a woman, Begga, the daughter of Pippin I. Her brother Grimoald died in the political struggles of the mid-seventh century, and is not attested as having left a male heir. His only known daughter Wulfetrudis entered the nunnery of Nivelles as a child, and subsequently became abbess, and thus had no children.[8]

Of course it is possible to regard the line as Arnulfing, passing through Arnulf's supposed son, Ansegisus. This, indeed, is how a number of Carolingian writers, beginning with Paul the Deacon, saw the matter. Paul was one of several authors to make particular play of the oddity of the name Ansegisus, and its similarity to that of the Trojan Anchises, father of Aeneas, and hence ancestor of the founding dynasty of the Romans.[9] Yet the reading of the family as Arnulfing does not appear to have been common before the late eighth century. The earliest clear statement that Arnulf was the father of Ansegisus comes in Paul's account of the bishops of Metz.[10] A family relationship between Arnulf and Pippin II is alluded to in a charter of the latter from 687, where the bishop is described as *avus noster*, which might mean 'our grandfather' or more generally 'ancestor', which is certainly the meaning of the phrase in a charter drawn up by four of Pippin's grandsons in 715.[11] It is possible to doubt whether Ansegisus was the son of

---

[8] *Vita Geretrudis*, ch. 6, ed. B. Krusch, *MGH SRM* II (Hanover, 1888). There is a translation and commentary in P. Fouracre and R. Gerberding, *Late Merovingian France: History and Hagiography 640–720* (Manchester, 1966), pp. 301–26. A different recension of the text is translated by J. A. McNamara and J. E. Halborg, *Sainted Women of the Dark Ages* (Durham, NC, 1992), pp. 220–8.
[9] Paul, *Libellus*, cols. 705–6; Waitz, *Genealogia* II, III, IV.   [10] Fouracre, *Charles Martel*, pp. 33–4.
[11] K. A. Pertz, *MGH Diplomata imperii* I, *Diplomata maiorum domus regiae* (Hanover, 1872), nos. I, 8. See now I. Heidrich, *Die Urkunden der Arnulfinger* (Bad Münstereifel, 2001), pp. 55–8, 71–5. The use of *avus* in the 715 charter casts doubt on the case of G. Halsall, *Settlement and Social Organisation: The Merovingian Region of Metz* (Cambridge, 1995), p. 263 n. I.

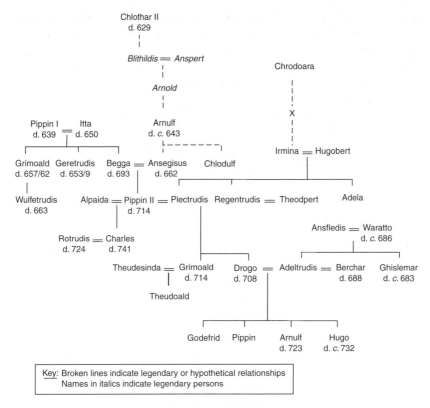

11   Genealogical table of the Pippinids and their women.

Arnulf – although it would be rash to deny any family connection between them. It is surely significant that Chlodulf, another supposed son of Arnulf and his successor as bishop of Metz, is portrayed in the *De Virtutibus quae facta sunt post dicessum beatae Geretrudis abbatissae* (*The Miracles which were performed after the death of the blessed abbess Geretrudis*) as being particularly knowledgeable about the saint:[12] a close family relationship would explain the knowledge. More important, whether or not the family was directly descended from Arnulf, its choice of names suggests a closer identification with Pippin I, certainly during the seventh and eighth centuries. There was at least one Pippin in every other generation, while the only known Arnulf in the family during the same period, other than the bishop of Metz, was

---

[12] *De Virtutibus quae facta sunt post dicessum beatae Geretrudis abbatissae*, ch. 2, ed. Krusch, *MGH SRM* II, trans. McNamara and Holborg, *Sainted Women*, pp. 229–34. The relationship of Chlodulf to Arnulf is not attested early: see Paul, *Libellus*.

a grandson of Pippin II.[13] This choice of names – one of the indicators that we have of collective identity – would seem to suggest that, until the late eighth century, the family thought of itself primarily as Pippinid, and thus by implication as descended through Begga, rather than Arnulfing and descended through Ansegisus. Even in the early ninth century, when the Arnulfing interpretation was coming into vogue, Begga was not forgotten. Indeed the *Annales Mettenses Priores (The Earlier Annals of Metz)* is the first text to give Begga her due in a narrative account of the family's history.[14] The Metz Annals were compiled in either 805 or 806, apparently 'to justify the royal and imperial power the Carolingians exercised'.[15] For the present argument it is more important to note that on a number of occasions these Metz Annals put unusual stress on the importance of women, whether good or bad: a point which may have some significance for the debate as to whether or not they were written by a nun of Chelles.[16] Certainly, there is a strong case for thinking that they were produced for Gisela, abbess of Chelles, and sister of Charlemagne.[17] A female author or patron might have been particularly sensitive to the influential roles played by members of her own sex.

HEIRESSES

The second introductory point, that a large proportion of the landed wealth of the Pippinids was acquired through marriage, is well known, if disputed in detail – not least because much of what we know about family property has to be deduced from its alienation to monasteries.[18] As Paul Fouracre has remarked, 'the "rise of the Pippinids" depended in large part on the

[13] Pertz, *Diplomata*, nos. 7, 8; Heidrich, *Urkunden*, pp. 69–75. There is also an Aunulf, son of Chlodulf: Pertz, *Diplomata*, nos. 36, 38, 43; Heidrich, *Urkunden*, pp. 147, 148, 150.

[14] *Annales Mettenses Priores* (hereafter *AMP*), s.a. 688, ed. B. von Simson, *MGH SRG* (Hanover, 1905): the first part of the text is translated with commentary by Fouracre and Gerberding, *Late Merovingian France*, pp. 329–70: the relevant passage is p. 351. The importance of women in the text is signalled by J. Nelson, 'Gender and genre in women historians of the early Middle Ages', in her *The Frankish World, 750–900* (London, 1996), p. 193, and picked up by Y. Hen, 'The Annals of Metz and the Merovingian past', in Y. Hen and M. Innes (eds.), *The Uses of the Past in the Early Middle Ages* (Cambridge, 2000), p. 177, where the point is not pursued: his article is the most recent discussion of the text.

[15] Fouracre and Gerberding, *Late Merovingian France*, p. 340.

[16] Nelson, 'Gender and genre', pp. 191–4. Fouracre and Gerberding, *Late Merovingian France*, p. 338, doubt the suggestion that the *Annales Mettenses Priores* were written by a woman at Chelles. The doubts are dismissed by R. McKitterick, 'Political ideology in Carolingian historiography', in Hen and Innes (eds.), *The Uses of the Past*, pp. 166–8.

[17] Nelson, 'Gender and genre', pp. 191–4.

[18] M. Werner, *Der Lütticher Raum in frühkarolingischer Zeit* (Göttingen, 1980), pp. 341–475; with the comments of R. Gerberding, *The Rise of the Carolingians and the Liber Historiae Francorum* (Oxford, 1987), pp. 95, 120–4.

acquisition of land from two heiresses, Begga and Plectrudis'.[19] Itta, the wife of Pippin I, seems to have brought with her estates in the region of Nivelles and Fosses, while her daughter Begga founded the monastery at Andenne.[20] Pippin II's marriages were equally important in building up landed possessions.[21] Plectrudis's family certainly held considerable property around Echternach,[22] while that of Alpaida seems to have been centred on Liège and its environs.[23]

Exactly how much land was brought to the Pippinid family in these cases is an open question. Begga, of course, was the daughter of Pippin I. Perhaps just as important in assessing her position as an heiress, she had no surviving brother. Plectrudis, equally, is not known to have had a brother – but it is also unclear whether Charles Martel, as her step-son, would have had any legal right to her land, as opposed to his father's treasure,[24] at least during the lifetime of any of her descendants, one of whom survived until after Charles's death.[25] Martel must have had a better claim to the land of his mother, Alpaida, but she may well have had a brother, in which case she could only have been the inheritor of a proportion of her parents' property.[26] Although the Pippinid family certainly did build up a strong landed base, it is as well to remember that marriages would have brought alliances as much as territory: the need to try to preserve one such alliance may well explain the complex attitudes of the Carolingian sources towards Plectrudis, which will concern us later.

---

[19] Fouracre, *Charles Martel*, p. 47.

[20] For Nivelles, *Vita Geretrudis*, ch. 2: Fosses, *Additamentum Nivialense de Fuilano*, ed. B. Krusch, *MGH SRM* IV (Hanover, 1902), with A. Dierkens, *Abbayes et chapitres entre Sambre et Meuse (VIIe–XIe siècles)* (Sigmaringen, 1985), p. 72. The *Additamentum* is translated by Fouracre and Gerberding, *Late Merovingian France*, pp. 327–9. For Andenne, *De virtutibus beatae Geretrudis*, ch. 10.

[21] R. Le Jan, *Famille et pouvoir dans le monde franc (VIIe–Xe siècle)* (Paris, 1995), p. 272.

[22] Fouracre and Gerberding, *Late Merovingian France*, pp. 311–12; Fouracre, *Charles Martel*, p. 43. See also J. M. Wallace-Hadrill, 'A background to St. Boniface's mission', in P. Clemoes and K. Hughes, (eds.), *England before the Conquest* (Cambridge, 1971), pp. 39–41, repr. in J. M. Wallace-Hadrill, *Early Medieval History* (Oxford, 1975), pp. 142–4.

[23] Gerberding, *Rise*, pp. 95, 120–4: R. Gerberding, '716: a crucial year for Charles Martel', in J. Jarnut, U. Nonn and M. Richter (eds.), *Karl Martell in seiner Zeit* (Sigmaringen, 1994), pp. 206–7; F. Theuws, 'Maastricht as a centre of power in the early Middle Ages', in M. de Jong, F. Theuws and C. van Rhijn (eds.), *Topographies of Power in the Early Middle Ages* (Leiden, 2001), pp. 188–92, 210, 213.

[24] Fredegar, cont. 10, ed. B. Krusch, *MGH SRM* II; see also the edition, translation and commentary by J. M. Wallace-Hadrill, *The Fourth Book of the Chronicle of Fredegar* (London, 1960).

[25] R. Collins, 'Deception and misrepresentation in early eighth-century Frankish historiography: two case studies', in Jarnut, Nonn and Richter (eds.), *Karl Martell*, pp. 229–35.

[26] Gerberding, *Rise*, pp. 118–19; the information is gathered by W. Joch, 'Karl Martell – ein minderberechtige Erbe Pippins?', in Jarnut, Nonn and Richter (eds.), *Karl Martell*, pp. 152–4, with notes 21–2.

MEMORIES OF GERETRUDIS AND WULFETRUDIS

Turning to the changing ways in which women were remembered by their families, we may begin with Geretrudis, since she alone among Pippinid women was the subject of a saint's *Life*. Geretrudis was the daughter of Pippin I and Itta, and was the first abbess of her mother's foundation of Nivelles. She died in 653.[27] Although she herself is portrayed as having led a somewhat uneventful life, that of her successor as abbess, her niece Wulfetrudis, was extremely troubled because of the crises surrounding the coup and overthrow of her father, Grimoald, who was the brother of Geretrudis and son of Pippin I.[28] Not that Wulfetrudis herself is likely to have stood above politics. It was almost certainly at Nivelles, under her auspices, that meetings took place that led to a political coup involving the exile of the young king Dagobert II.[29] Despite the silences of the texts, which in the case of hagiography are easily explicable, it is unlikely that Geretrudis was any less involved than her niece in the political scene.

That Wulfetrudis should have been affected by her father's fall from power is scarcely surprising, quite apart from the fact that she herself was probably in the thick of political machinations. Families were closely associated with their monastic foundations, and especially with the convents they founded.[30] Abbesses retained very close links with their families – indeed their links were more exclusively familial than were those of abbots.[31] Their tombs could be important to their relatives.[32] Nivelles, as the foundation of Grimoald's mother, housing the tomb of his sister Geretrudis, and with his daughter Wulfetrudis as abbess, was an obvious target for the enemies of the fallen *maior palatii* (technically the senior figure in the palace, and effectively the most influential secular official of the kingdom) – even if one ignores the probability that Wulfetrudis herself was deeply immersed in politics.

The position of the Pippinid family after Grimoald's death, and indeed of Wulfetrudis and Nivelles, must provide some context for the composition of the *Vita Geretrudis*, which has been dated to the period 663–670.[33] During the period between Grimoald's fall in 657 and the death of Ebroin in *c*. 680

---

[27] For a brief description of the career of Geretrudis, see Fouracre and Gerberding, *Late Merovingian France*, pp. 301–2.

[28] *Vita Geretrudis*, ch. 6.

[29] *Additamentum Nivialense*; Fouracre and Gerberding, *Late Merovingian France*, p. 329 n. 132.

[30] R. Le Jan, 'Convents, violence and competition for power in seventh-century Francia', in de Jong, Theuws and van Rhijn (eds.), *Topographies of Power*, p. 268.

[31] Le Jan, 'Convents', p. 266.   [32] Le Jan, 'Convents', p. 268.

[33] Fouracre and Gerberding, *Late Merovingian France*, pp. 303, 309.

the family was on the defensive. A slightly earlier date, of 650–657, has been given to another text with Nivelles links, the *Additamentum Nivialense de Foilano* (the *Nivelles Addition on Foilan*),³⁴ since both Grimoald and Clovis II would seem to have been alive at the time of composition. A slightly later date in the 690s has been given to the *De Virtutibus quae facta sunt post dicessum beatae Geretrudis abbatissae*.³⁵ These texts form a compact group, with one antedating the crisis caused by Grimoald's death, the second – like the Chronicle of Fredegar³⁶ – falling directly within the period of crisis, and the third dating to the period after the re-emergence from obscurity of the Pippinid family.

The *Vita Geretrudis* may show signs of the context in which it was written. While the saint's father and mother are mentioned,³⁷ there is no reference to her brother, although the *Additamentum* makes it clear that he was a visitor to Nivelles in his niece's day.³⁸ While Wulfetrudis's problems as abbess are referred to, albeit in the vaguest of terms, there is no indication in the *vita* that she was the daughter of Grimoald, or that his fall occasioned her difficulties.³⁹ Geretrudis's own life is presented as uneventful. The silences here are surely deliberate. One task of the hagiographer must have been to promote the saint in such a way as to benefit the Pippinid family in a period in which it was under threat. An easy strategy to follow was to avoid associating her with her controversial brother, by omitting any reference to him. A successful cult, in turn, might help revive the family's fortunes.

The *De Virtutibus quae facta sunt post dicessum beatae Geretrudis abbatissae* continues the promotion of the saint's cult, which by this time could boast the occurrence of miracles. It also adds a little more to the family history, revealing that Geretrudis had a sister called Begga, who founded the nunnery of Andenne, and sought relics from Nivelles.⁴⁰ Since Begga was the mother of Pippin II,⁴¹ we may guess that by the 690s the cult of Geretrudis was indeed benefiting the Pippinid family. Further, the role of Bishop Chlodulf of Metz in identifying an apparition of the saint also suggests that their Arnulfing relatives, to whom Geretrudis was related through her sister's marriage, were involving themselves in the cult.⁴² Even so, it is

---

³⁴ Fouracre and Gerberding, *Late Merovingian France*, p. 307.
³⁵ Fouracre and Gerberding, *Late Merovingian France*, p. 303.
³⁶ I. N. Wood, 'Fredegar's Fables', in A. Scharer and G. Scheibelreiter (eds.), *Historiographie im frühen Mittelalter* (Vienna, 1994), p. 366.
³⁷ *Vita Geretrudis*, chs. 1, 2, 3.   ³⁸ *Additamentum Nivialense*.   ³⁹ *Vita Geretrudis*, ch. 6.
⁴⁰ *De virtutibus beatae Geretrudis*, ch. 10.
⁴¹ On the importance of the *De virtutibus beatae Geretrudis* for the reconstruction of the Pippinid family, see Fouracre and Gerberding, *Late Merovingian France*, pp. 310–11.
⁴² *De virtutibus beatae Geretrudis*, ch. 2.

only with the *Annales Mettenses Priores* that Geretrudis is fully integrated
into a written account of the Pippinid family. The very same section of the
text that extols Begga draws attention to the piety of Geretrudis and her
mother Itta.[43]

Geretrudis and, albeit less prominently, her niece Wulfetrudis are unusual
among leading Pippinid women in being daughters rather than wives
of Pippinids. They were worthy of remembrance because their sanctity
brought distinction to the family. Begga – technically a Pippinid daughter, as the offspring of Pippin I – merited some attention as foundress of
Andenne, but, as wife of Ansegisus and mother of Pippin II, she was also
the vital figure in the survival of the Pippinid dynasty. As wife and mother
she played a role more akin to that of other women of the family, to attract
attention: not that that attention was always complimentary.

PIPPINID WIVES

Of the women who married into the Arnulfing family, the first case to
require discussion is almost certainly legendary. According to the early
ninth-century *Commemoratio genealogiae domni Karoli gloriosissimi imperatoris* Anspert, a man of senatorial family, married a daughter of Chlothar II,
called Blithildis. They had four children, one of whom, Arnold, was the
father of Arnulf of Metz.[44] This same story is repeated in the later *Genealogia regum Francorum*.[45] Interestingly this latter text effectively regenders
the princess, making her the dominant party in her marriage. The normal
form for expressing descent involves presenting the male in the nominative,
the offspring in the accusative, and the woman in the ablative, following
the preposition 'ex': thus, *Chilpericus genuit Lotharium magnum ex Frede-
gunde* ('Chilperic begat Chlothar the Great by Fredegund').[46] In the case of
Arnold's birth, however, the text has *Blithildis genuit Arnaldum ex Ansberto*

<hr>

[43] *AMP*, s.a. 688: see Fouracre and Gerberding, *Late Merovingian France*, p. 352.

[44] Waitz, *Genealogiae* II, p. 245; Tremp, *Studien zu den Gesta Hludowici*, pp. 33–4; Reimitz, 'Anleitung
zur Interpretation', pp. 169–71; Le Jan, *Famille*, p. 203. The question of Merovingian blood is
discussed by Hlawitschka, 'Merowingerblut'.

[45] Waitz, *Genealogiae* IV, pp. 246–7. On the manuscript, St Petersburg, Bibl. Saltykova F.IV.4, see also
E. Tremp, *Die Überlieferung der Vita Hludowici imperatoris des Astronomus*, *MGH Studien und Texte* I
(Hanover, 1991), pp. 128–39: R. McKitterick, *The Carolingians and the Written Word* (Cambridge,
1989), p. 239. Also M. Tischler, *Einharts Vita Karoli, Studien zur Entstehung, Überlieferung und
Rezeption*, MGH Schriften 48, 2 (Hanover, 2001), pp. 1163–77, where the manuscript is dated to the
tenth century; and H. Reimitz, 'Der Weg zum Königtum in historiographischen Kompilationen
der Karolingerzeit', in *Der Dynastiewechsel von 751* (forthcoming).

[46] Rosamond McKitterick reminds me that a fine example of this is to be found in Einhard's account
of Charlemagne's children, *Vita Karoli*, 18, ed. M. Holder-Egger, *MGH SRG* XXV (Hanover, 1911).

illustri viro ('Blithildis begat Arnold by the illustrious man Ansbert').[47] The existence of a Merovingian princess called Blithildis is, however, attested in no document of the seventh century. Her presence in the genealogy could be a fiction propagated in Charlemagne's reign to help legitimise Pippin III's usurpation,[48] while Anspert and their offspring, including Ferreolus of Uzès, a Gallo-Roman bishop known from the pages of Gregory of Tours,[49] may constitute an attempt to give the family some Gallo-Roman blood.[50] Charlemagne may have had a better claim to descent from the Merovingians through his mother Bertrada, but that fact (if indeed it was genuine) was left unexploited, which suggests that it counted for little.[51]

Wives of Pippinids in generations subsequent to Blithildis's have rather better basis in historical fact. Pippin I's wife Itta, the mother of Geretrudis and founder of Nivelles, seems to have brought her husband lands in the region of the *Silva Carbonnaria*, the Charbonnière forest of modern Belgium. More interesting still are the two wives of Pippin II, Plectrudis and Alpaida.[52] The landed base of the former, in the region round Echternach, has already been mentioned. Liège and its environs seem to have been central to the territorial holdings of Alpaida's family,[53] but there is some indication of elements hostile to her and her kin even in that region. Liège was the site of the murder of Bishop Lambert of Maastricht, at the hands of henchmen of the *domesticus* Dodo.[54] According to a fifteenth-century gloss added to a ninth-century manuscript, this Dodo was the brother of Alpaida: although the tradition is clearly questionable it should perhaps be borne in mind.[55] Equally uncertain is the claim in a number of texts of

---

[47] I owe this observation to Helmut Reimitz.   [48] Le Jan, *Famille*, p. 203.

[49] Gregory, *Decem Libri Historiarum* IV, 7, ed. B. Krusch and W. Levison, *MGH SRM* I (Hanover, 1951).

[50] Reimitz, 'Networks', p. 266.

[51] The evidence is in dip. 16, ed. E. Mühlbacher, *MGH Diplomata Karolinorum* I (Hanover, 1906). J. L. Nelson, 'La famille de Charlemagne', *Byzantion* 61 (1991), repr. in her *Rulers and Ruling Families in Early Medieval Europe* (Aldershot, 1999), p. 194; Le Jan, *Famille*, pp. 202–3. On the need for legitimation see Hen, 'Annals of Metz', pp. 175–90. Dip. 16 is discussed by W. E. Wagner, 'Zum Abtwahlprivileg König Pippins für das Kloster Prüm von 762', *Deutsches Archiv für Erforschung des Mittelalters* 57 (2001), pp. 149–56.

[52] I follow Joch, 'Karl Martell', pp. 149–69, in calling Alpaida wife.

[53] Gerberding, *Rise*, pp. 118–20; Theuws, 'Maastricht', p. 190.

[54] *Vita Landiberti episcopi Traiectensis vetustissima*, cc. 11–17, ed. B. Krusch, *MGH SRM* VI (Hanover, 1913).

[55] The evidence is gathered in *AASS Sept.*, 3rd edn, vol. V, pp. 539–46. See Gerberding, *Rise*, pp. 118–19. The case is put into question by Joch, 'Karl Martell', pp. 152–3, with n. 22; W. Joch, *Legitimität und Integration*, Historische Studien 456 (Husum, 1999), pp. 130–45. A. Dierkens, '*Carolus monasterium multorum eversor et ecclesiasticarum pecuniarum in usus proprios commutator*? Notes sur la politique monastique du maire du palais Charles Martel', in Jarnut, Nonn and Richter (eds.), *Karl Martell*, p. 288 n. 78, leaves the question open. For information on the manuscript, Paris, BN 10911, I am indebted to Helmut Reimitz.

the ninth century and later that the murder was prompted by Lambert's criticism of Pippin and his household, and more specifically of Pippin's bigamous association with Alpaida.[56] Although this claim has been almost universally rejected in recent years, there may be some support for it in the fact that Grimoald, Pippin II's son by Plectrudis, was murdered while on the way to Lambert's shrine at Liège.[57] There might have been every reason for Grimoald to visit the shrine of a martyr killed by the brother of his mother's rival, and certainly a pilgrimage to any shrine situated in the heartlands of his stepmother's family could easily have been understood as having political resonance. The cult of Lambert could initially have provided a focus in the Liège region for Plectrudis and her offspring, in opposition to Alpaida.[58] If this were indeed the case, Liège was not only in the heartland of Alpaida's family, but also boasted the shrine of her leading ecclesiastical critic.

The cult of Lambert was promoted by Hubert of Liège,[59] who appears to have been a relative of Plectrudis.[60] As such he was not a natural ally of either Alpaida or Charles Martel, and yet he seems to have been co-operating with Pippin's son by 716.[61] Charles in his turn seems very quickly to have taken on the promotion of the cult of Lambert[62] – which might well have been a *quid pro quo*: in acknowledging the sanctity of a bishop killed by a member of his own family and culted by relatives of his stepmother, Charles may have been attempting to conciliate them.[63]

Alpaida is a rather shadowy figure even in Carolingian tradition.[64] She was certainly a woman with important family connections, and she was the mother of Pippin II's son Charles – the one son of the *maior palatii* to outlive his father. Yet she receives remarkably little comment in early sources. The continuator of Fredegar's chronicle, writing perhaps around

---

[56] Ado, *Martyrologium*, 30 May, ed. J. Dubois, *Le Martyrologe d'Adon* (Paris, 1984), p. 319; Gerberding, *Rise*, p. 119 quite reasonably points out the moral purpose to Ado's account, but that is not enough to dispose entirely of the story. A fuller listing of the documentation is in Joch, 'Karl Martell', pp. 152–4, with nn. 21–2, but it does not refer to the evidence of Ado's martyrology.

[57] Fredegar, cont. 7.

[58] It is, of course, possible that Grimoald's visit was itself an attempt to develop the cult.

[59] *Vita Huberti*, I, *AASS Nov.*, vol. I, p. 799. The text appears to be of the eighth century.

[60] Gerberding, *Rise*, pp. 129, with n. 84, 133–4.

[61] Gerberding, *Rise*, pp. 133–4, and Gerberding, '716', pp. 213–14.   [62] Gerberding, '716', p. 214.

[63] Here I part company with Gerberding's reading: there are plenty of parallel examples of martyr-cults which the persecuting party had to accept: for instance those of Praeiectus and Leodegar in Merovingian Francia: Fouracre and Gerberding, *Late Merovingian France*, pp. 200, 266–7. Carolingian concern to dominate the cult may further be implied by the later association of the translation with Charles' son Carloman: *AASS, Sept*, vol. V, p. 539. The date given (743–744) is, however, incompatible with Hubert's translation of the relics, which must antedate the bishop's death in 727.

[64] Joch, 'Karl Martell'.

751, himself a Pippinid or a Pippinid dependant,[65] says simply: 'The afore-said Pippin took a second wife, the noble and lovely Alpaida. She gave him a son, and they called him in his own language Charles.'[66] The com-ment is favourable but surprisingly slight, given that the chronicle is closely associated with Childebrand who may have been a relative of Alpaida.[67] The comment by the Fredegar continuator, however, is more than can be found in the *Annales Mettenses Priores*, which ignore her altogether in their account of Charles Martel.[68] Equally silent are Paul the Deacon and the Carolingian genealogies. Alpaida gave Pippin a son, Charles Martel, and indeed in 714 he was crucial to the survival of the dynasty. Yet she was ignored in the telling of family history. Why Alpaida should be so ignored is a mystery: the fact that she was either a concubine of Pippin or a big-amous wife, and the influence of factions hostile to her, might be sought as explanations. Strangely Plectrudis, Pippin's other, lawful, wife, was more frequently remembered although neither of her sons outlived their father. It is worth exploring the picture of her presented in the *Liber historiae Francorum* (*Book of the History of the Franks*), the Fredegar continuations and the Metz Annals, as well as that to be found in the *Vita Trudonis* (*Life of St Trond*) of Donatus.

Of course Plectrudis was not remembered in the context of the Car-olingian genealogies edited by Waitz, and she receives no mention in Paul the Deacon's account of the bishops of Metz. On the other hand, she does appear, rather surprisingly, as the *inclitissima coniunx* ('most famous wife') of Pippin in the *Vita Trudonis* of Donatus, which, like Paul's work, was commissioned by Bishop Angilram of Metz (768–91).[69] While Paul went out of his way to present an Arnulfing genealogy, Donatus recalled the wife of Pippin from whom the Carolingians were not descended.[70] The *Liber historiae Francorum* of c. 727 was also enthusiastic about Plectrudis,[71] but then the author of the work was not a member of the Pippinid fac-tion.[72] The continuators of Fredegar, by contrast, were firmly associated

---

[65] R. Collins, *Fredegar* (Aldershot, 1996), pp. 32–5.

[66] Fredegar, cont. 6: the translation is that of J. M. Wallace-Hadrill, p. 86.

[67] Collins, *Fredegar*, pp. 33–4.

[68] *AMP*, s.a. 714: see Fouracre and Gerberding, *Late Merovingian France*, p. 365.

[69] Donatus' *Vita Trudonis*, ch. 23, ed. W. Levison, *MGH SRM* vi (Hanover, 1913). On the *Vita Trudonis*, B. Rosenwein, *Negotiating Space* (Ithaca, 1999), pp. 127–30.

[70] Donatus, *Vita Trudonis*, ch. 23, does also mention that Pippin II was the son of Ansegisus, but does not comment on the relationship between Ansegisus and Arnulf.

[71] *Liber historiae Francorum* (hereafter *LHF*), 48, ed. B. Krusch, *MGH SRM* ii; there is a translation of the relevant chapters in Fouracre and Gerberding, *Late Merovingian France*, pp. 79–96.

[72] Gerberding, *Rise*, pp. 146–72.

with the Carolingian house.[73] The first of their references to Plectrudis is taken directly from the *Liber historiae Francorum*,[74] but the tone of subsequent references, as she comes into conflict with Charles, is somewhat frostier: she is merely *matrona praefata* ('aforesaid matron'), *praefata femine* ('aforesaid woman'), and *praefata Plectrudis* ('aforesaid Plectrudis').[75] The term *matrona* may well be respectful,[76] but the repeated adjective *praefata* scarcely suggests any affection. Much worse is the image presented by the *Annales Mettenses Priores* of her cunning and cruelty, as she attempted to deprive Charles of his legitimate position.[77] On the other hand, in talking of Plectrudis's attempt to rule in the name of her grandson, the Metz Annals present her directly as acting as regent, that is, they acknowledge her as being an active player. The *Liber historiae Francorum* had talked of her direction of the state 'with her grandchildren and the king',[78] while the Fredegar continuator talked of her taking 'everything under her control', and commented on the fact that this led to a Frankish revolt.[79] Where the *Liber Historiae Francorum* attributes the revolt to the instigation of the devil, *instigante diabolo*, the continuator has the laconic *demum*, 'finally'. Of these last three texts, the account of the *Liber Historiae Francorum* is the most neutral towards Plectrudis, and that of the *Annales Mettenses Priores* the most overtly hostile.

The picture presented of Plectrudis in the Metz Annals is scarcely surprising: Charles's stepmother posed a very substantial obstacle to his obtaining control of his father's resources. What is strange, in many respects, is the mild presentation of her by the Carolingian Fredegar continuator, and the positive epithet granted her in the *Vita Trudonis*. As a significant opponent of Charles Martel she could have expected outright condemnation or a *damnatio memoriae*. Her grandsons certainly suffered at his hands: two were imprisoned and another was killed.[80] A fourth survived until 741, when he was killed, probably in the context of Charles's own death.[81] A fifth, Hugo, became bishop of Rouen, Paris and Bayeux, as well as abbot of St Wandrille (*c.* 725–732).[82] He co-operated with his uncle, although, as we shall see, there may have been some distance between them. The fact that Plectrudis was not condemned outright by Carolingian sources of the

---

[73] See most recently, Collins, *Fredegar*, pp. 32–7.   [74] Fredegar, cont. 5.

[75] Fredegar, cont. 8–10.   [76] Gerberding, *Rise*, p. 138.

[77] *AMP*, s.a. 714; trans. Fouracre and Gerberding, *Late Merovingian France*, p. 365.

[78] *LHF* 51; trans. Fouracre and Gerberding, *Late Merovingian France*, p. 94.

[79] Fredegar, cont. 8.

[80] Fouracre, *Charles Martel*, pp. 74–5. See also Collins, 'Deception', pp. 229–35.

[81] Collins, 'Deception', pp. 229–35.

[82] *Gesta abbatum Fontanellensium* (hereafter *GAF*), ch. 4, ed. P. Pradié, *Chronique des abbés de Fontenelle (Saint-Wandrille)* (Paris, 1999).

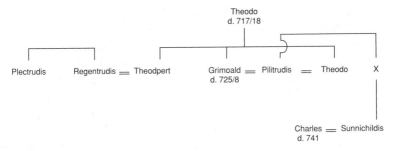

12 Table of eighth-century Bavarian marriages.

eighth century suggests that there were people who thought well of her, or at least cultivated her memory as a benefactress, and who needed to be appeased by Charles and his descendants.

One group of supporters might have been found within the various monastic foundations she endowed: Kaiserwerth and Süsteren, for instance.[83] Another centre which had reason to remember her well was Echternach, given to Willibrord by Irmina of Oeren,[84] who is traditionally, and probably correctly, identified as her mother.[85] On the other hand Willibrord was supporting Charles by 718, and arguably did so as early as 716.[86] Although the Echternach charters make clear the importance of Irmina and Plectrudis to the monastery,[87] it is not immediately apparent that the community helped extol the reputation or preserve the memory of the two women in the world outside in the years after 716.

There are a number of indications, however, that Charles recognised the need to appease Plectrudis's family, despite his conflicts with her and later with her sons. There is a possibility that Charles's first wife, Rotrudis, was a member of his stepmother's kin-group.[88] Charles's second wife, Swanahild (Sunnichildis) was related to Plectrudis, but only distantly, and by marriage (see Fig. 12). She was the niece of Pilitrudis, who married in turn Theodo/Theodolt (696–717/18), *dux* of Bavaria, and then his brother and successor, Grimoald (d. 725/8).[89] Her sister-in-law, Regentrudis, who was

[83] Gerberding, *Rise*, pp. 101, 114, 116, 127.
[84] C. Wampach, *Geschichte der Grundherrschaft Echternach im Frühmittelalter*, I, 2: *Quellenband* (Luxemburg, 1930), no. 3, pp. 17–20.
[85] Le Jan, *Famille*, p. 203, n. 108; Fouracre, *Charles Martel*, pp. 44–6.
[86] Gerberding, *Rise*, pp. 134–6; Gerberding, '716', pp. 208–13.
[87] Wampach, *Geschichte der Grundherrschaft Echternach*, *Quellenband*, nos. 2, 3, 4, 6, 9, 10, 12, 14, 15, 24.
[88] N. Gauthier, 'Une grande dame, Chrodoara d'Amay', *Antiquité Tardive* 2 (1994), pp. 259–60.
[89] Fredegar, cont. 12. For Pilitrudis's marriages, Arbeo of Freising, *Vita Corbiniani*, chs. 24, 31, ed. B. Krusch, *MGH SRG* (Hanover, 1920).

married to an older brother, Theodpert, *dux* of Bavaria from *c.* 702 to *c.* 716, was Plectrudis's sister.[90] Sunnichildis was, therefore, the niece of a sister-in-law of Plectrudis's sister. These connections scarcely suggest that Charles had his stepmother in mind when he married Sunnichildis. He had more reason to marry her because of the *entrée* she gave into the political world of the Agilolfing dukes of Bavaria. And the *Annales Mettenses Priores* had reason to curse Sunnichildis, because her son, Gripho, caused so much distress to Carloman and Pippin III.[91]

Other significant women have also been identified as sisters of Plectrudis. There is the redoubtable Adela, abbess of Pfalzel,[92] who was an influential figure in the days of Boniface.[93] So too, Bertrada the Elder, grandmother of Pippin III, and thus great-grandmother of Charlemagne himself, has been proposed as being another.[94] Unfortunately this last identification is merely conjectural, although it would certainly explain the continued attention paid to Plectrudis in the Carolingian period.

There are, however, more plausible indications of attempts by Charles Martel to appease his stepmother's kin – notably through the promotion of saint cults, or at least through acquiescence in their promotion. As we have seen, acceptance of the cult of Lambert of Liège is one possible indication that Charles was prepared to make concessions to Plectrudis's family and supporters, even to seek conciliation with them. Equally interesting is the evidence for the development of a cult of another woman: Chrodoara.

CHRODOARA

Chrodoara, who almost certainly died before 634, was the founder of the monastery of Amay, and it was there that she was buried.[95] She may have been culted at her tomb soon after her death, since the will of Adalgisel-Grimo of 634 defines the monastery as the place where an unnamed aunt, probably Chrodoara, was buried.[96] Her body was translated in 730 and placed in a splendid new sarcophagus bearing a full-length image of her as

[90] H. Wolfram, *Salzburg, Bayern, Österreich* (Vienna, 1995), pp. 237, 239.

[91] *AMP*, s.a. 741, 743, 746, 748–51; see I. N. Wood, *The Merovingian Kingdoms 450–751* (London, 1994), pp. 288–90.

[92] Fouracre, *Charles Martel*, pp. 44–5.

[93] Liudger, *Vita Gregorii*, 2, ed. O. Holder-Egger, *MGH SS* xv, 1 (Hanover, 1887).

[94] Fouracre, *Charles Martel*, p. 197.

[95] Gauthier, 'Chrodoara d'Amay', pp. 257–60; Dierkens, '*Carolus monasterium multorum eversor*', pp. 282–5.

[96] Ed. W. Levison, *Aus rheinischer und fränkischer Frühzeit* (Düsseldorf, 1948), pp. 118–38 esp. p. 133, 'et [basilica] domni Iorgii in Amanio constructa, ubi amita mea requiescit'; Gauthier, 'Chrodoara d'Amay', p. 258.

abbess[97] – one of the earliest surviving near life-sized stone carvings of a historical individual from the early Middle Ages. Chrodoara was not herself an abbess,[98] but she was made to look like one. As already mentioned, the tombs of abbesses in family monasteries seem to have had a particular cachet.[99] Transforming Chrodoara into an abbess may have enhanced her value to her kin. Subsequently she was remembered as Oda, and ultimately, but perhaps only in the thirteenth century, she was honoured with a saint's *Life*.[100]

Chrodoara's family connections are the subject of much hypothesis, but there is a strong case for thinking that she was the grandmother of either Hugobert or his wife, Irmina of Oeren, and thus the great-grandmother of Plectrudis.[101] To have culted her in the 730s could have been a way of reintegrating Plectrudis's family into the world of Frankish politics now dominated by Charles Martel. Chrodoara might have been a very convenient figure for the promotion of family unity. According to her *vita* she was the mother of Arnulf of Metz.[102] If this were the case, and the evidence is far too late in date to be relied upon, then Chrodoara could have been a figure to attract the kin both of Plectrudis and of Charles Martel. The *Vita Odae* also makes the saint a Merovingian, although in identifying her father as Childebert and her brother as Dagobert, it is clearly mistaken.[103] Obviously the claims of the *Vita Odae* are no more reliable than are those of the late Carolingian genealogies. Scepticism about the more extreme claims made about Chrodoara's family, however, does not detract from the notion that a female saint from the early seventh century could have been culted to reintegrate family groups torn apart by political conflict in the early eighth. Moreover, there is one element in the cult that is remarkably reminiscent of that of Lambert. Amay itself is in territory that appears to have been closely associated with the kin of Alpaida.[104] Chrodoara's cult could well have drawn together the kin of Charles, Alpaida and Plectrudis, just as Charles's acceptance of the cult of Lambert could have been a concession to his stepmother's family.

The success of Charles Martel essentially necessitated the removal of Plectrudis's descendants, and indeed the political elimination of Plectrudis herself. At the same time, her kin probably remained a force to be reckoned

[97] Dierkens, '*Carolus monasterium multorum eversor*', pp. 284–5; Gauthier, 'Chrodoara d'Amay', pp. 260–1.
[98] Dierkens, '*Carolus monasterium multorum eversor*', p. 285 n. 53. [99] Le Jan, 'Convents', p. 268.
[100] Gauthier, 'Chrodoara d'Amay', p. 258 n. 45.
[101] Gauthier, 'Chrodoara d'Amay', p. 259, with n. 63.
[102] Gauthier, 'Chrodoara d'Amay', p. 259. [103] Gauthier, 'Chrodoara d'Amay', p. 259.
[104] Dierkens, '*Carolus monasterium multorum eversor*', pp. 282–3.

with – not least because of her sister's marriage to Theodpert of Bavaria. As we have seen, she may have had other influential sisters.[105] It is also possible that some in Frisia, who had been supporters of the marriage of Plectrudis's son Grimoald to Radbod's daughter Theudesinda, remained loyal to the family.[106] The acknowledgement of the importance of Plectrudis in Carolingian sources could well reflect a willingness to appease her family, while the promotions of the cults of Lambert and Chrodoara, even in territory dominated by the kin of Charles's mother, could reflect the need to make some concessions towards the kindred of Pippin II's first wife.

HUGO, GRANDSON OF ANSFLEDIS

An exploration of some of the complexities of Charles's connections with Plectrudis's family has suggested some reasons for the continuing attention paid to her. Despite the fact that her own direct line of descent came to an end, and contributed nothing biologically to the Carolingian family, because of the deaths of her sons and the treatment of her grandsons, Charles Martel may well have had to conciliate her kin. Looking back, the Carolingians had no cause to remember Plectrudis as an ancestor. Yet curiously, eighth-century sources have more to say about her than about Alpaida. One descendant of Pippin and Plectrudis did, however, survive and prosper, and he seems to have had a rather unexpected attitude towards his ancestors.

Hugo, the son of Drogo, and grandson of Plectrudis and Pippin, did well under Charles, perhaps because he became a cleric. After Pippin's death Hugo was brought up in Rouen by his maternal grandmother Ansfledis, as we are told in a surprising passage of the *Annales Mettenses Priores* which was subsequently copied into the *Gesta Abbatum Fontanellensium*.[107] Hugo was to become bishop of Rouen before *c.* 725, when he was appointed abbot of St Wandrille: he later became bishop of Paris and Bayeux, as well as abbot of Jumièges.[108] He has been seen as an ally of Charles and his career as an indication of Carolingian control of the lower Seine valley.

There are, however, reasons for some scepticism about the supposed warmth of their relationship.[109] His long list of ecclesiastical offices might

---

[105] Fouracre, *Charles Martel*, pp. 44–5.   [106] *LHF*, ch. 50.
[107] *AMP*, s.a. 693; Fouracre and Gerberding, *Late Merovingian France*, p. 362; *GAF*, ch. 4, 1; Gerberding, *Rise*, p. 98.
[108] L. Duchesne, *Fastes épiscopaux de l'ancienne Gaule*, vol. II (Paris, 1899), p. 208.
[109] Gerberding, *Rise*, pp. 137–9; Fouracre, *Charles Martel*, pp. 48–9.

be an indication as much of the need to keep him sweet, as of his closeness
to his uncle. Although the monks of St Wandrille later boasted that their
founder, Wandregisil, was related to Pippin I,[110] this claim would not seem
to have been based on fact, and does not appear to have been made before
the end of the eighth century. Instead the monastery seems to have been
unenthusiastic about the policies of Charles Martel and Pippin III.[111]

Further, a monk of St Wandrille, writing perhaps between 823 and 833,[112]
described Hugo's family in a striking way. First, he mentioned Hugo's father
Drogo and his mother Adeltrudis (or Anstrudis). Only at the end of his
account of the family did he state that Hugo was the (step-)nephew, *nepos*,
of Charles. In dealing with the subject of the abbot's lineage the monk
had already explained that Adeltrudis was the daughter of Waratto and
Ansfledis. He then described Hugo's upbringing at the hands of Ansfledis,
setting out a panegyric of her, all of which is derived, oddly enough, from
the *Annales Mettenses Priores*.[113]

It is worth noting here who is left out of this genealogy: Plectrudis and
Pippin, and their ancestors. Clearly there is no straightforward hostility to
Plectrudis and her family, because Drogo is mentioned: equally there is
no simple passing over of the Pippinids, because Charles Martel is referred
to. In the main, however, this is a matrilineal genealogy: Hugo was the
son of Adeltrudis and Drogo: Adeltrudis was the daughter of Waratto and
Ansfledis: and it was Ansfledis who brought up the young boy. Of course this
genealogy may have been St Wandrille's view of matters, rather than Hugo's.
In 715 Hugo joined his brothers in endowing St Arnulf's Metz,[114] which
suggests that in that year he was keen to acknowledge his Arnulfing ancestry.
In 715, however, it still appeared that Plectrudis would succeed in excluding
Charles Martel from his father's succession. The most likely candidate to
establish himself as *maior palatii* was Hugo's brother, and fellow benefactor,
himself boasting the name of Arnulf. Thus, before Charles Martel's seizure
of power, it was possible to see Hugo as Arnulfing, but that option was
ignored later, in favour of an emphasis on his maternal kin. Here, the fact
that the paean of praise for Ansfledis first occurs in the *Annales Mettenses*

---

[110] *GAF*, ch. 1, 2; the same point is made in the *Vita II Wandregisili*, ch. 1, *AASS, Jul.*, vol. v, pp. 272–81.
Wandregisil is also integrated into Waitz, *Genealogia* 11; Tremp, *Studien zu den Gesta Hludowici*,
pp. 33–41.

[111] I. N. Wood, 'Teutsind, Witlaic and the history of Merovingian *precaria*', in W. Davies and
P. Fouracre (eds.), *Property and Power in the Early Middle Ages* (Cambridge, 1995), pp. 31–52;
I. N. Wood, 'Saint Wandrille and its hagiography', in I. N. Wood and G. A. Loud (eds.), *Church
and Chronicle in the Middle Ages* (London, 1991), pp. 10–12.

[112] See most recently Pradié, *Chronique des abbés de Fontanelle*, p. xxvii.

[113] *GAF*, ch. 4, 1; *AMP*, s.a. 693; Fouracre and Gerberding, *Late Merovingian France*, p. 362.

[114] Pertz, *Diplomata*, no. 8; Heidrich, *Urkunden*, pp. 71–5.

Priores – a pro-Carolingian source if ever there was one – from which it was borrowed by a monk of St Wandrille, is surely significant. Hugo could well have seen himself as his maternal grandmother's offspring, especially after the seizure of power by his uncle. Even if one takes the description as a later reading of the family, it does, nevertheless, give a striking insight into how communities could imagine descent groups in different ways. In the early Middle Ages it was perfectly possible to emphasise attachment to one's mother's lineage.

It is worth pausing on Ansfledis a little longer, because there were reasons for the Pippinids to remember her well. She was the wife of the Neustrian *maior palatii* Waratto, who on the whole received a good press from early eighth-century writers and from the *Annales Mettenses Priores*.[115] They had a son, Ghislemar, who was condemned by the Neustrian *Liber Historiae Francorum*, by the Fredegar continuator and by the Metz Annals. Ghislemar forced his father from office and pursued his own aggressive policy towards Austrasia, attacking Pippin (*c*. 684). In the event, he died, struck down, as the chroniclers said, by God. Waratto resumed his position, but he too died soon after. His son-in-law, Berchar, assumed the office of Neustrian *maior*, but quickly alienated the Neustrian nobility, and ended up fighting Pippin at Tertry in 687. After his defeat he was murdered at the instigation of Ansfledis.[116] Shortly after Berchar's death Pippin arranged for his widow Adeltrudis to marry Drogo.[117] It is at this point in the narrative of the *Annales Mettenses Priores* that the panegyric of Ansfledis, with its comments on the upbringing of Hugo, is inserted. The Pippinids, it seems, had good reason to accept a flattering depiction of Ansfledis. She had, after all, aided them by helping remove Berchar, and by facilitating Drogo's marriage to Adeltrudis. At the same time Neustrians could still respect her as a representative of their mayoral dynasty. In ninth-century St Wandrille, a monastery that by then claimed connections with Pippin I,[118] it was thus acceptable to describe Hugo as the child of Adeltrudis, brought up by Ansfledis. Such a claim also allowed a certain distancing from the Pippinids in Neustria, which may have been welcomed by those who disliked the policies of Charles Martel and Pippin III.

---

[115] *LHF*, ch. 47; Fredegar, cont. 4; *AMP*, s.a. 688; Fouracre and Gerberding, *Late Merovingian France*, p. 354.

[116] *LHF*, ch. 48; Fredegar, cont. 5; *AMP*, s.a. 689–90; Fouracre and Gerberding, *Late Merovingian France*, pp. 354–9 – although interestingly the *AMP* do not mention Ansfledis in the context of the murder.

[117] *AMP*, s.a. 693; Fouracre and Gerberding, *Late Merovingian France*, p. 362.

[118] *GAF*, ch. 1, 2; *Vita II Wandregisili*, ch. 1.

RETROSPECTIVE REPRESENTATIONS OF THE PIPPINID FAMILY

The marriage alliances of the Pippinids were crucial to the survival of the family. They also meant that a member of the family could trace his or her ancestry back through more than one significant lineage. Indeed, short of listing all one's ancestors, a selection, and not always a historically accurate one, had to be made. Such retrospective representation was usually patrilineal, but it did not have to be. Hugo could privilege descent from Ansfledis rather than from Pippin II. The fact that he, or a ninth-century monk of St Wandrille, did so, is an indication of the dangers of relying on modern reconstructions of family trees that are essentially patrilineal.

One particularly curious outcome of the leeway afforded by such retrospective representation is to be found in a ninth-century historical compilation, Vienna, ÖNB MS lat. 473, whose final section contains an account of the Frankish kings and kingdoms from Priam to Louis the Pious.[119] Here, the text relates that the Franks elevated Waratto to the position of *maior domus* on the death of Ebroin, and that after him Berchar was appointed. According to this text, Berchar had two sons by Plectrudis, Drogo and Grimoald, and one by Alpaida, Charles. Clearly the author has made a slip, substituting Berchar for Pippin, and this is indeed confirmed by the fact that the text goes on to mention Pippin's death, followed (incorrectly) by the death of Drogo and the murder of Grimoald. Yet the slip is all the more astonishing in that the manuscript seems to have been intended for Charles the Bald (840–877).[120] It was possible in a historical compilation, intended for a far-from-ignorant Carolingian ruler,[121] to substitute Berchar for Pippin II. By contrast the women in the story, Plectrudis and Alpaida are rightly remembered, as are their sons, although the chronology of the deaths of Drogo and Grimoald is inaccurate. The slip could, of course, be explained by an accident of copying, although even that points to a continuing interest in the family of Waratto, the husband of Ansfledis.

Slips, inaccuracies and inventions are in many ways more revealing when it comes to tracing attitudes towards the past generations of a family, than is

---

[119] For the manuscript, H. Reimitz, 'Ein karolingisches Geschichtsbuch aus Saint-Amand. Der *Codex Vindobonensis palat. 473*', in C. Egger and H. Weigl (eds.), *Text – Schrift – Codex: quellenkundliche Arbeiten aus dem Institut für Österreichische Geschichtsforschung* (Vienna, 2000), pp. 35–90; for a description of the manuscript, pp. 35–9; for an edition of the text in question, pp. 52–3.

[120] R. McKitterick, 'Charles the Bald (823–877) and his library: the patronage of learning', *English Historical Review* 95 (1980), p. 32; Reimitz, 'Ein karolingisches Geschichtsbuch', pp. 60–76; McKitterick, 'Political ideology', pp. 162–74.

[121] J. M. Wallace-Hadrill, 'A Carolingian Renaissance prince: the emperor Charles the Bald', *Proceedings of the British Academy* 64 (1978), pp. 155–84.

an accurate genealogy – although even an 'accurate' genealogy is important because of what it leaves out and what it includes. The Carolingian genealogies themselves are relatively silent on women: the presence of the legendary Blithildis is easily explained in terms of a search for legitimation, and that of Begga in terms of the fact that the Pippinid line passed through her, rather than her husband Ansegisus. The first narrative text to deal extensively with a Pippinid woman is the *Vita Geretrudis*, a work of hagiography written at a time of particular crisis for the family. The subsequent narratives to add to the picture are the standard texts relating the history of late Merovingian Francia: the *Liber Historiae Francorum*, the Fredegar continuations and the *Annales Mettenses Priores*. The first two of these present Plectrudis's role in a neutral light, while the first of them refers to Alpaida only in passing, and the second, curiously given their Pippinid origins, says nothing about her at all. The Metz Annals are, equally curiously, silent on Alpaida, but they otherwise give much more space to women within their narrative – and the number of women recalled is also greater. This may be significant, as already suggested, in assessing the possibility of the work being written by a woman.

The different sources show a range of possibilities in presenting the women of the family. They also show several conceptualisations of the family. It was possible, even in the *Annales Mettenses Priores*, to think of Hugo of Rouen as the descendant of his maternal grandmother. Such a cognatic view – that is, a view recognising descent from female as well as male ancestors – need not surprise.[122] In the fifth century Sidonius Apollinaris commented on the importance of maternal kin[123] – and although Roman and Germanic family patterns differed, the Carolingians of the late eighth century envisaged their family as including the Gallo-Roman Ferreolus of Uzès,[124] and they drew attention to the name Ansegisus as being akin to Anchises.[125] A stronger parallel is presented at the beginning of the *Life of Liudger*, by his nephew Altfrid, written in the second quarter of the ninth century,[126] that is, within a generation of the composition of the *Gesta Abbatum Fontanellensium*. There Altfrid recalled the ancestors of

[122] See Bullough, 'Early medieval social groupings', and Leyser, 'Maternal kin'. See also Le Jan, *Famille*, pp. 31–58, and E. van Houts (ed.), *Medieval Memories: Men, Women and the Past, 700–1300* (London, 2001), p. 6.

[123] Sidonius Apollinaris, ep. 4, 21, ed. W. B. Anderson (Cambridge, MA, 1936–65). For some commentary, I. N. Wood, 'Family and friendship in the West', in A. Cameron, B. Ward-Perkins and M. Whitby, *Cambridge Ancient History*, vol. xiv: *Late Antiquity, Empire and Successors A.D. 425–600* (Cambridge, 2000), pp. 420–1.

[124] Waitz, *Genealogia* ii.   [125] Paul, *Libellus*.

[126] See I. N. Wood, *The Missionary Life* (London, 2001), pp. 113–15.

the saint, on both his paternal and maternal sides, presenting a cognatic reading of the kin-group[127] – and women played crucial roles in the religious history of the family. Individuals and kin-groups remembered female ancestors, just as they remembered male ancestors, as and when they needed to. Begga was a *sine qua non* of the Pippinid family, and Geretrudis as a family saint could be of enormous value. But families also remembered less obvious individuals: Plectrudis played a major role, but it was one which the Pippinids could have done without – on the other hand, she also had important kin who needed conciliating: this concern may have encouraged the translation of Chrodoara. Ansfledis brought with her connections to the leading Neustrian family: she was worth remembering, even if she lay outside the blood-line of the Pippinids. All of these examples make the silences over Alpaida yet more curious. Her biological role apart, have she and her kin been overestimated in the development of Pippinid power? Or, perhaps more likely, did her bigamous marriage to Pippin lead her descendants to say as little as possible about her?[128]

Families, of course, cannot survive without the biological contribution of women: the Pippinid family would not have existed without Begga's marriage to Ansegisus. The vast extent of the family's land-holdings was dependent on what women brought with them. Also important, women played a major role in the definition of the family, even when they did not contribute to its biological survival: Geretrudis and the other monastic and holy women of the family shone in this respect more than any male other than Arnulf. Historical narratives of the late seventh and early eighth century tend to be dominated by war, which is largely the domain of men, although the career of Plectrudis presents a challenge to that picture. Moreover, the Pippinid family itself is usually presented – in Carolingian genealogies as in modern reconstructions of the family tree – as a male descent-group. Yet it was also a kindred which survived on alliances, estates and memories, and as such was dependent on its women as much as its men. Indeed, while it is impossible to think of women without thinking of their kin-groups, the reverse is also true. The point may surface only rarely in the genealogies, but the narratives, and especially that of the *Annales Mettenses Priores*, are much more forthcoming. That women were central to the survival and development of a family, biologically, economically and politically, should go without saying, yet it is not always acknowledged that, in the cognatic world of the early Middle Ages, maternal kin could be as

[127] Altfrid, *Vita Liudgeri* i, cc. 1–7, ed. W. Diekamp, *Die Vitae sancti Liudgeri* (Münster, 1881).
[128] Following this reading, the silences of the sources already imply those moral overtones detected in later sources by Gerberding, *Rise*, p. 119, and Joch, 'Karl Martell'.

important as paternal. On the other hand, when women do surface in the genealogies, we can be certain that they do so for a purpose: we should always ask who is and is not included and why. Sometimes a woman would be remembered in her own right; sometimes she would be remembered because of the kinship connections she brought with her. Married women could be deployed or deleted according to the agendas of an author. Sometimes a genealogist would see these connections as being more important than those of a husband. Indeed, in a world of cognatic kinship a genealogy could sometimes even seem to be matrilineal.[129]

[129] See also M. Innes, 'Keeping it in the family: women and aristocratic memory, 700–1200', in Van Houts, *Medieval Memories*, esp. pp. 21 with n. 20, 31 with n. 44. Le Jan, *Famille*, pp. 38–45.
   I am indebted to Helmut Reimitz, who gave considerable advice on the Carolingian genealogies, and who directed me to the consider Vienna, MS 473 in this context.

CHAPTER 14

Bride shows revisited: praise, slander and exegesis in the reign of the empress Judith

Mayke de Jong

A BRIDE SHOW IN AACHEN?

In the autumn of 818, after a victorious campaign against the Bretons, the Frankish emperor Louis the Pious (814–840) returned to Angers, where he had left his wife. The empress Irmingard was seriously ill; and two days after her husband's return, on 3 October, she died. According to the contemporary *Royal Frankish Annals*, the winter assembly which met after Christmas 819 dealt with the welfare of churches and monasteries, and drafted much-needed additions to written law. 'Once this was done, the emperor, after having inspected most of the daughters of the aristocracy, took Judith, the daughter of Count Welf as his wife.'[1] Two decades later, Louis's biographer, who is known as the 'Astronomer', was equally brief about the emperor's second marriage, but he added that the daughters of the great of the realm (*filiae procerum*) were 'brought from everywhere' for Louis's inspection, to the palace in Aachen.[2]

   This is all the evidence there is for what is widely regarded as a clear instance of the Franks having adopted the bride show, a supposedly Byzantine custom which enabled the emperor to choose his future spouse from the most desirable women in the realm paraded before him in the palace. When Louis chose Judith, so the traditional argument runs, this Byzantine bride show was the model he followed.[3] Whereas historians of the early medieval west generally agree that 'Byzantine custom' accounted for the

---

[1] *Annales regni Francorum* s.a. 819, ed. F. Kurze, *MGH SRG* (Hanover, 1895), p. 150: 'Quod peracto imperator inspectis plerisque nobilium filiabus Huelpi comitis filiam nomine Iudith duxit uxorem.'
[2] See note 11 below.
[3] E. Boshof, *Ludwig der Fromme* (Darmstadt, 1996), p. 152, based on H. Hunger, 'Die Schönheitskonkurrenz in "Belthandros und Chrysantia" und die Brautschau am byzantinischen Kaiserhof', *Byzantion* 35 (1965), pp. 150–8. Cf. also E. Tremp (ed.), *Thegan, Die Taten Ludwigs des Frommen (Gesta Hludowici imperatoris). Astronomus, Das Leben Kaiser Ludwigs (Vita Hludowici imperatoris)*, *MGH SRG* (Hanover, 1995), pp. 393, 432: 'Eine Art Schönheitswettbewerb nach dem Vorbild des imperialen Byzantinischen Zeremoniells', citing W. Treadgold, 'The bride shows of the Byzantine emperors', *Byzantion* 49 (1979), pp. 395–413. See also in this volume Janet L. Nelson, chapter 10,

distinctly odd way in which Louis came by his second wife, Byzantinists began to doubt the reality of this custom, pointing out that the texts which 'reported' on bride shows were mostly produced decades after the event, by authors with a particular agenda. Bride shows, fact or fiction? This was the question hotly debated throughout the 1990s, with 'fiction' gradually gaining the upper hand, although opinions as to its meaning and function still vary.[4] One view is that the literary theme of the bride show placated the families of potential brides who did not become empress, sustaining the fiction (and hope) that any girl would be eligible for this honour.[5] Another, argued in this volume by Martha Vinson, is that it was not the bride but the groom who was the lead player in the literary drama of the bride show. In the period of Iconoclasm, choosing a bride well became the hallmark of good rulership. Conversely, a mismanaged bride show could be used to discredit unsatisfactory emperors or to explain their failure. Most texts on the bride show did the latter, portraying emperors who bungled their bride shows and were therefore to be considered unsuitable as rulers. In short, the Byzantine textual tradition of the bride show mostly portrayed 'bad ritual' which, however, did not reflect badly on the brides, but all the more on the emperors involved.[6]

A Frankish imitation of a Byzantine literary *topos* does not seem likely either, for the two earliest Byzantine texts on the bride show, the *Life of Philaretos* and Theophanes' *Chronicle* date from the early 820s. Even if one allows for the possibility the Astronomer knew Theophanes' portrayal of the bride show of 807, this remained a highly unsuitable source of inspiration for Franks with imperial aspirations. After all, Theophanes painted a lurid picture of the emperor Nikephoros selecting the wrong bride for his son Staurakios and seducing other candidates in the process.[7] And there is more that argues against 'Byzantine influence', whether at the level of fact or fiction. Whereas the Byzantine bride show was a well-developed and persistent literary theme with many variations, the two Carolingian texts are brief references – almost afterthoughts tacked on to the main narrative.

---

p. 193, n. 35, with reference to E. Ward, 'The career of the empress Judith' (PhD dissertation, University of London, 2003). I have not been able to consult this work.

[4] L. Rydén, 'The bride shows at the Byzantine court – history or fiction?', *Eranos* 83 (1985), pp. 175–91; P. Speck, 'Ein Brautschau für Stauriakos?', *JÖB* 49 (1999), pp. 25–30; M. Vinson, 'The Life of Theodora and the rhetoric of the Byzantine bride show', *JÖB* 49 (1999), pp. 31–60.

[5] J. Herrin, *Women in Purple: Rulers of Medieval Byzantium* (London, 2001), pp. 136–8.

[6] On narratives about 'bad ritual' meant to undermine reputations, see Philippe Buc, *The Dangers of Ritual: Between Early Medieval Texts and Social Scientific Theory* (Princeton, 2001).

[7] Above, p. 112.

Furthermore, Louis's choice of Judith is the only instance of a Carolingian ruler's marriage being depicted as the result of a choice from a wide range of candidates, so the idea of the adoption of Byzantine 'custom' in Aachen does not make much sense. Where does this leave the supposed Carolingian bride show of 819? We shall see in the course of this chapter that the bride show was part of a passionate debate at the court about Judith, queenship and rulership in general in the early 830s. The answer to the question why Louis's marriage to Judith was portrayed in this exceptional fashion should be looked for not in Byzantium, but in the fact and fiction of the Carolingian world itself, and in the biblical models that guided it.

THE ASTRONOMER AND THE 'BRIDE SHOW'

The Royal Frankish Annalist's report on Louis's second marriage is so brief that some have doubted whether the author had any bride show in mind; it has been argued that the expression *'inspicere'* may have meant no more than that Louis carefully weighed his options.[8] The key text upon which the evidence for a bride show in Aachen rests, the Astronomer's *Vita Hludowici*, was written after Louis's death, in 840–841, by an as yet unidentified prominent courtier who remained staunchly loyal to Louis.[9] He owes his nickname to a celebrated passage in which he described the emperor and himself discussing the meaning of the signs of heaven from the sun-room of the palace.[10] Thus the Astronomer made it eminently clear to his audience that he was one of the men of the palace who enjoyed royal favour of the most intimate kind. Given that this author wrote about the royal marriage of

---

[8] Cf. note 1 above; S. Konecny, *Die Frauen des karolingischen Königshauses: die politischen Bedeutung der Ehe und die Stellung der Frau in der fränkischen Herrscherfamilie vom 7. bis zum 10. Jahrhundert* (Vienna, 1976), p. 92. But see J. Fleckenstein, 'Über die Herkunft der Welfen und ihre Anfangen in Süddeutschland', in G. Tellenbach (ed.), *Studien und Vorarbeiten zur Geschichte des grossfränkischen Adels* (Freiburg i/B, 1957), pp. 71–196 at p. 95, who interprets the *Royal Frankish Annals* in the light of later sources: Judith was chosen because of her beauty, by which she distinguished herself from her 'Mitbewerberinnen'.

[9] Tremp, Introduction to Astronomus, *Vita Hludowici*, pp. 66–8; see also E. Tremp, 'Thegan und Astronomus, die beiden Geschichtsschreibern Ludwigs des Frommen', in P. Godman and R. Collins (eds.), *Charlemagne's Heir: New Perspectives on the Reign of Louis the Pious* (Oxford, 1990), pp. 691–700. A recent identification of the Astronomer as Bishop Jonas of Orléans by M. M. Tischler, *Einharts 'Vita Karoli': Studien zur Entstehung, Überlieferung und Rezeption*, MGH Schriften 48, 2 (Hanover, 2001), pp. 1109–11, did not manage to convince me. Hugh Doherty's suggestion in 'The maintenance of royal power and prestige in the Carolingian regnum of Aquitaine under Louis the Pious' (unpublished MPhil dissertation, University of Cambridge, 1999) that this author was closely connected with Louis's half-brother, Archbishop Drogo of Metz, seems more plausible.

[10] Astronomus, *Vita Hludowici*, c. 58, ed. Tremp, p. 522. The expression used is *meniana*, correctly interpreted by Tremp as 'eine Art *solarium*'.

819 with considerable hindsight, one may expect the intervening turbulence surrounding Judith to reverberate in what may look, at first sight, like a straightforward description of this controversial queen's marriage. It is therefore worth citing the text in full:

In that same winter the emperor held a general assembly of his people and he heard reports about his whole realm from the *missi* whom he had sent out to restore what had fallen and to strengthen what was upright in the condition of the holy church. With holy devotion leading him on, he added whatever he thought was useful and he left nothing untouched that might possibly contribute to the honour of the holy church of God. Meanwhile certain chapters were added to the laws in those cases where judicial affairs seemed weak and right up to today they are retained as most indispensable. At that time, admonished by his men, he began to think about taking a wife again, for many were afraid that he might wish to give up the governance of the realm. But he finally acceded to their will, and after inspecting the daughters of the nobles who had been brought in from everywhere he married Judith, the daughter of the most noble count Welf.[11]

This is a portrait of a ruler who was a leader of the *sancta ecclesia* (the holy church), with principles to match his exalted position. The image of Louis as a ruler with one foot in the monastery, upon which the Astronomer dwelled repeatedly, was intended not as a badge of weakness, but rather as an indication that this was a true Christian emperor, for whom a withdrawal from secular life was a permanent option, only to be discarded because of his duties as a ruler; there may also have been some resonance of the events of the early 830s, when as a public penitent Louis came close to entering monastic life. According to a long Christian tradition, a second marriage should not be easily contracted, and was therefore a matter of suitable hesitation. The Astronomer's account of Louis's first marriage to Irmingard was that of a young king having to be urged into marriage 'by the counsel of his men (*cum consilio suorum*), and by his own fears that the innate desires of his body might cause him to fall prey to all kinds of wantonness (*luxuria*)'.[12] All the more so should Louis's second marriage be depicted as a matter of royal hesitation and ultimate persuasion by 'his men'.[13] Louis's alleged prevarication about remarrying should be taken

---

[11] Astronomus, *Vita Hludowici*, c. 32, ed. Tremp, pp. 390–2. My translation, barring some minor details, follows that of T. F. X. Noble.

[12] Astronomus, *Vita Hludowici*, c. 8, ed. Tremp, pp. 306–8. Cf. S. Airlie, 'Private bodies and the body politic in the divorce case of Lothar II', *Past and Present* 161 (1998), pp. 3–38 at pp. 25–7, about similar themes in the controversy over Lothar II and Theutberga. Adolescence was a dangerous time, but the 'taming' of the king's body was also a hallmark of Christian kingship, as was the integration of a monogamous marriage into the royal image.

[13] B. Kötting, 'Die Beurteilung der zweiten Ehe in der Spätantike und im frühen Mittelalter', in H. Kamp and J. Wollasch (eds.), *Tradition als historische Kraft* (Berlin, 1982), pp. 42–52.

with a grain of salt. After all, Irmingard had died in October 818, and in February 819 at the latest the emperor had chosen a new bride; this is hardly an example of Louis dragging his feet in what was clearly a matter of political survival. The 'senior palace' in Aachen, as it came to be called once Louis's sons were duly married and established palaces of their own,[14] could only be senior if the emperor had an empress at his side and another son ensuring the continuity of this particular royal household. All these hopes and ambitions were fulfilled by the birth of a son in 823 who was called Charles after his illustrious grandfather Charlemagne, the founder of the empire and the palace at Aachen.

Like Thegan, whose *Deeds of Louis the Pious* were written before the emperor's death, the Astronomer upgraded Judith's ancestry.[15] The 'daughters of the aristocracy' (*filiae nobilium*) of the *Royal Frankish Annals* became the 'daughters of the magnates' (*filiae procerum*), thus narrowing Louis's choice to the inner circle of those who fulfilled a 'ministry' in the empire; Count Welf became a *nobilissimus comes*, quite a significant feat, since the Astronomer only rarely bestowed the epithet *nobilissimus*.[16] But unlike Thegan, the Astronomer wrote this part of his biography with the *Royal Frankish Annals* on his desk. The narrative is subtly elaborated, with the net result that the Aachen winter assembly of 819, presumably a fairly restricted gathering, becomes an emphatically public affair involving all the leading Franks (this is how *conventum populi publicum* should be understood). Whereas the *Royal Frankish Annals* mention the well-being of churches and monasteries as part of the agenda, for the Astronomer the main issue was the 'honour of the *ecclesia*', which might well be translated as the honour of the realm. This very public and important assembly then serves as the Astronomer's background to Louis's 'inspection' of the potential marriage candidates in Aachen, which by implication becomes a public

---

[14] Agobard of Lyons, *Liber apologeticus* I, c. 5, ed. L. van Acker, CCCM 51 (Turnhout, 1981), p. 311.

[15] Thegan, *Gesta Hludowici*, c. 26, ed. Tremp, p. 214: 'Sequenti vero anno accepit filiam Huuelfi ducis sui, qui erat de nobilissima progenie Baioariorum, et nomen virginis Iudith, quae erat ex parte matris, cuius nomen Eigiluui, nobilissimi generis Saxonici, eamque reginam constituit; erat enim pulchra valde.' For a reconstruction of Judith's supposedly illustrious origins, see Fleckenstein, 'Über die Herkunft der Welfen'; cf. Konecny, *Die Frauen des karolingischen Königshauses*, p. 93: 'Er [Welf] gehörte kaum zu den Adligen die in unmittelbare Nähe des Königs lebten und an politischen Entscheidungen wesentlich beteiligt waren.' Similar doubts are expressed by M. Borgolte, *Die Grafen Alemanniens in Merowingischer und Karolingischer Zeit: eine Prosopographie*, Vorträge und Forschungen, Sonderband 31 (Sigmaringen, 1984), pp. 288–90. On the formation of an elite of *proceres*, to which Welf probably did not belong, see R. Le Jan, *Famille et pouvoir dans le monde franc (VIIe–Xe siècle): essai d'anthropologie sociale* (Paris, 1995), pp. 122–33.

[16] Tremp, Introduction to Astronomus, *Vita Hludowici*, p. 69.

event as well. The daughters of the *proceres* were 'brought from everywhere' (*undecumque adductas*), for Louis's inspection.

PRAISE

Judith's early years in Aachen are badly documented.[17] She only re-emerges in the Astronomer's narrative on the occasion of the birth of her son Charles in 823, which was ominously preceded by signs of cosmic disorder.[18] Charles's birth was not reported by the *Royal Frankish Annals* or Thegan, and nobody mentioned the birth of Gisela, Charles's elder sister who would later marry Count Eberhard of Friuli.[19] Thegan reintroduced Judith into his narrative on the occasion of the baptism of the Danish king Harald and his wife in Ingelheim in 826, when Judith became the godmother of the Danish queen.[20] The 824 entry of the *Royal Frankish Annals* offers a rare glimpse of Judith as an active queen working side by side with her husband. After a punitive expedition in Brittany, Louis returned to Rouen, 'where he had ordered his spouse to take care of matters at hand'.[21] This was the style of Judith's queenship, as appears from some of Louis's letters telling assorted courtiers that if he himself could not be present, they might find his beloved wife to take care of their pressing business.[22] Judith's star in Aachen clearly began to rise after she had given birth to Charles, and above all, once it became clear that this son would live. From 825 onwards members of her family rose to prominent positions. Her mother Heilwig became abbess of the venerable royal nunnery of Chelles (825). Her sister Imma married Louis's son Louis the German (827); this was the second daughter of Welf who made it into a royal bed. Her brothers Conrad and

---

[17] The best treatment of the first decade of Judith's queenship is E. Ward, 'Caesar's wife: the career of the empress Judith, 819–829', in Godman and Collins (eds.), *Charlemagne's Heir*, pp. 205–77; an informative survey of her entire reign is provided by P. Depreux, *Prosopographie de l'entourage de Louis le Pieux, 781–840* (Sigmaringen, 1997), pp. 279–88.

[18] Astronomus, *Vita Hludowici*, c. 37, ed. Tremp, pp. 420–2, based on *Annales regni Francorum*, s.a. 823. On Charles's birth and youth, see J. L. Nelson, *Charles the Bald* (London, 1992), pp. 75–104.

[19] On the famous will of this illustrious couple, with references to older literature, see C. La Rocca and L. Provero, 'The dead and their gifts. The will of Eberhard, count of Friuli, and his wife Gisela, daughter of Louis the Pious', in F. Theuws and J. L. Nelson, *Rituals of Power from Late Antiquity to the Early Middle Ages* (Leiden, 2000), pp. 225–80.

[20] Thegan, *Gesta Hludowici*, c. 33, ed. Tremp, p. 220; cf. Ermoldus Nigellus, *Carmen in honorem Hludowici casesaris* IV, ed. E. Faral, *Poème sur Louis le Pieux et épitres au roi Pépin* (Paris, 1964), pp. 166–90, who depicts Louis, Judith, Lothar and the Frankish *proceres* as godparents to their Danish counterparts, the king, the queen, the eldest son, the leading men.

[21] *Annales regni Francorum* s.a. 824, ed. Kurze, p. 165.

[22] Einhard, *Epistolae* nos. 21–2, cf. also nos. 13–14, ed. K. Hampe, *MGH Epp.* V (Hanover, 1899), pp. 120–1, 116–17, trans. P. E. Dutton, *Charlemagne's Courtier: The Complete Einhard* (Toronto, 1998), pp. 139 and 149–52. Cf. Depreux, *Prosopographie*, pp. 279–86.

Rudolf became sufficiently prominent to merit the punishment meted out to really powerful political opponents: in 830 they were tonsured and sent to a monastery.[23]

In the late 820s the empress Judith was at the pinnacle of her might. She was beautiful – on this everyone agreed. In 836, when Judith was a matron, Thegan remembered her comeliness as one of the reasons, apart from her illustrious ancestry, why Louis had married her: 'For she was very beautiful' (*enim erat pulchra valde*).[24] Thegan could rely on a panegyric tradition in which Judith's youth and beauty were a central theme. In 829 Freculf of Lisieux dedicated the second volume of his *Histories* to Judith, to assist her in the education of her son Charles, with a letter full of praise of Judith's wisdom and comeliness. 'With regard to physical splendour, let me say what is true, without any corruptive adulation: that in beauty you surpass all the queens of whom little me has seen or heard.'[25] He also called her the *domina augustarum*, the mistress of all empresses. The obvious competition in 829 came from the other *augusta*, Lothar's wife, another Irmingard, the daughter of Hugh of Tours. In the same year, Walafrid Strabo who was then young Charles's tutor and therefore very much part of Judith's entourage, wrote several poems in praise of his patroness, one of which evoked Judith as 'the beautiful Rachel, leading Benjamin, the comfort of grandfathers by the hand'.[26] The grandfather in question was Charlemagne, but this passage may also have referred to Louis, who in 829 was fifty-one years old, comforted by a young and beautiful wife and a son, as Jacob had once been. There may also have been an implicit slight to Judith's predecessor Irmingard and her three sons, for Jacob had preferred Rachel over Leah, his first spouse. Like Judith, Rachel was 'beautiful and well favoured' (*decora et venusto aspectu*; Gen. 29.17), and therefore the ideal biblical heroine for Walafrid's purpose, which was portraying Judith as the mother of Benjamin/Charles, a king-to-be with a great future.

A year before, Ermold the Black (Ermoldus Nigellus) had finished his panegyric poem in honour of Louis, in the hope that it would get him recalled from exile.[27] Judith figures in this repeatedly, and so does her beauty. Attending a hunting expedition, 'pious Judith, the most beautiful wife of Caesar, dressed and coiffed to magnificence, mounted a horse. The

[23] Thegan, *Gesta Hludowici*, c. 36, ed. Tremp, p. 222.

[24] Thegan, *Gesta Hludowici*, c. 26, ed. Tremp, p. 214.

[25] Freculf, *Prologus ad Iudith imperatricem*, ed. M. I. Allen, *Frechulfi Lexoviensis episcopi opera omnia*, CCCM 169A (Turnhout, 2002), pp. 435–7 esp. p. 435.

[26] Walafrid Strabo, *De imagine Tetrici*, ed. L. Traube, *MGH Poet.* II, pp. 370–8, lines 177–8. Cf. P. Godman, *Poets and Emperors: Frankish Politics and Carolingian Poetry* (Oxford, 1987), pp. 133–45.

[27] On Ermold's *Carmen in honorem Hludowici Pii*, see Godman, *Poets and Emperors*, pp. 109–29.

highest *proceres* and a troop of mighty men (*potentes*) preceded and followed the lady (*domina*).'[28] In Ingelheim, on the occasion of the baptism of the Danish visitors, Caesar proceeded from church, dressed in gold, like his wife and children who followed him, with the clerics suitably adorned in white; at the subsequent feast, he had beautiful Judith placed next to him, who kissed his knees.[29] Ermold evoked the image of a beautiful *and* dutiful wife, the wise mother and educator of her son Charles who tried to restrain the little boy from going off intrepidly in chase of a deer, but also that of Judith 'glittering with royal dignity', escorted by the most important *proceres* at the time, Counts Matfrid and Hugh, who duly honoured the virtuous queen (*domina honesta*).[30] Begging to be recalled from exile, Ermold also appealed to Judith: 'You, also, worthy wife to him, most beautiful Judith, you who hold the highest authority with him: grant help to one who sins.'[31]

This was Caesar's wife, the powerful queen who made her mark by her efficient and magnificent care of the royal household in fitting style, as Elizabeth Ward expressed it: holding the keys of the treasury together with the chamberlain, dispensing gifts, mediating between the ruler and his supplicants, and standing in for Louis when pressing business called him elsewhere. She was also the guardian of the *honestas* – the honour, virtue and integrity – of the palace over which she presided. But is all the praise of Judith's beauty sufficiently explained by the home truth that queens are usually beautiful in the eye of those seeking their patronage?[32] I doubt it. Connecting beauty and virtue was part and parcel of traditional panegyric – and hagiographical – strategies, but there was more to this than the mere recycling of *topoi*: 'appearances' mattered in a world which perceived external demeanour and beauty as a sign of inner virtue.[33] Building on this principle, those who praised Judith in writing went a step further: her splendour became the visible expression of her royal dignity (*munus regalis*). There is a lot to be said for translating this expression as 'royal office', and for reading the allusions to Judith as *domina* as 'ruler', rather than as the more neutral 'lady', even if Ermold makes it clear that the great men who escorted this *domina* did so 'in honour of the pious king'.[34]

[28] Ermold, *Carmen*, lines 2241, 2378–80, 2644–5, ed. Faral, pp. 170, 182, 200.
[29] Ermold, *Carmen*, lines 2354–5, ed. Faral, p. 180.
[30] Ermold, *Carmen*, lines 2302–7, ed. Faral, p. 176.
[31] Ermold, *Carmen*, lines 2644–5, ed. Faral, p. 200.   [32] Ward, 'Caesar's wife', p. 217.
[33] On the importance of external demeanour as not merely a reflection of inner states but also a way to foster internal virtue, in a monastic context, see M. de Jong, *In Samuel's Image: Child Oblation in the Early Medieval West* (Leiden, 1996), p. 263, inspired by T. Asad, 'On discipline and humility in medieval Christian monasticism', in Asad, *Genealogies of Religion: Discipline and Reasons of Power in Christianity and Islam* (Baltimore, 1993), pp. 125–67.
[34] Ermold, *Carmen*, line 2380, ed. Faral, p. 182.

A comparison of Ermold's fulsome praise with a work that inspired him, the narrative verse *Karolus Magnus et Leo Papa* of 799, reveals the extent to which the position of the queen had changed in the intervening years, also in the imagination of panegyrists.[35] In this poem Charlemagne's 'most beautiful spouse' (*pulcherrima coniunx*) Liutgard is depicted, emerging upon the scene from the 'proud bedchamber' where she had long lingered, surrounded by her entourage. Like Judith in Ermold's *Poem*, Liutgard was resplendent in royal attire, with jewels glittering and clothes shimmering with purple and gold. But unlike Judith, she had competition from 'an orderly file of virgins' led by Charles's daughter Rotrud on horseback; upon each of the six daughters the author lavished as much praise as on Queen Liutgard, and each of these daughters entered upon the public stage with a female retinue. The 'throng' (*caterva*) which accompanied Liutgard consisted of maidens who preceded her from the 'proud bed' to the public limelight.[36] By contrast, Ermold portrayed Judith exclusively in male company. At public occasions such as the royal hunt and the baptism at Ingelheim, she was escorted by counts Matfrid and Hugh,[37] surrounded by *proceres* and *potentes*,[38] joining the emperor at the head of the dinner table[39] or watching anxiously over her son Charles, together with his tutor.[40] Comparing these two panegyrics, it is as if all the women at the court, with the exception of Judith, had disappeared from the limelight.

Did Ermold deliberately omit other women in order to move Judith, upon whose assistance he relied, to the undisputed centre of the stage? Possibly – yet his praise of an empress who had *proceres* rather than *puellae* as her preferred retinue may also reflect a fundamental change in the way Caesar's wife presented herself during ceremonial occasions in relation to a court consisting of men and women: instead of being surrounded by a flock of girls, she was escorted by powerful magnates. The Astronomer, writing with Einhard's *Life of Charlemagne* on his desk, depicted Louis's succession in 814 as the take-over of Aachen, and the subsequent cleansing of a palace that had been contaminated by women. Einhard had already commented on the problems facing an emperor who had kept his

---

[35] On Ermold's dependence on *Karolus Magnus et Leo Papa*, see Godman, *Emperors and Poets*, p. 111.

[36] *Karolus Magnus et Leo Papa: ein Paderborner Epos vom Jahre 799*, ed. H. Beumann, F. Brunhölzl and W. Winkelmann (Paderborn, 1966), pp. 72–8. See also Theodulf's poem on the court, which also puts the daughters in the limelight: P. Godman, *Poetry of the Carolingian Renaissance* (London, 1985), p. 154.

[37] Ermold, *Carmen*, lines 2302–6, ed. Faral, p. 176.

[38] Ermold, *Carmen*, lines 2377–80, ed. Faral, p. 182.

[39] Ermold, *Carmen*, lines 2354–5, 2418–20, ed. Faral, pp. 180, 184.

[40] Ermold, *Carmen*, lines 2394–400, ed. Faral, p. 182.

daughters with him in his house until his death, saying he could not do without their company (*contubernium*). 'And because of this, though he was otherwise happy, he encountered the evil of bad fortune. This, however, he ignored, as if on their account no suspicion of any immoral conduct arose or no scandal (*fama*) was spread.'[41] Given that Einhard wrote as Louis's courtier, in a palace accustomed to be ruled by one empress only, his *Vita Karoli* may well be a first articulation of changing attitudes in the royal household.[42] The daughters who had once been exuberantly praised now became the source of *fama* – the kind of scandal that might undermine the reputation of the palace. Elaborating on Einhard's veiled intimations, the Astronomer minced no words. 'Although he [Louis] was most mild by nature, he had nevertheless long since made up his mind about the behaviour of his sisters in his father's household, by which stain alone his father's house was branded.' Accordingly, the emperor ordered 'the entire troop of women, which was huge' (*omnem coetum – qui permaximus erat*) to be excluded from the palace, except the very few (*paucissimi*) deemed suitable for royal service.[43] The daughters' goings-on in their father's *contubernium* had been the only real stain which had soiled Charles's palace. There is no doubt that the Astronomer's use of the word *contubernium*, borrowed from Einhard, carries connotations of sexual sin, but it should also be kept in mind that this author wrote after Louis's death, and with first-hand experience of the scandal surrounding an empress accused of adultery and incest. As with Charlemagne's daughters, the reality of Judith's sexual transgression remains a matter of speculation. What is clear, however, is that the sexual scandal endangering the palace became an issue only during the reign of Louis the Pious. It was only in this period that authors first included 'the dangers of women' in their representations of the court of

---

[41] Einhard, *Vita Karoli*, c. 19, ed. R. Rau, *Quellen zur karolingischen Reichsgeschichte* 1 (Darmstadt, 1974), p. 190.

[42] Recent attempts to date Einhard's *Vita Karoli*: K. H. Krüger, 'Neue Beobachtungen zur Datierung von Einhards Karlsvita', *Frühmittelalterliche Studien* 32 (1998), pp. 124–45, who opts for *c.* 823, in connection with the birth of Charles the Bald, and Tischler, *Einharts 'Vita Karoli'*, pp. 151–239, who assigns the work to *c.* 829, departing from the traditional and unfounded assumption that Einhard wrote this biography as an implicit critique of Louis the Pious. Whatever the case, the Einhard whom we know from his work was Louis's and Judith's courtier, not Charlemagne's.

[43] Astronomer, *Vita Hludowici*, cc. 21–3, ed. Tremp, pp. 348–52. For a challenging discussion of this text, with the suggestion that Charlemagne's relations with his daughters were indeed of an incestuous nature, see Janet L. Nelson, 'Women at the court of Charlemagne: a case of monstrous regiment?', in J. L. Nelson, *The Frankish World, 750–900* (London, 1996), pp. 223–42. My inclination would be to ascribe suspicions of incest to a later tradition, which was based on the Astronomer's representation of the take-over of 814. As Rosamond McKitterick pointed out to me, and as also appears from Nelson's 'Women at the court of Charlemagne', at most four of Charlemagne's daughters were alive at the time, which hardly accounts for the Astronomer's 'huge troop of women'.

Charlemagne. Einhard's veiled intimations and the Astronomer's explicit accusations represent two successive stages of this process. The intervening scandal surrounding Judith went a long way towards creating a more articulate discourse of purity and danger, which defined female sexuality as the major source of contamination of the palace and the polity.

SLANDER

On Ash Wednesday 830 Louis left Aachen for a badly timed and much-criticised campaign against the rebellious Bretons, leaving Judith behind in Aachen. In Louis's absence, a palace revolt erupted. Interpretations of its causes vary. Some have contended that this was a 'loyal palace rebellion' on the part of prominent courtiers such as Hilduin and Wala, who valiantly defended the unity of the empire against Judith and her clan.[44] Others have stressed the crucial role of Pippin of Aquitaine, who, resentful because of his father's persistent interference in what was once his own kingdom, accused his stepmother of having dishonoured his father's bed.[45] Yet as important as such 'political' motives, which are too complex to do justice to here, was the atmosphere of crisis and fear at the court. Military defeat, famine, pestilence and crop failure had led to anxious discussions in Aachen, which revolved around one central question: What have we done to offend God?[46] This was a climate of self-incrimination and mutual blame, in which scapegoats were singled out. In 830 it was the turn of Bernard of Septimania, the imperial chamberlain, to be brought down by accusations of dangerous sin, as the accomplice of the empress Judith. But whereas Bernard was allowed to flee to Barcelona, Judith was first sent to the convent of Sainte-Marie in Laon, and then to the royal nunnery of Sainte-Croix in Poitiers, to take the veil and do penance for her sins.

According to Thegan, the emperor never really lost his grip on the situation. During an assembly in Nijmegen in October 830, only half a year after the revolt broke out, Louis dealt efficiently with his adversaries; he returned to Aachen, 'and there came his wife to him', whom he 'received honourably, on the orders of the Roman pontiff Gregory and because of

---

[44] For a summary of this argument, cf. Boshof, *Ludwig der Fromme*, pp. 182–91.

[45] J. L. Nelson, 'The Frankish kingdoms, 814–898: the West', in R. McKitterick (ed.), *The New Cambridge Medieval History*, vol. II: *c. 750–900* (Cambridge, 1995), pp. 142–68 at p. 117. Nelson provides the best survey of events, and an up-to-date context, but for more detail see B. von Simson, *Jahrbücher des fränkischen Reiches unter Ludwig dem Frommen* I (Leipzig, 1874), pp. 341–66.

[46] This is the central theme in a letter issued by Louis the Pious and Lothar in the winter of 828/9; *Hludowici et Hlotharii epistola generalis*, MGH Conc. II, 2, pp. 599–601.

the just judgement of the bishops'.[47] The Astronomer's view of the matter was different. Judith was meant to be the instrument of Louis's downfall, for she should persuade her husband 'to lay down his arms, receive the tonsure, and take himself off to a monastery and she herself would also take the veil'.[48] And neither was Judith's 'honourable reception' in Aachen as easy as Thegan or the author of the *Annales Mettenses Priores* made it out to be. The latter portrayed the return of the beautiful Judith to the palace as a triumphant royal *adventus*: a multitude of magnates rode out to fetch Judith from Poitiers, and as she approached Aachen, her son Charles came to meet her, accompanied by Archbishop Drogo of Metz and other truly great men. Finally, Louis himself joined his wife in Aachen and restored her to her 'former honour'.[49] By contrast, the *Annals of Saint-Bertin* and the Astronomer both emphasised that Judith's full reinstatement in the palace was not a foregone conclusion. A winter assembly gathered in Aachen on 1 February to deal with the consequences of the revolt. Here, Judith 'purged herself according to the judgement of the Franks of all the things of which she had been accused'.[50] There is some ambivalence as to the measure of coercion involved; Judith was 'ordered' to appear in front of her husband and his sons, but also 'declared her willingness to purge herself'. Something of a tightrope had to be walked. The Astronomer later noted that Judith was 'not judged worthy of conjugal honour until she had purified herself in the prescribed manner from the accusations', which suggests that she spent the period from October 830 until February 831 in a liminal state – pardoned in Nijmegen by the pope and the *Germani*, but not yet among the magnates in Aachen. The Astronomer's precise date for Judith's final exoneration was a suitable one: 2 February 831, the Feast of the Virgin's Purification.[51]

What did Judith have to purify herself from?[52] According to Thegan her impious adversaries had accused her of actions it would be scandalous to repeat or believe. It was said that the queen had been violated by 'a certain duke' Bernard who belonged to the royal family and was also the emperor's godchild.[53] This is worth stressing, for there was more at stake than Judith's

---

[47] Thegan, *Gesta Hludowici*, c. 37, ed. Tremp, p. 224.

[48] Astronomer, *Vita Hludowici*, c. 45, ed. Tremp, p. 460.

[49] *Annales Mettenses priores*, s.a. 830, ed. B. von Simson, *MGH SRG* (Hanover, 1905), pp. 97–8.

[50] *Annales s. Bertiniani* s.a. 831, ed. R. Rau, *Quellen zur karolingischen Reichgeschichte*, ii (Darmstadt, 1958), p. 14; trans. J. L. Nelson, *The Annals of St Bertin* (Manchester, 1990), p. 23.

[51] Astronomer, *Vita Hludowici*, c. 46, ed. Tremp, p. 464; this author also mentions the celebration of the Purification of the Virgin in Aachen under Charlemagne (c. 14) and Louis's celebration of this feast in Thionville (c. 56).

[52] See G. Bührer-Thierry, 'La reine adultère', *Cahiers de Civilisation Médiévale* 35 (1992), pp. 299–312.

[53] Thegan, *Vita Hludowici*, c. 36, ed. Tremp, p. 222.

alleged adultery with her chamberlain. Like Queen Theutberga in the 850s, she was accused of having committed incest, a much more serious sexual transgression than mere 'adultery'.[54] Charges of incest were levelled selectively,[55] but there is no doubt as to their effectiveness as an instrument of slander. Most of what was said 'impiously' never made it into writing. Only Archbishop Agobard of Lyons's vitriolic prose against Judith survives as a contemporary witness to the drift of her enemies' invective.[56] He wrote two apologetic treatises defending the revolt of the sons against their father. In the second, written in the autumn of 833, Judith's return to the palace still rankled; she had taken the veil and then discarded it. Here she is portrayed as Jezebel, in a supporting role next to Ahab/Louis, who should save his soul by doing penance.[57] In the first treatise, Judith takes centre stage. It breathes all the frustration of a justified revolt gone wrong, with Judith, the cause of all evil, having gained a stronger foothold in the palace than ever, and the emperor valuing her advice more than that of his legitimate counsellors. Agobard may well have written this tract in 831, venting his anger about the unexpected turn of events in Judith's favour.

In this first treatise Agobard made the most of inverting the two interconnected qualities praised most by Judith's supporters: her beauty and virtue which upheld the honourable reputation (*honestas*) of the palace. The beauty that had only shortly before been the hallmark of the empress's royal dignity now became the visible sign of her moral depravity, polluting the palace and dishonouring the Franks; it was associated no longer with inner virtue and regal *gravitas*, but instead, with the irresponsibility and levity of youth. All the peoples to the end of the earth should know that Louis's sons had justly risen against their father, in order to expurgate the palace from sordid crimes and the factions perpetrating them. In this palace Louis had reigned peacefully, duly performing his marital duties to his still

---

[54] Airlie, 'Private bodies', p. 19; about incest legislation and its early medieval ramifications, see M. de Jong, 'An unsolved riddle: early medieval incest legislation', in I. Wood (ed.), *Franks and Alemanni in the Merovingian Period: An Ethnographic Perspective* (Woodbridge, 1998), pp. 107–20, with references to older literature.

[55] In 827 Judith's sister Emma married Emperor Louis's eponymous son without protest.

[56] On Judith's two chief literary foes, see above all E. Ward, 'Agobard of Lyons and Paschasius Radbertus as critics of the Empress Judith', in W. J. Sheils and D. Wood (eds.), *Women in the Church*, Studies in Church History 27 (Oxford, 1990), pp. 15–25. But it should be noted that Paschasius Radbertus wrote in 856 or even later, so his was a view recorded long after the events of 830; cf. D. Ganz, 'The *Epitaphium Arsenii* and opposition to Louis the Pious', in Godman and Collins (eds.), *Charlemagne's Heir*, pp. 537–50. An excellent analysis of accusations of adultery against Judith and subsequent queens is provided by Bührer-Thierry, 'La reine adultère'.

[57] Agobard, *Liber apologeticus* ii, cc. 3–4, ed. Van Acker, pp. 316–17. See also Agobard's personal charter confirming Louis's penance in 833: *Agobardi cartula de poenitentia ab imperatore acta*, ed. A. Boretius, *MGH Cap.* ii, pp. 34–5.

young wife, but then his age had made him tepid and frigid, allowing the queen to become lascivious, first secretly, then openly. This filled the sons with justified zeal, for they saw 'the paternal bed defiled, the palace soiled, the kingdom thrown into turmoil, and the name of the Franks, which until then had sparkled in the entire world, obscured'.[58] The sons had restored order by relegating Judith to the cloister, but by female wiles and seduction she managed to be recalled to the palace 'as if she were a legitimate queen' (*legitima domina*), regaining the emperor's trust. The oaths which accompanied Judith's rehabilitation, and especially those sworn to the boy Charles, were all false. They upset the right order of things, as became clear from the barbarian nations now attacking the Most Christian Emperor, while they should be subjected to him.

The revolts of 830 and 833 were both aimed at royal authority, but in 830 it was the empress and her captivating but dangerous beauty which provided the means of attack. Severe doubt was cast on Louis's virility, and therefore on his ability to govern well. Yet Agobard's vitriolic comments on young Judith's supposedly wanton behaviour far extended the register of a young wife making a fool of her elderly husband. The royal marriage bed had moved to the centre of the palace, which in turn had become the moral centre of the empire. A polluted palace endangered the realm, which by consequence became 'confused'. The expression *confusio* was a strong one, used also in connection with the dangers of incest;[59] it referred to the kind of contagious sin and public disturbance of the right order that elicited divine retribution, causing crops to fail and barbarians to lord it over the Christian emperor. The fear of the empire-wide polluting force of royal sin had a biblical basis, but it had further crystallised in the course of the 820s in the work of authors influenced by the seventh-century Irish treatise *De duodecim abusivis saeculi*.[60] These 'twelve reprehensible personalities of the world' include the *rex iniquus*, the unjust king who is incapable of ruling, for he cannot govern himself; the fifth reprehensible figure is the

---

[58] Agobard, *Liber apologeticus* I, c. 2, ed. Van Acker, p. 309.

[59] M. de Jong, 'To the limits of kinship: anti-incest legislation in the early medieval West, 500–900', in J. Bremmer (ed.), *From Sappho to De Sade: Moments in the History of Sexuality* (London, 1989), pp. 36–59 at pp. 51–3.

[60] On Ps.-Cyprian's *De duodecim abusivis saeculi*, cf. Michael. E. Moore, 'La monarchie carolingienne et les anciens modèles irlandais', *Annales HSS* 51 (1996), pp. 307–24, but from the limited perspective of this treatise serving primarily as a building block in Frankish episcopal ideology. For a broader and primarily biblical context of the dangers of royal sin, see M. Blattmann, 'Ein Ungluck für sein Volk. Der Zusammenhang zwischen Fehlverhalten des Königs und Volkswohl in Quellen des 7.-12. Jahrhunderts', *Frühmittelalterliche Studien* 30 (1996), pp. 80–102; also Rob Meens, 'Politics, mirrors of princes and the Bible: sins, kings and the well-being of the realm', *EME* 7 (1998), pp. 345–57. Both Blattmann and Meens provide extensive reference to further relevant literature.

woman without modesty (*femina sine pudicitia*).[61] Agobard's prose helped to articulate further these notions, but it also conflated the images of the unjust king and the immodest woman. It was not just any woman's immodesty that Judith had displayed, but queenly immodesty, and it rendered her incapable of governing.

The drift of Agobard's invective reveals the high expectations he and his contemporaries had come to harbour about the queen and her leading role in the palace and the realm. Apart from what was alleged about the *domina senioris palatii*, in secret or openly – Agobard referred to the accusations of incest and adultery – some said she was playful like a girl, luring those who should preach to play with the *domina ludens*, the frisky empress. Such behaviour went against what the Apostle had written about the qualities of a man to be elected bishop: 'He should be fully in charge of his house, with sons subjected to him and in total chastity; for if someone does not know how to lead his own household, how shall he be capable of cherishing the Church of God?' (I Timothy 3.5).[62] Not only bishops were chided but also Louis, unable to rule his *domus*, including Judith with whom he was jointly in charge of the palace. It was upon this point, after citing St Paul's ominous words with regard to the virtues of a truly episcopal household, that Agobard posed the crucial question: 'If the queen is incapable of governing herself, how then can she guard the honour (*honestas*) of the palace, or how can she effectively handle the reins of the realm?'[63] The implications are clear. Like the king and his bishops, the queen also had her ministry, which included the chastity that ensured the honour of the palace.

From this perspective, 'playing with bishops' was about the most under-mining accusation there was. In his second treatise, the bishop of Lyons defined a good queen as the king's helper in ruling and governing the palace and the realm (*adiutrix in regimine et gubernacione palacii et regni*).[64] Any apparent subservience in this expression is entirely in the eye of the mod-ern beholder, for in other contemporary contexts it was bishops who were characterised as the 'helpers' of the ruler, and, vice versa, the ruler as the *adiutor* of the bishops.[65] A queen who was an *adiutrix* shared in the royal

[61] J. M. H. Smith, 'Gender and ideology in the early Middle Ages', in R. N. Swanson (ed.), *Gender and Christian Religion*, Studies in Church History 35 (Woodbridge, 1998), pp. 51–73 at pp. 59–60.

[62] Agobard, *Liber apologeticus* I, c. 5, ed. Van Acker, pp. 311–12.

[63] Agobard, *Liber apologeticus* I, c. 4, ed. Van Acker, p. 311: 'si qua regina semetipsam regere non novit, quomodo de honestate palatii curam habebit? aut quomodo gubernacula regni diligenter exercet?'

[64] Agobard, *Liber apologeticus* II, c. 2, ed. Van Acker, p. 316.

[65] *Admonitio ad omnes regni ordines* (823–825), *MGH Cap.* I, no. 150, pp. 303–7. For a percipient analysis of this capitulary, see O. Guillot, 'Une *ordinatio* méconnue. Le capitulaire de 823–825', in Godman and Collins (eds.), *Charlemagne's Heir*, pp. 451–86.

and episcopal ministry of governance. Instead, Judith was said to have been loved illegitimately (*inofficiose*) by a man. At first glance this seems to refer to Bernard, but Agobard may also have had Louis in mind, the elderly husband besotted with his young and beautiful queen. Beauty is vain, and a god-fearing woman should be praised, Agobard concluded, citing Proverbs 31.30. In other words, with friend and foe, Judith's levity, youth and beauty were made the key issue.

EXEGESIS

Such mud stuck, and it was Hraban Maur, the abbot of Fulda (d. 856), who rushed to the rescue, dedicating his commentaries on the books of Judith and Esther to the empress in distress. He probably did so between October 830, when Judith had already returned to Aachen, and her final purification in February 831; his dedicatory letter speaks of a queen who had already conquered many of her enemies, but was 'still struggling' and therefore needed to implore God's help.[66] By then Hraban had become an authoritative biblical commentator, the author of a commentary on Kings that had been received favourably, though not without criticism, by Hilduin and other courtiers; Hraban offered it to Louis on the occasion of the latter's visit to Fulda in 832, quite possibly in Judith's presence.[67] By this visit Louis may well have expressed his appreciation of Hraban's staunch support during the first crisis, and he had equal reason to be grateful in 834, when Fulda's abbot once more threw his formidable weight on Louis's side. Still, in the winter of 830/831 Hraban's career as the undisputed authority concerning biblical exegesis, polishing off one commentary after the other, still lay ahead of him. As one of the faithful *Germani* the Astronomer wryly commented on, he stuck his neck out for an empress in distress. Did he quickly compose the commentaries with Judith's plight in mind, or had he written them before, ready to send them off when the occasion arose? It is difficult to say.[68] Hraban's overall aim was to offset the image of Judith as

---

[66] Hraban Maur, *Epistolae*, no. 17a, *MGH Epp.* v, ed. E. Dümmler (Berlin, 1899), pp. 420–1, lines 34–8. On Hraban's commentary for rulers, see M. de Jong, 'The empire as *ecclesia*: Hrabanus Maurus and biblical *historia* for rulers', in Y. Hen and M. Innes (eds.), *The Uses of the Past in the Early Middle Ages* (Cambridge, 2000), pp. 191–226, and de Jong, 'Exegesis for an empress', in E. Cohen and M. de Jong, *Medieval Transformations: Texts, Power and Gifts in Context* (Leiden, 2001), pp. 69–100, with references to older literature; also, with respect to Hraban's perceptions of the priesthood, Lynda Coon, chapter 15 below.

[67] About this visit, see H. P. Wehlt, *Reichsabtei und König, dargestellt am Beispiel der Abtei Lorsch, mit Ausblicken auf Hersfeld, Stablo und Fulda*, Veröffentlichungen des Max-Planck-Instituts für Geschichte 28 (Göttingen, 1970), p. 236.

[68] For a more extensive discussion of this question, see de Jong, 'Exegesis for an empress'.

playful, wanton and unworthy of her exalted office by that of two biblical heroines who saved their people and embodied the *ecclesia* that was, in contemporary terms, also the empire.

According to Hraban, Judith was the empress's namesake, Esther her equal in dignity.[69] Judith and Esther were both intrepid and vengeful women who outwitted kings and generals, making the most of male susceptibility to female attraction. Their biblical tales had an elusive historical setting which gave Hraban, an expert exegete *and* historian, a lot of headaches, but he still managed to turn these two heroines into dutiful Carolingian matrons. Unlike his exegesis of Judith, which remained closely associated with the eponymous empress, Hraban's commentary on Esther became detached from its original recipient. The author rededicated it in 840–841 to Lothar's wife, the empress Irmingard. From the ninth-century point of view, this was a commentary which legitimated an empress, the spouse of a new emperor. The story of Queen Esther was set in the Persian empire, at the court of Ahasuerus and his huge harem. After having repudiated his main wife Vashti, Ahasuerus ordered his eunuchs to bring all the beautiful girls of his realm to Susa, so he might choose a new bride. The king's eye fell on the gorgeous Esther, the ward and niece of Mordecai, one of the Jews exiled to Persia. Mordecai earned the king's favour by uncovering a plot against him, hatched by Haman, the second man at the court. Haman plotted revenge, but Esther made sure that Ahasuerus discovered that it was Haman who had been unfaithful, and who now planned to revenge himself on her people. Haman prostrated himself in front of Esther's couch asking for pardon, a gesture mistaken by the king as an act of seduction. After Haman died at the gallows he had prepared for Mordecai, the latter took his place, and the Jews were allowed to exterminate their enemies. To a Carolingian audience, Ahasuerus was an emperor *par excellence*, for he ruled many *gentes*, including the persecuted Jews; by proxy, Esther became the image of the legitimate empress.[70]

Hraban was on shaky ground when he embarked on his commentaries for Judith. Apart from Jerome's introductions to these biblical books and his typology, there was no reliable patristic model to guide him. But according to authoritative tradition, both Judith and Esther were 'types' of the

---

[69] Hraban Maur, *Epistolae*, no. 17a, ed. Dümmler, pp. 420–1.

[70] F.-R. Erkens, '*Sicut Esther regina*. Die westfränkische Königin als *consors regni*', *Francia* 20 (1993), pp. 15–38. Judith was not yet expressly called a *consors regni*, like her daughter-in-law Ermentrude and many subsequent queens, particularly Ottonian ones, but Hraban's exegesis certainly set the parameters for this interpretation.

church (*ecclesia*), which provided Hraban's main exegetical clue.[71] With some lengthy apology and explanation, the harem-loving king Ahasuerus thus became Christ, the betrothed (*sponsus*) of the victorious *ecclesia*,[72] and his repudiated wife Vashti the synagogue which had been ousted by the church;[73] Mordecai was cast as the preachers of the faith, especially St Paul,[74] and so on. The commentary should be read by its recipient at two different levels. On the one hand, there was the biblical narrative, but on the other – and more importantly – the spiritual and allegorical interpretation which transformed the former into a more meaningful story that belonged not to the past but to the present, and to the future, in terms of salvation: the *ecclesia* of the 820s had become synonymous with the Frankish empire.

This is not to say that Hraban wrote direct political commentary of any kind. His ultimate aim was to show how the *ecclesia* moved inexorably towards salvation, vanquishing its enemies. By implication, the same held true of the empress Judith who was Esther's 'equal in dignity'. Yet in passing, many of Hraban's exegetical explanations could be read as reactions to current events, at least for those who read closely and saw which shoe fitted whom. Haman was of course the *typus* of the Spiritual Enemy and of Satan who threatened order within the *ecclesia*. At the literal level, Hraban presented Esther as a model queen who had court etiquette at her fingertips and made the most of it in her deft and humble intercession with Ahasuerus. The commentary on Esther abounds with comments on the proper behaviour of a royal consort, and therefore has the flavour of a veritable 'queen's mirror' (*speculum reginae*). Yet the kind of exegesis Hraban adhered to, faithfully following the 'footsteps of the fathers', had its own rules. Its crux was the transformation of the literal meaning of biblical history into the spiritual truth of the victorious *ecclesia*. The synagogue had been superseded by the church; the preachers (*praedicatores*) and authoritative interpreters of scripture (*sancti doctores*) had prevailed over the Jews, the pagans and, above all, the heretics and schismatics. Within this traditional exegetical frame of reference, Hraban identified the empress Judith with two biblical heroines who counted as *typus* of the church.

---

[71] Cf. Isidore of Seville, *Allegoriae quaedam scripturae sacrae*, *PL* 83, cols. 99–130, which along with Jerome's prefaces to biblical books served as a typological 'Who's who' in the Old and New Testament. See *PL* 122, col. 116A: 'Judith et Esther typum Ecclesiae gestant, hostes fidei puniunt, ac populum Dei ab interitu eruunt.'

[72] Hraban Maur, *Expositio in librum Esther*, c. 1, *PL* 109, cols. 637D–638A.

[73] Hraban Maur, *Expositio in librum Esther*, c. 2, col. 642B.

[74] *Expositio in librum Esther*, c. 3, col. 646B. For a more detailed analysis of the exegesis involved, see De Jong, 'Exegesis for an empress'.

Given that by the 820s the *ecclesia* had become an expression that denoted the Christian polity,[75] this was powerful ammunition on Judith's behalf, even if it was fired obliquely. In Hraban's two prefatory dedications to the empress, no holds needed to be barred by the rules of exegesis, however. An acrostic poem was incorporated in the image of Judith as a ruler blessed by the hand of God; in his prose preface Hraban further underlined the empress's legitimacy, this time by calling himself 'a particle of the people committed to you by God'.[76] He also referred to the incessant prayer he, abbot of Fulda, and his monks offered on behalf of 'you, as well as your lord and son',[77] which suggests a heightened prayer activity at a time when the crisis still had not quite subsided. Prayer mattered deeply, as clerics liked to remind their rulers, but in Hraban's prose, there was no note of admonishment. Judith was hailed as a queen worthy of this indispensable support.

A topic Hraban pointedly avoided was beauty. This the empress had in common with her biblical namesake Judith, and most of all with Esther who had been chosen by Ahasuerus for her looks. Hraban skirted this delicate issue, even in the guise of physical beauty being transformed into its moral counterpart. His commentary on the bride show in Susa is telling.[78] The stunningly beautiful (*pulchra nimis et decoris facie*) orphan Esther, niece and ward of Mordecai, came to Susa to compete with many beautiful virgins (*multae pulchrae virgines*) in a bride show managed by eunuchs. Every single item of this passage is assigned its spiritual meaning: Esther is the *ecclesia gentium* ousting the synagogue, the parents' death is the error and superstition of the heathens, Mordecai stands for the apostles (*doctores gentium*), and the eunuch Egeus embodies the monastic order, both male and female. Beauty is nowhere in sight, for by 830/831 this had become a dangerous quality in a queen, be it in Aachen or in Susa. Instead, as Paolo Delogu has pointed out, Hraban stressed that Judith was the legitimate consort of the emperor, who fully and rightly shared the burdens

---

[75] N. Staubach, '*Cultus divinus* und karolingische Reform', *Frühmittelalterliche Studien* 18 (1984), pp. 546–81; de Jong, 'The empire as *ecclesia*'.

[76] Hraban Maur, *Epistolae*, no. 17a, ed. Dümmler, p. 420, lines 28–9: 'nos etiam quantulacumque pars plebis a Deo vobis commissae sub pietate vestra degentes'; Geneva, Bibliothèque Publique et Universitaire, lat. 22. Cf. E. Sears, 'Louis the Pious as *Miles Christi*: the dedicatory image in Hrabanus Maurus' *De laudibus sancti crucis*', in Godman and Collins (eds.), *Charlemagne's Heir*, p. 620; M. Perrin, 'La représentation figurée de César-Louis le Pieux chez Raban Maur en 835: religion et idéologie', *Francia* 24/1 (1997), pp. 39–64.

[77] Hraban Maur, *Epistolae*, no. 17a, ed. Dümmler, p. 420.

[78] Hraban Maur, *Expositio in librum Esther*, c. 3, *PL* 109, col. 645C: 'Repulsa igitur Judaea a consortio regali, diversae gentes ac diversae personae singularum gentium ex diversis partibus mundi ad societatem regiae dignitatis per praedicatores sanctos, qui ministri fuerint evangelici verbi, adducebatur.'

of government.[79] The image of God's hand above her head expressed this, but also the exegesis of Esther replacing Vashti as Ahasuerus' favourite wife. Vashti was 'excluded from the royal bed, that is, from partnership with God (*consortium Dei*)'. This refers to Vashti as the type of the synagogue ousted by Esther, the *ecclesia*, but it was clearly also Judith's role as imperial consort (*consortium regale*) which was on Hraban's mind when he elucidated the Book of Esther for his empress and the courtly audience surrounding her. This was one of the reasons why this particular text was deemed suitable to be rededicated to a later empress, Irmingard,[80] and why Esther became a model for future Carolingian queens: Hraban's commentary offered an implicit *speculum reginae* portraying a queen who allegorically represented the *ecclesia*, for jointly with her husband, she ruled the Christian polity.

AACHEN AND SUSA

By a few words the Astronomer turned the brief and equivocal passage from the *Royal Frankish Annals* describing Louis the Pious's second marriage, which only stressed 'choice', into something more specific. The notion of daughters being brought for his inspection 'from everywhere' finally provides the Carolingian bride show with a location: the palace at Aachen. It is the Astronomer's text, rather than the *Royal Frankish Annals*, which has convinced historians that a Byzantine custom of selecting imperial brides had found its way to the west. The words *undecumque adductas* indeed evoke an image of many potential brides travelling to Aachen to be paraded in front of Louis, but it was not Constantinople that was on the Astronomer's mind. Instead it was Susa. Just as Thegan borrowed a turn of phrase from Luke's Gospel[81] when he wrote about Judith's marriage, the Astronomer has the Book of Esther on his mind. When King Ahasuerus repudiated his wife Vashti, his courtiers (*pueri regis et ministri*) said:

Let there be fair young virgins sought for the king, and let the king appoint officers in all the provinces of his kingdom, that they may gather together all the fair young virgins until Sushan the palace. (Quaerantur regi puellae virgines ac speciosae, et constituantur, qui considerent per universas provincias puellas speciosas et virgines et *adducant* eas ad citivatem Susan. Esther 2.2–3).

---

[79] P. Delogu, '"Consors regni": un problema carolingo', *Bolletino dell'Istituto Storico per il Medioveo e Archivo Muratoriano* 76 (1964), pp. 85–98; Erkens, '*Sicut Esther regina*'.

[80] Hraban Maur, *Epistolae*, no. 46, ed. Dümmler, p. 500, lines 31–3; Hraban rededicated the commentary on Esther to Lothar's spouse Irmingard in 841, when he had declared himself Lothar's faithful man. For the political context of Hraban's exegesis, see de Jong, 'The empire as *ecclesia*'.

[81] Luke 1.27: 'et nomen virginis'.

This search throughout the kingdom yielded Esther, the ward and niece of the Jew Mordecai, who was taken into Ahasuerus' harem: 'And the king loved Esther above all women, and she obtained grace and favour in his sight more than all the virgins; so that he set the royal crown upon her head, and made her queen instead of Vashti' (Esther 2.17). Was the association with Susa and the brides 'brought from everywhere' for Ahasuerus' inspection a deliberate one? If not, this automatic association of the empress Judith with Queen Esther is all the more revealing. The Astronomer was a skilled author who wrote for a sophisticated audience capable of understanding oblique and fleeting biblical references; this was a world which had scripture at its fingertips. The connection between the empress Judith and Queen Esther had not yet gained currency at the time of Judith's marriage in 819, but it certainly had in the early 840s, when the Astronomer looked back on the empress's turbulent career. The two intervening decades saw the emergence of an increasingly articulate discourse on the position of the queen within the Carolingian polity. The allegorical exegesis of Old Testament history played a key role in this process, for it enabled commentators such as Hraban to transform the history of Esther into a persuasive and influential reflection on the nature of contemporary Christian queenship. Hraban's exegesis of the story of Esther stressed the interconnectedness of the queen and her people, be it Israel saved by Esther's courageous intervention, or the Christian people committed to the empress Judith by God. From a ninth-century perspective, the biblical history of the bride show in Susa conveyed a clear message: earthly rulers may choose their queens, but ultimately, both kings and queens are God's choice.[82]

---

[82] I am grateful to Barbara H. Rosenwein and Rosamond McKitterick for their supportive comments on earlier versions of this text, and to Thomas F. X. Noble for allowing me to use his working translations of Thegan, the Astronomer and Ermoldus Nigellus (the latter by Carey Dolores Fleiner, with annotations by Noble).

CHAPTER 15

'What is the Word if not semen?' Priestly bodies in Carolingian exegesis

Lynda Coon

'What is the Word if not semen?'[1] Even in a world used to artists dipping the crucifix in urine and bedecking the Madonna with buffalo dung, the question still startles. It is asked in *Explanations of Leviticus* (*c.* 820) by Hraban Maur (*c.* 780–856), abbot of the great monastery of Fulda and later archbishop of Mainz, but a writer dismissed by Henri de Lubac, a Jesuit scholar of Christian exegesis, as lacking in 'profound originality'. According to de Lubac, Hraban's towering pile of biblical commentaries represent no more than 'huge, colorless compilations'.[2] In a similar vein, the anthropologist Mary Douglas observes that 'Leviticus is the Bible book to which many little Jewish children are first introduced. Friends have confided that this early confrontation has put them off the book for life.'[3] This chapter compares one off-putting book of the priestly Torah with its allegedly drab Carolingian commentary.[4] While Hraban's *Expositiones in Leviticum*

---

[1] *PL* 108, col. 403: 'Quid est sermo, nisi semen?'

[2] Henri de Lubac, *Exégèse médiévale: Les quatre sens de l'écriture*, 2 vols. (Paris, 1959), citation from the English translation of vol. 1 by Mark Sebanc, *Medieval Exegesis: The Four Senses of Scripture* (Grand Rapids, 1998), p. 106. De Lubac does admit Hraban's importance as a transmitter of important exegetical traditions. For a brief overview of Hraban's life, see Franz Brunhölzl, *Histoire de la littérature latine de moyen âge I/2: L'époque carolingienne* (Turnhout, 1991), pp. 84–98. The first of Hraban's works on the Pentateuch, the commentary on Genesis, was finished *c.* 822 (Brunhölzl, *Histoire*, p. 93). The dating for Hraban's most important biblical commentaries is *c.* 818–822, the time when he was working under Abbot Eigil of Fulda (see M. Perrin (ed.), *Rabani Mauri, In Honorem Sanctae Crucis*, CCCM 100 (Turnhout, 1997), p. vi). The chronology and the manuscript tradition of these Torah commentaries are notoriously problematic; see Mayke de Jong, 'The Empire as ecclesia: Hrabanus Maurus and biblical historia for rulers', in Yitzhak Hen and Matthew Innes (eds.), *The Uses of the Past in the Early Middle Ages* (Cambridge, 2000), pp. 191–226. De Jong (p. 193, n. 5) discusses the manuscript transmission of Hraban's exegetical works. The seventeenth-century edition by George Colvenerius (adapted by J. Migne in the *PL* version (vol. 108)) remains the standard scholarly version of Hraban's corpus as there still is no critical text available.

[3] Mary Douglas, *Leviticus as Literature* (Oxford, 1999), pp. 14–15.

[4] For the full text of Hraban's *Expositiones*, see *PL* 108, cols. 247–586. For a treatment of issues of purity and defilement in Hraban's interpretation of Leviticus, see Raffaele Savigni, 'Purità rituale e ridefinizione del sacro nella cultura carolingia: l'interpretazione del Levitico e dell'Epistola agli Ebrei', *Annali di Storia dell'Esegesi* 13 (1) (1996), pp. 229–55.

is largely a redaction of the great patristic interpreters of this third book of Torah, his version also speaks to the sacred gender of Fulda's virginal men. The topic has significant implications, however, since Hraban's exegesis of Leviticus had the ultimate goal of justifying priestly authority over the princely powers, a notion that later informed the reform papacy and church–state relations in the medieval world.[5] The seemingly esoteric explication of an ancient Hebrew text also contributed to conceptualising the Frankish kingdom as the New Israel.[6]

In Hraban's inventive exegesis, Christian preachers are receptacles of God's semen, hence the equation of the Word of God with human ejaculate. Simultaneously, Christ's ministers of the Word are inseminators of other men: 'When the Word is emitted in an orderly fashion, the hearing mind – like a conceiving uterus – is impregnated for the offspring of good works.'[7] For Hraban, the worldly authority of the chaste Christian priest stems from a sensual relationship with Christ enacted within the all-male environment of the cloister, where mentor–disciple bonds flourished as a kind of earthly counterpart to a God-centred, spiritual eroticism. Hraban's allegorical reading of priestly bodies in Leviticus thus offers the modern gender theorist a glimpse into how one Carolingian churchman preserved and redeployed some of the most provocative Christian and rabbinical exegetical traditions concerning male mystical pregnancies. Hraban's decision to focus on male defilement in Leviticus compels his reader to understand semen not as a seed-metaphor, but as a bodily fluid. In Hraban's hands, Leviticus becomes not merely a fossilised text of arcane Hebrew praxis, but a theological blueprint for the ritual process of men impregnating other men through the agency of the Word.

Hraban's *Expositiones* also leads us to a very different interpretation of Carolingian masculinity than do more traditional studies of diplomacy,

---

[5] For a discussion of the influence of Leviticus on the medieval papal reform movement, see Dyan Elliott, *Fallen Bodies: Pollution, Sexuality, and Demonology in the Middle Ages* (Philadelphia, 1999). Elliott notes that the Levitican background to medieval Christian notions of clerical purity and reform 'continued to enjoy a covert and almost eerie afterlife' (p. 6).

[6] For early medieval ideologies of the 'New Israel', see Mary Garrison, 'The Franks as New Israel? Evidence for an identity from Pippin to Charlemagne', in Hen and Innes (eds.), *Uses of the Past*, pp. 114–61.

[7] *PL* 108, col. 403: 'Quid est sermo, nisi semen, qui dum ordinate mittitur, audientis mens, quasi concipientis uterus, ad boni operis prolem fecundatur.' Here, Hraban draws on the exegetical work of Gregory the Great, *Moralia in Iob*, CCSL 143B, pp. 1164–5. Conrad Leyser (*Authority and Asceticism from Augustine to Gregory the Great* (Oxford, 2000), p. 168) discusses Gregory the Great's views on the symbolic relationship between fluxes of semen and speech. See also his 'Nocturnal emission and the limits of celibacy in the early Middle Ages', in D. M. Hadley (ed.), *Masculinity in Medieval Europe* (London, 1999), pp. 121–42.

honour codes and lineage. Biblical exegesis, a largely untapped source for cultural constructions of masculinity, is an excellent starting point for any revised paradigm of medieval manhood.[8] Exegetical texts often deal quite explicitly with issues of male defilement, the body and sexuality, and Hraban's *Expositiones in Leviticum* is no exception.[9] Hraban's commentary on Leviticus enables its reader to revisit some very familiar themes in Frankish history in a new way, including the gender dynamics of the all-male cloister, the contribution of sacred gender to the Carolingian ideology of 'New Israel', and the Carolingian appropriation of both patristic and rabbinic interpretations of Torah. Finally, this particular biblical commentary is crucial for understanding how Carolingian monastic leaders used erotic and mystical imagery to sustain church hierarchy.

HRABAN: 'A FOURSQUARE MAN' OF SCRIPTURE

Anticipating de Lubac's later opinion of him, Hraban once confessed with characteristic monastic humility that he was a little man (*homunculus*), who wrote little biblical commentaries (*commentarioli*).[10] In fact, his over seventy homilies on the Bible are stunningly long and arduously organised masterworks of medieval exegesis.[11] In spite of his own critical assessment (and even harsher criticism at the hands of many historians of exegesis), Hraban's calculated interpolations of patristic exegesis are artistic, playful and, at times, even shocking. For example, the ritual oven (*clibanus*) used by Hebrew priests to bake sacrifices is likened by the abbot to the Virgin's

---

[8] For the theoretical and historiographical background to the study of medieval masculinity, see Clare A. Lees (ed.), *Medieval Masculinities: Regarding Men in the Middle Ages* (Minneapolis, 1994). Lees ('Introduction', p. xv) underscores the importance of studying medieval masculinity beyond the more traditional focus on '"hegemonic males" – the kings, princes, lawmakers, and so forth'. See also Julia M. H. Smith, 'Gender and ideology in the early Middle Ages', in R. N. Swanson (ed.), *Gender and Christian Religion*, Studies in Church History 35 (Woodbridge, 1998), pp. 51–73.

[9] Early medieval penitential literature is also an excellent source for male defilement and sexuality. See Allen J. Frantzen, *Before the Closet: Same-Sex Love from Beowulf to Angels in America* (Chicago, 1998), esp. 'Introduction: straightforward', pp. 1–29.

[10] Epistle 10, *MGH Epp.* v, p. 396: 'mirari me, quare ad tale studium vilem et inertem homunculum eligeres'. Here, Hraban confesses to Bishop Freculph of Lisieux to whom the *Expositiones* is dedicated, that he was shocked to be chosen for such a pious task. In his Epistle 28 to Lothar (*MGH Epp.* v, p. 443), Hraban humbly describes his commentaries as being nothing more than 'little works (*opuscula*)'.

[11] Franz Brunhölzl, 'Zur geistigen Bedeutung des Hrabanus Maurus', in Raymund Kottje and Harald Zimmermann (eds.), *Hrabanus Maurus: Lehrer, Abt, und Bischof* (Mainz, 1982), p. 5, reminds us that being a 'compiler' in the medieval era was not necessarily considered an inferior vocation. Compilers performed the almost impossible by taking disorderly, incoherent material and reordering it in an accessible manner.

womb, which cooked the flesh of a sacrificial Jesus.[12] Hraban muses extensively on male chastity as an important offering on the altar of heaven, and
asserts that the ritual purity of altar servants is most effectively preserved
by donning spiritual chastity belts.[13] A study of how Hraban reshaped and
reorganised the patristic corpus on Leviticus within the new arena of Carolingian monasticism reveals a creative and challenging exegetical mind.

Hraban's unique and seemingly indefatigable ability to decipher some
of the most complex writings of Holy Scripture for both royal and clerical
audiences stemmed from his own experience as a member of the intensely
erudite and privileged circle associated with Alcuin, abbot of St Martin's
at Tours.[14] In *c.* 801, the young Hraban's monastic mentors at Fulda sent
him to join the select company of the biblical exegetes working under
Alcuin's tutelage.[15] In the dedicatory poem to his first work, *In honorem
sanctae crucis* (*c.* 814), Hraban elaborates on the reasons behind this scholarly
pilgrimage – Alcuin was to instruct the young monk in the difficult arts
of poetic metre, ethics and philosophy.[16] At Tours, Hraban acquired his
first taste of the precocious court culture of Charlemagne's reign, wherein
gifted students ferreted out tidbits of esoteric knowledge from a variety

---

[12] *PL* 108, col. 259.
[13] *PL* 108, col. 252 (on male chastity as offering) and cols. 328–9 (on male chastity belts). Hraban's male chastity belts are discussed below.
[14] On Hraban's intended audiences, see Philippe Le Maitre, 'Les méthodes exégétiques de Raban Maur', in Claude Lepelley *et al.* (eds.), *Haut moyen-âge: culture, éducation et société, études offertes à Pierre Riché* (Paris, 1990), p. 344, and Mayke de Jong, 'Old law and new-found power: Hrabanus Maurus and the Old Testament', in J. W. Drijvers and A. A. MacDonald (eds.), *Centres of Learning and Location in Pre-Modern Europe and the Near East* (New York and Cologne, 1995), p. 165. Mary Carruthers (*The Book of Memory: A Study of Memory in Medieval Culture* (Cambridge, 1990), pp. 175–6) notes how Hraban's *De universo*, 'a promptbook for memoria', aided ecclesiastical administrators in their recollection of sacred texts they had studied as young men.
[15] For the chronology of Hraban's life, see Wilhelm Wattenbach and Wilhelm Levison, *Deutschlands Geschichtsquellen im Mittelalter: Vorzeit und Karolinger* VI (Weimar, 1990), pp. 698–705. For a discussion of Alcuin's work within the larger context of the history of the Bible, see Ernst Würthwein, *Der Text des Alten Testaments* (Stuttgart, 1988), citation from the English translation by Erroll F. Rhodes, *The Text of the Old Testament* (Grand Rapids, 1995), p. 98.
[16] CCCM 100, p. 5. Hraban addresses this dedicatory poem to St Martin of Tours (*pater*) and writes the verses in the voice of his master, Alcuin:

> Nempe ego cum fueram custos humilisque minister
> Istius Ecclesiae, dogmata sacra legens,
> Hunc puerum docui divini famine verbi
> Ethicae monitis et sophiae studiis.
> Ipse quidem Francus genere est, atque incola silvae
> Bochoniae, huc missus discere verba Dei.
> Abbas namque suus, Fuldensis rector ouilis,
> Illum huc direxit ad tua tecta, pater,
> Quod mecum legeret metri scholasticus artem,
> Scripturam et sacram rite pararet ovans.

of manuscript sources, including Anglo-Saxon *computus*, Jewish history and antiquities, and Roman poetry. Hraban also was part of a linguistically erotic – yet simultaneously ascetic – world wherein celibate men exchanged love poems and called each other by amorous epithets.[17] Hraban, the 'young raven' (Germanic *Hrafn*; Latin, *corvulus*) was the favourite of his teacher, Alcuin (*Albinus*)[18] (Fig. 13).

The tender relationship between Alcuin and his little *corvulus* was short-lived, however. By 804, Alcuin was dead, and Hraban was back at Fulda, administering its famous monastic school and eventually becoming abbot (*c.* 822–842). As custodian of this great intellectual centre of the eastern half of the Carolingian empire, Hraban oversaw the material and spiritual welfare of about 600 monks, supervised thirty sacred building projects, and amplified the *cultus* of Fulda's saintly founder, Boniface.[19] He also extended

Translation:

> As everyone knows when I was a custodian and lowly minister
> Reading the holy dogma of our own church,
> I taught that boy with hunger for the divine word,
> By means of advice for ethics and instruction for wisdom.
> Indeed he himself is a Frank by birth,
> And also an inhabitant of the Buchenwald forest,
> Sent to this place to learn the words of God.
> For his own abbot, the rector of the flock at Fulda,
> Directed him to this place to your dwellings, O Father,
> So that he as a student might read with me the art of meter,
> And so that he – triumphing – might be prepared, with suitable ceremony,
>   for Holy Scripture.

For the dating of *In honorem sanctae crucis*, see Michele Camillo Ferrari, Il *'Liber sanctae crucis' di Rabano Mauro: Testo, immagine, contesto* (Bern, 1999), p. 17.

[17] Discussed by John Boswell, *Christianity, Social Tolerance, and Homosexuality* (Chicago, 1980), pp. 188–94, and by Stephen C. Jaeger, *Ennobling Love: In Search of a Lost Sensibility* (Philadelphia, 1999), pp. 42–50.

[18] In recognition of Hraban's special status, Alcuin added the prestigious cognomen Maurus to that of Hraban in memory of Benedict of Nursia's most beloved disciple, Saint Maurus. See Hraban, Epistle 14 (*MGH Epp.* v, p. 403): 'M litteram Mauri nomen exprimentem, quod meus magister beatae memoriae Albinus mihi indidit'. For a discussion of Hraban's name, consult Maria Rissel, *Rezeption antiker und patristischer Wissenschaft bei Hrabanus Maurus: Studien zur karolingischen Geistesgeschichte*, Lateinische Sprache und Literatur des Mittelalters 7 (Frankfurt, 1976), p. 8, and J. M. Wallace-Hadrill, *The Frankish Church* (Oxford, 1983), pp. 199, 315.

[19] Rudolf of Fulda, *Miracula sanctorum in fuldenses ecclesias translatorum*, *MGH SS* xv/1, p. 340: 'Aliorum autem sanctorum reliquias de diversis partibus orbis plurimas congregavit atque in oratoriis, quae tempore sui regiminis numero 30 construxerat, et ab episcopis, in quorum diocesi fuerant, dedicari fecerat, honorifice collocavit.' For a discussion of the size of the monastic community, see Karl Schmid, 'Mönchslisten und Klosterkonvent von Fulda zur Zeit der Karolinger', in Karl Schmid (ed.), *Die Klostergemeinschaft von Fulda im früheren Mittelalter* II/2 (Munich, 1978), pp. 612, 632. Bat-Sheva Albert discusses Hraban's role in the promulgation of Fulda as pilgrimage site in her *Le Pèlerinage à l'époque carolingienne*, Bibliothèque de la Revue d'Histoire Ecclésiastique 82 (Brussels, 1999), pp. 198, 215.

MAVRVS·ALBINVS· S͞CS MAR   TINVS

13 Alcuin presenting Hraban Maur and his work to St Martin of Tours. Hraban Maur,
De laudibus sanctae crucis, Vat. Reg. Lat. 124, fol. 2v.

the reputation of this Bonifatian house by attracting future luminaries of
the Carolingian period, including Lupus, Rudolf and Walafrid, to study
there. By the end of his abbacy (842), Fulda's scriptorium housed forty-
six texts of the Bible, classical histories and a variety of patristic writers,
including Origen of Alexandria (c. 185–254).[20] Hraban's later years were

[20] Wallace-Hadrill, *Frankish Church*, pp. 336–7. See also Wattenbach-Levison, *Deutschlands Geschichtsquellen* VI, p. 688 n. 104, for the extensive bibliography on Fulda's library. Hraban himself acknowledges in several places his debt to Origen's commentaries: Epistle 5 (*MGH Epp.* v, p. 388), Epistle
10 (*MGH Epp.* v, p. 396), Epistle 26 (*MGH Epp.* v, p. 440), Epistle 28 (*MGH Epp.* v, p. 443), and

spent as an exiled hermit-scholar, holed up in a cramped *cellula* at Fulda's mountain refuge, the Petersberg (842–847). Then, in 847, Louis the German appointed him custodian of the *sedes* of Mainz, the place of his birth. The former abbot remained in that position until his death in 856.[21]

Hraban's reputation as stellar biblical exegete made him famous and thereby served to protect him when he backed the Carolingian emperor Lothar I against the victorious Louis the German during the civil wars of the sons of Louis the Pious. In Carolingian Europe, biblical hermeneutics gained the practitioner a special kind of political authority. In this recondite environment, Hebrew scripture in particular provided the framework for a new political ideology of sacred kingship, an ideology based not only on the historical books of the Hebrew Bible, such as Kings and Chronicles, but also on its most difficult legal and priestly sections.[22] Even Louis the German, Hraban's one-time enemy, made the pilgrimage to the Petersberg to consult the holy man on matters of scripture, for the ex-abbot's commentaries continued to be prized commodities even after his exile in 842. Louis, as Mayke de Jong observes, remained one of Hraban's 'best customers'.[23] Hraban provided royal politicians with helpful Hebrew models for emulation by drawing on his vast knowledge of biblical kingship and military history. For royal women, as de Jong argues, Hraban allegorised the heroic virtues of Esther and Judith.[24] As the expert on Leviticus, Hraban also settled disputes over incest taboos.[25] This kind of wide-ranging exegetical

---

Epistle 44 (*MGH Epp.* v, 493–4). Hraban also emphasises that Origen was not among the 'catholic' fathers of the church ('Doctores enim ipsi omnes catholici fuerant excepto Origene', Epistle 23, *MGH Epp.* v, p. 430). Fulda possessed a late ninth-century manuscript of a fragment of Origen's most controversial work, *Peri Archon*, discussed by Robert G. Babcock, 'Häresie und Bibliothek: Die Fuldaer Handschrift von Origenes' *Peri Archon*', in Gangolf Schrimpf (ed.), *Kloster Fulda in der Welt der Karolinger und Ottonen* (Frankfurt, 1996), pp. 299–313. Babcock believes that the manuscript post-dates Hraban's death; yet the abbot himself was keenly interested in Origen's exegetical corpus.

[21] On Hraban's exile and subsequent election to the archbishopric of Mainz, see de Jong, 'Old law and new-found power', pp. 168–9; Rissel, *Rezeption antiker und patristischer Wissenschaft bei Hrabanus Maurus*, p. 14; and M. Perrin, CCCM 100, p. vii.

[22] Avrom Saltman, 'Hebrew scholarship in the Carolingian Renaissance', introduction to his *Pseudo-Jerome: Quaestiones on the Book of Samuel* (Leiden, 1975), p. 3.

[23] De Jong, 'Old law and new-found power', p. 168. See also Bernhard Bischoff, 'Bücher am Hofe Ludwigs des Deutschen', in his *Mittelalterliche Studien* III (Stuttgart, 1981), pp. 187–8.

[24] See Mayke de Jong, 'Bride-shows revisited' in this volume and 'Exegesis for an empress', in Esther Cohen and Mayke de Jong (eds.), *Medieval Transformations: Texts, Power, and Gifts* (Leiden, 2001), pp. 69–100. Elizabeth Ward, 'Caesar's wife: the career of the Empress Judith', in Peter Godman and Roger Collins (eds.), *Charlemagne's Heir: New Perspectives on the Reign of Louis the Pious, 814–840* (Oxford, 1990), p. 224, and Elizabeth Sears, 'Louis the Pious as *Miles Christi*: the dedicatory image in Hrabanus Maurus' *De laudibus sanctae crucis*', in Godman and Collins (eds.), *Charlemagne's Heir*, pp. 620–1.

[25] De Jong, 'Old law and new-found power', p. 171.

skill secured Hraban's eminence as one of the most important writers for the monasteries and pastoral workers of the north.[26]

Yet the degree to which Hraban's celebrated biblical acumen included a systematic knowledge of Judaism is a crucial and controversial concern. Indeed, scholars of Judaica have been much more willing than have many of their colleagues in early medieval Christian studies to attribute to the abbot a rigorous grasp of Judaism and its extra-biblical traditions and texts.[27] Avrom Saltman, in a ground-breaking essay on Hebrew scholarship during the Carolingian period, believes that both Theodulf of Orléans (c. 750–821) and Hraban had access to Aggadic and Talmudic materials through Jewish texts and/or Jewish converts to Christianity.[28] Saltman hypothesises that Theodulf attempted to re-create a Latin version of the *Hexapla*, Origen's sixfold Hebrew-Greek edition of scripture. For this purpose, Theodulf may have brought with him to Orléans a Jewish scholar who had converted to Christianity, who could be consulted on the most intricate aspects of ritual practice and biblical interpretation.[29] As Bernhard Bischoff argues, finding a scholar of Hebrew in Francia was a much more likely scenario than was chancing upon a Greek linguist.[30]

Hraban, the second great Judaica scholar of the Carolingian empire after Theodulf, 'may well have attended Claudius's [of Turin] lectures on the Pentateuch at the Court of Louis the Pious'.[31] Claudius of Turin was another important interpreter of the Torah, who apparently used Jewish exegetical and Talmudic sources.[32] Hraban himself claims to have conferred with a 'certain Hebrew of modern times, who was well-versed in the

---

[26] Le Maitre, 'Les méthodes exégétiques de Raban Maur', p. 343.

[27] A notable exception is the work of scholar of early medieval Christian exegesis Jean-Louis Verstrepen, 'Raban Maur et le Judaïsme dans son commentaire sur les quatre livres des rois', *Revue Mabillon* 7 (1996), pp. 23–55.

[28] Saltman, 'Hebrew scholarship in the Carolingian Renaissance', and 'Rabanus Maurus and the Pseudo-Hieronymian Quaestiones Hebraicae in Libros Regum et Paralipomenon', *Harvard Theological Review* 66 (1973), pp. 43–75. Jean-Louis Verstrepen ('Raban Maur et le Judaïsme', p. 45) hypothesises that Hraban (or a member of his intellectual circle) was well acquainted both with rabbinical exegetical traditions and with Jewish communities in the Frankish empire of his own day.

[29] Saltman, 'Hebrew scholarship in the Carolingian Renaissance', pp. 6, 18. See also Bat-Sheva Albert, '*Adversus Iudaeos* in the Carolingian Empire', in Ora Limor and Guy G. Stroumsa (eds.), *Ancient and Medieval Polemics between Jews and Christians* (Tübingen, 1996), pp. 119–42. Albert (p. 121) discusses how Theodulf's Hebraeus added marginal notations (e.g., *Hebraeum non habet*) to Jerome's translations at each point where the Hebrew and Latin appeared not to correspond.

[30] 'The study of foreign languages in the Middle Ages', *Mittelalterliche Studien* 2 (Stuttgart, 1967), p. 234.

[31] Albert, '*Adversus Iudaeos*', p. 128.

[32] Albert, '*Adversos Iudaeos*', pp. 124–8, deals with Claudius' knowledge of Judaism and his Jewish contacts.

law', but the precise meaning of this rather cryptic phrase is less clear.[33] Furthermore, in his commentary on the Gospel of Matthew, Hraban discusses the possible meaning of an Aramaic word, *racha*, which he interprets as indignation.[34] Even if Hraban did not consult a Jew personally, his writings do display a familiarity with Jewish culture that goes beyond standard Christian allegory.[35]

The willingness of the Carolingians Theodulf and Hraban to delve into Jewish exegesis of scripture parallels the biblical work of their patristic predecessors, Origen and Jerome (*c*. 345–420). And, as Saltman observes, after Jerome, 'there had been a steep decline both in the knowledge of Hebrew and in the interest in Jewish exegesis'.[36] Hraban would have known the famous *Vita* of Origen through Latin translations of Eusebius of Caesarea's *Ecclesiastical History* (book 6), and it is quite possible that he purposefully imitated the pedagogical style of the neoplatonist. Both Origen and Hraban achieved reputations as brilliant teachers who specialised in interpreting labyrinthine passages from Hebrew scripture. Origen, an Egyptian who lived and taught in Palestine in the same century when the *Mishnah* was produced, may have had hired Jews to transcribe his oral homilies. He probably attended synagogue services, and certainly had his own personal Hebrew teacher. Aside from Jerome, he was the best-versed patristic writer in the Judaism of late antiquity.[37] Like Hraban, Origen claims to have consulted a 'certain Hebrew' when he was composing his commentary on Isaiah.[38] Both men specialised in the delivery of oral homilies on

[33] 'Praetera Ebrei cuiusdam, modernis temporibus in legis scientia non ignobiliter eruditi', Epistle 14 (*MGH Epp*. v, p. 403). The secondary bibliography for the identity of Hraban's Hebrew is quite extensive and divided. See de Jong, 'Old law and new-found power', pp. 172ff.; Bernhard Blumenkranz, *Juifs et chrétiens dans le monde occidental 430–1096* (Paris, 1960), pp. 48ff.; Saltman, 'Hebrew scholarship in the Carolingian Renaissance', pp. 24ff.; and Albert, '*Adversus Iudaeos*', pp. 128ff.

[34] *Racha*, an Aramaic term of abuse, appears in Matthew 5.22. For Hraban's interpretation of *racha*, see *PL* 107, col. 279: '*Racha* enim proprie interjectio est Hebraicae linguae, non voce aliquid significans, sed indignantis animi motum exprimens.' Hraban's use of the word *racha* is noted by Solomon Katz, *The Jews in the Visigothic and Frankish Kingdoms of Spain and Gaul* (Cambridge, 1937), p. 70.

[35] See Saltman, 'Rabanus Maurus and the Pseudo-Hieronymian', p. 45, and de Jong, 'Old law and new-found power', p. 173.

[36] 'Rabanus Maurus and the Pseudo-Hieronymian', p. 44.

[37] N. R. M. De Lange, *Origen and the Jews: Studies in Jewish–Christian Relations in Third-Century Palestine* (Cambridge, 1976), pp. 1–39. See also David J. Halperin, 'Origen, Ezekiel's Merkabah, and the Ascension of Moses', *Church History* 50 (1981), pp. 261–75.

[38] '. . . quemdam Hebraeum', cited by De Lange, p. 25. M. L. W. Laistner once noted that several of Hraban's comments concerning his Jewish informants are exactly the same as earlier statements made by patristic authors, including Jerome. See 'Some early medieval commentators on the Old Testament', in Chester G. Starr (ed.), *The Intellectual Heritage of the Early Middle Ages: Select Essays by M. L. W. Laistner* (Ithaca, 1957), p. 182.

Torah, which were then transcribed by teams of copyists.[39] The two exegetes intended these texts to serve as teaching tools, and their audiences included both lay and clerical hearers and readers. Hraban's attraction to the controversial corpus of Origen reflects what Jean Leclercq once called the 'renewed Origenism' of the ninth century.[40] For Carolingian Benedictines, Origen embodied the ideal qualities of monk and spiritual sage.[41]

The lifework of both Origen and his Carolingian emulator, Hraban, testifies to late antique and early medieval Jewish–Christian intellectual interactions wherein 'convergence is as possible as divergence'.[42] As Saltman emphasises: 'a fair case can be made for Rabanus as an original and tolerant commentator, judging him by the standards of the period'.[43] Yet for Hraban, study of *Torach*, as he referred to it, was no mere academic diversion. It was one of the four cornerstones on which the 'foursquare' Heavenly Jerusalem (Revelation 21.16) was built, and Hraban was its 'foursquare genius'.[44]

Rudolf of Fulda, Hraban's pupil, preserved for posterity the list of his foursquare mentor's interpretations of Torah: four books on Genesis, four on Numbers, four on Deuteronomy and seven on Leviticus.[45] Although the greater attention to Leviticus may suggest that this was the most important text in Torah for the abbot, there is another possible explanation. Hraban could be calling attention to the priestly number (seven), a number

[39] Hraban's scribes discussed by Le Maitre, 'Les méthodes exégétiques de Raban Maur', p. 347. For Origen's copyists, see Eusebius of Caesarea, *Ecclesiastical History* 6.23, in Roy J. Deferrari (trans.), *Eusebius Pamphili, Ecclesiastical History*, 2 vols., Fathers of the Church Series (New York, 1953 and 1955), vol. II, p. 44.

[40] Jean Leclercq's reference to the *renouveau origénien* of the ninth century is in his *Origène au XIIe siècle* (Chevetogne, 1951), p. 428, cited by Babcock, 'Häresie und Bibliothek', p. 312. See also Raffaele Savigni, 'Alcune considerazioni sulla fortuna di Origene nella cultura carolingia: le opera esegetiche di Rabano Mauro', *Studi e Ricerche sull'Oriente Cristiano* 15 (1992), pp. 67–86.

[41] Particularly in the writings of Benedict of Aniane, discussed in Babcock, 'Häresie und Bibliothek', pp. 311–12.

[42] See Daniel Boyarin, *Dying for God: Martyrdom and the Making of Christianity and Judaism* (Stanford, 1999), p. 9, who offers a new model of Jewish–Christian interaction in late antiquity.

[43] 'Rabanus Maurus and the Pseudo-Hieronymian', p. 46.

[44] In his dedicatory letter to Freculph at the beginning of the *Expositiones*, Hraban refers to the books of Moses as Torach: 'ut quinque libros Mosaicae legis, quos Hebrei torach appellant' (Epistle 10, *MGH Epp.* v, p. 396). The phrase 'foursquare man' is that of de Lubac (*Medieval Exegesis*, p. 112), who points out the abbot's use of architectural metaphors from the Bible, particularly the number four which is associated with the building of heavenly Jerusalem (Revelation 21.16: 'Et civitas in quadro posita est' (Vulgate); 'The city [Jerusalem] lies foursquare'). Hraban himself, as de Lubac points out, used the phrase 'foursquare' frequently: *carmina quadrata, orbis quadratus, lapides quadrati, homo quadratus* (de Lubac, p. 351, n. 48).

[45] Rudolf of Fulda, *Miracula sanctorum, MGH SS* xv, 1, p. 340: 'hoc est in Genesim libros 4, in Exodum libros 4, in Leviticum libros 7, in Numeros libros 4'.

associated with activities that would have been of great interest to the clois-
tered males of Fulda. Seven is the number of creation and human reproduction in Genesis 1 (a text authored by the same priestly group that compiled
Leviticus 1–16). Not coincidentally, it is also the priestly ritual reproduction
number in Leviticus, for just as God creates in seven-unit sequences, so too
do Hebrew priests engage in most ritual activity in increments of seven.
For example, Hebrew priests ritually cut the penis of an infant boy on the
eighth day to mark the end of the seven-day birthing period. These same
priests enclose themselves within the sacred precincts of the tabernacle for
seven days, a period during which their sacred powers intensify. Hebrew
altar servants activate ritual objects and vestments by sprinkling blood on
them seven times. Seven is the symbolic number for rites of passage, from
carnal to spiritual.[46]

Leviticus is a book that emphasises the difference between carnal and
spiritual reproduction: 'It [Leviticus] opposes natural fertility to the ritual for making heirs to God's promise. Descent by the seed of the loins
on the one hand, and the cut and blood of the circumcised penis on the
other, its laws keep the two bodily fluids, semen and blood, meticulously
apart.'[47] Hraban recognises this connection between the fleshly fertility of
humankind and the spiritual fecundity of male priests. His exegetical musings on mystical male pregnancies incorporate a multi-cultural, gendered
discourse that fuses together rabbinic allegories on the fathering of children
through Torah instruction,[48] the Platonic trope of the male soul-womb,[49]
and late antique neoplatonic Christian redactions of these two traditions.[50]
For Hraban, one of the most important functions of celibate men is to
inseminate the ears of the righteous with God's semen.

Hraban's sexually charged *Expositiones* owes a great deal both to the
patristic sources he consulted and to the priestly Torah itself. Half a

---

[46] See Jacob Milgrom's translation of and commentary on Leviticus in his *Leviticus 1–16*, Anchor
Bible 3 (New York, 1991), pp. 234, 566–9.

[47] Douglas, *Leviticus as Literature*, p. 5.

[48] For a discussion of the feminised rabbis of late antiquity, see Daniel Boyarin, 'Thinking with virgins:
engendering Judeo-Christian difference', chapter 3 of his *Dying for God*, pp. 67–92, and Howard
Eilberg-Schwartz, 'A sexless father and his procreating sons', chapter 9 of his *God's Phallus and Other
Problems for Men and Monotheism* (Boston, 1994), pp. 223–37.

[49] On the Platonic traditions, see Ruth Padel, *In and Out of the Mind: Greek Images of the Tragic Self*
(Princeton, 1992).

[50] Most notably in the writings of Origen of Alexandria, Didymus the Blind and Gregory of Nyssa
(under the crucial influence of the Jewish platonist Philo of Alexandria). For the neoplatonic traditions, see Verna E. F. Harrison, 'The allegorization of gender', in Vincent L. Wimbush and Richard
Valantasis (eds.), *Asceticism* (Oxford, 1996), pp. 520–34, and for an overview of ascetic masculinity
in late antique Christianity, see Virginia Burrus, *Begotten, Not Made: Conceiving Manhood in Late
Antiquity* (Stanford, 2000).

millennium after Origen of Alexandria delivered sermons on Leviticus to a group of Christian catechumens, Hraban gave his own performance to a priestly audience. The abbot's text relies heavily on a variety of earlier Christian commentators on Leviticus in addition to Origen: Hesychius (fifth century),[51] Jerome, Augustine (*c.* 354–430) and Gregory the Great (*c.* 540–604). In Hraban's idiosyncratic method of exegesis, he typically would use Jerome for more literal translations of scripture, Gregory for moral interpretations, and Origen for difficult allegorical readings. Augustine bridged the gap between the literal and allegorical realms and thus could be used for both. Hraban himself would offer his own opinion, particularly when he lacked an authoritative voice from the past on particular issues.[52] He instructed his scribes to indicate in the margins of manuscripts which church father was being invoked.[53] For the most complex sections of the priestly Torah, Origen emerges as the 'master of allegory'.[54]

The priestly Torah (P) itself, which Hraban knew well through his public teachings on Genesis, Exodus and Leviticus, is the largest of the independent narrative strands (JEPD) that form the 'five books of Moses' and is usually dated to the sixth century BC.[55] The priestly sabbath commandment and the Levitican categorisation of 'clean' foods (Genesis 1), the meticulous descriptions of Noah's ark (Genesis 6–7), the 'tabernacle Torah' (Exodus 25–40), and the handbook on priestly sacrifice and ritual ablutions

---

[51] Hesychius, a fifth-century Jerusalem exegete, wrote a lengthy commentary on Leviticus which was translated into Latin in the sixth century (Migne's edition preserves the Latin translation, *PG* 93, cols. 787–1180). Hraban acknowledges his debt to Hesychius' earlier work in the dedication to the *Expositiones* (Epistle 10, *MGH Epp.* v, p. 396): 'repperi hunc a venerabili presbytero Hierosolimorum Esychio satis pene expositum'. See Silvia Cantelli Berarducci, 'L'esegesi della rinascita carolingia', in Giuseppe Cremasco and Claudio Leonardi (eds.), *La Bibbia nel medioevo* (Bologna, 1996), p. 171, as well as A. Wenger, 'Hésychius de Jérusalem. Notes sur les discours inédits et sur le texte grec du commentaire, "In Leviticum"', *Revue des Etudes Augustiniennes* 2 (1956), pp. 457–70.

[52] Hraban himself comments on kashrut laws (*PL* 108, cols. 354–5) and leprosy (*PL* 108, cols. 390–1), which he believes is an affliction of the body connected with Adam's fall from grace.

[53] Dedicatory letter to *In Genesim commentarium* addressed to Freculph (Epistle 8, *MGH Epp.* v, p. 394) describes in some detail how this system works: 'Feci enim sicut postulasti, et sanctorum patrum libros, in quibus rebar aliquid de sententiis legis expressum esse, quantum licuit perlegi et singula secundum opportunitatem loci, prout mihi satis esse videbatur, inserui, eorum nominibus ante in pagina prenotatis.' See also de Jong, 'Old law and new-found power', p. 169.

[54] Le Maitre, 'Les méthodes exégétiques de Raban Maur', p. 348.

[55] The *torat-cohanim* ('instruction for priests') has been further subdivided into two major sections: the holiness code (H = LEV 17–26) and the priestly Torah (P = LEV 1–16). The dating of both H and P is highly disputed, but it is generally agreed that both were formalised during the sixth century BC. For discussion of both P and H, see Israel Knohl, *Sanctuary of Silence: The Priestly Torah and the Holiness School* (Minneapolis, 1995), and Milgrom, *Leviticus 1–16*. Douglas views P and H as a unified whole: 'However, according to the anthropological analysis, the differences between the two halves of Leviticus do not quite follow these lines. Both halves of the book use analogies in the same way, and neither demonstrates "causal," "logical," "discursive," or "dialogic" reasoning' (see *Leviticus as Literature*, p. 34).

(Leviticus 1–16) are all influential sections of the priestly Torah, particularly for the subsequent Christian reinterpretation of Hebrew holiness. For a Carolingian exegete and abbot, there is much fodder here for allegorical play, including detailed sections on blood and semen taboos, the numinous vestments and bodies of Hebrew holy men (*cohanim*), and the consecrated material culture of the *mishkan* (God's dwelling-place).[56] Furthermore, unlike the narrative (and hence more famous) portions of Hebrew scripture, Leviticus makes no mention of kings or the magical arts, two topics that much of modern scholarship has emphasised in Hraban's writings.[57] In the *Expositiones in Leviticum*, we are dealing with a text solely devoted to multivalent manifestations of priestly power. Hraban himself underscores the intensity of that power in his dedication of the *Expositiones* to Freculph, the bishop of Lisieux. Hraban exhorts his friend and fellow scholar to unravel the mysteries of Leviticus, a book in which there is 'such great power' (*tanta vis*).[58]

PRIESTLY BODIES AND LEVITICUS

One of these Levitican powers is that of virginal men to generate offspring. This anagogic motif is part of Hraban's allegorical interpretation of Leviticus 8.1–36, the 'investiture' of Hebrew priests. Leviticus 8 details how Moses washes, anoints and ritually dresses Aaron and his sons. This gruesome process involves slaughtering a bull and two rams, pulling out and smoking their innards, purifying with blood the sacred objects in the tabernacle, and throwing blood on priestly garments. Moses also dabs blood on the right big toe, thumb and ear lobe of the *cohanim* (the priests), a ceremonial exercise that parallels the anointing of the extremities of the altar; hence, the body of a Hebrew priest is a kind of activated altar.[59] The last part of

---

[56] For a discussion of the larger late antique and medieval contexts for Christian appropriations of the sacrificial powers of the Hebrew priesthood, see Paul Beaudette, '"In the world but not of it": clerical celibacy as a symbol of the medieval church', in Michael Frassetto (ed.), *Medieval Purity and Piety: Essays on Medieval Clerical Celibacy and Religious Reform* (New York, 1998), pp. 23–46.

[57] To date, a great deal of the secondary literature on Hraban has focused on his exegesis of scripture in the service of Carolingian monarchy and his even more famous attacks on magic. For an example of the political reading, see de Jong, 'Empire as Ecclesia', as well as Sears, 'Louis the Pious as *Miles Christi*', and Ward, 'Caesar's wife'. For the anti-magical invective, see Valerie Flint, *The Rise of Magic in the Early Medieval West* (Princeton, 1991), pp. 55–6.

[58] Epistle 10, *MGH Epp.* v, p. 396: 'Accipe opus quod postulasti et Levitici libri multiplicia mysteria in eo legendo revolve. Cuius libri tanta vis est, ut beatus Hieronimus in eius laude alicubi dixerit, quod singula sacrificia, immo singule poene sillabe et vestes, Aaron et totus ordo Leviticus celestia inspirarent sacramenta'. Here, Hraban agrees with Jerome that even the most minute sections of Leviticus hold the key to the mysteries of the Christian sacramental system.

[59] Milgrom, *Leviticus 1–16*, pp. 527–9, offers several explanations for the anointing of various body parts. One scholarly interpretation suggests that the anointing of these organs symbolises the consecration

the ceremony involves the cloistering of Aaron and his sons in the *mishkan* (sanctuary) for seven days, a ritual activity strangely parallel to that of the seclusion of unclean women.[60] During their isolation in the *mishkan*, the priests are to eat the remaining sacrifices.

Drawing heavily on Hesychius and Origen, Hraban uses Leviticus 8 for two different purposes. He creates an allegory of the cosmic body of Christ, whose feet represent ordinary humanity and whose head – personified on earth by the anointed bodies of priests – signifies divinity.[61] Hraban also connects the girding of priestly loins with the chastity of Christian preachers.[62] He equates the penis's ability to discharge semen with the mouth's ability to expel the Word.[63] In these shocking sections, Hraban pieces together disparate threads of patristic discourses on Leviticus to refashion the spiritual body of a Frankish priest. For Hraban, Christian priests are both receptacles of God's seed and inseminators of others, just as Christ himself 'is semen', and, as semen, the Son of God penetrated the bodies of his apostles.[64] As Christ's successors, the apostles carry on the process of filling the bodies of their disciples with divine mysteries. In turn, altar servants and theologians continue impregnating catechumens: 'Indeed in the Church there are priests and doctors who are able to generate sons.'[65] Hraban's exegesis on the spiritual reproductive powers of chaste men is based on the Apostle Paul's reflections on a similar theme: 'My little children, for whom I am again in the pain of childbirth until

---

of the entire body. Another theory posits that this anointing awakens the powers of hearing, touching and walking to God's will. Even more persuasive is Milgrom's contention that the anointing of these various members of the human body corresponds to the parts of the altar of the tabernacle: 'Thus it can be seen that the blood-daubing of the altar's extremities – its horns – closely resembles the blood-daubing of the extremities of the priests' (p. 528).

[60] Douglas, *Leviticus as Literature*, p. 187.

[61] *PL* 108, col. 327: 'Et si Christi caput, secundum Pauli verbum, divinitas intelligitur, non frustra tamen nec extra ordinem in hoc mysterio sacerdotis ungi nunc caput legislator scripsit, ut cognoscamus quoniam quemadmodum caput a pedibus dividi non potest, sic neque Christi divinitas post unitionem ab humanitate dividitur . . . Secundum hunc modum, caput intelligibilis sacerdotis ungebatur et ipse sanctificabatur.' Here, Hraban is associating the anointed head of the Christian priest with the divine aspect of Christ. Priests clearly share in both parts of the divine body, the human and the godly.

[62] *PL* 108, cols. 325–9 for the exegesis on Hebrew investiture. This section is pure Origen. For the Latin text of Origen's allegorical interpretation of Leviticus, see Marcel Borret (ed. and trans.), *Origène: Homélies sur le Lévitique*, SC 286–7 (Paris, 1981). For an English translation, see Gary Wayne Barkley, *Origen: Homilies on Leviticus 1–16*, Fathers of the Church 83 (Washington, DC, 1990). In this passage, Hraban incorporates the language of Origen's Homily 6.6, SC 286, pp. 290–6.

[63] *PL* 108, cols. 328–9. See also his discussion of Leviticus 15 (*PL* 108, cols. 403–4, analysed below).

[64] *PL* 112, col. 1048: 'Semen est Christus', and 'id [semen] est in Christo sancta praedicatio'. These musings on Christ as semen are from Hraban's *Allegoriae in sacram scripturam*.

[65] *PL* 108, col. 328: 'Possunt enim et in Ecclesia sacerdotes et doctores filios generare' (paraphrasing Origen, Homily 6.6, SC 286, p. 294).

Christ is formed in you' (Galatians 4.19), as well as on patristic interpretations of the spiritual functions of the sacred garments of Hebrew priests
(Leviticus 8).

In his exposition of the fleshly and spiritual meanings of the liturgical clothing of the *cohanim*, Hraban points to an apparent inconsistency
between the old dispensation and the new: whereas the apostles are to possess only one tunic (Matthew 10.10), Moses commands his priests to wear
two (Leviticus 8.7). For Hraban, this disparity in sacred fashion is no mere
accident because it is related to the other major difference between Christ's
male heirs and their Hebrew ancestors: 'the cut and uncut penis'. Moses's
High Priest is circumcised, and this ritual cut on his flesh parallels his work
as God's butcher, who offers unblemished animals as carnal sacrifices to the
Lord. As Hraban explains, the High Priest wears two tunics, one exemplifying his carnal ministry and another denoting his spiritual discernment of
that ministry.[66] The apostles, in contrast to their Hebrew prototypes, don
only an 'interior' or spiritual tunic, one that speaks to their repudiation
of the bloody sacrificial code of the *cohanim* and also acknowledges that
the great sacrifice – Christ on the Cross – has ended all other ceremonial carnage.[67] For Hraban's priests, sacrifice has become an esoteric affair:
Christian circumcision is a spiritual cut on the heart, and Christian holy
men find altar offerings not in the entrails and skins of animals but within
themselves, within their souls.[68]

Among Hraban's interpretations of the various vestments of Hebrew
priests, one passage stands out: the girding of the loins of the *cohanim* with
aprons as a material representation of their chief duty as holy butchers.
These aprons or *campestria* cover the thighs (in Hebrew, a euphemism for
the genitalia) and restrain the kidneys and loins. *Campestre* (pl. *campestria*)
is a specialised Latin word that appears infrequently in the classical
(Horace, *Epistle* 1.11.18) and late antique corpus of texts (Augustine, *Civ.
Dei* XIV.17). According to classical authors, the *campestre* was a leather
apron worn about the loins, or a 'wrestling apron'. The name itself stems
from the *locus* of its public display, the Field of Mars (*Campus Martius*,
an ancient district of Rome initially dedicated to military training and

---

[66] *PL* 108, col. 326: 'Sciebat ergo pontifex ille quem tunc ordinabat Moyses, quia esset circumcisio,
incircumcisus pontifex esse non poterat. Habebat ergo iste duas tunicas: unam ministerii carnalis,
et aliam intelligentiae spiritualis. Sciebat quia et sacrificia spiritalia offerri debent Deo, offerebat
tamen nihilominus et carnalia: non enim poterat esse pontifex eorum qui tunc erant, nisi hostias
immolaret.' For a discussion of patristic allegory and circumcision, see Elizabeth A. Clark, *Reading
Renunciation: Asceticism and Scripture in Early Christianity* (Princeton, 1999), pp. 225–30.

[67] *PL* 108, col. 326.

[68] *PL* 108, col. 304: 'istas hostias intra teipsum require, et invenies eas intra animam tuam'.

the election of high-ranking officials). Augustine of Hippo, in his famous Book 14 of the *City of God* (his re-creation of 'sex in paradise'), uses the term *campestria* to describe the garments in which God clothes both Adam and Eve after they had been expelled from Eden (Genesis 3.21). Augustine, who understood the athletic origins of the word, notes that during his own day the young men who were to participate in the public games were stripped naked and reclothed with *campestria*.[69] Augustine thus connects the physical combat of the arena with the postlapsarian struggle to control the loins that now suffer from disobedient desire.[70] Other late antique rabbinic *midrashim* also associate liturgical clothing with Adam's expulsion from Eden, for the rabbis advocate a celestial lineage for priestly vestments, beginning with Adam, who handed his skin-garment down to his heirs, who then passed it on to subsequent patriarchs until it eventually made its way into the priestly cult centred on the tabernacle.[71]

Hraban, following Augustine's lead, links the *campestria* of Hebrew priests with the earthly combat of the postlapsarian *pudenda*. He argues that these 'wrestling aprons' were used to restrain both the kidneys and the loins (*constringi renes videntur ac lumbi*), the innermost parts of the body connected by ancient Hebrew tradition with emotions and thoughts, and reread by Hraban as metaphors for the libido.[72] As the abbot makes clear, these first-covenant altar servants were not, as were their Christian descendants, chaste men.[73] In fact, God granted the *cohanim* certain concessions to ensure the 'posterity of the race and the success of offspring'.[74] For chaste Christian priests, Hraban believes that this section of the priestly

---

[69] Augustine, *De civitate Dei* 14.17 (CCSL 48, p. 440): 'Porro autem campestria Latinum quidem verbum est, sed ex eo dictum, quod iuvenes, qui nudi exercebantur in campo, pudenda operiebant; unde qui ita succincti sunt, campestratos vulgus appellat.'

[70] Augustine, *De civitate Dei* 14.17 (CCSL 48, p. 440): 'Quod itaque adversus damnatam culpa inoboedientiae voluntatem libido inoboedienter movebat, verecundia pudenter tegebat.'

[71] Michael D. Swartz, 'The semiotics of the priestly vestments in ancient Judaism', in Albert I. Baumgarten (ed.), *Sacrifice in Religious Experience*, Numen Series on Studies in the History of Religions 93 (Leiden, 2002), pp. 57–80. Discussion of the primordial priestly vestment is on p. 66.

[72] *PL* 108, col. 328 (Origen, Homily 6.6, SC 286, p. 292). For a discussion of the spiritual significance of the kidneys and loins, see Douglas, *Leviticus as Literature*, p. 80. See also *PL* 108, col. 308, on the sacrifical offerings of the kidneys and the fatty mass at the opening of the liver. Here, Hraban equates the purging of these interiors of animals with the eradication of the libido: 'ut purgentur omnia interiora tua'. For the specific connection between the kidneys and the libido, *PL* 108, col. 308: 'Quod si ablatum fuerit omne quod pingue est de renibus et de omnibus interioribus viscerum, tunc vere purgatus omni vitio libidinis jugulasti hostiam pro delicto, et obtulisti sacrificium Domino in odorem suavitatis.'

[73] For a discussion of the ritual purity of the Carolingian priesthood and its appropriation of Hebrew models, see Mayke de Jong, 'Imitatio morum: the cloister and clerical purity in the Carolingian world', in Frassetto (ed.), *Medieval Purity and Piety*, pp. 49–80.

[74] *PL* 108, col. 328: 'Aliquando enim et de posteritate generis et successu sobolis indulgetur.'

Torah relates an important mystery (*sacramentum*), one that remained concealed to the circumcised *cohanim* of Moses.[75] Acting as a kind of numinous chastity belt, the *campestria* serve to uphold the commandments (detailed in Leviticus 18 and Deuteronomy 22) not to spill seed in inappropriate orifices. Hraban explains for his priestly audience that in imitation of the Apostle Paul, who begat children through the *logos*, Christian altar servants similarly form Christ within the bodies of their votaries. Priests, the abbot argues, at times must bind their thighs and abstain from such spiritual procreation because there are some hearers in whom they cannot produce any fruit.[76] Such would-be disciples, described here as hypocrites and false ones (*simulatos et hypocritas auditores*), have incapable ears (*incapaces aures*). The mystical impregnation of such individuals would cause God's seed to die (*semen periret*).[77] The *campestre* and the thigh coverings (*femoralia linea*) thus are a kind of divine prophylactic for the discerning priest who does not waste a single drop of the Lord's semen.[78] Addressing his virginal male audience, Hraban exhorts: 'put on the *campestre*!' and 'use the thigh coverings!'[79]

PLATONIC AND RABBINIC PREGNANCIES

The major Christian precedent for Hraban's recasting of the ritual reproductive potency of Hebrew priests is Origen of Alexandria's *Homilies on Leviticus* (*c.* 240 CE).[80] In fact, the sections of Hraban's *Expositiones* covered

---

[75] *PL* 108, col. 328: 'Sed ego in sacerdotibus Ecclesiae hujusmodi intelligentiam non introduxerim, alio namque rem video currere sacramento' (Origen, Homily 6.6, SC 286, p. 292).

[76] *PL* 108, col. 328: 'imposita habuisse femoralia et continuisse se ne filios generarent, quia scilicet tales erant auditores in quibus et semen periret, et non possit haberi successio'.

[77] *PL* 108, cols. 328–9.

[78] Hraban's other important work, *De institutione clericorum* 1.14–23, also 'reads' the vestments of Christian priests as numinous chastity belts: the *podere* is a tight linen tunic designed to maintain continence; the *cingulum*, or belt, prohibits an ill wind from flowing up the tunic; the *casula* ('little house'), the garment that goes on last, defends priestly virtue; the *pallium*, with its purple cross, causes the chaste priest to be ever mindful of the dead body of the crucified Christ. For the text, see Detlev Zimpel (ed.), *Hrabanus Maurus, De institutione clericorum libri tres*, Freiburger Beiträge zur mittelalterlichen Geschichte 7 (Frankfurt, 1996), pp. 309–15.

[79] *PL* 108, col. 329: 'imponant campestre' and 'utantur femoralibus'.

[80] Latin text is in SC 286–7 (see note 62 above). The original Greek text of Origen's *Homilies on Leviticus* did not survive antiquity and scholarship on this topic has relied on Rufinus' Latin translation/interpretation (*c.* 403–405) of Origen's original exegesis of the priestly Torah. For major scholarly interpretations of Origen's life and writings, see Jean Daniélou, *Origène* (Paris, 1948), English translation by Walter Mitchell, *Origen* (New York, 1955); Henri Crouzel, *Origène et la philosophie* (Paris, 1962); Henri de Lubac, *Histoire et esprit: l'intelligence de l'écriture d'après Origène* (Paris, 1950); and de Lubac, *Exégèse medievale*. For a review of scholarly theories on Rufinus' alteration of Origen's

in this essay are largely lifted from Origen's more famous commentary on priestly *vis*, known in the west through Rufinus' early fifth-century Latin translation. In his allegory of Christ's salvific preaching, Origen employs explicitly sexual language: 'The soul conceives from this seed of the Word and the Word forms a fetus (*conceptum*) in itself until it gives birth to a spirit of the fear of God.'[81] Proselytising therefore takes the form of spiritual impregnation, a kind of mystical pregnancy that replicates Christ's own conception. In Origen's allegorical invention, those converted to the teachings of Christ are transformed into receptacles of the *logos*. Whereas women are the repositories of male seed, Christian converts are feminised vessels for divine revelation; true birth begins only when the human soul unites with Christ.

Of course, Origen is not the inventor of this concept of mystical male pregnancy. The *logos* as foetus is a product of a multi-cultural discourse with roots in platonism and rabbinic *midrashim*. In Plato's *Thaetetus* (150–1), Socrates refers to himself as a midwife to men.[82] Whereas women's wombs are the *locus* of their carnal pregnancies, men become pregnant in their souls and 'bring forth the fruits of moral, intellectual, artistic, and civic creativity'.[83] The male mind (*noos*) acts as a kind of spiritual womb that is capable of a superior kind of birth – the birth of intellectual discipleship. The Jewish and Christian heirs to this Platonic notion include Philo of Alexandria, Origen of Alexandria, Didymus the Blind and, through Origen, Hraban Maur. Yet, as Verna Harrison illustrates, the original homoerotic context of Plato's musings on male pregnancies is 'allegorised' out of the Jewish/Christian exegetical tradition.[84] No longer do the beautiful bodies of Socrates' inner circle serve as visual aids for instructing future philosophers on how to make the ascent from physical *eros*. In late antique Christianity and Judaism, a bodiless God becomes the sole focus of that desire, to be achieved only through the transformation of ascetic male bodies into perfect wombs for divine penetration.

Greek text, see Barkley, *Origen*, pp. 20–3. For a discussion of the western manuscript transmission, see Borret, *Origène*, pp. 52–6. Marilyn Dunn, *The Emergence of Monasticism: From the Desert Fathers to the Early Middle Ages* (Oxford, 2000), p. 69, places Rufinus' translations of Origen within the larger context of the development of western monasticism.

[81] Homily 12.7 (SC 287, p. 194): 'Concipit ergo anima ex hoc verbi semine et conceptum format in se Verbum, donec pariat spiritum timoris Dei.'

[82] Noted by Harrison, 'Allegorization of gender', p. 526.

[83] Harrison, 'Allegorization of Gender', p. 526.

[84] Harrison, 'Allegorization of Gender', p. 526: 'among early Christian writers such as Origen and his follower, Didymus of Alexandria, though for them the homosexual dimension is absent'.

In late antique Judaism there is a series of *midrashim* and martyr texts
that describe 'virgin rabbis', who marry Torah and maintain their purity
within the 'whore-house' that is the Roman empire, a political system
that had outlawed the public teaching of Hebrew scripture.[85] The martyr-
rabbi of late antiquity guards his outlawed bride (Torah) from Roman
gaze: 'Rabbi Hiyya taught: Anyone who studies Torah in front of one of
the people of the land is like one who has intercourse with his fiancée in
front of them.'[86] Furthermore, the primary occupation of these late antique
rabbis was – in spite of Roman opposition – to disseminate Torah. The
Avot and the *Mishnah* (200s AD) both compare the teaching of Torah with
procreation. The successful rabbinic sage is said to have 'never lost a drop'
of Torah.[87] The connection with the biblical command not to waste semen
(also echoed in Hraban Maur's discussion of the *campestria* as prophylactic
belts for men) is obvious. Not unlike the neoplatonic tradition of separating
the physical body from its more perfect spiritual form, the rabbis of late
antiquity divided the male body into two registers: the lower body which
is marked off by the circumcised penis, symbolised earthly kinship and
procreation, while the upper body, represented by the mouth, housed the
organ of Torah dissemination. The mouth thus replaced the phallus as
the part of the body responsible for making heirs and, implicitly, the ears
became orifices of conception.[88]

Incorporating both Origen and Gregory the Great, the abbot of Fulda
offers his celibate audience a unique instruction on the male body: the male
mouth is a mystical phallus which expels semen through public preaching.[89]
That semen then enters the attentive male mind, which is conceived of as
a fecund uterus (*audientis mens, quasi concipientis uterus*) through ears that
serve as the uterine canal. The male mind-womb then gives birth to virtuous
discipleship. In this reversal of the natural process of human birth, men
become like God, who breathes life into the lifeless body of Adam. Christian
priests who possess this Godlike power of spiritual generation, however,
must ensure that their 'fluxes of semen' are emitted in an orderly fashion,

---

[85] Boyarin, *Dying for God*, p. 73.   [86] Cited by Boyarin, *Dying for God*, p. 70.
[87] Cited by Eilberg-Schwartz, *God's Phallus*, p. 214.
[88] Hraban incorporates the platonic motif of the ears as birth canals in his *Expositiones*, see *PL* 108,
cols. 328–9 and 403–4. For a discussion of the rabbinical refashioning of the ascetic male body, see
Eilberg-Schwartz, *God's Phallus*, p. 214, and his 'The nakedness of a woman's voice, the pleasure in a
man's mouth: an oral history of ancient Judaism', in Howard Eilberg-Schwartz and Wendy Doniger
(eds.), *Off with Her Head! The Denial of Women's Identity in Myth, Religion, and Culture* (Berkeley,
1995), pp. 165–84.
[89] See *PL* 108, cols. 328–9 (Origen's exegesis on Leviticus 8, investiture of Hebrew priests) and cols.
403–4 (Gregory the Great's exegesis on Leviticus 15, unclean discharges of semen).

or else they run the risk of ritual pollution. The Christian preacher who is a babbler (Latin, *seminiverbius*, Greek, *spermologos*) or speaker of vain words is compared to a phallus tainted by unclean discharges or defiled by the careless waste of semen, a mystical form of the biblical 'onanism' (Genesis 38.9–10).

CAROLINGIAN SACRED GENDER

Unlike scholars of late antiquity, Carolingianists do not often think about Frankish men in terms of body, gender and mystical pregnancies. Rather, scholarship on early medieval priests and lay nobles has sought to envision their masculinity almost exclusively through the lens of politics and diplomacy. Is it the case then that the 'dazzling, metaphysical bodies' of male ascetics and virgin rabbis die out with late antiquity?[90] Is Origen, whom Peter Brown once described as antiquity's 'walking lesson in the basic indeterminacy of the body', only possible in the late Roman empire?[91] The example of Hraban Maur, an influential abbot of a prominent monastery in northern Europe, who gave public lectures on Origen's theories of male 'indeterminacy', suggests otherwise. Preserving one of the most heterodox statements in Origen's *Homilies*, the abbot instructs his disciples on the power of their own bodies: 'Understand that you are another world in small and that there is inside of you the sun, the moon, and the stars.'[92] A better statement of the remaking of the ascetic male into a dazzling vessel of the divine could not have been made.

Through his teachings on Leviticus and his writings on liturgical clothing, the abbot envisions a rarefied Frankish male body built upon a series of theological reversals: the Carolingian priest is a spiritual gladiator,

[90] Jean-Pierre Vernant's theory of the 'divine, dazzling body' of ancient Greek religious discourse and its Christian ascetic redaction is discussed by Patricia Cox Miller, 'Dreaming the body: an aesthetics of asceticism', in Wimbush and Valantasis (eds.), *Asceticism*, p. 281.

[91] Peter Brown, *The Body and Society: Men, Women and Sexual Renunciation in Early Christianity* (New York, 1988), p. 169.

[92] *PL* 108, col. 304: 'intellige te alium mundum esse in parvo, et esse intra te solem, esse lunam, esse etiam stellas'. See Origen, Homily 5.2 (SC 286, p. 212). For a discussion of the neoplatonic implications of this statement, see Alan Scott, *Origen and the Life of the Stars: A History of an Idea* (Oxford, 1991); pp. 154–8. Hraban, in several places in his *Expositiones*, creates an image of the cosmic body of the Christian priest: by associating the laity with Christ's feet and priests with Christ's head, by maintaining that the bodies of priests house the universe in small, and by promoting a theology of ascetic body as esoteric sacrifice, Hraban's teachings take part in the larger arena of world asceticism that includes certain forms of medieval Hindu and Islamic esotericism. For a discussion of Hindu and Islamic parallels, see Gavin Flood, *Body and Cosmology in Kashmir Saivism* (San Francisco, 1993), pp. 1–25, and Vince Cornell, *Realm of the Saint: Power and Authority in Moroccan Sufism* (Austin, TX, 1998), pp. 211–14.

protected from bouts of lust by his leather *campestre*; his loins are restrained from their carnal impulses by a tight-fitting, linen *balteus* (belt) and his purifying *casula* (chasuble) enables him to approach the altar.[93] Made more spiritually fertile through his militant chastity, the priest marries Jesus at the altar and there fathers numerous children, an anagogic activity mirrored in reality through the intense teacher–disciple relationships experienced by Carolingian monks, including Alcuin's *corvulus*, his little raven. Even the monastery is a 'chamber of the bridegroom', where male virgins muse on a sensual Christ, whom they see, hear, smell, taste and touch.[94]

In Christian Europe, this kind of mystical, erotic power, enacted within the confines of a male cloister, was closed to the laity. Herein lies the major motivation behind Hraban's study of Leviticus, for no other text in Torah is better suited for the propagation of priestly authority over the non-consecrated. Leviticus creates for its Frankish readers an imagined community of ancient Israelite priests, whose powers can be channelled only by their second-covenant descendants. The priestly Torah, the major source for this imagined community, spells out how God designed the altar vestments of his *cohanim* (Exodus 28), provided the architectural blueprints (Exodus 25ff.) for the sacred spaces that only they could penetrate, and appointed them privileged custodians of sacrificial atonement and ritual cleansing (Leviticus 1–16). Hraban used these politically significant Hebrew lessons in his own liturgical writings to emphasise the superiority of the church hierarchy over its lay counterpart.[95]

In Hraban's recasting of this idealised community, Frankish priests possess an exterior body which they display to the laity and an interior, or occult, body which they reserve for mystical contemplation within the monastery's hallowed spaces. Hraban underscores the tension between the exterior and interior body by pointing to the use made by the *cohanim* of two different sets of liturgical garments: one vestment for the ministry to the laity and another, more mystical garb reserved for the 'experienced' and

---

[93] *De institutione clericorum* 1.17, 1.21: 'Ergo lineas induunt sacerdotes, ut castitatem habeant; accin-guntur baltheis, ne ipsa castitas sit remissa et neglegens' and 'Sine hac [casula] nec sacerdos ipse ad altare appropinquare debet, nec munus offerre, nec preces fundere.'

[94] *PL* 108, col. 292: 'Deum videmus, vel aures habemus ad audienda ea quae docet Jesus, vel odorem capimus illum, quem dicit Apostolus, *quia Christi bonus odor sumus* (II Cor.v); vel etiam gustum sumimus illum, de quo dicit Propheta: *Gustate et videte quoniam suavis est Dominus* (Psal. xxxiii), vel tactum illum, quem dicit Joannes: *Quia oculis nostris perspeximus et manus nostrae palpaverunt de verbo vitae* (I Joan. 1).' Origin, Homily 3.7 (SC 286, p. 150).

[95] Wallace-Hadrill, *Frankish Church*, p. 318, notes that Hraban was an intensely hierarchical thinker, who consistently maintained the superiority of priests over the laity. For a discussion of religious 'imagined communities', see Benedict Anderson, *Imagined Communities* (London, 1983), pp. 12–18.

'more perfect', who dwell within the sanctuary.[96] Anointed priests are 'more excellent' (*praestantior*), 'more wise' (*doctior*) and 'more holy' (*sanctior*) than the unconsecrated laity.[97] The priestly body, clothed in its esoteric garb, also is more holy because of its proximity to God's altar, and because of its ability to purge the libido.[98] The laity (*filii Israel*), who live outside the sacred precincts of the monastery, are imperfect and lack the capacity for the true contemplation of God; sanctified priests alone may receive the vision of the Godhead.[99] Cleansing the 'inner man', Christian altar servants invite Jesus, 'who is semen', into the tabernacle-like spaces of their own bodies. This allegorical vision of the sacred gender of Carolingian holy men forms the basis for the Church hierarchy's claims of authority over the *filii Israel*.

Carolingian churchmen, including Hraban, have left us with a wealth of texts that preserve part of a platonic and rabbinic tradition of 'allegorical gender'.[100] Hraban Maur's *Expositiones in Leviticum* certainly is not colourless, as de Lubac once claimed, nor is it purely derivative. The abbot of Fulda decided which exegetical traditions to preserve from late antiquity and how to organise, emend and even reinterpret those passages. Hraban approached the complex third book of Torah from the perspective of a vastly changed cultural context – a same-sex monastery in northern Europe. This preservation and reception make Hraban's *Expositiones*, the 'little' commentary compiled by Fulda's foursquare genius, an excellent perspective for an examination of Carolingian sacred gender and its contribution to the making of the Frankish New Israel.[101] The ritually reproducing priests of Hraban's allegorical text rise superior to the authority of lay potentates. They do so precisely because of the gendered nature of Hraban's allegorical treatment of Leviticus. Thus a reading of the *Expositiones* adds a novel, unexpected aspect to the study of Carolingian church history, a field which has been approached almost exclusively through institutional history,

---

[96] Hraban's exegesis of Leviticus 8, where the High Priest and the *cohanim* wear specialised garments within the sacred precincts of the tabernacle (*PL* 108, cols. 320–33).

[97] *PL* 108, col. 325.

[98] *PL* 108, col. 295 (on sanctification through the altar), and *PL* 108, col. 308 (on purging of the libido).

[99] Hraban's reading of Exodus 24, where God commands the people of Israel not to approach him (*PL* 108, cols. 342–3).

[100] Whether or not this pedagogical paradigm was directly influenced by rabbinical commentaries (rather than indirectly through patristic citations of those commentaries) is something we may never know.

[101] As Mary Garrison argues, most studies of early medieval ideologies of 'New Israel' have focused on kingship ('The Franks as New Israel?'). A notable exception is Mayke de Jong ('Imitatio morum'), who has dealt with the Hebrew roots of Carolingian clerical purity and its contribution to the making of 'New Israel'.

clerical reform movements and the cataloguing of monastic library collections. Hraban Maur's *Expositiones in Leviticum*, with its subtle homoerotic mysticism, its male appropriation of female birthing power and its implicit statements of priestly supremacy, suggests that biblical exegesis can make a singular contribution to studies of gender and power in Carolingian Europe.[102]

[102] The author would like to thank the following individuals who helped enormously with the completion of this chapter: JoAnn D'Alisera, John Arnold, William Diebold, Robert Finlay, Jeremy Hyman, Suzanne Maberry, Tom Noble, Barbara Rosenwein and Michael Swartz.

CHAPTER 16

Negotiating gender, family and status in Anglo-Saxon burial practices, c. 600–950

Dawn Hadley

Burial archaeology has long played an important role in discussions of early medieval migrations, revealing much of the material culture through which ethnic identities may have been signalled.[1] However, this is not the only debate about social identities to which burial archaeology can usefully contribute. Indeed, archaeologists have recently suggested that ethnicity may not have been the major factor determining burial display in early medieval England. Rather, factors relating to gender, age and social status are now often seen as more important in determining burial practices in the fifth, sixth and seventh centuries. Although precisely how this happened remains open to much debate, one issue that most archaeologists are agreed upon is that by the eighth century burial rite had ceased to be a medium of social display and differentiation. They also generally accept that there was a gradual transition towards the medieval pattern of burying the dead, in unelaborate fashion in churchyards, which apparently became widespread from the eighth century. This chapter proposes a different model. First, it suggests that gender was both erratically determined and variously expressed in Anglo-Saxon burial display, but was particularly important at times of great social stress. Second, it argues that the decline in the use of grave goods must not be allowed to obscure the ways in which burial continued to be a medium of social expression after the seventh century. To this end, it maintains that while gender remained relevant to burial practices after the seventh century, we need to situate gender analysis within the broader context of the family, lordship and landholding.

[1] See chapter 9 by Bonnie Effros above.

301

BURIAL PRACTICES OF THE FIFTH TO SEVENTH CENTURIES:
EXPRESSING GENDER, AGE AND SOCIAL STATUS

Anglo-Saxon cemeteries of the fifth and sixth centuries are characterised
by elaborate burial displays, involving both cremation and inhumation
accompanied by grave goods. Numerous studies have commented on the
distinction between the burial of adult males with weapons and of females
with jewellery in cemeteries of this date, and on age-related distinctions,
suggesting that age and gender both determined and were signified in
funerary ritual.[2] Although weapons are occasionally found in the burials
of females, and jewellery assemblages occasionally occur in the burials of
males, the fact that weapons and jewellery virtually never appear together
confirms the significance of the dichotomy between the two forms of burial.
Moreover, the exceptions are so few (and often based on uncertain sexing of
the skeleton) that it seems unhelpful to deny that on the whole weapons carried masculine connotations, and jewellery carried feminine connotations.[3]
We should not forget, however, that not all burials were elaborated in this
way. As many as one third to a half of burials in most early Anglo-Saxon
cemeteries either have no grave goods or have assemblages common to
both male and female graves (often dubbed 'gender-neutral' assemblages).[4]
Heinrich Härke has suggested that both those individuals buried without grave goods and those with gender-neutral assemblages were lesser
members of the household, such as servants or slaves.[5] Support for this
hypothesis is provided by evidence in some cemeteries – such as Andover
(Hants.), Petersfinger (Wilts.) and Sewerby (Yorks.) – for clusters of gender-
neutral burials around gendered adult male and female burials, which may
have been household groups.[6] By contrast, Guy Halsall has interpreted

---

[2] N. Stoodley, *The Spindle and the Spear: A Critical Enquiry into the Construction and Meaning of Gender
in the Early Anglo-Saxon Burial Rite*, British Archaeological Reports 288 (Oxford, 1999), pp. 24–52;
see also the reviews in D. M. Hadley and J. Moore, '"Death makes the man"? Burial rite and the
construction of gender in the early Middle Ages', in D. M. Hadley (ed.), *Masculinity in Medieval
Europe* (London, 1999), pp. 21–38, and in T. M. Dickinson, 'What's new in early medieval burial
archaeology?', *EME* 11 (2002), pp. 71–87.

[3] For a paper emphasising the apparent exceptions to this norm see S. J. Lucy, 'Housewives, warriors
and slaves? Sex and gender in Anglo-Saxon burials', in J. Moore and E. Scott (eds.), *Invisible People
and Processes: Writing Gender and Childhood into European Archaeology* (London, 1997), pp. 150–68.
For a contrary view see Stoodley, *The Spindle and the Spear*, pp. 29–30, 76–7.

[4] Lucy, 'Sex and gender', pp. 157–62.

[5] H. Härke, 'Early Anglo-Saxon social structure', in J. Hines (ed.), *The Anglo-Saxons from the Migration
Period to the Eighth Century: An Ethnographic Perspective* (Woodbridge, 1997), pp. 125–70 at p. 132;
see also, Stoodley, *The Spindle and the Spear*, pp. 126–35.

[6] Stoodley, *The Spindle and the Spear*, pp. 131–5. Throughout this chapter site references give the pre-1974
counties.

sixth-century burials around Metz (France) as indicating that generally neither the very young nor the very elderly were given gendered burials, and that those burials expressing masculine and feminine differentiation appear to have been the preserve of males and females between puberty and middle age. He concluded that those individuals whose death proved the greatest loss to their family and community – apparently those of marriageable and childbearing age – prompted the greatest funerary investment. He also remarked that the use of expensive grave goods was confined to a period of great social fluidity and stress, and that competitive investment in death ended when a more stable aristocracy emerged in the seventh century.[7] Similarly, study of some Anglo-Saxon cemeteries has revealed that the young and the elderly tended to have gender-neutral assemblages.[8] Thus it may be that a variety of factors, including claims to social status, wealth, occupation and age, determined which individuals were accorded gendered burials in early Anglo-Saxon cemeteries.[9]

Recent studies have suggested that the seventh century witnessed a decline in the signalling of gender, in terms both of the gendered associations of grave goods and of the number of burials in which gender was signalled. For example, Nick Stoodley's study of West Saxon cemeteries reveals that fifth- and sixth-century burials in which gender was signified account for 53 per cent of all inhumations, whereas in the seventh century gendered burials account for only 24 per cent of the total.[10] At the same time there was an increasing separation of the more wealthy and elaborate burials, often in or near barrows and prehistoric landscape features, from the less elaborate burials in the row-grave cemeteries. There was also an increasing standardisation of the feminine burial kit, which was more commonly found in the row-grave cemeteries, while the masculine version became limited to very high-status burials, often associated with prominent landscape features.[11] It has been argued that by the seventh century increasingly stratified societies had emerged, and that weapon burials – which

---

[7] G. Halsall, 'Female status and power in early Merovingian central Austrasia: the burial evidence', *EME* 5 (1996), pp. 1–24.

[8] S. Lucy, *The Early Anglo-Saxon Cemeteries of East Yorkshire*, British Archaeological Reports 272 (Oxford, 1998), pp. 43–8.

[9] Ethnicity has generally fallen out of favour as an explanation for differences in Anglo-Saxon burial practices, but see H. Härke, 'Changing symbols in a changing society: the Anglo-Saxon weapon burial rite in the seventh century', in M. Carver (ed.), *The Age of Sutton Hoo* (Woodbridge, 1992), pp. 149–65 at pp. 152–5; and also Effros in this volume.

[10] N. Stoodley, 'Burial rites, gender and the creation of kingdoms: the evidence from seventh-century Wessex', in T. M. Dickinson and D. Griffiths (eds.), *The Making of Kingdoms* (Oxford, 1999), pp. 99–107 at p. 101.

[11] Stoodley, *The Spindle and the Spear*, pp. 97–8, 141.

were fewer in number than at an earlier date – may now have been less markers of gender than markers of a regionally important social elite, more secure in their position and announcing their exclusivity through both place and manner of burial.[12] The use of burial strategies in this way by regional elites is also apparently reflected in the replacement of regionally distinctive assemblages of grave goods by more uniform assemblages across most of England.[13] The fact that some of this signalling of elite status was achieved through what had hitherto been symbols of masculinity has been interpreted by Stoodley as an indication of changing household structures, with lines of descent and claims to regional authority being increasingly traced through the male line alone.[14] Whether or not this is the case, it does seem to be true that the symbolic expression of femininity had declined in importance by the seventh century, while symbolic expressions of masculinity and of elite status had become intertwined. By the seventh century, weapons in burials were effectively symbols of elite status and relatively limited in number, whereas assemblages of jewellery were still primarily markers of feminine gender and were found across a wider spectrum of graves.[15]

This is not to say, however, that female graves were no longer used to signal issues of contemporary concern. For example, there was a notable emergence of supra-regional burial rites drawing on the Roman heritage, and these Romanising influences were most clearly expressed in female graves through pendants, necklaces, dress-fittings and chatelaines.[16] It is also primarily in female graves that we find cross-shaped pendants in the seventh century.[17] Although the use of crosses as decorative motifs may have had no particular Christian significance, actual crosses in the form of pendants may, as John Blair has observed, 'replicate the artistic repertoire of

---

[12] Stoodley, 'Burial rites', pp. 103–6.
[13] H. Geake, *The Use of Grave-Goods in Conversion-Period England, c.600–c.850*, British Archaeological Reports 261 (Oxford, 1997), pp. 125–6, 132–4. Although the documentary evidence indicates the existence of a multiplicity of kingdoms in the seventh century, they are archaeologically indistinguishable in their burial practices. It has been suggested that this is the result of the various kingdoms drawing on Roman influences, in an active adoption of *romanitas*, to underpin the legitimacy of their rulers: H. Geake, 'Invisible kingdoms: the use of grave-goods in seventh-century England', in Dickinson and Griffiths (eds.), *The Making of Kingdoms*, pp. 203–15.
[14] Stoodley, 'Burial rites', pp. 104–5.
[15] Wealthy female barrow burials of the seventh century are not unknown. However, the range of accompanying grave goods tends to be less distinct from those of contemporary female burials in other cemetery contexts than is the case for male barrow burials, which contrast sharply with their less elaborate counterparts in the row-grave cemeteries: H. Geake, 'Persistent problems in the study of Conversion-period burials in England', in S. Lucy and A. Reynolds (eds.), *Burial in Early Medieval England and Wales* (London, 2002), pp. 144–55 at pp. 147–8.
[16] Geake, 'Invisible kingdoms', pp. 205–11.
[17] Geake, *Conversion-Period England*, pp. 146, 148, 164, 166, 175; J. Blair, *Anglo-Saxon Oxfordshire* (Stroud, 1994), pp. 70–1.

self-evidently Christian crosses in sculpture and manuscripts'.[18] This need not reveal that women were more receptive to Christianity, but rather that the jewellery they wore was more suited to displaying religious symbols. Seventh-century women's dress and burial items could thus mark a range of cultural attributes distinct from, but complementary to, the expressions of status signalled in men's graves.

BURIAL PRACTICES OF THE EIGHTH TO TENTH CENTURIES: DIVERSITY AND DIFFERENTIATION

The burial practices of the eighth to tenth centuries have not been investigated to the same extent as those of earlier centuries, yet a number of generalisations have entered the scholarly literature. For example, Helen Geake has commented that 'we know from historical sources that Anglo-Saxon society was ranked during the eighth century, but funerary practice has completely masked this in favour of an ostensibly egalitarian rite', and Sarah Tarlow has similarly described Christian burials as expressing 'an ideology of egalitarianism'.[19] The following paragraphs challenge this notion of an 'egalitarian rite', for there is rather more to be said from an archaeological perspective about the continuing role of burial practices in signalling various aspects of social status, including gender. Such comments based on archaeological data also overlook aspects of funerary provision that leave no or few archaeological traces, such as processions, feasts and performance of the liturgy, and the documentary evidence for cultural beliefs about death, the fate of the soul and the value of commemoration and intercession.

Given the relative lack of scholarly attention paid to burial practices after the seventh century it is first necessary to identify the available evidence. As we shall see, it is more diverse than some recent studies have led us to believe. Documentary and archaeological evidence reveals that burial occurred in a variety of locations from the eighth century. The inhabitants

---

[18] J. Blair, *The Church in English Society* (forthcoming).

[19] Geake, *Conversion-Period England*, p. 127; S. Tarlow, 'The dread of something after death: violation and desecration on the Isle of Man in the tenth century', in J. Carmen (ed.), *Material Harm: Archaeological Studies of War and Violence* (Skelmorlie, 1997), pp. 133–42 at p. 139. These are not isolated views: see also I. Hodder, 'Social structure and cemeteries: a critical appraisal', in P. Rahtz, T. M. Dickinson and L. Watts (eds.), *Anglo-Saxon Cemeteries*, British Archaeological Reports 82 (Oxford, 1980), pp. 161–9 at p. 168, where Christian burials are said to promote an ideology of 'equality, humility and non-materialism which is blatantly in contrast with the way we live our lives in practice'; M. Carver, 'Cemetery and society at Sutton Hoo: five awkward questions and four contradictory answers', in C. Karkov, K. Wickham-Crowley and B. Young (eds.), *Spaces of the Living and the Dead: An Archaeological Dialogue* (Oxford, 1999), pp. 1–14 at p. 8, where it is claimed that 'the Christian dead proclaim equality, which there was not'.

of religious communities, bishops and kings were buried in churchyards, and occasionally within churches, from the seventh century. The aristocracy may also have buried their dead at such churches, or at the churches they were evidently building on their own lands.[20] However, there is also evidence to suggest that burial location remained variable and not invariably associated with a church until at least the tenth century. The tradition of burial in or near barrows and prehistoric landscape features is widely considered to have been a largely seventh-century phenomenon, but recent radiocarbon dating of skeletal remains from Thwing (Yorks.), Swinhope (Lincs.), and Harting Beacon and Winton Hill, Alfriston (Sussex) suggests that this practice continued later.[21] Burial grounds of eighth-century and later date unassociated with any known contemporary church have been excavated at a number of sites.[22] Admittedly, to interpret this evidence as an indication that churchyard burial was not extended to everyone by the eighth century depends on accepting that absence of evidence for a church at these sites is, indeed, evidence of absence. None the less, limited documentary evidence suggests that it may not have been until the tenth century that the church sought actively to control burial for the majority.[23] Excavation of these eighth-century and later cemeteries gives rise to another, more secure, archaeological interpretation: that the eighth century did not witness the establishment of a pattern of burial location that was to persist, and many cemeteries contracted in size or went out of use relatively quickly.[24]

In terms of burial rite, there is much variation identifiable both within and between cemeteries from the eighth century. Although the body was often placed directly in the ground, there is also evidence for both stone and wooden coffins of varying degrees of complexity. We also find

---

[20] For examples, see D. M. Hadley, 'Burial practices in the Northern Danelaw, c.650–1100', *Northern History* 36 (2) (2000), pp. 199–216 at pp. 200–5.

[21] To which can be added Bevis's Grave, Bedhampton (Hants.) where the associated grave goods include a ninth-century strap-end: Geake, *Conversion-Period England*, pp. 154, 159, 183–4; Hadley, 'Burial practices in the Danelaw', pp. 210–11.

[22] Examples include Garton-on-the-Wolds, Kemp Howe (Yorks.), Bevis's Grave, Bedhampton, Aylesbury (Bucks.), Shipton-under-Wychwood, Beacon Hill, Lewknor, Kidlington (Oxon.), Burrow Hill (Suffolk) and Caister-on-Sea (Norfolk): Geake, *Conversion-Period England*, pp. 145, 154, 158, 170, 178; Blair, *Anglo-Saxon Oxfordshire*, pp. 66, 73.

[23] D. Bullough, 'Burial, community and belief in the early medieval West', in P. Wormald, D. Bullough and R. Collins (eds.), *Ideal and Reality in Frankish and Anglo-Saxon Society* (Oxford, 1983), pp. 177–201; J. Blair, 'Introduction', in J. Blair (ed.), *Minsters and Parish Churches: The Local Church in Transition, 950–1200* (Oxford, 1988), pp. 1–19 at p. 8.

[24] Sometimes associated churches also disappeared: see, for example, Cherry Hinton (Cambs.), J. Bradley and M. Gaimster, 'Medieval Britain and Ireland', *Medieval Archaeology* 44 (2000), pp. 235–354 at p. 252.

stone grave covers, stone or mortar linings of graves, charcoal in graves, and stones placed around the head in a 'pillow' or 'ear-muff' arrangement (Fig. 14).[25] Excavation at some cemeteries, such as Winchester Old Minster and Hereford Castle Green, reveals that through the ninth and tenth centuries graves become increasingly diverse and complex, in terms of grave preparation – including the use of charcoal and grave linings – and the use of various forms of coffin.[26] The archaeological evidence of diversity is paralleled in Christian texts of the period. As Victoria Thompson has recently commented, tenth-century homilies and penitentials suggest that experimentation in burial rites, funerary rituals, masses, forms of commemoration and expressions of humility and penance characterised the period.[27]

This range of burial practices makes it difficult to maintain that what went into the ground was really any longer the primary focal point for expressions or negotiations of social status. In order to understand the messages conveyed by burial from the eighth century, we need to scrutinise in more detail both location of burial and the use of above-ground markers. In these respects, we can indeed detect forms of social differentiation. Excavation at sites such as Ripon (Yorks.), Repton (Derbs.), and Hartlepool and Monkwearmouth (Durham) indicates that early medieval religious communities may have had more than one burial ground. Judging by the demographic profiles of the populations buried in them, these were perhaps restricted to members of the religious house and the local population respectively.[28] There is also some evidence for zones within cemeteries, characterised by different types of grave or demographic profile. At Hartlepool, for example, in one of the two known seventh- and eighth-century cemeteries associated with the religious community there, over seventy burials of adult males, females and infants were arranged in five distinct groups, which may relate to social, age-related or occupational status. There were two separate groups of adult burials arranged in rows, a group of burials focused on a primary interment in a coffin, a group of

[25] C. Daniell, *Death and Burial in Medieval England* (London, 1997), pp. 158–64.
[26] B. Kjølbye-Biddle, 'Dispersal or concentration: the disposal of the Winchester dead over 2000 years', in S. R. Bassett (ed.), *Death in Towns: Urban Responses to the Dying and the Dead, 100–1600* (London, 1992), pp. 210–47 at pp. 224–33; R. Shoesmith, *Excavations at Castle Green, Hereford City Excavations I* (London, 1980), pp. 24–5.
[27] V. Thompson, 'Constructing salvation: a homiletic and penitential context for late Anglo-Saxon burial practice', in Lucy and Reynolds (eds.), *Burial in Early Medieval England and Wales*, pp. 229–40 at pp. 232–4, 238–40.
[28] Reviewed in D. M. Hadley, 'Burial practices in northern England in the tenth and eleventh centuries', in Lucy and Reynolds (eds.), *Burial in Early Medieval England and Wales*, pp. 209–28.

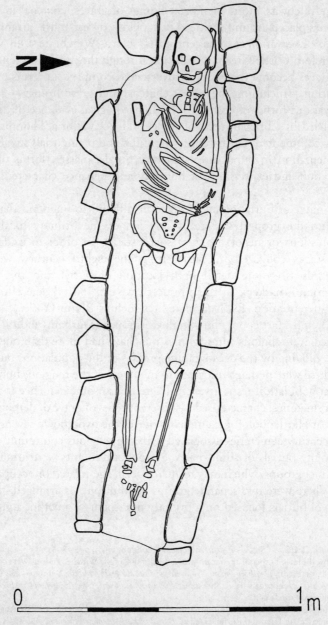

0   1m

14 Late Anglo-Saxon grave from Fillingham (Lincs.). The grave is lined with stones
and additional stones are set on either side of the skull. This practice was common
in the tenth and eleventh centuries.

burials edged with pebbles and a concentration of infant burials.[29] Evidence for zones with different demographic profiles has also been noted in eighth- to tenth-century cemeteries at Winchester, Raunds (Northants) and Withorn (Dumfries).[30] The most common form of zoning involved the separation of infant burials, often around the walls of the church. The significance of this is unclear, but it reflects the care that was taken over infant burials, unlike in some earlier cemeteries.[31]

Another development of this period was the increasing use of above-ground markers to draw attention to a grave. These included stone sculpture and churches, chapels and mausolea. Although stone crosses may not normally have marked individual graves or served commemorative functions much before the tenth century, commemorative inscriptions on the eighth- or ninth-century cross-shafts at Hackness (Yorks.), and Carlisle and Urswick (Cumbria) suggest that they sometimes did, and others may have become foci for burial.[32] In contrast, a number of recent studies of later Anglo-Saxon burial practices have pointed to the high incidence of riverine deposits of artefacts, particularly swords, and hoards typically containing weapons and coins, as possible indications that while deposition of artefacts in graves had declined, other forms of ritual deposition of artefacts may have continued.[33] Thus, while graves might themselves be unostentatious, this need not mean that funerary display was not elaborate in other respects.

This evidence combines to suggest that messages about the status of a person were conveyed as much by *where* the corpse was buried, as by *how* it was interred. The church's control of cemetery topography may have provided an additional impetus, by hinting at the post-mortem fate believed to await individuals. By way of an analogy it is worth citing an incident recorded by Gregory of Tours (d. 594) concerning Palladius, count

---

[29] R. Daniels, 'The Anglo-Saxon monastery at Hartlepool, England', in J. Hawkes and S. Mills (eds.), *Northumbria's Golden Age* (Stroud, 1999), pp. 105–12 at pp. 108–10 for the cemetery at Church Walk.

[30] Kjølbye-Biddle, 'Winchester dead', pp. 226–8; A. Boddington, *Raunds Furnells: The Anglo-Saxon Church and Churchyard* (London, 1996), pp. 55–7; P. Hill (ed.), *Whithorn and St Ninian: The Excavation of a Monastic Town 1984–91* (Stroud, 1997), pp. 164–72.

[31] Boddington, *Raunds Furnells*, p. 69, where it is argued that these 'eaves-drip' locations for infant burials may have been linked to a belief in the ongoing baptismal qualities of the rainwater falling on to the burials.

[32] Discussed in Hadley, 'Burial practices in northern England', p. 211. St Cuthbert requested burial 'near my oratory towards the south on the eastern side of the holy cross which I have erected there': Bede, *Vita S. Cuthberti*, in *Two Lives of Saint Cuthbert*, ed. B. Colgrave (Cambridge, 1940), c. 37. According to *De Abbatibus* Abbot Sigewine was laid 'by the figure of the tall cross which he himself had set up': *De Abbatibus*, ed. A. Campbell (Cambridge, 1967), p. 43.

[33] G. Halsall, 'The Viking presence in England? The burial evidence reconsidered', in D. M. Hadley and J. D. Richards (eds.), *Cultures in Contact: Scandinavian Settlement in England in the Ninth and Tenth Centuries* (Turnhout, 2000), pp. 259–76 at pp. 267–8.

of Javols: he committed suicide, and although his body was accepted for burial at the monastery of Cournon (France) he was buried in ground away from the rest of the Christian community because of the stigma attached to his death.[34] Occasionally burials located on the outskirts of Anglo-Saxon churchyards display unusual characteristics, indicating that the individual was either physically or socially distinctive, and these burials imply that some individuals were segregated from the rest of society in death. For example, at North Elmham (Norfolk) an adult male with a severely deformed leg was buried just beyond the boundary wall, in the only burial with the head placed to the east rather than the west, and an adult male who had apparently met a violent death was buried beneath the boundary wall of the same cemetery.[35] At Ripon the monastic cemetery was later used for a series of distinctive burials, including a multiple burial and the burial of a severely deformed individual, and it has been suggested that by the tenth century the cemetery was being used to bury the socially excluded.[36] As with the unfortunate count of Javols, burial strategies may have been intended to convey strong messages about the fate of the souls of the deceased.

The reasons why burial ritual and location were different in the eighth century from preceding centuries cannot be attributed solely to the influence of Christianity, however. The great diversity of funerary practices itself strongly suggests that a wide range of other factors were at work. Thus we must also look to the continuing development of regional elites and state formation, the emergence of more regular trading networks and urbanism, and changes in the nature of land-holding. We must doubtless also bear in mind the possibilities for the elite to invest their wealth in such undertakings as church building and developing their estate centres, rather than in burial display.[37] Whatever factors determined the form of burial accorded an individual, the notion that there was an egalitarian principle

---

[34] B. Effros, 'Beyond cemetery walls: early medieval funerary topography and Christian salvation', *EME* 6 (1) (1997), pp. 1–23 at pp. 1–2.

[35] P. Wade-Martins, *Excavations in North Elmham Park 1967–72*, East Anglian Archaeology 9 (1) (1980), p. 189.

[36] R. Hall and M. Whyman, 'Settlement and monasticism at Ripon, North Yorkshire, from the 7th to 11th centuries A.D.', *Medieval Archaeology* 40 (1996), pp. 62–150 at pp. 112–13, 122. It should, however, be noted that individuals suffering severe physical afflictions were not routinely isolated from mid- to later Anglo-Saxon cemeteries: J. L. Buckberry and D. M. Hadley, 'Caring for the dead in later Anglo-Saxon England' (forthcoming).

[37] M. Carver, 'Kingship and material culture in early Anglo-Saxon East Anglia', in S. R. Bassett (ed.), *The Origins of Anglo-Saxon Kingdoms* (London, 1989), pp. 141–58 at p. 157; H. Geake, 'Burial practice in seventh- and eighth-century England', in Carver (ed.), *The Age of Sutton Hoo*, pp. 83–94 at pp. 91–2.

governing funerary treatment from the eighth century is simply untrue. Yet although burial did remain an arena for social display after the eighth century, this cannot be linked to any single or simple factor relating to gender, social status, wealth, religious beliefs or occupation. Although it is clear that funerary arrangements in the eighth and ninth centuries did occasionally distinguish between men, women and infants, the recognition of this must be tempered by the apparent lack of general conventions, with practices varying enormously from cemetery to cemetery.

Some distinctions in the treatment of men, women and infants can certainly be related directly to factors other than age and gender. For example, the clusters of male burials at Ripon, Hereford, Burrow Hill (Suffolk) and Beckery Chapel, Glastonbury (Somerset) can be explained as monastic burials.[38] In contrast, other sites with clusters of male burials can sometimes be identified as execution sites, either from evidence for decapitation or from documentary evidence.[39] Although we can hardly suppose that men were more inclined to criminal activity than women, the evidence does suggest that men were more likely to be executed for their criminal behaviour than women, and to be denied burial in consecrated ground as a consequence.[40]

Analysis of Anglo-Saxon churchyard burials confirms that elaborate burials (including various types of coffin or grave lining, and those with evidence for above-ground markers) were not generally age or gender sensitive. For example, at York Minster tenth-century burials marked by stone sculptures include those of adult males, adult females and infants (Fig. 15).[41] There were also four coffins that have been interpreted as reused domestic chests, which were used in the ninth century for the burial of an adolescent, a young adult male, a middle-aged female and an elderly male. The similarity of

---

[38] Hall and Whyman, 'Settlement and monasticism at Ripon', p. 95; Shoesmith, *Castle Green, Hereford*, pp. 24–30, 39–45; V. Fenwick, 'Insula de Burgh: excavations at Burrow Hill, Butley, Suffolk', *Anglo-Saxon Studies in Archaeology and History* 3 (1984), pp. 35–54 at p. 37; P. Rahtz and S. Hirst, *Beckery Chapel Glastonbury* (Glastonbury, 1974), pp. 27–34.

[39] For example, Walkington Wold (Yorks.), Stockbridge Down, Meon Hill (Hants.), Goblin Works, Ashtead (Surrey) and Roche Court Down (Wilts.): J. Bartlett and R. Mackey, 'Excavations on Walkington Wold', *East Riding Archaeologist* 1 (2), (1972), pp. 1–93; G. Hayman, 'Further excavations at the former Goblin Works, Ashtead', *Surrey Archaeological Collections* 81 (1991–2), pp. 1–18; D. Liddell, 'Excavations at Meon Hill', *Proceedings of Hampshire Field Club and Archaeological Society* 12 (1933), pp. 127–62; N. Hill, 'Excavations on Stockbridge Down 1935–36', *Proceedings of Hampshire Field Club and Archaeological Society* 13 (1936–7), pp. 247–59; J. Stone, 'Saxon interments on Roche Court Down, Winterslow', *Wiltshire Archaeological and Natural History Magazine* 45 (1932), pp. 568–99. I am grateful to Annia Cherryson for bibliographic assistance on this issue.

[40] A. Reynolds, *Late Anglo-Saxon England: Life and Landscape* (Stroud, 1999), pp. 105–10.

[41] D. Phillips, 'The Pre-Norman cemetery', in D. Phillips and B. Heywood (eds.), *Excavations at York Minster*, vol. 1 (part 1) (London, 1995), pp. 75–92 at pp. 89–90.

15 Tenth-century burials from York Minster. The sculpture depicts the heroic figure
Sigurd with his sword and a serpent. It was excavated *in situ* above a grave. Unfortunately
there are no available details about the occupant of the grave.

the unusual coffins and the proximity of these burials has been taken as a
possible indication that the individuals concerned were in some way connected with each other in life; perhaps a family group. If this hypothesis
is correct, it is worth noting that the burials inter-cut each other, and they
appear to have been made over several decades, rather than being contemporary.[42] At the seventh- and eighth-century cemeteries at Brandon
(Suffolk) both adults and infants had coffins, and at least one adult and
one infant had a pebble-lined grave in the partially excavated seventh- or
eighth-century cemetery at Church Walk, Hartlepool.[43] In the cemetery
at Black Gate, Newcastle-upon-Tyne, which was in use from the eighth to
the eleventh century, wooden coffins, stone cists and 'pillow-stones' surrounding the head were found in the burials of both adults and infants.[44] In

[42] Phillips, 'The Pre-Norman cemetery', pp. 83–4; B. Kjølbye-Biddle, 'Iron-bound coffins and coffin-
     fittings from the pre-Norman cemetery', in D. Phillips and B. Heywood (eds.), *Excavations at York
     Minster*, vol. 1 (part 2) (London, 1995), pp. 489–521 at pp. 489–99.
[43] R. Carr, A. Tester and P. Murphy, 'The middle Saxon settlement at Staunch Meadow, Brandon',
     Antiquity 62 (1988), pp. 371–7, at p. 374; Daniels, 'The Anglo-Saxon monastery at Hartlepool', p. 110.
[44] University of Sheffield archive report.

Winchester, at both Old Minster and New Minster, there were numerous forms of burial available in the tenth century (simple earth graves, wooden coffins, graves with pillow-stones, charcoal graves, graves with yellow sand, graves with a stone coffin, and burials in a monolithic coffin), and these appear to have been accorded to both adults and infants.[45]

The evidence suggests, then, that neither gender nor age was central to determining the form of burial accorded an individual between the eighth and tenth centuries, and that other factors need to be addressed. In some cases the relatives of the individuals concerned may have been using their wealth to try to protect burials from later disturbance, while the presence of charcoal in burials may have been a symbol of humility and penitence.[46] Victoria Thompson has drawn attention to contemporary homilies and poems that reveal a fear of bodily corruption – worms are described as biting the body in the grave, and this process is linked with damnation – and she has suggested that the increasingly enclosed form of graves may have been a response to these fears.[47] Wealth, the status of the family group as a whole and perhaps also knowledge of ecclesiastical teachings relating to death and the fate of the soul may have combined to shape burial form.

Whether burial continued to be used to negotiate claims to power or land is less evident. If this was the case, it is more likely to have been achieved through a combination of location within the churchyard, and the nature of any above-ground markers. It may be significant then in this context that some excavations have revealed a higher proportion of adult male burials in some seemingly favoured and prominent locations near to access routes through the churchyard or near to elaborate funerary monuments. For example, at Raunds in the tenth and eleventh centuries there were more adult male graves on the south side of the church near the only stone monuments of the cemetery, and this sector was also characterised by a greater number of coffins, grave covers and markers.[48] At Old Minster, Winchester, most of the burials clustered around the supposed grave of St Swithun (d. 862) west of the church contained adult males, but such clustering is not otherwise a notable feature of burials associated with this church, and

---

[45] The relative percentages of adult male, adult female and infant burials are difficult to assess because many skeletons are unsexable, and while the excavations were extensive only a small proportion of the cemeteries has been excavated: Kjølbye-Biddle, 'Winchester dead', pp. 227–31.

[46] Kjølbye-Biddle, 'Winchester dead', pp. 228–33.

[47] Thompson, 'Late Anglo-Saxon burial practice', pp. 234–8.

[48] Boddington, *Raunds Furnells*, pp. 55, 69. This distribution was taken by one author to 'indicate status lowering' of women: D. Hinton, *Archaeology, Economy and Society: England from the Fifth to the Fifteenth Century* (London, 1999), p. 131.

so these burials may have been monastic rather than lay.[49] Whatever claims to power or influence were being staked through such burial strategies they are a long way off from the clearly defined gendered burial strategies of the fifth and sixth centuries. If statements about family status were made, it is most likely that this was done through male churchyard burials. In sum, burial in the eighth to tenth centuries was not the preferred way of negotiating those forms of status which either age or gender might convey. Amidst the variety of observable burial practices, three distinctions are particularly apparent. The first is between those burials that express, in varying degrees, a Christian identity and those that appear to lack any such connotations. The second marks out certain social and 'occupational' categories, whether monks, criminals or those socially excluded by physical deformity. The third distinction is of those burial practices available to individuals or groups who were wealthy enough to afford them. To that extent, burial practices did continue to register those aspects of social status which wealth might bring, although they no longer paid much attention to either age or gender. In general, we can conclude that the use of burial practices to mark social distinctions persisted, but that both the signals and their significance had changed.

FAMILY AND STATUS IN NORTHERN AND EASTERN ENGLAND, C. 900

These observations do not, however, apply when we look at the more elaborate funerary displays that are found for a short period in northern and eastern England around about 900. At that time male burials and explicitly masculine symbolism dominate the negotiation of social strategies. The evidence consists of a small number of scattered burials accompanied by grave goods – mostly weapons, or items with agricultural or trading connotations – some of which are placed in barrows. All of these burials were of adults, mostly, it appears, men, or at least the burials contained items that had strong masculine associations, in particular weapons.[50] This transitory display represents a brief return to the display of symbols of power in the grave, perhaps prompted by the Scandinavian onslaught, and at a time of great stress in local power politics. While it might be tempting to ascribe these graves solely to the Scandinavians (but if so, with whom were they communicating, why are there so few and why are so many near churches?), there is a notable similarity of symbolism between these funerary displays of

[49] Kjølbye-Biddle, 'Winchester dead', pp. 223, 228.   [50] Halsall, 'The Viking presence', pp. 270–1.

weapons and other accoutrements of elite male lordship and the symbolism of the broadly contemporary stone funerary sculpture. The production of stone sculpture was an indigenous tradition, scarcely known in Scandinavia, which proliferated in the tenth century, and it appears to represent the new-comers and the indigenous population working through the processes of accommodation and integration in an artistic medium. The regional distribution of similar types of monument has recently been interpreted not simply as signifying the location of particular workshops – since we know that individual workshops were inclined to produce a variety of types and styles of monuments[51] – but also as an indication that particular forms of monument were commissioned to enable lords to display their regional, political allegiances.[52]

Some of these stones employed warrior images or scenes from heroic culture, on occasion alongside overtly Christian imagery. Examples include the sculptures depicting warrior figures at Middleton, Old Malton, Weston and Brompton (Yorks.), Alstonefield (Staffs.), Brailsford and Norbury (Derbs.), Lowther (Cumbria), and Gainford, Chester-le-Street and Sockburn (Durham), hunt scenes on sculptures at Neston (Cheshire), Heysham (Lancs.) and Staveley (Yorks.), the images of Sigurd the dragon-slayer found on sculptures at York, Ripon and Kirby Hill (Yorks.) and Halton (Lancs.), images of Wayland the Smith on sculptures at Leeds, Sherburn and Bedale (Yorks.), the depictions of Thor and Odin on sculptures at Gosforth (Cumbria), and the apparent depiction at Ovingham (Durham) of Heimdallr and Fenris the wolf (Figs. 15–17).[53] Older interpretations of the heroic and mythological scenes as overt statements of paganism have been replaced by an acceptance that there is nothing essentially un-Christian about such scenes, and by emphasis on their secular qualities.[54] It is not unlikely that the warriors incorporated in some of these sculptures were interpreted – if not intended – as depictions of real people, perhaps serving as memorials to those men. Indeed, one sculpture from Chester-le-Street bears an inscription in runes and capitals of the name Eadmund set above a

[51] Demonstrated by recent work on cutting techniques linking diverse sculptural schemes to the same workshop: J. Lang, 'Recent studies in the pre-Conquest sculpture of Northumbria', in F. H. Thompson (ed.), *Studies in Medieval Sculpture* (London, 1983), pp. 177–89 at p. 185.

[52] D. Stocker and P. Everson, 'Five towns funerals: decoding diversity in Danelaw stone sculpture', in J. Graham-Campbell, R. Hall, J. Jesch and D. Parsons (eds.), *Vikings and the Danelaw* (Oxford, 2001), pp. 223–43 at pp. 229–40.

[53] J. Lang, 'Sigurd and Weland in pre-Conquest carvings from northern England', *Yorkshire Archaeological Journal* 48 (1976), pp. 83–94; R. N. Bailey, 'The hammer and the cross', in E. Roesdahl (ed.), *The Vikings in England and in their Danish homeland* (London, 1981), pp. 83–94.

[54] R. Bailey, *England's Earliest Sculptors* (Toronto, 1996), pp. 85–94.

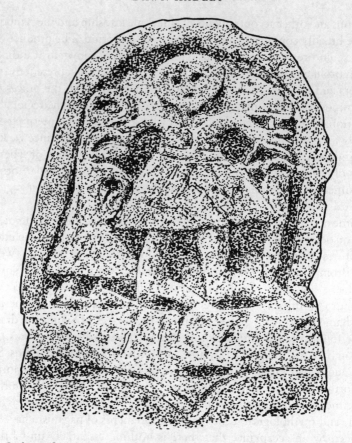

16 Sculpture from Weston (Yorks.) (height of section shown 22 cm). The sculpture
depicts a warrior with his sword, who is grabbing, or alternatively protecting, a woman.
On the reverse, the warrior is depicted alone with his sword and battle axe. The warrior
carvings were added to an existing cross-shaft in the tenth century.

horseman with shield.[55] The scenes that referred to heroic stories both served
as reminders of Scandinavian culture and, in some cases, were used to draw
parallels with Christian themes, but they may also have served to commemorate the heroic, martial ethos of aristocratic society, if not of specific individuals. It is, admittedly, difficult to offer precise dating either for the burials

[55] Bailey, 'The hammer and the cross', pp. 93–4. A sculpture from Crowle (Lincs.) depicts three men,
one grasping a sword and another on horseback, and it bears an inscription, which, although much of
it is lost owing to subsequent cutting of the monument, was clearly commemorative, incorporating
the element *licbæcun*, 'corpse monument, memorial stone': P. Everson and D. Stocker, *Corpus of
Anglo-Saxon Stone Sculpture*, Vol. v: *Lincolnshire* (Oxford, 1999), pp. 147–52.

17 Examples of tenth-century sculpture from northern England: *a* Sockburn (Durham) (length 63.5 cm); *b* Leeds (Yorks.) (height of section shown 82.5 cm); *c* Sockburn (Durham) (height 48 cm); *d* Middleton (Yorks.) (height 56 cm). The mounted warriors (*a*) are from a fragment of a hogback monument. The cross-shafts from Middleton (*d*) and Sockburn (*c*) depict armed warriors. The warrior on the Middleton shaft appears to be seated, and on the reverse of the shaft is a serpent-like beast. The Sockburn warrior is depicted above a stag. The Leeds cross-shaft (*b*) depicts the flight scene from the story of the heroic figure Wayland the Smith, and is accompanied by a series of ecclesiastics and evangelists.

with grave goods or for the sculptures. None the less, we are permitted to say that for a generation or so either side of 900, both in graves and on stone sculpture, displays of elite masculinity, emphasising warrior prowess, were used to negotiate local power politics in parts of northern and eastern England.

What was the context for these elaborate displays? It is tempting to point simply to the general context of the turbulent political and military circumstances of northern and eastern England between the later ninth and the mid-tenth centuries. Indeed, elaborate burial is a transitory statement suited to the circumstances of social upheaval, yet stone sculptures were expensive monuments, painted and sometimes decorated with precious stones, and they seem unlikely to have been commissioned and manufactured during turbulent times without there being some potential for them to have a longer-term value. Some of these sculptures may have had some liturgical role, but they also seem to have been symbols of elite status and wealth. These sculptures are a distinctive group within the corpus of Anglo-Saxon carved stones, different in both style and function from those of preceding centuries. In the tenth century more sculpture was clearly funerary (including grave covers and markers) than at an earlier date, and much of it also had a more overtly secular flavour than previously. Although there is no doubt that the monasticism of the seventh to ninth centuries shared the concerns of the secular aristocratic world beyond the monastic enclosure, this was rarely expressed in the medium of stone sculpture.[56] The tenth-century sculpture of parts of northern England, by contrast, provides numerous examples of warriors and hunting imagery. This surely reflects the change in patronage of stone sculpture, which was now found at three times as many sites, and at five times the quantity as in the eighth and ninth centuries.[57] It has been suggested that many of the sculptures were the founding monuments of a new generation of local churchyard, since large numbers are to be found at churches that appear to have been established no earlier than the tenth century.[58] Thus, the sculptures may reflect local lords exercising a novel form of conspicuous display at their

[56] Notable exceptions are the royal figure on a cross at Repton, and a portrait of a man in secular clothing accompanied by falconry equipment on a cross at Bewcastle (Cumbria): Bailey, *England's Earliest Sculptors*, pp. 66–8, 85. The figural inhabitants of vine scrolls on earlier sculptures at, for example, Hexham, Jarrow and Auckland (Durham) included hunters and archers, which 'could have been interpreted allegorically and may reflect classical models. They are certainly to be viewed as distinct from the armed men in apparently contemporary dress that appear in the post-Viking period': R. Cramp, *Corpus of Anglo-Saxon Stone Sculpture*, Vol. 1: *County Durham and Northumberland* (Oxford, 1984), p. 20.

[57] Bailey, *England's Earliest Sculptors*, p. 79.

[58] Stocker and Everson, 'Danelaw stone sculpture', pp. 225–7.

newly founded churches. The sparse documentation for northern and eastern England during the tenth century provides only glimpses of the nature of lordship at this time, but what does emerge, as Julia Barrow has recently observed, is the rapidity with which land changed hands. This suggests that it may have been difficult for prominent families to maintain their status locally by land-ownership alone, and they may have had to employ other strategies to maintain rank. Barrow suggests that the church had a vital role to play because it provided careers for members of kin-groups, who in turn could offer assistance to their relatives.[59] It can also be argued that the outward trappings of the church must have helped to give these local lords some stability. Thus, the founding of local churches, which seems to have been much more advanced in eastern and parts of northern England than elsewhere, and funerary stone sculptures both with and without heroic or warrior imagery, appear to have been symbols of a particular type of dynamic, but insecure, local lordship.

Unlike urban environments, where the greater concentration of wealth seems to have made it common for many individuals to be commemorated with stone monuments, it is rare to find more than a couple of monuments at any one rural site. This is true even for those churches that have experienced extensive renovation or excavation.[60] These sculptures were, then, the markers of an elite rural minority. That they were probably made for male heads of households, or male heirs, is suggested by the fact that the only clearly gendered symbolism identifiable on the monuments displaying secular images is masculine. Moreover, documentary evidence suggests that heads of households were normally male, and that Anglo-Saxon women generally only had access to land when it suited family interests or in default of a male heir.[61] A rare secular female image appears on a cross-shaft at Weston, and this may have something to reveal about the relative status of women in this artistic medium, and more generally about secular attitudes to lordship, as the woman is shown being either grabbed, or perhaps protected, by a male warrior brandishing his sword (Fig. 16).[62] Monuments in this group may have been intended to serve as markers of

[59] J. Barrow, 'Survival and mutation: ecclesiastical institutions in the Danelaw in the ninth and tenth centuries', in Hadley and Richards (eds.), *Cultures in Contact*, pp. 155–76 at p. 170. Stone sculpture was comparatively rare in East Anglia, but the number of churches built during the later Anglo-Saxon period was enormous, and many villages have two or more churches, generally associated with separate manors: T. Williamson, *The Origins of Norfolk* (Manchester, 1993), pp. 154–61.

[60] Stocker, 'Stone sculpture in Yorkshire and Lincolnshire', pp. 180–91.

[61] J. Crick, 'Women, posthumous benefaction and family strategy in pre-Conquest England', *Journal of British Studies* 38 (1999), pp. 399–42.

[62] P. Addyman, 'The attackers return', in Roesdahl (ed.), *The Vikings in England*, pp. 55–68 at p. 61.

the status of the whole family, and not simply of the status of the individual over whose grave they were placed.

This interpretation is supported by the iconography of the so-called hogback monuments, which became popular in the tenth century in northern England and southern Scotland, and which appear to have been grave covers. They are typically house-shaped monuments, with some actually depicting house features, such as doors and a roof.[63] The house may have symbolised the lord and his family, and may reflect an emphasis on the family in burial strategies and forms of commemoration in the tenth century.[64] That the deaths of individuals focused attention on the family unit is supported by the evidence of later Anglo-Saxon wills. Wills regularly reveal a concern to dispose of family property, to provide for heirs, to place obligations regarding property and commemoration on future generations and to carry out the wishes of already-deceased family members concerning both their property and the welfare of their soul.[65] Burial strategies – involving both location and the provision of monuments – may, then, have been a material manifestation of the contemporary concerns expressed in Anglo-Saxon wills.

The use of stone grave markers in rural contexts seems to have had significance for later burials in the same cemeteries, which on occasion clustered around them. Excavation at Raunds revealed that the churchyard expanded outwards from a core of burials close to the church, two of which were elaborated with carved stone monuments – those of a middle-aged man buried in an exclusive plot, and an infant in a stone-lined grave.[66] Such monuments may have been as much family monuments as individual monuments – indeed, the sculpture placed over the infant had been recut and reused, perhaps from the disturbed adult male burial beneath. Here we seem to have evidence for the local elites in northern England promoting family burial grounds in the tenth century at churches, many recently founded, which were integral parts of their holdings. The status of both the lord and his family was then expressed through burial near to both the church and elaborate monuments many of which, if for a short time, in a turbulent situation employed warrior imagery.

[63] J. Lang, 'The hogback: a Viking colonial monument', *Anglo-Saxon Studies in Archaeology and History* 3 (1984), pp. 85–176.

[64] D. Stocker, 'Monuments and merchants: irregularities in the distribution of stone sculpture in Lincolnshire and Yorkshire in the tenth century', in Hadley and Richards (eds.), *Cultures in Contact*, pp. 179–212 at pp. 198–9.

[65] J. Crick, 'Posthumous obligation and family identity', in W. O. Fraser and A. Tyrell (eds.), *Social Identity in Early Medieval Britain* (London, 2000), pp. 193–208 at pp. 199–205.

[66] Boddington, *Raunds Furnells*, p. 45.

It is difficult to say who commissioned stone sculpture as inscriptions are rare, and there is no relevant documentary evidence. Yet in trying to understand the context of the production and display of sculpture it might be worth remembering the historically attested role of aristocratic women in commemoration and in preserving dynastic memory, and their part in the transmission of cultural and artistic traditions through their marriages into new families, often far from their homelands.[67] We do not know the relative proportions of Scandinavian men and women who settled in England, but the likelihood that there were many more men is suggested by the fact that far fewer female than male Scandinavian personal names are recorded in documentary sources of the tenth to twelfth centuries. This is arguably a reflection of the smaller number of female settlers introducing fewer female names and naming models.[68] The male settlers must sometimes have married into indigenous families, perhaps for political or pragmatic reasons to secure their claims to land, as did Sihtric, the Hiberno-Norse king of York, who married a sister of King Æthelstan of Wessex in 926.[69] It may be that marriage strategies were a significant means by which the Scandinavian settlers, the majority of whom appear from available evidence to have been men, secured their position and authority in England. If so, marriage must have been a context where both ethnicity and religious affiliation were renegotiated. The stone sculptures and their role in expressing family status thus take on a new dimension, as they employ both indigenous and Scandinavian motifs, as well as innovative forms of secular display. If they were produced in the context of cultural assimilation, and in the context of the emergence of new types of local lordship, then they were also formed in the context of marriages and families.

That funerary sculptures may have been used in the tenth century to promote dynastic and lordly concerns among the laity is made more plausible by evidence suggesting that even at an earlier date, when stone sculpture was largely a monastic concern, it was sometimes used for dynastic purposes. Catherine Karkov has recently discussed a possible example of the strategic use of sculptures within an eighth-century monastic environment. Abbess Ælflaed of Whitby (Yorks.) (d. 714) appears to have played a major role in preserving the memory of members of her family and abbey, and also in determining who was excluded from both the documentary record

---

[67] E. Van Houts, *Memory and Gender in Medieval Europe, 900–1200* (Basingstoke, 1999), pp. 65–120.

[68] C. Clark, 'Clark's first three laws of Applied Anthroponymics', *Nomina* 3 (1979), pp. 13–19 at pp. 17–18.

[69] D. Whitelock (ed.), *English Historical Documents I, c.500–1042* (London, 1955; 2nd edn 1979), no. 1, s.a. 926.

and commemoration in stone. Thus the names of her relatives are recorded in the Lindisfarne *Liber vitae*, and several members of her family are commemorated in stone at both Whitby and its daughter-house at Hackness (Yorks.), but the name of the founder of the monastery, Hild, is notably absent from this record. It appears that Ælflaed had been successful in promoting the commemoration of her own family members above those of others, including Hild.[70] The commemoration and the manipulation of the dead by women was an important means by which family power and authority could be established and maintained even in a monastic environment. If this was true of the eighth century, how much more pressing a concern the maintenance of family power and status must have been during the tenth century when patterns of land-holding were comparatively much less stable. We might hypothesise that women commissioned at least some of the sculpted funerary monuments of tenth-century northern England.

CONCLUSIONS

The role of burial display in the negotiation of gender had undergone major transformations since the fifth century. From the seventh century onwards, above-ground markers (barrows, prehistoric landscape features, churches, monuments) were increasingly used to convey messages about the deceased and his or her family. Moreover, burial practices did not just transform gradually, but experienced periods of rapid change, and we must keep this in mind in order to understand the role of gender in mortuary customs. In the early Middle Ages, gender was not a constant determining how burials had to be arranged or marked out, but rather a category of distinction that could be drawn upon in burial when required in specific social situations. Attempts by recent studies to read gender difference into the incidence of coffins, charcoal burials or pillow-stones are missing the point. Gender was not being invoked in that context, so much as wealth or notions about humility and the need to protect the corpse from the sacrilege of disturbance connected to fears about the ultimate reunification of body and soul. Throughout the Anglo-Saxon centuries, the more prominent and elaborate graves were restricted to certain individuals within society. However, those excluded varied. In the earlier centuries it appears to have been the very young, the very elderly and perhaps also those without economic, social or political influence. At a later date, however, it appears

---

[70] C. Karkov, 'Whitby, Jarrow and the commemoration of death', in Hawkes and Mills (eds.), *Northum-bria's Golden Age*, pp. 126–35 at pp. 133–5.

to have been family status that determined who was accorded particular burial rites. In referring to family status, we must, of course, acknowledge that this phrase may mask a complex social reality. Documentary sources suggest that early medieval family affiliations were sometimes extensive, and may have included members of the wider kin group and foster-children, not to mention illegitimate offspring, whether knowingly or not.[71] For this reason we should be cautious of the claims by scientists to be able to identify familial links from skeletal remains, since early medieval 'families' were at least as much social constructs as biological realities.[72]

During moments of intense social stress notions of masculinity were commonly re-evaluated in the early Middle Ages. In this respect, there is an interesting parallel between the early years of Germanic settlement in the fifth century and the period around 900. In both periods there was more signalling in burials of the masculine gender than of the feminine.[73] This surely reflects the fact that in times of social transformation it was invariably to men that communities looked to ameliorate that disruption, to renegotiate local power structures, to make claims to land and to return the community to its status quo. Those men were also members of families, and it was within the family, and through restructuring of the gendered roles of family members, that some of the most complex transformations of the early medieval world were played out. A study of the graves of these family members can provide us with richer and more nuanced pictures of the ongoing and regionally varied expressions of those transformations.[74]

---

[71] S. Crawford, *Childhood in Anglo-Saxon England* (Stroud, 1999), pp. 122–38.

[72] For a recent attempt to use DNA evidence to identify family relations see K. Lidén and A. Götherström, 'The archaeology of rank, by means of diet, gender and kinship', in Dickinson and Griffiths (eds.), *The Making of Kingdoms*, pp. 81–7 at pp. 83–4.

[73] Stoodley, *The Spindle and the Spear*, pp. 80–1.

[74] I would like to thank Andrew Reynolds and Nick Stoodley for their comments on an earlier version of this chapter, and Jo Buckberry and Annia Cherryson for discussion of various sites. I am grateful to Oliver Jessop for preparing the illustrations, and to the British Academy for funding the research on which much of the chapter is based.

Index